The BUSINESS ONE IRWIN Guide to

TRADING SYSTEMS

The BUSINESS ONE IRWIN Guide to

TRADING SYSTEMS

by

Bruce Babcock, Jr.

Publisher of
Commodity Traders Consumer Report

BUSINESS ONE IRWIN
Homewood, Illinois 60430

This book is dedicated to my friends in the commodity industry (they know who they are) who helped me reach the point where I could write it.

Project editor: *Suzanne Ivester*
Production manager: *Ann Cassady*
Cover designer: *Ed Letwenko*
Compositor: *Weimer Typesetting Co., Inc.*
Typeface: *11/13 Century Schoolbook*
Printer: *The Maple-Vail Book Manufacturing Group*

Library of Congress Cataloging-in-Publication Data

Babcock, Bruce, Jr.
     The BUSINESS ONE IRWIN guide to trading systems.

     Includes index.
     1. Commodity futures. I. Title.
HG6024.A3B33 1989   332.64′4   88–31441
ISBN 1-55623-126-1

Printed in the United States of America
     5 6 7 8 9 0 V 6 5 4 3

Foreword

You are about to experience an interesting unveiling . . . as Bruce Babcock removes the shroud of secrecy and mumbo-jumbo from what many speculators have long been in awe of . . . trading systems.

Trading systems, for stocks and commodities, have been with us almost as long as the markets. The first system I have in my library comes from 1858. So Bruce's subject matter has been around a long time. But not until now has anyone dissected it like this for the public's inspection.

Step by step, Bruce will take you through commodity trading basics and then explain trading system theory, development and construction. He will show you how to create many kinds of simple and advanced systems and then give you approaches to money management, the final touch of any successful system. Thus, this book is for the neophyte as well as the experienced commodity trader, system follower, or system developer.

While I have taught commodity systems to perhaps more people than anyone in the history of the markets, I was surprised how much I learned from reading Bruce's book. There were several ideas that were new to me, twists to system development and application I had not thought of. I'm just chomping at the bit to run them through my computers.

Bruce's detail work has always been among the best in the industry, and this book is certainly no exception. He gives you hundreds of examples in clear, "man on the street" English, so anyone can understand how the systems are constructed. And then, more importantly, you see the actual trading results: how the system would have performed in real-time trading had one chosen to follow the system. This is invaluable. It shows you what types of systems work the best in which markets and which publicly-recognized systems don't work. It is certain to ignite new ideas and suggest new ways you can develop system applications for commodity trading.

I hope you will pay particular attention to Bruce's chapters on money and equity management. I am absolutely convinced, beyond any shadow of a doubt, that while we need a good system to follow, the rapid hypothecation of one's account is not as much contingent upon the system, as it is contingent upon the type of markets one gets to trade. Thus, you should read and reread his chapter on Systems and Markets . . . and then the application of correct money management.

It gets down to this: a winning system in a nonvolatile market with poor money management isn't going to do very well. However, a good system in a volatile market with superb money management can achieve phenomenal results. It is with the correct combination of locking in on highly volatile markets, using decent systems and applying an intelligent form of money management that I think you will experience your greatest rewards.

Bruce specifically teaches you about each of those three significant phenomena: system, market and money management. When you finish, you will know when to trade, what to trade, and how to trade it.

Until this book, trading system construction has been in the hands of maybe twenty to one hundred people in America. Thanks to Bruce Babcock, now everyone can understand how systems are put together. After reading it, you will be a better system developer and a far more knowledgeable system buyer, should you decide to purchase a commercially-available system or computer program.

I've always thought that when it comes to understanding trading systems, if Bruce Babcock has written about it, I'd better read it. This book is no exception. I hope you enjoy it as much as I have.

Larry Williams

Preface

Commodity futures traders have always been fascinated with mechanical trading systems. Short-term stock market players have been anxious to transfer the technology to their arena as well. The reason systems have been popular is that speculative trading is so frustratingly difficult. Peter Aan described it as "Like sitting in a chair next to a conveyor belt with $1,000 bills going by. You keep trying to grab them, but they're always a little bit out of reach."

Because he finds it so difficult, the average trader assumes that the small percentage of successful speculators must know some inside secrets of how the markets work. A natural conclusion is to assume that a trading system will somehow reveal and exploit this secret market code. System vendors are skillful at exploiting this misapprehension.

The truth is that there is no market code. There are no inside secrets only the professionals understand. The essential principles of successful trading are well-known, but almost no one can implement them consistently. The reason is that natural human emotions interfere and are extremely difficult to overcome.

I know. I have been trading myself since 1975. I first began investigating trading systems in 1976. My most successful years have come when I followed a purely mechanical approach. I have been writing and publishing *Commodity Traders Consumer Report* since 1983. In that capacity I have had the opportunity to evaluate nearly every important trading system and computer software program available in the public domain. I have designed and produced a good number myself. I know how to create a trading system and how to evaluate trading systems created by others.

While there have been a number of books written which describe various commodity trading methods and systems, few make any attempt to demonstrate the effectiveness of the methods described. I suspect this is partially because over the long run most of them don't work. Traders continue using these methods because they assume that if they are in a book, they must be effective. They do work sometimes which keeps things confusing.

We have arrived at an age where powerful computer technology is available to anyone with enough capital to consider commodity speculation. There is no longer any excuse for trading with untested methods.

Even if you have never traded commodities before, this book will tell you what you need to know to understand the problems you face. It will explain why such a high percentage of traders eventually lose. It will show you why a completely mechanical approach is your best route to profits. It will guide you step by step through the process of creating your own system and teach you how to evaluate those created by others. It will introduce you to the newest computer technology available to help you at remarkably low cost.

In addition to describing the theory of trading system creation and testing, I have also included for the first time in this kind of book, a systematic examination of what actually works and what does not. You will see historical tests of various trading system approaches in ten markets over a five-year period. I will teach you a simple long-term system I created especially for this book which trades rings around all the popular approaches.

I must caution, however, that reading this book will not guarantee trading riches and early retirement. We can only test our systems in the past, but we trade for profits in the future. As someone said, "The future will be just like the past, only different." There is much randomness in market behavior which will always make trading a struggle. Though it is a challenge, it is an entertaining one, certainly never boring. You will need sufficient capital, sufficient patience, sufficient discipline, sufficient courage and sufficient determination to succeed. Above all, if you can master yourself, you can master the markets. Good luck.

Bruce Babcock, Jr.

Acknowledgments

This book is a product of over a decade of interaction and learning from many people involved with commodity trading. Although it is impossible to thank them all by name, I appreciate their unselfish assistance.

All the computer charts in the book were produced on my Commodity Quotegraphics equipment. The help and friendship of its President, Tim Mather, and his staff over the years have been greatly appreciated. I am also grateful to Gerald Becker and Knight-Ridder Commodity Perspective for permission to reproduce their weekly charts in the Appendix. IBM/PC/XT/AT are trademarks of International Business Machines Corporation. Perpetual Contract is a trademark of Commodity Systems, Inc. Market Profile is a trademark of the Chicago Board of Trade. CQG System One and Volume Profile are trademarks of Commodity Quotegraphics, Inc.

Without the help of my Research Director and programmer, Stephen Winter, this book would not have been possible. His inventive mind and attention to detail were as necessary to the finished product as his endless tolerance of my perfectionism. The casino-system research in Chapter 17 was the brainchild of Robert E. Lehman. Joe Bristor conducted the equity-curve-management research in Chapter 17. My thanks go to each of these gentlemen.

My years in this business would not have been as enjoyable without the help of Larry Regg. Larry handles all assignments with good humor, dedication and care. He also happens to be the best proofreader imaginable. His work on this book was up to his usual standards.

I wish to thank Larry Williams for writing the Foreword. His fertile mind has been a source of ideas for everyone he touches. He should be the first inductee into the Commodity Trading Hall of Fame. Jake Bernstein deserves special mention for the inspiration he gave me to tackle this project. He must be the kindest person and most prolific worker in human history.

Finally, I am grateful to Alison and Scooter for their indulgence and support during this project. They encouraged me even though they knew that when it was finished, it would inevitably be replaced by something else just as time-consuming.

B.B.

Contents

The Test Period Using Different Time Segments
Using Different Markets
Costs of Trading
Special Problems of Testing with Daily Data
Evaluating Tests Results

Total Number of Closed Trades
Total Number of Profitable (or Losing) Trades
Percentage of Profitable Trades
Cumulative Closed Profit or Loss
Open Equity
Average Profit per Closed Trade
Maximum Drawdown
Greatest Number of Consecutive Losses
Average Profitable Trade
Average Losing Trade
Ratio of Average Win to Average Loss
Profit Factor
Biggest Profitable Trade
Biggest Losing Trade
Number of Closed Trades That Were Buys (or Sells)
Percentage of Long (or Short) Trades Profitable
*Average Profitable (and Losing) Trade Length in Market
   Days*
Total Slippage and Commissions
Return on Margin
Effectiveness Ratio for Closed Trades
Effectiveness Ratio with Open Equity

List of Exhibits

1

An Introduction to the Commodity Trading Problem

In this introductory chapter, I will teach you exactly what is involved in trading commodity futures, why it can be risky but need not be, and what principles you will need to follow in order to be successful. To understand this, you do not need to have had any previous exposure to commodity trading.

The last 10 years have seen an explosion in the volume of futures trading. One of the most important reasons for this is the introduction of a whole new class of markets to trade—financial futures. The decade of the 1970s saw increasing inflation. The hot markets were the traditional agriculturals and precious metals. In the 1980s inflation receded, and these markets declined—both in price and in popularity. The favorites of this decade have been the futures contracts based on financial instruments: Foreign currencies, T-bonds, Eurodollars, and stock market indexes. Professional traders do not distinguish between the traditional commodity markets and the new financial futures. To them, they are all potential markets to trade, and traders approach them the same way. However, the press often refers to speculation in the financial markets as "futures trading" while reserving the term *commodity trading* for traditional markets with actual products. For the purposes of this book, I will refer to all speculation in the futures markets as "commodity trading." The principles and concepts I will teach you apply to all the markets.

Another whole new area for speculative activity has grown up in the 1980s—listed commodity options. These options are especially popular with brokerage firms because buying puts and calls appears to offer the same large (theoretically unlimited) profit potential as commodity trading, while having absolutely fixed maximum risk (the cost of the option plus the commission). This is an effective selling point to those with great profit aspirations and little knowledge. The public always buys the options; it never sells them.

I don't know a single professional trader who prefers buying puts and calls to trading futures contracts. While the option buyer's risk is strictly limited to the price he pays for the option, that risk is substantial in relation to the probable reward. For a quick appreciation of the attractiveness of buying puts and calls, consider this. When a brokerage firm customer buys a put or call, there is someone on the other side of the transaction selling it to him. That person is always a professional options trader. The seller is assuming a position with strictly limited profit potential and theoretically unlimited risk. Of the two, who do you think has the greater expected reward, the professional trader or the amateur? In my opinion, it is impossible to make money in the long term buying puts and calls. However, selling them requires too much attention and expertise for the average investor. Therefore, this book will ignore options. I suggest you do so as well.

The popular conception of commodity trading is far removed from the reality. This should not be especially surprising. It is remarkable that a substantial percentage of those who have actually traded commodities do not have a good understanding of what the realities are. Contrary to what you might expect, learning how to trade commodities is relatively easy. What is difficult is applying the knowledge consistently. In other words, traders know what they should do, but they just cannot do it consistently enough to make money over time. I will explain why in Chapter 2.

You Never Really Buy or Sell Anything

One of the hoary myths of commodity trading is that the inattentive trader is liable to receive an unexpected delivery of a not-very-useful product. Nontraders have humorous visions of trucks arriving to dump tons of soybeans on the front lawn or of carloads of squealing pigs showing up one morning before breakfast.

This misapprehension stems from the idea that commodity traders are madly buying and selling such tangible products. However, the reality is that commodity traders do not buy or sell anything. When you call a broker and buy 100 shares of General Motors stock, you are actually buying a small piece of the company. You can take delivery of the share certificate and hold it in your hand as proof of your new possession. You hold a small part of the profit-making potential of the company and are entitled to participate in managing the company as well as to receive dividends.

On the other hand, a commodity speculator who calls his broker and tells him to buy 5,000 bushels of March corn does not intend to own any corn. He places the order because he believes the price of corn will soon rise. If it does, he will profit. This is known as a "long" position. At about the same time someone else may call another broker and place an order to sell 5,000 bushels of March corn. He is not a farmer with a corn crop in the fields. He does not own any corn. How can he sell something he does not own? When he tells his broker to sell, it is just a shorthand way to say that he is betting the price of corn will drop. If it does, he will profit. This is known as a "short" position. Neither trader will ever own any corn.

You Are Gambling on Price Movement

Commodity speculation is nothing more than (theoretically) intelligent gambling on the future direction of price movement. How intelligent it is will depend on the person doing the trading. Every time you take a position, someone is matched with you, taking the opposite position. That is one of the purposes of the commodity exchange: To match up traders with opposite opinions who wish to make bets by taking a position. Your broker deals through the exchange on your behalf. In the above example, the buyer's broker and the seller's broker would transmit the orders to the floor of the exchange, where they would be executed at the current price. Assume that price is $2. The buyer will be long one March corn contract at $2; the seller will be short one March corn contract at $2. A "contract" is one trading unit.

In order for you to participate in commodity trading, your broker will require that you deposit money in an account. The brokerage firm sets a minimum deposit for your account as a whole. As a general rule, most commodity brokerage firms require that you make a deposit of at least $5,000 to open an account. Unlike the stock market, where the broker uses money in your account to buy shares, the money in your commodity account is not used to buy anything. It is the guarantee that when you are wrong about the price change, the broker will have the money to pay off the person on the other side of the transaction.

For each commodity, the exchanges and your brokerage firm set an amount that you must have available in your account for this guarantee before initiating a trade in that market. This is called "margin." The exchange where corn is traded, the Board of Trade in Chicago, sets a minimum margin that every corn trader must have in his account to trade corn. Your brokerage firm may set a higher amount at its discretion. The amount of the margin is based upon the value of the contract. A contract of corn involves 5,000 bushels and is quoted in cents per bushel. The value of the contract is the current price times 5,000. For the past few years, corn has been averaging about $2 a bushel, so the value of the corn contract has averaged around $10,000. Another factor determining margin is a commodity's daily volatility. *Volatility* means the distance price moves in a given period. Corn does not have very large daily price moves and is considered a low-volatility market. Corn has one of the lowest margins. The current exchange margin for corn is $350 per contract. If you deposited $5,000 in your account and your broker allowed you to trade with the exchange margin, you could trade as many as 14 contracts of corn.

In contrast, coffee has a margin of $2,000. A coffee contract involves 37,500 pounds of coffee and is quoted in cents per pound. Coffee has been averaging about $1.50 per pound, so that the average value of a coffee contract has been $56,250. It is also a more volatile market, so that its margin is considerably higher than corn. Using the exchange margin, your broker would allow you to trade only two contracts of coffee with your original $5,000 deposit. Required margin is cumulative. You must have the margin separately available for each contract you trade. Since those two coffee contracts would only use up $4,000 in margin, you could trade two corn contracts in addition without going over your $5,000 limit. Or you could trade one coffee contract and eight corn contracts.

The market with the largest margin is currently the S&P 500 stock index. This contract originated in 1982 with a margin of $6,000. As the stock market rose and the contract's price increased, the margin rose to $10,000. After the extreme volatility demonstrated in October 1987, the margin went up to $20,000. At that level, you would need $20,000 in your account to trade just one S&P contract.

When you buy or sell (gamble on) corn, the payoff is the difference in price from when you initiated your position times 5,000 (bushels). If the price of corn moves 10 percent (a 20-cent move), you stand to make or lose $1,000. Our buyer would make $1,000 if the price of corn moved to $2.20; the seller would lose $1,000. If the price dropped to $1.80, the results would be the reverse. The buyer would lose $1,000, and the seller would gain $1,000. In coffee, a proportional move (15 cents) would result in a gain or loss of $5,625. In the S&P 500, a proportional move (25 points) is worth $12,500.

The profit/loss adjustment, which credits winners and debits losers, takes place at the end of every trading day. To the extent that price moved in your favor on your positions during the day, your broker adds money to your account after the markets close. To the extent that price moved against your positions, your broker removes money from your account.

If your account grows in value because of profitable price moves, your margin available for trading increases, and you can assume new positions. If your account decreases in value because prices are moving against you, you may be required to add more money or exit enough positions so that you are not trading above the margin available in your account. The amount you need to enter a position is called "initial margin." You need a slightly lower amount, called "maintenance margin," to maintain an existing position that is moving against you. Thus, even if you use your entire account value as initial margin, you are not necessarily required to add more money or dispose of a position the first day if price immediately moves the wrong way.

It is possible for people who trade futures contracts to take delivery of the product or deliver the product to someone else. The players who do this are called "commercials." They are producers, such as farmers, who want to guarantee a certain selling price for their corn (or other product). Or they may be users of the product, such as cereal manufacturers, who want to guarantee a certain price for the corn they need to buy. In our example, if the corn buyer was a commercial, he would have guaranteed that he could take delivery of 5,000 bushels of corn in March at a price of $2 per bushel. If the seller was a commercial, he would have guaranteed that he could deliver 5,000 bushels of corn in March and receive $2 per bushel.

However, the speculator who buys and sells futures contracts does not want to deal in the product. He wants to deal only in money. He is betting on the direction that price will move. If he is right, he makes a profit in proportion to the size of the price move. If he is wrong, he suffers a loss. The terms *buy* and *sell* are just shorthand expressions for "I bet the price is going up" and "I bet the price is going down."

To avoid dealing with the product, the usual practice is to exit the position prior to what is called "first notice day." You may have noted that when the buyer and seller called their respective brokers to place their corn orders, they referred to *March* corn. Each contract traded is connected to a particular delivery month in the future. At a particular day (which varies from market to market during the delivery month), the contract expires, and the final closing price on that day fixes the delivery price for the contract. Commercials who are short and still hold their positions must deliver the appropriate amount of the commodity at the final closing price. Commercials who are long must accept delivery and pay the final closing price. These deliveries occur at specified delivery locations and are often handled by exchanging warehouse receipts. Speculators routinely exit their March positions no later than the last trading day in February to avoid any problems with delivery. However, even if you are on vacation in Africa and forget to close out your position, you may still avoid the consequences of delivery. Your broker arranges this for an additional fee.

To exit a position, you call your broker and place the opposite order from your entry. If you have a long position, you originally bought; so now you sell the same amount. If you have a short position, you originally sold; so now you buy the same amount. Again, you are not actually buying or selling anything. It is merely shorthand to tell your broker to close out your original position. Your final profit or loss on a trade is the difference between the value of the contract when you entered the trade and the value when you exited. If the price of corn rose 25 cents between entry and exit, the buyer would make a profit of $1,250 (25 cents times 5,000 bushels) and the seller would suffer a loss of $1,250 for each contract traded.

The Effect of Leverage

In the last example, the corn speculator made a $1,250 profit on a 25-cent move in corn. But corn can move 25 cents in only a few weeks, sometimes in one week! Where else can you invest $5,000, place two telephone calls, and make a return of 25 percent on your investment in only a few weeks?

That return assumes you traded only one contract. However, remember that using the exchange margin of $350, you could have traded 14 corn contracts at once with your $5,000 deposit. If you had traded the full number of contracts your account allowed, you could have made a profit of $17,500—a return of 350 percent—in the same couple of weeks. And corn is one of the tamest markets there is. Now do you see how it is possible to "get rich quick" trading futures?

It is the principle of leverage that allows such stupendous profits. You are controlling about $10,000 worth of corn with only a $350 investment. If the price of corn changes by only 1 percent, the value of your investment changes by 28.6 percent. If the price of corn changes by 10 percent, the value of your investment changes by 286 percent. You have probably already figured out that there is a dark side to this. You can lose money just as fast as you can make it. If you had decided to trade the full 14 corn contracts allowed by your $5,000 account, you could have been wiped out by only a 7-cent move against you. Corn can move 7 cents in one day.

That, in microcosm, is an explanation of the riskiness of trading commodities. Regardless of any horror stories you may have heard about huge losses in trading, the truth is that the trader himself controls his risk. He is the one who decides how many contracts he will trade. He is the one who decides how long he will hold a position that is moving against him. The trader who insists on trading 14 corn contracts with his $5,000 account will lose all his money after a 7-cent move against him. The trader who trades one corn contract and chooses to exit his position after the same 7-cent move against him will lose only $350. He will have plenty of money left to trade again.

That is why I say commodity trading has received a bad rap. It is, in fact, no riskier than you want to make it. Do you think roulette is too risky to play? Probably not. You can go to Las Vegas or Atlantic City with $5,000 and bet a few dollars on each spin of the wheel. There's nothing terribly risky about that. You could probably play for days without losing all your money. The problem is that if you did win, you would not win very much. If you are impatient and want to make big money quickly, you can play at the same wheel and bet $2,500 or $5,000 on each spin. Now all of a sudden it becomes very risky. You can lose everything in only one or two spins. It is the same wheel and the same game. The only difference is the player's approach.

The reason commodity traders lose big money is because they get impatient and take big risks. In trading, like any investment, the risks are always commensurate with the rewards. If you control yourself and have a limited goal, the risk will also be limited, and you will have a reasonable chance to achieve your goal. If you get excited about the possibilities and try to get rich too quickly, you will increase the risk to the point where you have virtually no chance of success. You will probably be quickly wiped out. This is precisely what happens to a substantial percentage of new traders. They have no one to blame but themselves. It is usually those with the smallest accounts who have the most unrealistic expectations.

What is a reasonable return for trading commodities? After many years of trading and discussing this with professionals, the number I use is 50 percent return per year. This is an amount most professionals would be comfortable with if they could do it consistently year after year. In good years, they would hope to do better. In bad years, they would not want to do much worse. Certainly they would not like to have net losses for a whole year. But even that can happen eventually to a very good professional trader. You can trade conservatively and comfortably with a goal of a 50 percent return per year.

To someone starting with only $5,000, a return of 50 percent does not sound like very much. To make only $2,500 for a whole year of commodity trading seems ridiculous. We've already seen that you could trade only two corn contracts and make that in a few weeks. Or you could trade one corn contract and make it on two 25-cent moves over the one-year period. It is precisely this appearance of easy profits that gives novice traders unrealistically high expectations.

Easy profits may not be attractive if the risks are too high. Let's go back to the roulette table. You could bet $2,500 on red at the roulette table and have almost a 50 percent chance of achieving a $2,500 return in a few seconds. Would you take that chance? Most people who expect to make big money in commodities would not be caught dead in a gambling casino, much less bet like that.

If you demand gargantuan returns from your trading, you will probably fail. If you have only limited capital, your best chance of success is to play it safe, settle for a reasonable return from your trading, earn more money on the side to add to your account, and count on the power of compounding to build a significant fortune. If you pay your income taxes from other earnings, you could start with $5,000, earn 50 percent per year, and have about $1 million in only 13 years. If you started with $20,000, it would take only 10 years. If that's too long for you to wait, I recommend you play a state lottery instead of the commodity markets. Your chances of eventual success are probably better.

The leverage available to commodity traders is what permits relatively large profits in relation to capital. The potentially devastating effect of leverage when the market is moving against you adds an additional dimension to the selection and management of trades. In order to make a profitable trade, you must correctly choose the future direction of price movement. In addition, the timing must be precise because there is little margin for error.

We already saw how much money you can make or lose from even small price movements. The greater the number of markets or contracts you choose to trade at once, and the smaller your available capital, the less margin for error you will have. In the corn example, the person trading the maximum number of contracts would have been wiped out by only a 7-cent move against him. That means, not only must he correctly choose the direction of price movement, price must never move more than 6 cents against him. If it does, the broker will liquidate his positions immediately, and his capital will be gone forever. It will be little consolation if the next day price moves back in the correct direction so that the trade eventually would have yielded thousands of dollars in profit. He will be gone—out of the market.

Although most traders are careful not to trade up to the limit of their account and leave so little margin for error, the same principle of avoiding ruin applies on every trade. When the market is moving against you, you never know whether it will turn around before you are wiped out. Even if it stops moving against you, it may never come back to the point where you entered. In a highly leveraged situation, you cannot just hold your position forever until you make a profit. You must have a point where you admit you were wrong, abandon the trade, and take your loss.

This raises a dilemma. The greater the loss you are willing to take before admitting you were wrong, the less likely it is your capitulation point will be reached. However, if it is reached, it will be very difficult to recover from the large loss. If you suffer a 50 percent loss, you have to achieve a 100 percent return on your new account size just to get even. If you then suffer another 50 percent loss, you have to achieve a 300 percent return just to get even. Even if your mandatory exit point is not reached, the trade may still result in a loss only slightly smaller than your maximum allowable disaster. On the other hand, if you try to avoid catastrophic losses by exiting losing trades quickly, there is a much greater chance your exit points will be hit. The problem is finding the happy medium where your exit point will result in tolerable losses when you are wrong, but with a reasonable likelihood that you will not take too many losses.

Thus, high leverage adds an extra dimension to the price-prediction problem. You must choose the direction of future price movement correctly. In addition, you must also time your trade so that price moves in the correct direction *and* you take your profit *before* price moves against you to the extent that you must abandon the trade.

The Costs of Trading

In order not to complicate the trading examples we have looked at so far, I purposely left out an important consideration in the commodity-trading equation. These are the three costs of trading: brokerage commissions, slippage, and the bid/asked spread. You will pay two of these costs on every trade and often all three. While they seem relatively insignificant on a per trade basis, they add up quickly over time and have a significant impact on profitability. As you will see later, it is important to remember to include them when judging the profitability of a trading system.

Commissions

On every trade you pay your broker a commission for his work in completing the transaction. Stock brokerage commissions usually depend on the number of shares involved and the dollar size of the transaction. The bigger the transaction, the more you pay. Stock brokers charge a separate commission on both the buy and the sell side. The bigger your profit, the bigger the commission. In commodities, the trader has an advantage in that commissions are fixed at a certain amount per contract. It does not matter how much the contract is worth, the commission is the same. Also, there is only one commission for both the entry and exit, which you do not pay until you complete the trade. (A few brokerage firms charge half the commission after the entry and the other half after the exit, but the total is the same.) Thus, you can make a huge profit and still pay the same small commission. Standard commodity commissions range from $100 per contract per trade, charged by some full-service firms, down to as little as $18 charged by so-called discount firms for clients who do not require any advice or assistance from the broker.

To see the difference between stock and commodity commissions, assume that you had bought one S&P 500 futures contract at the opening on Monday morning, December 14, 1987. The price was 236.00, which meant you controlled the equivalent of $118,000 worth of stock. You could have sold your contract on Friday's close, December 18, at 248.45, a profit of $6,225. Using the rates of a major stock discount firm and assuming you had bought 1,000 shares of a stock at $118 and sold it for $124, the total commission would have been $510 on the two stock market transactions. Your discount commission on the one futures contract would have been $25 or less.

With any firm you are free to negotiate the commission rate on the basis of the size of your account and the amount of trading you do. I strongly suggest that you press for the lowest possible commission rate regardless of the firm with whom you decide to do business. Individual commissions are small, but over the course of a year's trading they add up. Every dollar you save in commissions is as good as a guaranteed dollar in profitable trading.

Slippage

Slippage refers to the difference between the price at which you want to execute your trade and the price at which it is actually executed. Depending on the type of orders you use and your trading tactics, slippage can reduce profits or increase losses significantly. Unfortunately, the best tactical trading approaches result in the most slippage. Here are some examples.

Assume you are watching the corn market on your computer quote machine. It is trading at 1.98. You decide that if it goes up to 2.00, that will confirm an uptrend, and you want to buy. When you see it hit 2.00, you call your broker and place an order to buy at the market. He calls you back and tells you your order was executed at 2.00½. The market moved up another half cent in the time it took to transmit your order to the floor. The difference between where you wanted to enter and the actual price where the order was filled is slippage, in this case $25 per contract. You could have prevented the possibility of slippage by placing an order to buy at "2.00 or better" instead of "at the market." Then you would have been guaranteed that if your order was executed, the price would be no higher than 2.00. However, if after your order reaches the floor, the price is over 2.00 and never goes back down to 2.00, your order will not be filled. The market may then go up without you.

There is another type of order that is very popular, the "stop" order. When the market was trading at 1.98 and you decided to buy if it rose to 2.00, you did not have to wait and watch the market yourself. You could have placed an order to buy at "2.00 stop." This instructs the broker on the exchange trading floor to hold your order until the price hits 2.00 and then execute it as soon as possible. You will probably pay a little more than 2.00. On some exchanges you can attempt to control the slippage by placing a limit on the price at which the floor broker can execute your order by saying "buy . . . at 2.00 stop limit" or "buy . . . at 2.00 stop with a limit of 2.01." (Floor brokers at the Board of Trade, where corn is traded, do not accept limit orders. Most other exchanges do, however.) The order will not be executed at a price greater than your limit, but you run the risk of having the market move through your entry trigger price before your order can be executed. You might then miss a very profitable trade.

Good traders almost always use stop orders to exit a trade automatically when the market is going against them. For instance, if he entered an order to buy corn at 2.00, a good trader would simultaneously determine how far he would let the position move against him before getting out. He would then place a stop order to sell his corn at that price, for example, "sell . . . at 1.90 stop, good until cancelled." This order would remain on the exchange floor to be automatically executed if and when the price of corn dropped to 1.90.

Stop orders eliminate the delay caused by your having to communicate the order to your broker and his having to deliver it to the trading floor, but in most markets a stop order is invariably executed at a slightly worse price. Depending on the market and the current volume of activity, this difference can range from $25 to $75. In esoteric markets without much activity or in very volatile situations, slippage can amount to hundreds of dollars.

In another common situation, large slippage can reduce your profits or add to your losses. This is caused by the fact that the markets do not remain open for trading 24 hours a day. There can be a large gap between where the market stops trading on one day (the close) and where it starts trading the next (the open). In our corn example, assume the market dropped to 1.91, where it closed for the day. The resting stop order at 1.90 would not be executed because the market did not reach as low as 1.90. The next morning the market may not open at 1.91. Because of some news that came out during the night, such as a big storm in the Midwest, the market may open the next day at 1.88. Your stop order would be filled immediately, but you would still have lost an additional $100 per contract more than you had wanted. This is a classic example of slippage.

The Bid/Asked Spread

The bid/asked spread is a cost to traders off the exchange floor that is hidden from view so most traders are not aware of it. When a price is being quoted in the trading pit, there are actually two prices, the bid and the asked. They are usually, but not always, one tick apart with the bid being the lower of the two. For example, in the T-bond pit, the minimum price fluctuation is 1/32 of a point, which is worth $32.50 per contract. When the price is quoted at 90-00, that is the bid price. The simultaneous asked price is 90-01, or 1/32 higher.

The public trader always buys at the asked price and sells at the bid price, while the floor trader (who takes the other side of the transaction) will be buying at the bid and selling at the asked. Thus, if you bought and sold 100 contracts from the same floor trader without any price change, you would lose $3,250 and he would make $3,250. You would have bought at 90-01 and sold at 90-00, while he would have done the opposite. He would have a further advantage in that his transaction cost is only a few dollars per trade, while you have to pay a $20 or $25 commission on each trade.

This hidden cost may not be very large in itself, but when added to the costs of slippage and commissions, the total becomes significant. The more you trade, the more it adds up. For the sake of hypothetical historical testing of trading systems, I usually assume a transaction cost of $100 per trade. This is called "slippage and commissions," but it includes the bid/asked differential as well. If you trade 10 times per month, you would be paying $1,000 a month just to execute the trades. That's a tremendous burden on a small account. Perhaps now you can appreciate better why the professional is satisfied with less than 100 percent return on capital.

Trends

Some college professors, who have probably never traded commodities, have suggested that commodity and stock prices move randomly. By this they mean that there is no relationship between the past and future. Commodity trading, they say, is like flipping a coin. Heads gives you a winning trade and tails means a loss. Since you must always pay commissions on every trade, if you played for any length of time you would be almost guaranteed to lose. The profits and losses from trading would cancel each other out, and you would have to pay all the commissions. If prices are really random, it would mean that in the long run no one could expect to make money by trading commodities. Your only chance for profit would be a short-term lucky streak after which you had sense enough to quit. The realistic chance for continued success would be as hopeless as in casino gambling.

At the opposite extreme from the few academics who espouse the random-walk theory are the mystics who believe there is a perfect order behind the markets. They think that if they could only break the market's code, they would always be able to tell precisely what will happen next. This is wishful thinking, but it is impossible to convince these people otherwise. They just keep on looking. Millions, perhaps billions, of computer hours have been devoted to analyzing the markets in an effort to find a better method of predicting prices. If there were a foolproof method, someone would probably have found it by now.

He or she would quickly be able to amass huge wealth. Word would get out.

The most telling argument against the "random-walk" theory is the number of traders who consistently earn large amounts of money from their trading. Some of these traders have careers lasting 20 years and more. This does not seem possible if market activity is always completely random. The question can probably never be definitively resolved.

There is no evidence that anyone has been able to devise a method that is very good at precise market forecasting, despite heroic efforts. The reason is that there is, in fact, much randomness in price fluctuations, especially in the short term. I spent several years searching for a way to predict just the direction of the next day's close in the stock market. All I wanted to know was whether tomorrow's closing price would be higher or lower than today's. I found nothing with enough accuracy and statistical reliability to be useful in trading.

There is, however, one nonrandom characteristic of commodity market price movement that makes the difference between hopelessness and potential profitability. Markets tend to trend. That means that there is a stronger likelihood that a market will continue its

EXHIBIT 1-1 Monthly Chart of Swiss Francs

Does this look like random price action?

current trend than that it will reverse. Secular trends are caused by long-term fundamental forces that tend to persist. Look at Exhibit 1–1, a monthly continuation chart of Swiss franc futures, and Exhibit 1–2, a weekly continuation chart of crude oil futures. Do they look like random price activity? Other trends that are more short-term in nature are caused by shifts in market psychology. Such shifts are usually precipitated by news events relevant to the particular market.

One can speak of a trend only in relation to a given time frame. The trend for the last two years, the last two weeks, and the last two hours may have been up. At the same time the trend for the last two months, the last two days, and the last twenty minutes may have been down. Exhibits 1–3 through 1–6 illustrate the problem. Is the trend up or down? In Exhibit 1–3, over the longest term shown on the chart, the trend is down. In Exhibit 1–4, over the last two years, the trend is up. In Exhibit 1–5, over the previous six months, the trend is down, while in Exhibit 1–6, over the last two months, the trend is up.

All trends are not created equal. There are strong trends, in which price moves steadily in one direction for an extended period. There are weaker trends, where the market's main movement is slow and shows

EXHIBIT 1–2   Weekly Chart of Crude Oil

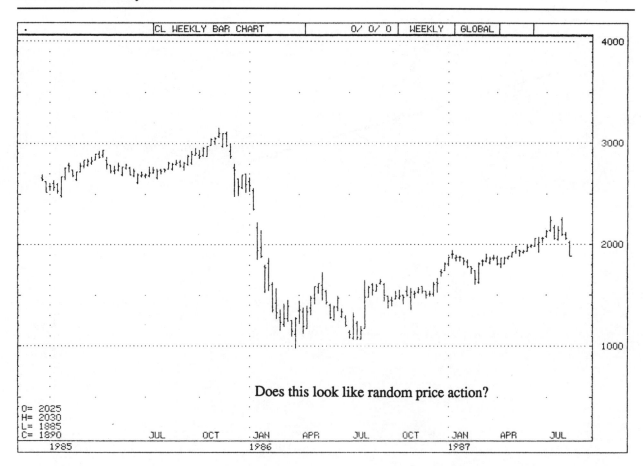

significant, periodic countertrend reversals. Often there is no significant trend in a particular time frame although there will be trends in longer and shorter time frames.

The commodity trader will do the best when he positions himself in the direction of a strong trend and stays with the trade as long as the trend persists. This is not as easy as it sounds because he can never be sure when the periodic countertrend moves, which always occur, will mark the beginning of a trend reversal.

Trading Time Frame

Each trader must operate in the time frame which matches his trading personality. Some people are very impatient and seek the excitement of numerous trades. It is psychologically impossible for them to trade in a long-term time frame where they must trade infrequently and hold positions for weeks and even months. There are many traders who feel most comfortable trading in a very short time frame. Known as "day traders," they enter and exit their trades on the same day,

EXHIBIT 1–3 Weekly Chart of Crude Oil with Very Long-Term Trend

often within an hour or even less. This kind of trading generates a large number of trades that result in relatively small individual profits and losses.

As we have seen, each trade you make has a cost. The smaller your average profit per trade, the larger will be the percentage of those profits offset by that cost. The more often you trade, the greater will be the likelihood that your trading profits will not be large enough to surmount the costs of trading. You have the greatest chance to overcome the costs of trading if you trade infrequently and shoot for long-term trades and large profits. This means watching trends on weekly and daily charts.

Another way to look at this is to think about maximizing your average profit per trade. To the extent that it is feasible, you want to maximize your average profit on profitable trades and minimize your average loss on losing trades. Sometimes, when you are wrong and the market goes strongly against you, your intention to seek a long-term profit can result in a very short-term loss. There's nothing wrong with that if the loss is small. The real problem arises when you take profits too quickly and have small average profits while taking losses too slowly, causing large average losses. That fatal combination results in

EXHIBIT 1–4 Weekly Chart of Crude Oil with Long-Term Trend

either net trading losses or trading profits too small to exceed the costs of trading.

It may be possible to be successful with a relatively small average profit per trade if you have an unusually high percentage of profitable trades and can keep the costs of trading down. This is feasible for floor traders in the exchange trading pits. However, for members of the public who trade off the floor, the greatest chance of success is with longer-term trading.

Predicting the Market

One reason people shy away from commodity trading is that they assume that in order to be successful, they will have to become an expert on all the markets they want to trade. I have good news. To speculate on a particular commodity, you do not have to know anything about its fundamentals. While supply and demand determine the price level, you as a speculator do not have to worry about trying to figure out those numbers. How could you hope to predict future supply and de-

EXHIBIT 1–5   Weekly Chart of Crude Oil with Intermediate-Term Trend

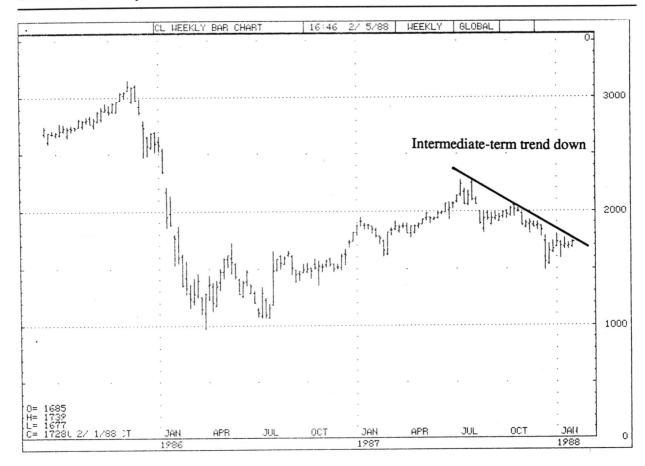

mand anyway? The Department of Agriculture publishes estimates of supply in many agricultural markets. But how accurate are they? Not very. You can estimate demand only on the basis of previous demand. How accurate can you expect to be at predicting changes in demand?

If you were going to trade, for instance, T-bond futures using such fundamentals, you would have to learn how to predict where long-term interest rates are going in the future. There are many experts who give such predictions, but they are not precise enough or reliable enough to assist a commodity trader. You could never hope to do better.

In commodity trading, the market's perception of supply and demand is even more important than the actual figures. Even if you knew something about supply and demand, you would still have to figure out how the market would react. Luckily, you do not have to.

Everything that market participants currently know about supply and demand and the market's perception of supply and demand is already reflected in the price. All you have to look at is the price history and the current price level. From those you can determine the current trend, if there is a trend. Look at the two price charts in Exhibits 1–7 and 1–8. Exhibit 1–7 is a weekly continuation chart of

EXHIBIT 1–6   Weekly Chart of Crude Oil with Short-Term Trend

orange juice futures prices. Your task is to predict from that chart the probable future direction of orange juice prices—up or down.

Suppose that at the time of this chart an alleged orange juice expert presented you with a comprehensive research report (in commodities, he would probably want to sell it to you) demonstrating that the price of orange juice must go down in the near future because there was too much supply and too little demand. Would you be convinced and sell the market? I would not. Do you think he is the only one in the world who understands the true fundamental situation in orange juice? Those who are closest to the market and know the most about it are active traders. They have been bidding the price up. If the price is so surely going to go down soon, why is it now going up? The expert could as easily have told you the same thing any time in the last two years and he would have been wrong every time. The better strategy is not to anticipate what will happen, but to wait for the market to agree with his analysis by changing to a downtrend.

Exhibit 1–8 is a weekly chart of S&P 500 stock index futures showing the spectacular bull market between 1985 and 1987. What if, at the time of this chart, you heard a famous guru on television predict that the stock market was about to go into a strong downtrend? Would

EXHIBIT 1–7   Weekly Chart of Orange Juice

Does the future direction of prices look up or down?

you sell? The reason he gave was the readings of his secret technical indicators. How do they know? The truth is that he is just guessing. No one *knows* the future direction of prices.

As it turned out, he would have been exactly right. That was the very time of the major stock market top in August 1987. You would probably have been very impressed with his stock market predicting ability and perhaps have subscribed to his newsletter, hoping to profit from his next inspired call. What you would not have known was that he had been predicting an imminent top every week for the previous year. Had you followed *that* advice, you would have had catastrophic losses. You will save yourself much wasted effort (and perhaps trading losses) if you accept the idea that it is impossible to predict future market action with the precision necessary to be useful in commodity trading.

To be successful as a speculator, you must follow rather than try to anticipate trends. Therefore, to determine whether to buy or sell, you do not need to make inspired predictions about future supply and demand. You do not have to anticipate the market's reaction to the latest political news. All you have to do is determine the current price trend and position yourself accordingly. If the trend is up, you

EXHIBIT 1–8   Weekly Chart of the S&P 500

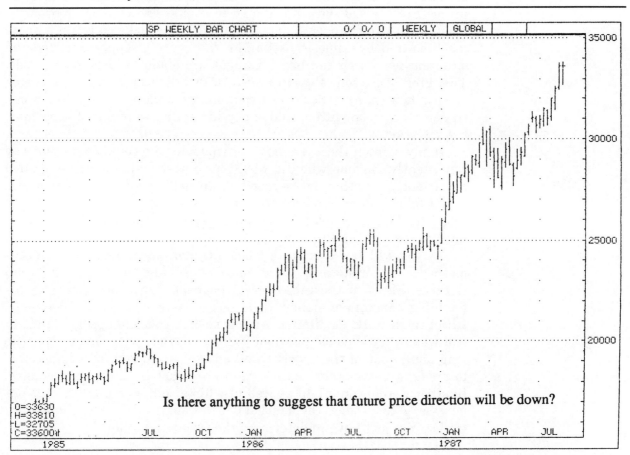

Is there anything to suggest that future price direction will be down?

always buy. If the trend is down, you always sell. What could be simpler than that?

One of my favorite caricatures of the commodity trader is the movie *Trading Places,* starring Eddie Murphy and Dan Ackroyd. Dan Ackroyd plays a professional commodity trader who works for a wealthy brokerage firm. Eddie Murphy plays a down-and-out ghetto dweller who has been reduced to pushing himself around on a cart pretending he has no legs. The brokerage firm's two senior partners make a bet about how Murphy and Ackroyd will manage if their roles in society are reversed. The partners bring Murphy into the firm to trade commodities.

At one point Murphy is in an opulent office with a commodity quote machine on the desk. He is watching the tick-by-tick price changes in pork bellies. (Although most references to commodity trading in such situations refer to pork bellies, in actuality this is not a popular market with speculators.) He watches intently as the price drops . . . 66.01, 65.93, 65.67, 65.49, 65.11. (Never mind that pork belly prices cannot end in 3, 9 or 1.) "The place to buy is 64.00," he confidently announces. After the partners place the order to buy hundreds of contracts, the price turns around and starts to climb, assuring the firm and its clients of huge profits.

The question is, how did Murphy know the price of pork bellies was going to stop dropping and start rising? The supposition is that some people are blessed with an ability to divine future price movement from past price changes. They sit watching the ticks go by on a quote machine and by osmosis assimilate the overall supply and demand situation for which the price changes are some kind of secret code. This kind of person is said to have "a feel for the market." It is surprising how many experienced commodity traders believe that some traders were born with a kind of psychic ability to predict future market direction.

In my opinion there are not many people who could trade this way consistently. Anyone who did would have specific methods he applied consistently, whether he realized it himself or not. These methods would follow sound trading principles. It would be the adherence to those trading principles that would generate the profits, not some mystical psychic ability.

As you will see later in this book, traders have devised numerous methods for predicting price movements and anticipating trend changes. Many of these have been packaged and sold, some for astounding amounts of money. We'll look at some of those in Chapter 7. All of them work for limited time periods. That time period tends to end when they are sold or when you try to trade with them. Over the long haul, none of them works well enough to rely on. It is impossible to *predict trend changes* with a reliability that is better than chance. In other words, you might as well just flip a coin. Fortunately, it is not necessary to predict the markets to be successful as a commodity trader. You just have to determine the trend and follow it.

The Three Cardinal Rules of Successful Commodity Trading

Successful commodity trading boils down to three principles. They are as old as trading itself, emphasized in every book on the subject, and well-known to every trader:

1. Follow the trend.
2. Cut losses short.
3. Let profits run.

Even though every losing trader knows these principles, he is nevertheless unable to follow them. We will examine why in the next chapter.

2

Why People Fail at Commodity Trading

It is fairly well known that the odds of making money consistently from commodity trading are low. Depending on the source of the statistics, you will hear that anywhere from 75 percent to 95 percent of traders lose money. A fairly high proportion stop trading within six months because of excessive losses. Some traders are fortunate to do well at the beginning. Invariably, they become overconfident and lose all their early profits. Because they have tasted limited success, they are likely to keep trading longer and lose more than somebody who has lost consistently from the beginning.

Other than gambling, there is probably no human endeavor with such a low success rate that continues to attract such a large number of participants. It is not because the newcomers do not understand the odds against them. It is because everyone thinks (or hopes) he or she will be the exception. Almost everyone, it seems, wants to get rich quick with a minimum of work. Commodity speculation looks like it will be faster and involve less work than real estate. It is much more complicated than gambling or entering sweepstakes or lotteries, but the odds of success appear far better. Even more important for many, perhaps, is the intellectual challenge. Success also carries prestige. In most circles successful speculators are respected and envied. So, while this is a steep mountain, the rewards for successfully scaling it are exceptional.

Once you begin trying to solve the riddles of commodity trading, it becomes addictive. Analyzing and trading the markets is a supreme challenge and lots of fun. It makes a great hobby. Unlike other hobbies the potential rewards of success are tangible and tremendous. Those who can afford to continue funding their losses will go on trading for years without a single profitable year. There is always the potential of discovering something significant. Their trading career begins anew with each new trade.

There are new advisory letters to try. There are new books and new trading systems to buy. In the last 10 years commodity trading education has made a quantum leap. Although people had been actively trading commodities in the United States for decades, when I started trading in 1975, there was only a handful of decent books on the subject. The perspective was limited. Just 12 years later, there is a large body of literature with excellent works on many different aspects of trading. Every aspect of the American information revolution has touched commodities. In addition to proliferating books and newsletters, there are audio tapes, video tapes, endless seminars, and computer software.

The advent of the affordable personal computer has had an enormous effect on commodity traders. The computer's calculating speed has brought the average trader incredible capacity to analyze the markets on a daily basis. You can come home from your office, turn on the computer and go eat dinner. Before you are finished the computer will automatically call a commodity data base, retrieve the day's prices in the markets you follow, perform complicated analyses of recent price history that might take days to do by hand, and then print charts and tables summarizing the results of all the markets. You can review them over coffee and decide on your trading tactics for tomorrow. In the early days of personal computers, this kind of computer work might take all night. Now you can complete it in an hour or less.

Satellite communications have made it feasible for small traders to receive instantaneous price quotations from the exchanges. Ingenious new software allows an inexpensive personal computer to transform this stream of tick-by-tick price quotations into price charts and

EXHIBIT 2–1   Five-Minute Chart of Japanese Yen with Analytic Studies (March 1988 contract)

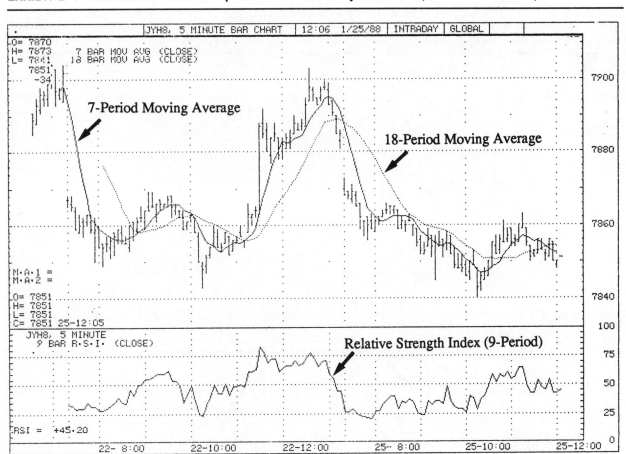

analytical studies almost instantaneously. For example, Exhibit 2–1 shows a Japanese yen bar chart with two up-to-date moving averages and an oscillator (Wilder's Relative Strength Index) displayed underneath. Exhibit 2–2 shows a pork belly bar chart with one moving average and a different oscillator (stochastics) displayed underneath. I was able to look at each chart on my computer screen during market hours within seconds of the last price change represented on the chart. I have great flexibility in displaying the price data and can apply over a dozen different analytical tools, most of which allow me to adjust the sensitivity to suit my taste and trading style.

Unlike the floor trader trying to think in the pandemonium of the pit, the off-the-floor trader can watch these sophisticated graphics in the comfort of his office or home. He can watch all the markets at once. Exhibit 2–3 shows an up-to-the-minute, simultaneous display of the Dow Jones Average and two different stock indexes trading in New York and Chicago. Perhaps a trader believes there is some short-term relationship between stock index futures and T-bond futures. As you can see in Exhibit 2–4, he could watch both at once and compare them even though they trade on different exchanges. For the first time, there are some real advantages to trading off the floor.

Sophisticated software is now for sale that makes historical testing of trading approaches simple and fast. Until a few years ago, this ca-

EXHIBIT 2–2   Four-Minute Chart of Pork Bellies with Analytic Studies (February 1988 contract)

pability was unavailable to the average trader unless he could write his own programs or afford to pay someone else who could. Later in this book, I will be showing you the results of hypothetically testing numerous trading approaches on historical data. These tests were all run with software available to anyone. You can test virtually any trading method specific enough to be expressed mathematically on any market over any time period for which you have data. It is precisely this kind of testing capability that has made this book possible.

In spite of all these educational and technological advances in the last 10 years, the trading success ratio has probably not risen at all. I expect it will continue to be low forever. The reasons people fail as speculators are not a secret. I divide them into six separate categories, although there are interrelationships between the categories.

Lack of Understanding

Although knowledge is usually power, knowledge is not enough in commodity trading. The hardest part is the doing. Lack of understanding is probably the least contributing factor of the six listed here. Nevertheless, there are some common misunderstandings among commodity

EXHIBIT 2–3   One-Minute Charts of Stock Indexes and the Dow Jones Average

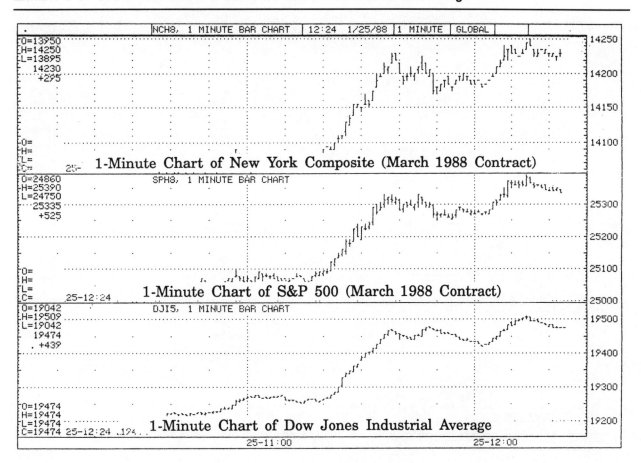

1-Minute Chart of New York Composite (March 1988 Contract)

1-Minute Chart of S&P 500 (March 1988 Contract)

1-Minute Chart of Dow Jones Industrial Average

traders that inhibit success potential. I have already addressed some of them in Chapter 1. Here are some more.

If you ask the average commodity trader why he trades, the answer is invariably some variation of, "To make money." This seems obvious. But like many aspects of speculative activity, what is most obvious is obviously wrong. It is safe to say that most commodity traders are in it primarily for the challenge, the experience, and the thrill rather than profits. They honestly do not care whether they make money or not. They would prefer to make lots of money but not because they want to spend it. Profits to them are the yardstick of performance, the measurement of success.

For most commodity traders the real driving force is ego, but many are not aware of it. They want to prove to themselves and others around them how brilliant they are compared to the other traders they are competing against. This causes two important mistakes. First, they tell other people the details of what they are doing so that they can brag about their successes. The problem is that when a trade is not working out, they are less concerned about monetary losses than losing face with the people they told. If you tell your golfing buddies one weekend that gold is going up and you just bought a bunch of contracts, how will you react during the next week when gold starts

EXHIBIT 2–4   One-Minute Charts of the S&P 500 and T-Bonds

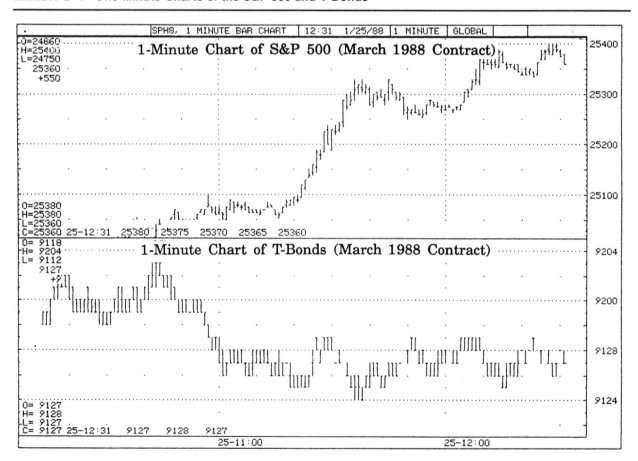

heading down? If you take your loss, you will probably have to admit it when the subject comes up again during next Saturday's game. If you hold on a little longer, gold may well rebound. You can tell your friends to be patient, that you will still be right. If you tell no one (not even your spouse), you can take your losses without any fear of looking bad to anyone.

This is also a good argument in favor of using a discount broker instead of a full-service broker. With a full-service broker, you talk a lot; you tend to become friends. You discuss potential trades and their rationale. When you originate the ideas, you will tend to have an emotional involvement in their success. When you take losses, it is natural to feel that in your broker's eyes you have failed. This is bound to affect your decisions in managing the trades. To the extent that trade ideas originate with your broker, he will have the same problem because he does not want to fail you either.

When you do business with a discount broker, you do not deal with an individual. You call a trading desk and speak to someone who only takes your orders. He has no idea why you are placing an order and does not care. His only concern is to carry out your instructions quickly and accurately. You have no reason to be embarrassed about taking a loss. You will not look bad to anyone. You can act without any ego involvement.

The second mistake that results from trading for ego reinforcement rather than pure profits is placing too much emphasis on predicting. That is the most satisfying aspect of trading for the ego: predicting what the market will do and being right. It puts you above everyone else trading that market. In Chapter 1, I stated that no one can predict the markets with the precision needed for highly leveraged commodity trading and that, furthermore, good predicting is not necessary for profitable trading. To the uninitiated, this is heresy.

Because it appears obvious that accurate predicting will assure profitable trading, almost all traders spend extraordinary time and money trying to learn better methods of predicting. It is well known that analyzing fundamentals is useless for predicting changes in trend. Price action invariably leads fundamental news. So traders turn to technical analysis.

Technical analysis is a vast labyrinth of techniques to analyze market action. Hundreds of books have been written on the subject. Although most have been directed toward the stock market rather than commodities, the approach is the same. There are countless ways to break down and organize price history. Each can be considered a "tool" of technical market analysis. Most of these tools require some judgment in their use. Technical analysis is referred to as an art rather than a science.

There are two results from the imprecise nature of technical analysis tools. First, learning to be a good technical analyst becomes a great and fascinating challenge. Second, no one can prove whether these methods really work. Proponents can always point to numerous examples where a particular tool (as they interpret it) correctly foretold future price movement. These are always easier to identify in retrospect. However, there can be no rigorous test because there are no precise rules to apply. If the trader diligently employs the tools of technical analysis and he loses money, he concludes it was his fault rather than the methods he was using. He tries harder. He learns more methods. He spends lots of money. He wastes his time.

To the extent that fancy technical analysis does no more than identify the trend within a particular time frame, it is harmless although unnecessary. To the extent that it gives the trader a structure in which he can rationalize trading decisions, be consistent, and take action, it is useful so long as the trader also follows the three important rules of trading listed at the end of the preceding chapter.

I have seen no evidence that technical analysis can consistently predict future market direction. I am not suggesting that all professional market technicians make unrealistic claims about their talents. Most of the ones I know are pretty realistic, even humble. It is the trading public's perception that is wrong.

A good example is the Elliott Wave Theory. This is a method of organizing market action described by R. N. Elliott in the 1930s. It has achieved great notoriety in the last few years because of the successful stock market predictions of Robert Prechter. Prechter has appeared on national television and been on the cover of several major magazines. He co-authored the definitive book on the subject and also writes a newsletter called *The Elliott Wave Theorist,* which analyzes the stock market, interest rate markets, and gold. Commodity traders assume the Elliott Wave Theory predicts the markets. They believe that if they learn its precepts or subscribe to a newsletter that gives advice based upon it, they will be able to predict the markets.

Elliott Wave professionals, however, including Prechter, make no such claims. Dan Ascani is the editor of *The Elliott Wave Commodity Forecast,* which Robert Prechter's company, New Classics Library, owns and publishes. Here is how Dan describes the value of Elliott Wave analysis for commodity traders:

> A magic system that can accurately predict the future does not exist. The Elliott Wave Principle is a dynamic and flexible method for reading the market you are trading. By listening to what the market is saying, we are deriving our strategies from the market itself. In this way, we let the market tell us what to do.

That is what I mean by following the markets rather than trying to predict them.

Lack of Capital

Lack of capital is the only reason for failure beyond your control. Either you have capital or you don't. Unfortunately, most potential commodity traders don't have enough capital. That is why they want to trade in the first place: to accumulate capital.

In commodity trading there are two kinds of capital: risk capital and nonrisk capital. Risk capital is usually defined as money you can afford to lose without changing your standard of living. You should also be able to lose it without great self-recrimination. As you will see, your attitude toward losing money will be a key factor. If you agonize and wring your hands over every losing trade, you will not be successful. If you transfer into your commodity account savings that you have earmarked for your children's college education, you will not be comfortable losing it. This is suicidal. Your conscience is your best guide as to what is risk capital and what is not. Although you will probably not lose every dollar you deposit in your commodity account, you still should accept the reality that you may well lose such a significant part of it that what remains will not matter much.

It helps to have a source of income to generate replacement capital if you do lose it. Retired people are attracted to commodity trading because it gives them something exciting to do that is not physically demanding and can be pursued on a part-time basis. They usually have a nice pool of capital available. The problem is they will not be able to replace any losses because they are no longer working.

Traders often play games with themselves in calculating how much capital they have available for commodity trading. They count money that is not deposited in their trading account as "available for trading." There is an intriguing bonus return available on commodity accounts that makes this deception unnecessary.

Commodity traders have a number of significant advantages over stock traders. We have already seen that they pay much smaller commissions as a percentage of each transaction. Here is another. In order to obtain leverage, stock buyers may borrow a certain amount from their brokers, using the stock as collateral. This percentage is set by the Federal Reserve and is currently 50 percent. That means you can buy $1,000 worth of stock with only $500 in your account. However, you must pay your broker interest on the amount of the loan. To the extent that your gains on the stock transaction do not exceed the interest you pay, you lose.

In commodities, as we have seen, there is natural leverage in buying and selling commodity contracts. In addition, you can earn extra interest on the money in your account by buying T-bills. Your broker will buy the T-bills for you and allow you to use the T-bills for margin just like cash. Thus, you get twice the bang for your buck. You use the same money to earn interest on T-bills and trade commodities. There is a minimum account size required for this (around $15,000). There are also limits on the percentage of the account that can be in T-bills, but the percentage is high (usually about 90 percent). To avoid the hassle of buying T-bills every quarter, some brokerage firms just pay you T-bill interest on a portion of your account.

Since you will be earning bonus interest on most of the money in your commodity account, there is no excuse for holding commodity risk capital outside your account. If you are reluctant to deposit some money in your account, you should ask yourself why. You either need it elsewhere or you don't feel comfortable losing it. Either way, it is not risk capital, and it will be detrimental to your trading to count it as such.

Lack of capital is relative. The more money you have deposited in your trading account, the more flexible and diversified you can be in your trading. The more you have and the more you are truly willing to lose, the better will be your chance for success provided you manage your trading properly. However, it is possible to trade with the brokerage minimum of $5,000. The same proper money management principles that apply to a $50,000 account also apply to a $5,000 account. Those will be discussed in detail in Chapter 16. If it were possible, one should be trading at one-tenth the level with the smaller account. As a practical matter, there are some limits to how small you can trade. In addition, it is very difficult for traders with small accounts to accept the limits this imposes on projected profits. They want to trade their small account as if it were much bigger. Therefore, they will be taking bigger risks in relation to their account size and have a far greater chance to fail.

The first important step in managing your capital is to make a realistic assessment of what is risk capital. Whatever you are going to risk in commodities, you must deposit in your account. Never deposit nonrisk capital in your account with the idea that you will stop trading before you lose it. If your account contains nonrisk capital, you cannot trade with the kind of indifference to losses so necessary for success. You must accept the total loss of all the money in your account as an expensive lesson you may have to learn. The more money you can devote to trading within these restrictions, the greater will be your chance for success.

Unrealistic Expectations

In Chapter 1, I alluded to the problem of the small trader who tries to trade like a big trader. He will have to take big risks and will therefore fail. I indicated that a reasonable goal for commodity traders is a consistent return of 50 percent a year on the total amount in your trading account. In the best years, you hope to do better. In the worst years, you hope at least to break even.

That is the goal for an experienced trader. The novice should have even lower expectations. If a new trader broke even in his first year, he would be far ahead of most others. If he was able to do that, he could go for perhaps a 20 percent return his second year. Then he would be ready to shoot for 50 percent his third year and thereafter.

These targets are far below the expectations of the usual trader who has limited risk capital and wants to get rich quick. I remember a seminar I gave several years ago where I asked individuals in the audience what their profit goals were. Some people really expected to make 30–40 percent per month! I wish I knew who they were so I could ask them how they have done and what their goals are now. I bet they are no longer even trading. Since the risks are inexorably related to the rewards, you can keep the risks manageable only by controlling your expectations. If you are trying for a return of only 50 percent per year, you don't have to trade every day or even every week. You can afford to wait for the best opportunities with the highest probability of success. Your costs of trading will be lower. You will make fewer mistakes. You can keep your anxiety low. You will probably live longer so you can enjoy your profits.

Lack of Patience

Lack of patience is related to unrealistic expectations. It most often manifests itself in two ways: overtrading and overrisking. These are both caused by trying to make too much profit too quickly.

We have already seen that because the costs of trading are high, it is better to trade less often and shoot for a higher average profit per trade. In addition, each trade has a particular risk/reward ratio that can be defined as the potential reward, divided by the risk assumed, times the probability of success. Naturally, for any trade there is considerable difficulty in assigning specific numerical values to these variables. If you evaluate each trade this way, at least in general, you should be taking only trades with relatively high risk/reward ratios. The average trader finds he cannot wait for these trades. He must be doing something all the time. This results from all the effort he puts into analyzing the markets. After spending three hours in the evening updating all his charts, running a computer program, and analyzing all the markets, it is hard to decide there is no trade to make. He ends up overtrading.

Many times a trader will be watching a market, waiting to enter a position. He has a point picked out for his stop-loss order that will give him a comfortable loss. All of a sudden the market takes off in the direction the trader was anticipating. By the time he wakes up to what is happening, the trader will have to take a much bigger risk than he planned because he wants to place his stop-loss order in the same place, but now his entry will be much farther away. The correct thing to do in this circumstance is to wait for the market to pull back, so you can keep your loss limited, or look for another trading opportunity. But the average trader sees the market as confirming his analysis, and he wants to profit from it. So he enters late, takes a trade he knows he should not be in, and usually ends up with a much bigger loss than his account can stand. There are other ways to fall into trades with a greater risk than is prudent. Each of these common mistakes is caused by lack of patience, the inability to wait for the perfect trading opportunity.

Lack of Discipline

Discipline is the most popular word used to describe the essence of good commodity trading. Trite though it may be, it does cover a multitude of sins that even the best traders seem incapable of avoiding . . . again and again. We know what we are supposed to do. We may even have a specific plan replete with details about how to react in every possible situation. Yet we constantly find ways to deviate from the plan. At the time we goof up, we always have what appears to be a good reason. Later, upon reflection, we realize we should have stayed with the plan. We keep making the same mistakes over and over. Until it happens to you, you cannot believe how easy it is for otherwise intelligent people intentionally to do things they know are unwise. This is a constant battle that every trader wages over and over throughout his career. The best traders not only have the best plans, they deviate from their plan the least often.

An easy way for ineffective traders to function without discipline is to trade without a plan. Most traders fall into this category. They don't have the faintest idea what they will do in a given situation until it develops and they are forced to make a decision. We will watch some of these people make their trading decisions in Chapter 3.

Any trading plan is better than no plan, but most plans are hopelessly general. The more general the plan, the more opportunity there is to make a mistake while making a decision under pressure. One of the purposes of this book is to persuade you to trade with a plan so specific that you always know in advance what to do in any given trading situation. There is no leeway for interpretation or judgment. Everyone who applies the rules correctly gets the same trading signals. That is called a mechanical system. Then, once you choose your system(s), the only thing you will have to worry about is always making your trading decisions according to the system rules. It sounds easy, but it isn't.

High Risk Aversion

Aversion to risk is the least mentioned and least understood reason why most commodity traders fail. Most human beings are naturally averse to risk. We all have a survival instinct. In caveman days survival depended upon the ability to find food and create shelter. In today's civilized society man trades money for food instead of finding it in the wild himself. He trades money for shelter instead of building it himself. Survival depends on having money. Generally, the more money we have, the more lavish is our lifestyle. Once we get used to a certain lifestyle, we do not want to give it up. We equate losing money with losing comfort and happiness. Most of us are very careful with our money.

How many people would want to drive a racing car around a track at 200 miles per hour when one little mistake can mean your life? How many people would want to jump out of a plane at 15,000 feet when the parachute could tangle and let you fall to instant death? How many people would want ski down a huge ramp at 60 miles an hour, leap 200 meters off into space, and then try to land on a steep downslope that is as hard as ice? Would you relish taking any of these risks? Almost everyone would politely decline such an opportunity. Yet there are a small number of people who are not only willing to do these things, they receive the most enjoyment in their life from them. Do you think you could ever learn to enjoy any of these activities?

The best commodity traders are like financial race car drivers, sky divers, and ski jumpers. They are not afraid of taking big financial risks; they actually enjoy it. One of the most successful private traders was once asked what his threshold of pain in trading was. In other words, how big did a loss have to be before it hurt. His answer was $250,000! He was talking about a loss from a single trade even though it may involve hundreds of contracts. That is the most significant reason to explain how this man is able to generate consistent profits in the millions of dollars per year.

Recent scientific evidence suggests there is an actual biochemical difference between the brains of risk takers and non-risk takers that may explain this compulsive behavior. If that is so, it means there is only so much that risk-averse traders can do to feel more comfortable with high-risk trading. Maybe in the future, we'll be able to take a pill to feel more comfortable taking risks.

In the meantime, one of the most important steps you can take toward profitable trading is to come to terms with your level of financial risk aversion. This will probably only become apparent when you actually start making real trades. One of the questions you have to answer on every trade is, Where will I place my automatic stop-loss order to abandon my position if the market goes against me? If you determine where you will place your stop-loss order and the trade feels uncomfortable, you are probably beyond your loss comfort level. You should not make such trades. There will be some loss level that divides the point where you do not really mind taking a loss from the point where it begins to hurt a little. That is your loss comfort threshold, and you must respect it.

I found two intriguing things about my comfort threshold. First, it has not changed much over the years even though my net worth and the amount of money I devote to commodity trading has risen substantially. This leads me to believe that financial risk aversion is much more a product of total lifetime experience than actual financial strength. Second, I have different levels of comfort depending on how I am selecting my trades. If I am trading a mechanical system where my judgment is not involved, I am comfortable with considerably larger losses than if I am making the trading decisions on my own. This is probably because I have more confidence in the performance of mechanical systems than in my own judgment. I have been able to test the mechanical system historically, and I know what the loss experience is. I know I will have to accept certain losses to trade the system. The historical testing gives me confidence that any equity drawdowns will be limited and that the system will be profitable overall.

Profitable commodity trading requires quick action. The markets move quickly. If you hesitate over a signal to enter or exit a trade, most times you pay a penalty. If the signal is an entry signal, you may miss the trade completely or end up with a much less favorable entry price. If the signal is an exit signal, you will usually increase your loss or decrease your profit, sometimes substantially. "Buck fever" is a term hunters use to describe the common phenomenon of a hunter's not being able to pull the trigger when an animal is in his gunsight. Commodity traders refer to the analogous phenomenon—of a trader's inability to take timely action—as not being able to "pull the trigger."

Not being able to pull the trigger has only one cause—fear of taking a loss. Those who suffer from it (almost everyone at one time or another) are operating beyond their natural risk aversion level. Many people are so risk averse that they will never be able to trade commodities. If you fall into this category, you might as well admit it before you start. Stick to the kind of investing you feel comfortable with. If you do think you can handle commodity trading losses, stay within your comfortable limits. If you don't, you will pay the price in poor decisions and added losses. If you find yourself worrying about your positions, you are probably exceeding your comfort level. It is time to cut back on your trading or stop altogether. Commodity trading is not worth ruining your emotional equilibrium for. Be sensible, and respect your natural limits.

With the exception of lack of capital, every one of the reasons for failure is psychological. This psychology, however, has nothing to do with raw intelligence. No one suggests superior intelligence is a prerequisite for success. If you can understand this book, you have all the intelligence necessary. If you have real risk capital, are willing to devote the required time, and can surmount the psychological impediments to successful trading, you have a real chance to be a profitable commodity trader.

Almost everyone approaches the decision-making process from the wrong direction. This is the key factor that makes them prisoners of their own natural psychology. The next chapter will describe this usual direction of market analysis and show you how another, simpler way is the best road to commodity-trading profits.

3

The Mechanical Approach to Trading

People who come to commodity trading invariably have already had success in some other field. Most of the time they have been extremely successful. Without that success they would not have accumulated the capital necessary to trade. They expect to apply the same rational approach to commodity trading that led to their previous successes. Unfortunately, it is precisely this seemingly intelligent methodology that steers them to disaster.

Dr. Marvin Modestmoney, a Professor of Virology at a large state college, was sitting comfortably in his study after dinner. He took a telephone call from a man with a friendly voice who asked if he would be interested in a short-term investment opportunity with the potential for a truly exceptional return. Marvin had nothing better to do at the moment so he agreed to listen. The caller was a commodity broker who eagerly launched into his pitch.

"Doctor Modestmoney, I know your time is valuable so I won't waste any of it getting to the point. I work for Superselective Commodities, a small firm here in Newport Beach, California. We are small in size, but we have developed some incredible sources of information around the world. We were able to alert our clients ahead of time to the silver squeeze in 1980. We also caught the drought scare in soybeans in the summer of 1983, the bull market in coffee in 1985, and many other big short-term moves in the commodities markets. Naturally, our clients were able to make many times their investments on these moves. Our computer analysis program was correctly positioned on the short side before the big stock market crash last October. With the help of our firm's research, you could have made four times your money in one day on that one. Doctor, does that sound like the kind of situation you'd like to be able to take advantage of?"

"Sure."

The broker lowered his voice and continued. "The reason I'm calling you tonight, doctor, is that we have just received a report from West Africa about the cocoa crop. Our source is located in the Ivory Coast, which is one of the biggest cocoa growing countries in the world. He is telling us that the crop there and in Ghana is going to be affected in a big way this year by pod rot, a very dangerous disease for cocoa trees. The cocoa market has been very depressed since 1983, so there's no telling how high prices could go. The important thing is to get a position before the news gets out. Do you think you might be interested?"

"What did you call this disease?" Marvin responded. He was thinking about how a cocoa disease might operate compared to a human virus.

"Pod rot, doctor. It can devastate a year's crop or even kill the whole tree. The crucial thing is to act quickly."

"How much do I have to invest?"

"We only deal with substantial people like yourself, doctor. Our minimum account for futures trading is $10,000, but this has so much potential, I would recommend that you invest more than that. How much were you thinking about, doctor?"

"How much can I make on a $10,000 investment? And what is the risk?"

"Well, I'm not permitted to promise you any particular return, doctor. But if the market just goes back to its old high, that's a potential profit of $20,000 per contract. Our firm's current margin on cocoa is $2,000 per contract so that's about 10 to 1. Does that sound like a good return?"

"What about the risk?"

"Again, doctor, I can't promise you there's no risk trading commodities. Actually, if you trade futures and the price goes against you, there's theoretically no limit on your losses. You can even lose more than you start with in your account. But I wouldn't want to subject you to a risk like that, doctor. I've got a much better way to go. If you want to guarantee yourself a maximum risk, we could buy you some cocoa options in London. That's what I recommend. That way your risk would be fixed at whatever price you pay for the options. You would still have unlimited upside potential. We could get you a three-month option for $3,000 tomorrow. You would get the profit on however far the market goes up in three months with a guarantee you couldn't lose more than your $3,000 per option. Remember, you will maximize your profit if you buy right away before the news gets out. I have a certain number of these options I can sell because we don't want to alert the market. How many shall I put you down for?"

Marvin finally bought 10 options. He had to borrow half of that using the line of credit on his house. Although he didn't know it, the commission was $1,000 per option. The market did move up some in the next three months, so he only lost half his investment. After the options expired, the market kept going up. Marvin could see that there was a great deal of money to be made. If he had only bought futures instead the options, he would have done very well. He decided to find a new broker who specialized in futures and to do some reading about commodity trading on his own.

A few months later Marvin eagerly checked *The Wall Street Journal* before breakfast. The headline on the commodity page was "Soybean Prices Soar on Planting Report." He called his new broker to suggest buying some soybeans as the government report indicated that farmers' planting intentions were down slightly from expectations. Prices had been up strongly yesterday, but they had tailed off considerably near the close. The story quoted some major brokerage firm analysts as saying that declines in the dollar and expected strong demand would probably continue to fuel the bull market. The paper also quoted a floor broker as saying the buying was mostly emotional as the fundamentals were still pretty bearish.

Marvin asked his broker whether he thought this would be a good time to buy. "I agree wholeheartedly," was the reply. "Our research department issued a bullish report on soybeans two weeks ago. If there is a drought this summer, we could see beans in the teens. Some of my other clients got in yesterday." Marvin made some quick calculations in his head. That would mean at least a $35,000 per contract profit, he nodded to himself. "Buy me two contracts at the market," he quickly instructed the broker.

That day marked the high in soybeans. Three days later Marvin was down $1,500 per contract. He called his broker to ask what to do. "I think the market still looks good, Marvin," his broker reassured him, "but just to be safe, maybe you better blow out of one of your contracts." The loss with commission was $1,685. A few days later, Marvin sold out the other contract with a $2,140 loss. Convinced that his broker didn't know what he was doing, Marvin sought help from some independent experts. He sent for some free samples of advisory services.

The first one Marvin received was called *The Top-Secret Commodity Report*. It had a nightly hotline. There was a brochure enclosed with a track record that showed that the service had been profitable every year for the last four years. Signals were given based on a secret proprietary method that allegedly had an 80 percent accuracy record picking intermediate tops and bottoms. One of the recent recommendations had been to sell soybeans right about the time Marvin was buying. "If I had been subscribing to this letter, I never would have taken that stupid trade," Marvin told himself.

The free sample did not include the hotline number so Marvin called and subscribed for the three-month trial at $110. He received the hotline number after he gave his credit card number. He could hardly wait until after 5:00 P.M. so he could see what the current recommendations would be. He was pleased to read in the newsletter and accompanying literature that he would also receive stop-loss recommendations so he would know what his risk would be before he took the trade.

There were no recommendations the first two nights. Marvin was ready to make another trade on his own, but he congratulated himself for having the patience to wait for his advisor to act. The third night, there were three recommendations: buy the S&P 500, sell T-bonds, and sell cattle. He did not have enough in his account to cover the margin for the S&P and the stop in T-bonds was $1,500 from the point of entry, so he elected to take the cattle trade. The risk was only $600. His trade went nowhere for four days. He was stopped out on the opening of the fifth day. Because the market opened beyond his stop order, he ended up losing $760 after commissions. He noticed that both the S&P and T-bonds trades were doing well.

Marvin enjoyed reading all the sample advisory letters he received. He liked the idea of having many recommendations to choose from with a good explanation of the merits of each one. He subscribed to four more letters, three of which had hotlines. He decided it would be safer to wait until at least four of the five services agreed on a particular recommendation.

He went through what was to Marvin a really unlucky period. Six of his next seven trades resulted in losses, even though each one was recommended by at least two of the services. Three of the losing trades were recommended by all five. The winning trade would have been even larger except he decided to take a $1,500 profit when several of his services took a contrary view. Reading the newsletters was very educational. He especially liked following the trading tactics on the charts reproduced in the letters. Marvin decided he should be getting his own chart service. From the illustrations in his advisory letters, he picked his favorite and dispatched a check by Federal Express.

The weekly *ChartWatcher* chartbook came with a little booklet describing some "classic chart patterns" allegedly favored by knowledgeable technical traders. Marvin was thus initiated into the arcane world of the head and shoulders, triangle, flag, pennant, rectangle, and wedge. It all seemed a little mysterious, but the illustrations in the booklet showed clearly how these chart patterns had preceded some very profitable moves. There were also some special indicators printed under the charts, which the booklet said could be used to determine the trend and predict tops and bottoms.

Marvin was especially intrigued by an indicator called "stochastics," which seemed to make a precise top or bottom just as the market was doing so. Marvin could not help noticing that just as he had been buying his two contracts of soybeans several months ago, stochastics was making a top. Here was something that would have been a big help, if only he had known about it at the time.

Three days after he received his first chartbook, Marvin saw a good trade developing. Gold was tracing out a triangle and appeared to be threatening an upside breakout. Marvin drew his trendlines carefully and identified the price where the breakout would occur. He was ready to call his broker and place his order when he noticed that stochastics was in the overbought zone, signalling a potential sale. He looked at some of the other charts to see whether he could find a similar situation in the past. He did find one in lumber, where the triangle pattern had worked perfectly in spite of the overbought stochastics reading. He placed the order.

It was filled on the same day, and the market closed strongly at almost limit-up. Marvin was very happy with his trade. He only wished he had traded more than two contracts. The next day, however, the market gapped down on the opening and quickly went to limit-down. The price was back inside the triangle. Stochastics had probably now completed a sell signal, but he wouldn't know until he received next week's chartbook. Marvin wondered whether to reverse his position to short or to give the trade some more time.

The next morning Marvin called his broker, who advised Marvin to reverse to short as it looked like a false breakout on the triangle. Marvin went along. The trade was profitable for two days before the market reversed strongly to the upside. He exited the short trade above the previous high registered on the first breakout. That day turned out to be the high of the move. Had Marvin held his short position just one more day, he could have earned a substantial profit. As it was, he ended up with two losses of two contracts each. He decided the problem was that he did not have up-to-date stochastics indicators. Marvin resolved to buy his own computer so he could calculate indicators for himself every day.

It took about a month for Marvin to acquire his computer, software, and data. He needed to borrow the money, but felt it was worth it in terms of the increased profits he could make with computer analysis. He resolved to earn the money back through his trading. His computer turned out to be quite a bit more complicated than he was expecting, though, so it took him another month and a great deal of frustration before he learned how to use it.

In the meantime he was reading all he could about all the new analytical studies he had available on his software. He found a few that really looked promising. He also continued to trade. He had a few small profits mixed in with the losses. The profits would have been larger except his broker convinced him to take them too quickly. "You'll never go broke taking a profit," his broker advised him. "Bulls make money, bears make money, but pigs never make money." His broker had one of those catchy sayings for just about everything, except his trading advice didn't seem to be very good.

Marvin's first trade using his computer was in the New York composite stock index. One of his advisory letters was going long the stock indexes, and the MACD study had a buy signal. Marvin didn't even know what MACD stood for, but he knew it was a respected study among professionals. He entered the position and waited. The market went in his favor only a little before heading south. Marvin dutifully calculated his MACD value every day with his computer, but there was no sell signal. Marvin was nervous about the loss but hopeful that the trade might turn around and be profitable in the end. Finally, when the loss was just over $3,000, the computer gave him his sell signal and Marvin closed out his position with a sigh of relief. He realized he should have used a stop, but did not want to second-guess his indicator.

The day before he closed out his ill-fated stock index trade, Marvin received a very exciting brochure in the mail. There was a new software package available for the *Trend-a-matic Trading System*. It was an obviously expensive brochure, 12 pages long and printed on glossy paper. The system results were breathtaking. Trading only 10 markets for the last three years, the system had made over $200,000. The inventor of the system was a consultant to Swiss bankers who had achieved some prominence in Europe. Some well-known Swiss financial consultants had been using the system to time their gold and currency trading. The system had never been offered in the United States before, and only 125 would be sold for $3,500 each. The system looked so good that Marvin was certain it would be oversubscribed immediately. He calculated that he could trade about half the 10-market portfolio with what was left in his account. That would give him an income of about $3,000 a month to start. He could pay off the cost of the system and increase his account to the size necessary to trade the full portfolio in no less than six months. After that he could make $6,000 a month. The system even had a guarantee. If it was not profitable over the six months after he bought it, he could ask for a refund. The system would work only with a computer. Marvin congratulated himself because he was probably already ahead of most other people who received the brochure. He owned the computer and had managed to teach himself how to use it. He was ready for just this kind of opportunity.

Marvin read the brochure over about five times. He could find nothing wrong although he wished the system weren't so expensive. He remembered seeing what looked like a good system with strong endorsements advertised for only $1,000. He concluded that the originator could not possibly sell a system for this much money if it wasn't pretty good. He decided to borrow the $3,500. He mailed his cashier's check the next day and started daydreaming about what life would be like when he was making money with *Trend-a-matic*.

The system arrived one week later. After some initial problems, Marvin was able to run it on his computer. He found out that the system was not compatible with his data format, so he had to arrange for dial-up data retrieval. He did not have time to enter all those prices by hand. It took him two weeks to be able to generate his first system signals. It took him another two weeks before he closed his first profitable trade. That followed two initial losses. The instructions had recommended waiting for a loss before starting to trade each market, but Marvin needed to make some money to help make the payments on his loans. Although the track record in the brochure had shown 51 percent profitable trades, Marvin was losing on three out of four. He decided to filter the system's trades with the recommendations of his best advisory service. When they both agreed, Marvin took the trade. He used whoever's stop was smaller. This strategy did not help.

Trend-a-matic was a disaster. After only 11 weeks and over $9,000 in losses, Marvin's account was below the broker's minimum. He had to stop trading. Marvin was not defeated, however. He vowed to earn the money to pay back his loans and start another account. He figured that would give him time to learn how to trade and find an effective system. "On the other hand, maybe I should find a professional money manager next time," he thought . . . .

The difference between Marvin Modestmoney and the average professional trader is that the professional has had enough experience to learn the limitations of analysis. While there is a repetitive similarity to market behavior, there is just enough uncertainty to make predicting the future an impossible task. The professional knows the importance of a consistent approach to the markets. He has a concrete plan of attack. Like the professional golfer who jokingly says, "I always swing hard in case I hit it," the professional commodity trader wants to take lots of positions in case there is a big move. The amateur assumes the pros have a good idea where the best opportunities are. Actually, however, professionals consistently admit they have no idea in advance which trades will work. Most often the ones that look the least promising turn out to be the big winners.

There is no favorite time frame for professional traders. Each finds the perspective that matches his or her trading personality. Some become floor traders who seldom hold trades for more than a few minutes. There are some floor traders, however, who hold positions much longer. Professionals trading off the floor may be day traders, intermediate-term traders, or long-term traders. What is consistent is that each tends to stick with only one time frame, the one that works best for him.

Each professional has his own unique way to identify potential trades. He enters the market when his plan dictates. He tends to follow the direction of the market in his time frame rather than anticipate a change in trend. The pros are all ruthless in getting rid of losing positions. The late Frankie Joe was one of the best and most famous of big-time speculators in the 1970s and 1980s. He had a very simple approach to trading. He once confided that his real secret was "never to go home with a loss." That means he never wanted to hold a position after the close unless it was already profitable. Frankie Joe's money management rule is the ultimate in cutting losses short. It sounds radical and unrealistic, but it makes a great deal of sense, especially for a short-term trader. If you study your successful trades, you will find that many, if not most, were immediately profitable and never were behind on a closing basis. Thus, you have little to lose and a great deal to gain by exiting losers as quickly as possible. The problem is that the Frankie Joe method will result in many, many small losses. The amateur wants as few losses as possible because to him, they are a sign of failure.

The professional has learned to handle the inevitability of losses. He knows that he can never avoid them. They are as much a part of his life as shaving in the morning. He pays almost no attention to losses unless they become bigger than permitted under his overall trading plan. There is little ego involvement for the professional in his next trade. He will seldom let his ego interfere with abandoning losing positions.

Although the professional has learned the importance of discipline and does a good job of following his plan, even he is subject to lapses. Every professional is guilty of trading outside his plan, violating good trading principles, and going against his better judgment. It is constantly amazing to us all how often this happens. Perfection is as elusive here as in any human endeavor.

For all traders there is a continuum between 0 percent mechanical trading and 100 percent mechanical trading. (You can also think of the continuum as going from 100 percent to 0 percent judgmental trading.) Someone who trades 100 percent mechanically never has to make any trading decision. He has a plan that tells him precisely what to do in any situation. All he has to do is monitor market activity, determine what actions his plan requires, and then place the required orders with his broker. Most often, these plans are computerized. The trader inputs market data and the computer program tells him what to do.

At the other end of the spectrum, someone who trades 0 percent mechanically has no fixed rules whatever. He makes every trading decision on the spur of the moment without any particular guidelines except his own idea of what will work best. Although he attempts to learn from previous mistakes, he will be unsuccessful at doing so because of the problem of random reinforcement.

Understanding the concept of random reinforcement is critical to learning how to trade correctly. Random reinforcement means that you are not always rewarded when you do something right and you are not always penalized when you do something wrong. Behavioral scientists found when testing animals that random reinforcement rather than consistent reinforcement made it much more difficult for animals to learn desired behaviors. Think about the implications of consistent reinforcement versus random reinforcement. If a burglar went to prison every time he entered someone else's home, burglaries would be infrequent occurrences. If a trader lost money every time he held a losing position more than two days, he would quickly learn to cut losses short. If all nonsmokers lived to at least 75, there would be darned few smokers. If a trader still made money on a trade every time he resisted the impulse to take a quick profit, all traders would be letting their profits run. This is all very obvious when you think about it. The problem is that people usually think in terms of consistent reinforcement. They expect to be rewarded when they do something right, and they assume when they are penalized, they have done something wrong. They are used to judging the correctness of their previous conduct by its result. Because of the randomness in market price behavior, this apparently rational approach is counterproductive in commodity trading. You can never judge the correctness of your trading decisions by whether they resulted in a profit or a loss. That makes learning correct trading behaviors extremely difficult.

The emotionalism of trading can be truly appreciated only by those who have tried it. The effects of fear and greed are remarkable. Human nature is such that, left to your own devices, these twin villains will invariably cause you to make the wrong decisions in the speculative arena. The most outstanding trait of professional speculators is that they have learned to control their fear and greed. They do this through self-discipline, which of necessity means their decision-making has a certain structure. I believe that successful traders all have a relatively mechanical approach even if they do not know it themselves. Therefore, all professional traders are grouped in the top half of the mechanical trading continuum. Most amateurs, on the other hand, will be found in the bottom half. Many professional money managers have a system that is 100 percent mechanical. Those who do not operate 100 percent mechanically allow personal judgment to override their system infrequently.

There are many professional traders who do not use mathematical systems. Chart pattern traders are a good example. Even these chartists have a very structured approach to their trading. They know exactly what patterns they want to trade. They have their own definitions of what constitutes a particular pattern. They know where they will place their stops for each kind of pattern. They have a precise plan of how to take profits.

The average person has the best chance to be a profitable trader if he or she adopts a 100 percent mechanical approach. If profit is your goal rather than massaging your ego or having fun, I recommend that you find one or more good mathematical systems and trade them in a diversified group of markets. You will also need sufficient capital and courage to withstand the inevitable equity drawdowns that occur regardless of trading approach.

Here is what I mean by a strictly mechanical approach. You will have a predetermined group of markets that you will follow. You will have mathematical formulas to apply to previous prices, which will tell you when to buy and when to sell. There will be entry rules, exit rules for losing trades, and exit rules for profitable trades. There will be rules for when to start trading and stop trading each system. Your only tasks will be to choose initially the systems and markets to trade, to apply the system rules to market price action, and to decide how to spend the profits that you hope to achieve. If your system is computerized, you will have to provide data to the computer, run the system software, and place the orders the system dictates. This should not take very much of your time. You can hire someone else to do it for you if you want.

Note that this approach requires no specialized knowledge about the markets you will be trading. You will not have to read government reports about this year's grain harvest and the current amount in storage. You need not become an expert in the relationship of economic statistics and interest rates. You can forget about agonizing over whether we are going to have inflation or deflation in the coming months or years. Your system will automatically exploit commodity price movements resulting from those trends without any expertise on your part. You will be able to profit regardless of whether markets move up or down and regardless of whether you correctly anticipated those movements.

What you will have to learn is the theory and creation of mechanical commodity trading systems. That's why you bought this book. The next chapter begins with an explanation of the two general approaches to creating trading systems.

4 Creating Mechanical Trading Systems

Today you can buy a personal computer system for less than $1,000 that will run almost any commodity trading software being sold. For about $2,000, you can afford a more powerful computer that will operate two to three times faster. For around $5,000, you can own a machine so powerful that it can do things only expensive, mini-main-frame computers could do several years ago. Coupled with today's fast programming languages, these computers can accomplish mind-boggling tasks in only seconds.

The advent of the inexpensive personal computer has been at the same time a boon and a nightmare for commodity system players. It has been a boon for two reasons. First, a computer permits any trader to use a trading system that is too complicated and time-consuming for hand calculation. Or it may permit a trader to follow more systems and more markets using approaches involving complex mathematical formulas. Second, and even more important, a computer permits a trader to give his system a rigorous historical test before risking real money with it. I will examine the subject of system testing in Chapter 5.

Computers have been a nightmare because they permit construction of systems that have an eye-popping historical record but that a trader will never be able to recreate as he trades with the system in the future, using real money. These are called "curve-fitted" systems. A curve-fitted system is one in which the system developer creates the rules by inspecting historical data to see what would have worked. Here are some examples of what I mean by curve-fitted.

Curve-Fitted Systems

Suppose someone had called you on a Sunday afternoon six weeks ago and told you the following. "Hello, my name is Greg Greenbacks. How would you like to make some easy money? I'm a broker with Future-land Commodities, and I have a dynamite commodity trading system which has an uncanny record of being able to predict gold prices. I don't want you to send me any money, however, until I prove the system is everything I say it is. Fair enough? OK, here's the system's prediction for this week. Buy gold on the opening tomorrow because it will be up for the week."

Every Sunday for the next five weeks he had called again with another gold recommendation for the coming week. Every one had been right. If you had traded one contract (margin about $2,000) on each recommendation, you would have made $4,650 even after paying commissions. Chances are you would be anxious to find out how you could begin exploiting the system with real money. You would probably be ready to pay a considerable sum for the secret.

Here is how Mr. Greenbacks did it. The first weekend he called 320 people and told half to buy and half to sell. The next weekend he called the 160 who had received the right advice and told half of them to buy and half to sell. Each succeeding weekend he called the remaining people who had received all correct recommendations and repeated the process. At the end of four weeks he would have had 20 people anxious to invest. At the end of six weeks, he would still have five people ready to mortgage their houses and get rich quick. Believe it or not, law enforcement authorities have indicated that this scam, called "The Great Predictor," has been regularly perpetrated around the country in the last few years.

We can create the *Greenbacks Mechanical Gold System* by looking at the last six weeks of gold data to find out whether to buy or sell on Monday's open to produce profits for the week. The system will tell you to buy week one, sell week two, sell week three, buy week four, etc. If we test the system historically, we will find it was 100 percent accurate and produced $4,800 in gross profits. Yet it is obvious that we should not expect to get rich if we start trading it next Monday morning instead of six weeks ago. This system is no more likely to work than just flipping a coin and buying on heads and selling on tails. It is a rudimentary example of a curve-fitted system.

Many commodity markets have a seasonal influence that traders use in gauging the likely future direction of prices. Because of the intellectual appeal of this approach, it is very popular. For example, agricultural markets have a consistent yearly harvest season. Price tends to decline in anticipation as the harvest season approaches and rise thereafter. This is a natural result of the increased supply caused by the harvest. Markets such as copper and lumber exhibit seasonal tendencies related to weather. They tend to decline in price going into the winter months and rise in anticipation of increased construction and manufacturing activity in the spring. The seasonal tendencies in the coffee and orange juice markets are strongly influenced by the potential for dramatic price moves during their winter freeze season. Such yearly seasonal trends are not infallible, and they are only general trends. You cannot pinpoint them to the day. There are just too many other factors that affect prices.

The popularity of basing trading decisions on seasonal factors has led to some classic curve-fitted systems. It is easy with the aid of a computer to examine the last 5 to 10 years of data for a particular market in order to find out what seasonal strategies for buying and selling would have been especially profitable. Let's see how we could create such a seasonal system. It will have two rules. Rule One will be to buy (or sell) on the close of the nth trading day of the year. Rule Two will be to hold the position for a certain number of days and then exit on the close.

Our computer will check all the possibilities for us. It starts by buying on the close of the first trading day of the year. It then sees what would have happened if you had held the position from 1 day to 250 days. Then it tests selling on the first trading day of the year. Then it moves to entering the trade on the second, third, fourth, etc., trading day of the year. It can also test entering and exiting the trades on the open instead of the close. There may be millions of possible trades to test, but with a computer it is quick and painless.

You should not be surprised that with so many possibilities, there would be a number of potential rules that tested 80 to 100 percent accurate over the last 5 or 10 years. If I told you that buying silver on the close of the first Tuesday in February and selling it exactly one week later would have been profitable every year for the last seven years, would you expect that trend to continue in the coming years? It just so happens that *selling* silver on the third Thursday in February and holding it for exactly one week would also have been profitable every year for the last seven years. Is there some mysterious market force that causes silver prices to go up and down at those times every year? Or is this just a coincidence that has only a 50:50 chance to repeat? If you had a computer to search diligently through the back data for 30 commodity markets, there are many such calendar coincidences it could find that were 100 percent profitable. If you require only 75 percent accuracy, there would obviously be many more.

Some researchers use this process to find "seasonal" spread trades where you simultaneously buy one market and sell another or where you simultaneously buy one contract month and sell another contract month of the same commodity. Such spread trades can involve many different contract months as well as all the different markets. For example, you could buy March silver and sell June silver at the same time, hoping to profit from a favorable change in the relationship between the two contracts. You could buy silver and sell gold at the same time for the same reason. Spread trading increases the universe of potential "seasonal" trades geometrically, but the research method is the same.

These calendar trading systems may be profitable in the future if there is truly a seasonal force in the marketplace that tends to produce similar price action at the same time every year. *However, the similarity of price action in the past does not prove that such a seasonal force exists.* Most of these trades result from coincidence.

There are a number of sources that sell such seasonal recommendations, although they do not usually call them systems. They may also tell you where to put a stop-loss that historically has never been hit. There are several advisory services devoted solely to them. One service has been glowingly reviewed in a major financial magazine. Many people trade them because they assume that the past performance of such a system is indicative of future performance. It may or may not be, but you cannot tell solely from the high historical accuracy.

It is easy to understand the curve-fitted nature of such simple calendar systems. The computer looks exhaustively at back data to find rules that would have worked in the past. However, as trading systems become more complicated and mathematically based, traders lose sight of what the computer is actually doing. There is something mysterious about computer research that seems to give it added credibility.

Before computers became so affordable, it was simple to identify curve-fitted systems. They were the ones with the frightfully complicated rules, exceptions, and exceptions to exceptions. The complexity arose because the system's inventor was trying to find an approach that worked consistently over a reasonable number of previous occurrences. He started with a simple set of rules. Every time he found an instance where the rules failed, he had to create exceptions or change them just enough so they still worked on the data he had previously checked while avoiding the failure he had just discovered. In the end the rules worked in every instance, but they had, by necessity, grown very elaborate. Here is an example of a seasonal system for trading a particular market that you could have purchased in 1976. A broker suggested it to me.

> Sell short the October contract at the market on the close of July 1st. Place an open reverse stop-loss of 75 points. Place an open order good through July to close out the short position at 100 points profit; if unable, then place a new open order good through September to close it out at 80 points profit; if unable, then place a new open order to close it out at 60 points profit. If the short position is closed out in July, place an open stop buy order at 15 points above the original short sale; if executed, place a stop-loss of 60 points and an open order to close it out at 200 points profit. If the short position is reversed on stop to a long position, place a stop-loss of 75 points and an open order to close it out at a 350 point profit; however, if the short position is reversed on stop to a long position within 10 trading days after the short position is taken, place an open order good through August to close out the long position at 1,000 points profit; if unable, then place a new open order good through the last trading day of September to close it out at 500 points profit or at the market on the close of this day. If a long position is taken on the reverse stop-loss order, wait eight trading days to place a stop-loss of 175 points; if during these eight trading days the price goes against the position by at least 175 points, then change the open order to close it out to 350 points profit. If the short position is not closed out by the next to the last trading day of the October contract, then close it out at the market on the close of this day.

You can be sure from the many rules and exceptions that it had been consistently profitable for a number of previous years. But its consistent historical performance should not persuade anyone that it would work again in 1976 or thereafter.

Non-Curve-Fitted Systems

The key to whether a system was curve-fitted is how the developer determined the rules. If he examined historical data to see what would have worked and then concocted the rules accordingly, the system was curve-fitted. The more curve-fitted the system was, the less likely it will be to work in the future. We have seen several examples of this. If, on the other hand, the developer created the rules based on theories about how the market works without reference to particular historical data, the system was not curve-fitted. If a non-curve-fitted system works when tested on sufficient historical data, it has a much better chance than a curve-fitted system to continue working in the future.

Here is an example of an elementary non-curve-fitted system and the theory behind it. Market trends shift from up to down and back up again. We want to buy when the market starts moving up and hold on until it stops moving up and starts moving down. At that point we want to exit our long position and go short, holding until the downtrend exhausts itself and the market moves back up. At that point we will cover our short position and go long, repeating the process. Since the best indicator of an uptrending market is an actual upward movement, we will buy when price moves up a certain amount. Since the best indicator of an downtrending market is an actual downward movement, we will sell when price moves down a certain amount. The system will always have a position in the market, either long or short. That way it is guaranteed that we will always be long in strong uptrends and we will always be short in strong downtrends. Here are the rules.

> Start by determining whether the trend for the last five days has been up or down. If today's close is higher than the close five days ago, the trend is up. If today's close is lower than the close five days ago, the trend is down. If the trend for the last five days was down, the first trade will be a buy. Buy when price reaches a level 2 percent above the lowest low for the last five trading days. Once long, hold the position until price moves 2 percent below the highest high for the last five trading days. At that point, close out the long position and go short. Once short, hold the position until price moves 2 percent above the lowest low for the last five trading days. At that point, close out the short position and go long. Continue trading this way.
>
> If when you start, the trend for the last five days has been up, the first trade will be a sell. Use the same rules as described above to change from short to long and back again. (You use the five-day trend indicator only to determine the direction of the first trade.)
>
> In the unlikely event that at the point the rules indicate a change in position, the price is 2 percent below the highest high of the last five days and 2 percent above the lowest low of the last five days at the same time, hold the current position for the rest of the day and start applying the rules again on the next trading day.

Exhibit 4–1 shows how the *Two Percent Reversal System* will work. Its trading performance over a five-year period in a number of markets appears in Chapter 8.

I chose the amount of price movement required for a change in trend as 2 percent without any historical testing. Based on my experience, it seemed like a reasonable amount that could be applied across all markets. If I had conducted exhaustive tests to see what amount would work the best, the system would no longer qualify as non-curve-fitted.

Some of the best examples of non-curve-fitted systems are in J. Welles Wilder's classic book, *New Concepts in Technical Trading Systems,* published in 1978. Wilder presented six mathematical trading tools and six complete mechanical trading systems. He based each upon a different mathematical algorithm that operated in some way using previous daily open, high, low, and closing prices. The book has been one of the most popular commodity trading books ever in spite of the fact that it presents no proof that any of the trading tools or systems is actually effective in trading the markets. For each system Wilder shows a worksheet with a month or two of calculations whose purpose is to demonstrate the operation of the system rather than its profitability. It is not surprising that Wilder picked periods where the system showed net profits. Those brief worksheets are the only evidence of trading efficiency, and the time periods involved are too short to demonstrate effectiveness. Later computer testing of the systems by

EXHIBIT 4-1 Two-Percent Reversal System (March 1988 contract)

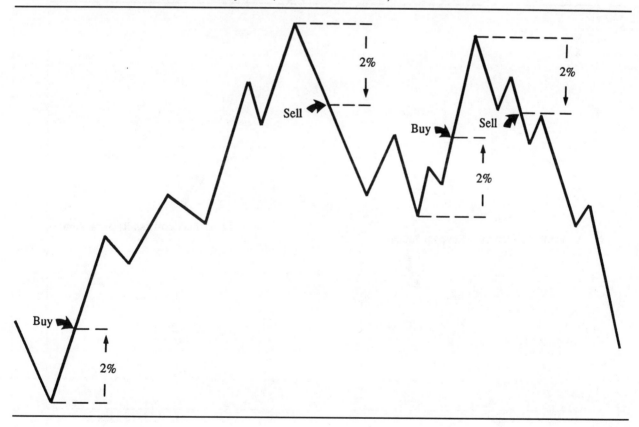

others was disappointing. The book has been praised not because of the profitability of its systems but because of its contribution to the theory of analyzing past price action.

The simplest (and most effective) of the book's systems is the *Parabolic Time/Price System*. Wilder based this system on a fluctuating stop-loss point. It works in the same general way as the Two Percent Reversal System described above. As it enters a position, the system employs a relatively large stop-loss-reversal point to accommodate the relatively wide price swings that normally occur as a trend change takes place. Then, as the new trend develops and the market becomes more directional, the system begins to trail the stop-reversal point closer and closer to the price action. As the trend matures, a trend reversal becomes more and more likely. The system moves the trailing stop-reversal point ever closer to protect profits on the current move and catch the trend reversal as soon as possible. When the price action turns sufficiently to hit the trailing stop, the system reverses position and begins trailing a stop in the other direction (on the assumption the market trend has changed). Exhibit 4–2 shows the operation of the system in a strongly and smoothly trending market, where it would naturally have the most success. In a choppier market, such as shown

EXHIBIT 4-2   Daily Chart of Swiss Francs with Wilder's Parabolic System (March 1988 contract)

in Exhibit 4–3, the trailing stop does not close in fast enough to generate profits.

Optimization

Wilder used an acceleration equation for the stop, which required increasing it by a factor of 0.02 for each day the market made a new price extreme for the move. He did not explain why he decided upon 0.02 as opposed to 0.01, 0.03 or some other number. So long as he chose 0.02 without historical testing, the system would not be curve-fitted. It would be natural, however, in designing such a system to see what acceleration factor worked the best in the past. A computer can run the tests for you. This process is called optimization. The computer will obediently test every value you specify and report the effect on profitability.

Suppose you find that over the last five years a different acceleration factor worked the best in each different market. Would you then trade each market using its own optimal value? You would probably also find that if you broke the test down into monthly periods, each monthly period for each market would have its own individual optimal value. Would you then change the value based on the current month?

EXHIBIT 4-3   Daily Chart of Cocoa with Wilder's Parabolic System (March 1988 contract)

For cotton would you use 0.15 in January, 0.203 in February, 0.146 in March, etc., because historically that was what performed the best? You could use the same process to change the acceleration factor in every market every week, or even every day. It should be obvious that a trading system created this way is no different from the earlier curve-fitted seasonal system examples.

If the computer examined the last five years of data in 10 individual markets and found the best acceleration factor to use in each month for each market, it would create 12 different sets of rules for each market, or a total of 120 separate rule-sets in all. You could still consider it as one system, however. The historical profits for the 120-rule-set system would be far higher than the profits for the original Wilder system, which had only one set of rules for all the markets.

If you had to guess which system would be more likely to be profitable in the future, would you select the more complicated system merely because it showed the most profits historically? If you said yes, you should reread this chapter. The correct answer is no. A curve-fitted system is, by its very method of creation, guaranteed to be profitable on the historical data used to create it. This says little about its likely profitability in the future.

The question of whether to use a different value for each market is more difficult. Suppose you found that for the last five years an acceleration factor of 0.025 worked best in silver, 0.108 worked best in gold, 0.022 worked best in T-bonds, etc. Would you use those values instead of 0.02 when trading the particular markets? If you did, you would be using an optimized system. This is curve-fitted, but to a much lesser extent than the one that used a different value for each month in each market.

If you were in commodity trading dreamland, you could create a system without any reference to historical data and then find that it was wildly profitable in every market during every time period you tested it. Then, unfortunately, you would wake up and have to face reality, where this does not happen. When dealing with the complexities of mathematical trading systems, there are usually many parameters you can change. The only way to know how to maximize the effectiveness of your system is to test it historically, using different values for the changeable parameters. Thus, some optimization is required. If you over-optimize, however, you end up with a highly curve-fitted system that will probably not be reliable in the future.

When doing historical testing, it is essential to remember what the goal is. It is not to create a system that generated the most hypothetical profits trading in the past. It is to create a system that will generate the most profits trading in the future. The future is the only arena where you can make real money.

Most traders do not know how to tell the difference between a system that has demonstrated only the ability to make money in historical testing and a system that is likely to make money in future real-time trading. The subject of historical testing is full of thorny questions that a system developer or evaluator must answer. We will examine these dilemmas in the next two chapters.

5

Testing Commodity Trading Methods

There are two extremes among commodity traders. There are those who are so impatient to trade and make money that they do very little historical testing to determine the previous effectiveness of their latest pet technique. They have faith that it will work because of where it came from or because they saw a few charts where it worked unbelievably well. On the other extreme are those traders who assume that anything that worked well in the past will almost certainly produce profits in the future. The more profitable the past performance, they reason, the more likely their chance to make big money with it in their trading. Both outlooks are equally dangerous to your pocketbook.

Federal law requires registered commodity trading advisors (CTA's) to warn their clients and customers that "past performance is no guarantee of future results." Like other important commodity trading truths, this reality is known by everyone but really accepted by almost no one. If I told you that I had found a particular price pattern in soybeans that over the last five years had been followed by at least a $5,000 upmove 80 percent of the time, you would certainly be interested, wouldn't you? If I told you the same price pattern had been 83 percent effective in predicting at least a $3,500 move in cotton, you would be even more curious, wouldn't you? See what I mean? This fallacy is so common that in the study of logic it even has a fancy Latin name: *Post hoc ergo propter hoc*. The fallacy is assuming that something has caused an event merely because it preceded it.

Subjecting a commodity system to an historical test is like living together before getting married. It does not assure a successful marriage, but it is an excellent way to gain greater confidence in the relationship and avoid some unpleasant surprises. You can gain the most advantage from historical testing by understanding the process and its limitations.

Before traders had computers, they had to take the word of the system developer as to its historical effectiveness. Before system developers had computers, not much testing was done. People traded the markets on cursory testing or faith. Now that computers and testing software are within the financial means of all but the most shoestring-oriented traders, there is no excuse for trading untested ideas. However, deciding to test a system is only the beginning of the problem. You must know how to conduct the test so as to obtain realistic results.

Data Interval

The first significant question the tester must answer is what kind of data to use. Naturally, you must test the prospective system on data that matches the time interval on which the system will trade.

Most systems use daily data points. That means the system obtains its entry and exit intructions by analyzing the four available daily data points: the open or first price of the day, the high or highest price of the day, the low or lowest price of the day, and the close or settlement price.

There is often a range of prices at the beginning and end of daily trading. Those who are executing orders "on the open" or "on the close" do not always trade at the same price. For instance, in the S&P 500, the market may have a closing range of 250.00 to 250.30. Buyers who have orders for action on the close may be filled near the high end of the range, 250.25 to 250.30. Sellers who have orders for action on the close may be filled near the low end of the range, 250.00 to 250.05. The exchange determines a settlement price somewhere in the middle of the closing range, probably 250.15 in the example. The exchange posts this settlement price a few minutes after the close, and it becomes the accepted "closing" price. The difference between where actual traders were filled on their closing orders and the published close is an example of the "slippage" described in Chapter 1 as a cost of trading.

There is also a range of prices at the opening. This results from matching opening buy and sell orders in the pit. Buyers will be filled in the top part of the range and sellers in the lower part. The usually accepted opening price, however, is not the midpoint of the opening range, but rather the first trade that the exchange reports for the day.

If your system is designed for intraday trading, it will use perhaps hourly prices or even five-minute prices to make its decisions. You cannot very well test such a system with daily prices. They would be meaningless. You would have to obtain what is called "tick data." This means the list of every price at which a trade took place in consecutive order along with the time of the trade. You can then segregate these trade prices by time period so there is an open, high, low, and close for each hour or other time segment. Such tick data is available along with software to handle the chore of segregating the data by the desired time period.

Some longer-term systems may be designed for use with weekly data. For weekly data, the open is the open on Monday (or first trading day of the week), the high is the highest price for the week, the low is the lowest price for the week, and the close is the settlement price on Friday (or last trading day of the week). While weekly data is available on a limited basis, the normal procedure is to obtain daily data and convert it to weekly by extracting the weekly open, high, low, and close. There is computer software to handle this for you also.

There are two other commodity data measurements that the exchanges publish and that may be used in systems: volume and open interest. Volume refers to the number of contracts traded during the day. Open interest refers to the number of outstanding contracts. When a new buyer and seller enter the market (although not necessarily matched together in the same trade), the open interest grows by one. When a buyer and seller close out an open position (although not necessarily with each other), open interest decreases by one.

Each commodity has a number of delivery months trading at the same time. While the exchanges publish volume and open interest figures for each individual contract, most data compilations use the total each day for all contracts of a given market. Although price data is available immediately during the day, volume and open interest figures do not become available until the next day, usually after the market has opened. Thus, volume and open interest statistics are always a day behind. This makes them less useful for trading systems that require today's prices to generate signals for tomorrow's trading. This book will ignore volume and open interest as an input for system trading signals.

Types of Data

Having decided to use daily data to test a system, the tester's data decision problem is still not over. There are three kinds of daily data commonly used for historical testing: actual contract data, Perpetual™ contract data, and continuous contract data. The choice of which to use will have effects on both the testing process and the test results.

On any given day there may be active trading in 2 to 12 delivery months per commodity. For instance, in the first week of January, you could trade January soybeans or March, May, July, August, September, or November soybeans for delivery in the current year, or January soybeans for delivery the following year. Contracts in interest rates and precious metals go out two years into the future. Which daily price do you pick for your testing? The answer requires a further explanation of how a speculator actually chooses between delivery months and what happens when a contract expires.

While a market may have trading occurring in a number of different months at once, speculative activity is concentrated in the closest month. Just before the end of the month before contract expiration, most markets have a "First Notice Day." On or after First Notice Day, someone holding a short position may notify someone holding a long position (through the exchange) that they intend to make delivery of the commodity involved in the contract (e.g., 5,000 bushels of soybeans). If the person holding the long position actually wants to take delivery, he does not mind. However, most participants in futures trading do not want to make delivery or take delivery. They avoid all these messy problems by offsetting their positions before First Notice Day. They may then take a similar position in the contract month next further out. The trader may make the two trades simultaneously. This process of closing out a position in the nearby month and re-establishing the same position in the next month out is called "rolling over."

The contract month that is closest in time but that has not yet reached First Notice Day is called the "nearby" month. There are many financial markets in which no delivery takes place. At contract expiration these markets are settled in cash. However, to avoid the settlement procedures speculators routinely exit positions in these markets in the weeks prior to expiration. If they want to maintain their position in a market, they re-establish a similar position in the contract month next further out by rolling over. As contract expiration approaches and these transactions occur, open interest and volume decline in the nearby month and increase in the next month out.

The amount of volume and open interest in a particular contract month are indexes of liquidity. The more liquid a market is, the easier it is to find willing buyers and sellers, and the smaller the price change between one trade and the next. The speculator wants the most liquid market possible so he can execute his orders with minimum price slippage between the time he decides to act and the time he can actually establish or offset his position. The closest month is the most liquid until a few weeks before expiration. Then the next month out becomes the most liquid. Financial markets such as T-bills, Eurodollars, and T-bonds have four contract months per year—March, June, September, and December. The nearby month is most liquid until the last week of the month prior to expiration. Thus, speculators will concentrate in the March contract from the last week in December to the last week in February. The June contract is most popular between the last week in February to the last week in May, etc.

Thus, the answer to the previous question about which contract's data to pick is the contract with the highest open interest. That is the most liquid month, where a speculator will most likely be trading.

Now assume you are going to test a T-bill system over the year 1987. If you are going to use actual contract data, you will obtain daily data for the March, June, September, and December 1987 T-bill contracts. You might use the March contract data between January 1 and February 28, the June contract between March 1 and May 30, and so on. Each contract will require a separate computer run that looks at the limited data segment. This means four computer runs for each year of the test. While the computer works very quickly, it is time-consuming to set it up for each separate run because programs generally work with only one data file at a time. Then you would have to combine the four separate sets of results to see the total performance over the year. There is also the problem of how to handle positions open at the end of one contract segment. You could close the position in the expiring contract and re-establish it in the next contract. But what if, considering the data in the next contract, the system would have had the opposite position? You could close the position in the expiring contract and wait for a new signal in the next contract. But what if the system would have retained the same position? You might be shaking yourself out of a good, long-term trade right in the middle. In actual trading you would probably roll over the position and hold it.

There is no simple solution to the problem of expiring futures contracts, but several different approaches are available. There are two types of artificial contracts that do not expire. You can use either one to test systems historically and to generate trading signals.

Robert Pelletier is the owner of Commodity Systems, Inc. (C.S.I.), which has the most popular commodity data base. He invented a type of nonexpiring futures contract called the Perpetual™ contract. For each market the Perpetual contract process looks at a fixed date in the future, usually 91 days ahead, and projects a price as of that date based on two forward contracts. It performs a kind of mathematical average on the prices of the contracts expiring immediately before and after the projection date. This average price in the future becomes today's Perpetual contract price. The advantage of this process is that it smooths the price action and eliminates any price gap when transferring from one contract to another. The disadvantage is that the Perpetual contract prices have no relation to contracts that a person can actually trade. He would have to test his system using Perpetual prices and then generate trading signals on actual contract prices or generate trading signals on Perpetual prices while placing orders using actual prices. Another disadvantage is that Perpetual prices are available only from C.S.I. You must pay for them, and if you are going to use them in your trading, you must access them daily by computer modem.

An alternative artificial contract that is not as artificial as the Perpetual contract is called a continuous contract. A continuous contract uses actual contract prices for the most recently traded contract during the three months it would actually be traded. When it is time to change to the next contract, you begin adding actual prices from that contract. To eliminate the price gap between contracts, you adjust all previous price data by the amount of the difference between the closes of the two contracts on the date before you begin using the new contract's prices. As an example, assume you were trading Eurodollars between December 1, 1988, and February 29, 1988. The continuous contract would contain the actual March contract prices for those dates because that is the contract speculators would be trading. On March 1, the continuous contract would switch to the June contract and begin adding those prices to the data file. There would be a gap between the prices on the day of the switch. On February 29, 1988, the March contract closed at 93.13 while the June contract closed at 93.00. To keep the correct relationship between the closes on February 29 and March 1 in your data file, it would be necessary to subtract 0.13 from all previous prices in the continuous file. This would also result in maintaining the correct relationship between all previous opens, highs, lows, and closes, which existed at the time the contract was the actually traded contract. The actual date the rollover takes place is not crucial. The best theoretical date would be the day the open interest in the next contract out exceeds that in the nearby month.

Using continuous files allows you to enter and use the current day's data in the nearby contract every day. Your data file always reflects current prices in the nearby contract, which you will most likely be trading. Signals and stops generated by the system will be expressed in terms of the nearby contract you are actually trading. The day-to-day relationships for all previous days in your data file are identical to those of the nearby contract at the time you would have been trading it. The only difference between the continuous file and the actual contract data you might have been trading several years ago is the price level, which may be higher or lower. However, the differences between daily opens, highs, lows, and closes—both intraday and from day to day—are the same as the nearby contract at the time. The price level difference does not affect trading signals except in some cases when they are based on a percentage of the actual price. Very few systems operate that way. All the other kinds of trading signals (such as moving averages, price patterns, and the like) will generate virtually the same entries and exits on a continuous file as they do on the actual nearby contract.

Because a continuous contract eliminates the jump in price from one contract to another when rolling over a position forward at contract expiration, it is easy to assume that this causes a distortion in historical testing results. In fact, except for the additional commissions incurred during rollovers, historical testing profits generated using continuous contracts should be nearly identical to those using actual contracts, no matter how many times a position is rolled forward from one contract to the next. The amount of the extra commissions is insignificant in the context of extrapolating past results to future performance, which is an inexact process to begin with. Thus, you lose nothing important by testing and trading with continuous data files created in this way. You save by avoiding the data management problems associated with contract expiration. If you want to maintain your data files manually, you can use daily prices available from a broker, a quote machine, or the newspaper at no charge. All system testing in this book used continuous contracts.

The Test Period

Another important consideration in testing a trading system is the length of the historical test. While on the surface it may appear that the longer the test the better, if the markets change their characteristics over time, a long test may actually be counterproductive. Remember that you can make money only trading the future. You must therefore design an historical test that you hope will be predictive of future trading. A system that would have been highly effective trading the markets of 1980–83 may do terribly trading the markets of 1988–89 if they are significantly different in price movement characteristics.

Although you constantly hear traders commenting about how difficult it has been to trade recent markets, compared to the past, this attitude is more a reflection of the speaker's trading success than the true nature of the markets. If you look at charts of markets over long periods of time, it is difficult to discern such a difference in price behavior in a particular market that would affect the success of a trading system. There are characteristics that definitely change. There are secular bullish periods and bearish periods. The markets often undergo cyclical changes in volatility. The problem is that you never know what kind of market you will be facing in the future. Therefore, your system must be capable of dealing with all these kinds of changes.

It is best to pick a period long enough to cover both a bullish and bearish cycle and times of relatively high and low volatility. On the other hand, you need to give some thought to the convenience of testing. There is only so much time available. It is probably better to devote more time to testing over a somewhat shorter period than to test over data going back 20 or 30 years.

Even more significant than the length of the test period is the number of trades generated by the system. Statistically speaking, the smaller the number of trades generated, the less reliable is the test. The same considerations statisticians use in determining the minimum size of a data sample are relevant to commodity traders testing their systems. Thirty data points is an acceptable minimum for general statistical reliability. To the extent that your test period is too short to generate at least 30 trades, the reliability of the results will suffer. Some people claim that if the test period is long enough, it must be a reliable test. Actually the length of the test period is irrelevant if the system does not generate enough trades over that period of time. Regardless of time period, the more trades the test generates, the more statistically reliable will be the results. Statistical reliability is important because it relates to the probability that your historical results will repeat in the future. That is the whole purpose of the test.

I believe a good figure to use is five years. This should give a good sampling of up and down trends and a cross-section of volatility levels. The last five years should still be relevant to tomorrow's trading. That period offers sufficient time to generate a good number of trades while being short enough to permit relatively rapid testing. If you are using a very long-term system that only generates a few trades per year, it will be necessary to extend the testing period so that the total number of trades in your test is close to 30. If you use the same parameters, you can accumulate the number of trades in several different markets. All systems described in this book were tested on a consistent five-year period.

In order to avoid distortions in your test results, you must also be cognizant of peculiarly aberrant periods in the data. If this past price action results in especially unfavorable or favorable results without a reasonable probability of repeating in the future, the test results will be less useful. Some good examples of this are the incredible silver market of 1979–80 and the stock market melt-down on October 19, 1987. In order to maintain a consistent five-year period for this book's testing while eliminating October 1987 from the data, I have chosen a test period between July 1, 1982, and June 30, 1987.

Using Different Time Segments

The next chapter discusses optimization, the process of refining a system by testing different values for its variable parameters. The more variable parameters there are in your system and the more you test them to isolate the very best values for each one, the better your system will be in historical testing. Unfortunately, as you are using optimization to squeeze the very best historical performance from your system, you will also be increasing the likelihood that the system will not be able to repeat its historical performance in the future.

One good way to guard against over-optimization is to set aside different segments of historical data for optimization and final testing. For instance, if you have five years of data, you might optimize on the first three years and then test the system on the last two years.

This is not a foolproof solution, however. In the first place, how do you decide which segment to use for optimization and which to use for final testing? If you reserve the latest data for final testing, you may be using out-of-date data for optimization and vice versa. Secondly, the more you repeat the process of optimizing on one set of data and testing on another, the more you end up actually optimizing on the entire set of data. In the ideal situation, you create a good system by using older data, and then it immediately works about as well on recent data. Assuming your system generated enough trades for statistical reliability, that system would have an excellent chance to be profitable in future trading.

Using Different Markets

Specialization is fashionable in commodity-trading systems these days. The reason is that it is far easier to design a system with superior historical performance in one market than it is to design a system that performs well in a variety of markets. It is easy for the system creator to argue that each market has its own peculiar trading characteristics so that each requires its own set of trading rules. But how valid is that excuse? I treat this question in detail in Chapter 12.

Costs of Trading

In Chapter 1, I discussed the inherent costs of trading which are a significant hurdle for a trader to overcome on his path to profits. These costs are commissions and slippage, which includes the bid/asked spread. They are easy to overlook when evaluating historical trading results. Although they may be relatively low as a percentage of one successful trade, they add up inexorably over time. As you trade more and your average profit decreases, they become very significant. Depending on the system and the markets, they can mean the difference between overall profit and loss. Therefore, in order to have a meaningful historical test, you must always incorporate a realistic deduction for commissions and slippage.

Each trader must consider his own commissions in arriving at a justifiable number. If you use a discount broker, you should be paying $25 or less per trade in commissions. Slippage varies between markets according to liquidity at the time. I use a total figure of $100 per trade to cover these costs. Some traders think this is too large, while others claim it is too low. In evaluating any system results you should always know what, if anything, was deducted for commissions and slippage. You are free to adjust the amount to correspond with your own experience. The important thing is to deduct something reasonable from every trade to simulate these very real costs. Otherwise the test is meaningless.

Special Problems of Testing with Daily Data

Two important limitations interfere with accurate testing using daily data. In order to assess the reliability of historical testing, you must be aware of these problems and know how the particular test deals with them.

I have previously discussed the concept of placing a stop-loss order to exit a position and limit your loss when price moves against you. Thus, if you took a long position in corn at $2.00 per bushel, you might decide to place a stop-loss at $1.90. This would, if executed precisely at 1.90, limit your loss to $500 per contract plus the commission. There are several ways to handle this kind of loss limitation. You can place your order in the market as an open order. It would be a stop order, which means that you would sell at the market as soon as price touched 1.90, but not before. If you place an open order, a floor broker in the corn pit will have your order in his deck and will be ready to execute it if and when the price drops to 1.90. Some traders prefer to use what is called a mental stop. This means that they or their broker do not actually send the order to the pit. Instead, they watch the price and phone it in as a market order when they see price hit the stop point.

The idea of using a mental stop usually results from bad experiences with stop orders placed in the market. Often the market reacts to the point where it touches your price before resuming its previous trend. This means you are taken out of your trade at a loss even though the market eventually goes in the direction you wanted. Sometimes you can be stopped out at the very extreme of the day before the market turns around. This is exasperating. Under such circumstances it is easy to become paranoid and assume there is some kind of conspiracy on the part of floor traders to move the market to the point where your stop will be touched before allowing it to resume the opposite trend. You could reason that if you did not place your stop order in the market, the floor traders would not know it was there and could not conspire against you. Take it from me, there is no conspiracy aimed at your orders. Most of the markets are too big for the floor traders to move around at will. The market is just as likely to move to your mental stop as it is to move to a stop you send to the floor broker as an open order.

I do not recommend mental stops because there are too many things that could happen to defeat your loss-limiting plan. You or your broker could fail to notice right away that price had declined to the exit point. This could result in a larger loss by the time you corrected the oversight. Even more important is the chance that you would rationalize ignoring the plan when the time came to execute it. You might tell yourself something like, "If corn was a good buy at 2.00, it is an even better buy at 1.90. I should be buying more instead of exiting my position. I'll just wait a little while longer and see if the market doesn't turn around." It doesn't, and you end up getting out at 1.70 with three times the loss you originally budgeted.

If you are trading with a mechanical system, there is even less reason to use a mental stop. The system tells you to get out or reverse your position at a certain point. You must follow the system. However, even if you follow my advice and place your order in the market, there is still no guarantee that it will be filled at or near your price. If the market trades to your stop point during market hours, there can be some slippage between the time the market hits your stop price and the time the broker can execute your order. In liquid markets, except in unusual circumstances, this will usually be a fairly small amount.

A problem can arise, however, because of events that occur overnight while the market is closed. Suppose that while you are holding your corn position, the market had dropped to 1.92, where it closed for the day. Your 1.90 stop is close but not reached yet. Then a story develops overnight that the Soviet Union will be buying its corn from another country rather than the United States this year. The market could open the next day as low as 1.82. Since there is an exchange-set 10-cent limit on how far the price of corn can move in one day, it cannot trade lower than 1.82 that day. Because of the shocking news, there may be no buyers at that level. Your broker will be unable to execute your stop-loss order because there is no one willing to take the other side. Eventually, price will move low enough to attract buyers, and you will be out. Your loss will be larger than the $500 you set when you entered the trade. Such "limit moves," as they are called, are a risk in trading, although they do not occur very often. However, a gap between the closing price one day and the opening price the next is quite common. These gaps can cause larger losses than you intend to tolerate.

In testing a trading system, it is important that the tester or computer program not assume that a stop order is filled at its exact price when the order occurs in a gap between the open and previous close.

Using the previous example, if the market opened the next morning after the news at 1.86, your 1.90 stop order would be filled at approximately 1.86, not 1.90. If the computer programmer is aware of the problem, it is easy to build the correct logic into a testing program. To insure results as accurate as possible, you should be sure your computer program accounts for opening gaps. All testing for the purpose of this book took such opening gaps into account in executing stop orders.

The other latent difficulty in testing with daily prices is not as easy to handle. It results from the limitation in the price data. You know what the opening, the high, the low, and the close were, but you do not know in what order they occurred.

Assume you are trading a system in the S&P 500 stock futures. It uses a 300-point reversing stop. This means that when you enter a long position, the system tells you to reverse your position to short if the market moves 300 points or $1,500 against you. You would at that point sell two contracts—one to cover your long position and the other to initiate a new short position. You would use the same kind of order to reverse back to long if the market whipsawed around and went back up. If you entered your initial long position at 250, your reversing stop goes at 247. Assume on the day of your entry, the market closes at 250.50. The next day the market goes into a tailspin. It opens at 248.50, has a high of 249.00, a low of 246, and closes at 246.25. Under the system rules, you would have closed your long position at 247 and gone short at that price as well. In addition, you would place another order to exit and reverse again at 250. With a high price of 249.00 for the day, we know there is no way the second stop and reverse could have been hit after the short entry at 247.

If the high of the day had been 250.25 instead of 249, there would have been a problem. Since the low of the day was below the stop and reverse point of 247, we know the 247 stop would have been triggered. But we have no way of knowing for sure that the market did not go back up to 250 and reverse the system to long after going short at 247. Since the market closed at 246.25, after going back up to 250, it would have gone back down through the 300-point stop again, creating two additional losses. Exhibit 5–1 illustrates the uncertainty.

There are two ways to solve this problem in historical testing. First, you can specify that the system will take only one entry during a day and no stops can be triggered until the following day. This guarantees that historical testing will not miss a day on which the system could have resulted in several trades during one day because the system by definition allows only one trade per day. The disadvantage of this solution is that in a volatile market, you may want to exit your trade or reverse your position on the same day as an entry. If you wait until the next day, you may unnecessarily enlarge a loss or reduce a profit.

Another possible solution is to make reasonable assumptions about the order in which the highs and lows were made, based upon their relationship to the open and close. If the open is closer to the high, you assume that the high was made before the low and that after the low,

EXHIBIT 5-1   The Uncertainty of Daily Price Action

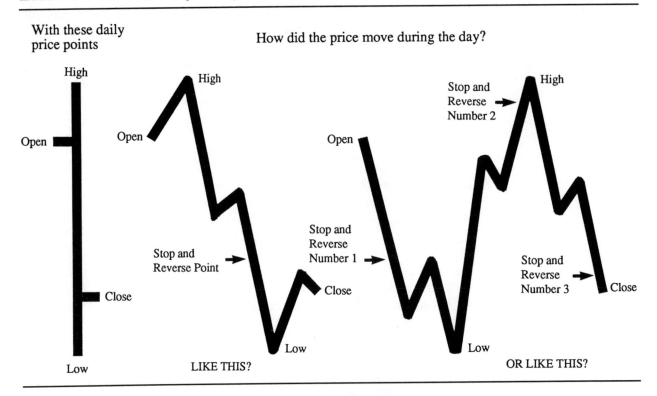

the market did not move higher than the close. If the open is closer to the low, you assume that the low was made before the high and that after the high, the market did not move lower than the close. Exhibit 5–2 illustrates these assumptions. This is usually the way the markets act and the assumptions will lead to nearly accurate test results unless you are using very tight stops. The tighter your stops in relation to the average daily range, the greater the chance your system will trigger several trades in one day. No historical test that uses only daily prices can accurately reflect such a system's actual performance.

Evaluating Test Results

Like beauty, successful performance of trading systems is in the eye of the beholder. Trader A may prefer the system that makes the most total profits. Trader B may prefer the system that has the highest average profit per trade. Trader C may prefer the system with the highest percentage of winning trades. Trader D may prefer the system with the lowest maximum loss. Trader E may prefer the system with the lowest drawdown. There is a reasonable basis for all these preferences, so it is normal practice to have a computer program express historical test results in a number of different categories. Exhibits 5–3 and 5–4 show a sample test report from two different programs. Here is a description of the most popular performance categories.

EXHIBIT 5-2 Assumed Daily Price Action

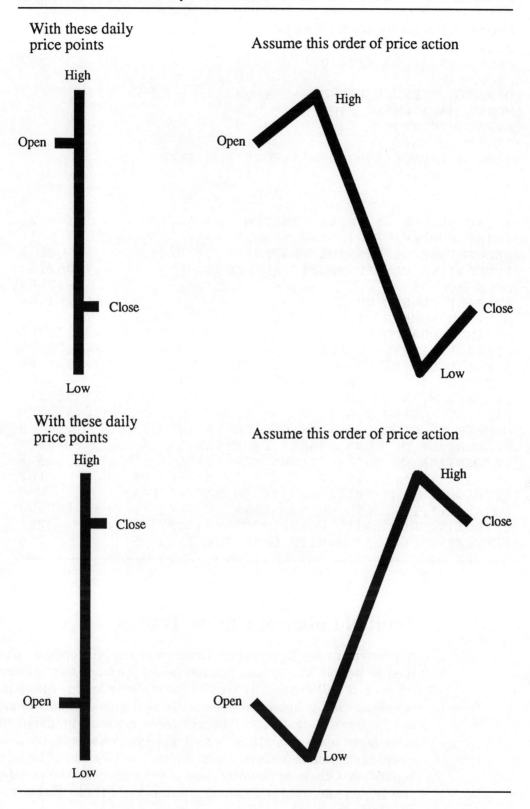

With these daily
price points

Assume this order of price action

With these daily
price points

Assume this order of price action

EXHIBIT 5-3   CTCR Software Performance Report

```
PROFESSIONAL TRADING SYSTEM.........................
JYHIST.PRN
FROM 820701 TO 870630
STOP TYPE                    =   P
DYNAMIC % ENTRY FILTER       =   32
MONEY MANAGEMENT STOP        =   0
BREAKEVEN STOP               =   0
PROFIT TARGET                =   0
$100 SLIPPAGE AND COMMISSIONS PER TRADE
```

```
TOTAL NUMBER OF CLOSED TRADES                    21
TOTAL NUMBER OF WINNING TRADES                   10
PERCENTAGE OF WINNING TRADES                   47 %
CUMULATIVE CLOSED PROFIT AND LOSS        $37,062.52
OPEN EQUITY                                   $0.00
AVERAGE CLOSED TRADE                      $1,764.88
MAXIMUM NUMBER OF CONSECUTIVE LOSSES              3
MAXIMUM DRAWDOWN                         -$2,375.00
AVERAGE WINNING TRADE                     $4,620.00
AVERAGE LOSING TRADE                       -$830.68
RATIO OF AVERAGE WIN TO AVERAGE LOSS           5.56
BIGGEST WINNING TRADE                    $23,562.50
BIGGEST LOSING TRADE                     -$2,375.00
NUMBER OF CLOSED TRADES ON LONG SIDE              9
PERCENTAGE OF LONG TRADES PROFITABLE           66 %
PERCENTAGE OF SHORT TRADES PROFITABLE          33 %
AVERAGE WINNING TRADE LENGTH IN MARKET DAYS     102
AVERAGE LOSING TRADE LENGTH IN MARKET DAYS        9
TOTAL SLIPPAGE AND COMMISSIONS            $2,100.00
EFFECTIVENESS RATIO FOR CLOSED TRADES           266
EFFECTIVENESS RATIO WITH OPEN EQUITY            266
```

Total Number of Closed Trades

A problem arises in treating trades that are still open at the end of the test period. The system has not exited the trade so you do not know whether it will eventually result in a profit or loss. If the open equity is substantial, to ignore it completely will give a distorted picture of the system's performance. Longer-term systems in particular may have large open profits, for which the system should receive credit. Some programs report any open equity at the end of the test period separately. Others artificially close out the trade on the last day of the test period and treat it as an additional closed trade. Either method is satisfactory.

EXHIBIT 5-4   System Writer Performance Report

```
/////////////////////////////////////////\\\\\\\\\\\\\\\\\\\\\\\\\\\\\\\\\\\\\\\\\\\\

                        HISTORICAL RESULT PRINTOUT

Summary        :      1 of      1           Today's Date : 06/27/1988 07:49am

Model Name     : Cruz Demonstration Model
Contract Name  : JYHIST              06/87
Calc Dates     : 07/01/82 - 06/30/87        Days :   1825

 Num. Conv. P. Value  Comm  Slippage  Margin  Format  Drive:\Path\FileName
 -----------------------------------------------------------------------------
   65    2  $ 12.500  $ 25   $ 75   $  2,500  Ascii   D:\SYSTEMS\HISTDATA\jyhis

 /////////////////////////////////// ALL TRADES \\\\\\\\\\\\\\\\\\\\\\\\\\\\\\\\\\\\\\

Total net profits       $33,637.50   Number of contracts           1
Gross profits           $57,487.50   Gross losses          $-23,850.00

Total # of trades              50    Percent profitable           38%
Number winning trades          19    Number losing trades          31

Largest winning trade   $10,925.00   Largest losing trade   $-2,062.50
Average winning trade    $3,025.65   Average losing trade    $ -769.35
Ratio avg win/avg loss        3.93   Avg trade (+ & - trades)  $672.75

Longest string + trades        3     Longest string - trades        5
Average days in + trades       43     Average days in - trades      12

Max closed-out drawdown $-5,675.00   Exchange required margin  $2,500.00
Max intra-day drawdown  $-6,125.00   Total required margin     $8,175.00
Profit factor                 2.41   Return on margin             411%

                   Dates of equity dips and peaks
        Description                    Date          Amount
        ---------------------------------------------------------
        Largest Winning Trade        05/22/87       $10,925.00
        Largest Losing Trade         09/23/85       $-2,062.50
        Largest String of + Trades   06/30/87            3
        Largest String of - Trades   02/03/84            5
        Maximum Closed-Out Drawdown  02/03/84       $-5,675.00
        Maximum Intra-Day Drawdown   02/10/84       $-6,125.00
```

Total Number of Profitable (or Losing) Trades

Most programs allow you to specify an amount to be deducted from all trades for slippage and commissions. A profitable trade should be defined as one that yields a profit after deducting those inherent costs. Some trades may break even, but it is confusing to give them their own category separate from profit or loss. A trade that breaks even should be considered a loss. It must have some profit to qualify as a profitable trade.

Percentage of Profitable Trades

The percentage of profitable trades is the number of winning trades divided by the number of closed trades and multiplied by 100. Traders tend to prefer a high percentage of winning trades. It is easier on the ego and the psyche to have a relatively small number of losers. Most professional traders, however, have winning percentages less than 40. Their egos can accept more losers than winners. A more important consideration is the relative size of the winners and losers. The professionals' average winners are always much larger than their average losers. If you strive for a higher percentage of winners, you must accept larger losers and smaller winners. This violates the essential principles of cutting losses short and letting profits run.

Cumulative Closed Profit or Loss

Total all profitable closed trades and all losing closed trades. Deduct the total losses from the total profits to produce the cumulative net closed profit or loss. Slippage and commissions should be included. This is probably the most popular way to compare the effectiveness of trading systems, but it can be misleading. A system that generates a great number of trades can produce large total profits without being a very effective system. If the average profit per closed trade is small there is little margin for error.

Open Equity

At the end of the run through the data, the system may have an open position. If so, the program compares the entry price to the closing price on the last day in the test run to compute an open equity figure. Some programs treat this amount as an additional closed trade and do not report it separately. As previously indicated, it is important not to ignore it completely.

Average Profit Per Closed Trade

To get the average profit per closed trade, the program divides the cumulative closed profit or loss by the total number of closed trades. This is the first figure I look at in judging system effectiveness. I would not be impressed by a system that made less than $200 per closed trade after deducting at least $100 per trade for slippage and commissions. The only exception would be a day trading system that always enters and exits on the same day. For a day trading system with at least 200 trades, performance over $100 per trade after a $100 deduction for slippage and commissions would be attractive.

Maximum Drawdown

Maximum drawdown is the dollar amount of the worst possible result you could have achieved by trading the system during the overall period tested. The program assumes you started trading at the worst possible time and subsequently stopped trading at the worst possible time. It reports how much you would have lost. This amount may or may not be coincident with the drawdown during the maximum number of consecutive losses because the worst drawdown period can contain profits. Slippage and commissions should be included, and only closed trades are considered. Maximum drawdown can be based on intraday trade equity as well as the results of trades after waiting for them to be closed out. The latter looks at the worst possible performance of closed-out trades, while the former identifies the worst position the account would have reached even if it was in the middle of a trade.

Greatest Number of Consecutive Losses

A good program reports the longest string of consecutive losses. This may or may not be coincident with the largest drawdown. Only closed trades are considered. All systems or methods have bad periods; you must be able to trade through these in order to use the system. This number, along with the maximum drawdown, will give you an idea of the pain you must be prepared to endure.

Average Profitable Trade

The program segregates and totals profitable trades only and divides the sum by the number of profitable trades. Slippage and commissions should be included. The result indicates how well the system is letting profits run. You should compare it to the next number, the average losing trade.

Average Losing Trade

The program segregates and totals losing trades only and divides the sum by the number of losing trades. Remember that break-even trades are normally considered losses. Slippage and commissions should be included. This result shows how well the system is cutting losses.

Ratio of Average Win to Average Loss

The program divides the average profitable trade by the average losing trade. Any ratio over 2:1 is usually good, depending on the percentage of profitable trades.

Profit Factor

The profit factor is the ratio of the total net profits from profitable trades divided by the total net profits from losing trades: a break-even system has a profit factor of 1. All other things being equal, I would prefer the system with the higher profit factor. Another possible measure, which is not normally used, would be the overall net profits divided by the total net losses from losing trades. This would be an expression of the number of net dollars won for each dollar lost. Since losses are a measure of risk, such a figure would be another way to express profit in terms of risk.

Biggest Profitable Trade

The largest profit on a closed trade, including slippage and commissions, is another reflection of how well the system lets profits run. Long-term systems tend to make most of their profits from a small number of trades, so that it is useful to determine what percentage of the total profits came from the largest trade. The higher this percentage, the lower the margin for error the system has, because it depended on one super trade, which probably will not recur.

Biggest Losing Trade

In searching for ways to improve system performance, the largest losing closed trade, including slippage and commissions, is a good place to start. If you can eliminate or reduce some large losses, system performance should improve dramatically.

Number of Closed Trades That Were Buys (or Sells)

Some programs give you the percentage of trades that were buys and sells. This can be useful in judging the effectiveness of the system in exploiting uptrending or downtrending markets.

Percentage of Long (or Short) Trades Profitable

The program can segregate the long and short trades and determine what percentage of each were profitable. These figures usually reflect the overall market trend more than the system's effectiveness. In general, long trades will be more successful in a bull market, and short trades will be more successful in a bear market.

Average Profitable (and Losing) Trade Length in Market Days

The program segregates profitable and losing trades and computes the average number of days each type was open. A trade closed out on the same day as entry is considered open for one day. This will give a measurement of whether the system is a long-term or short-term system. It also reflects how well the system lets profits run and cuts losses short.

Total Slippage and Commissions

The program multiplies the per-trade amount specified for slippage and commissions by the total number of closed trades. It is important to deduct a realistic amount from all trades to reflect the reality of the marketplace. For the purposes of this book, I deducted $100 from every trade for slippage and commissions.

Return on Margin

Some programs report a figure for return on margin. They compute the number of days on which trading occurred, incorporate the required margin, identify the cumulative net profit or loss, and then calculate the return on actual margin used. To me this figure is deceptive because margins change with some frequency, and traders normally have much more than the minimum margin in their accounts. If comparing similar systems trading in the same market, this number could identify the most efficient system. It would be the most efficient because it achieved its profits trading over fewer days. Trading on fewer days reflects lower exposure to risk.

Effectiveness Ratio for Closed Trades

The effectiveness ratio appears in historical trading reports generated by all my software. It is a proprietary measure of overall trading performance. The program computes the ratio without considering any open equity at the end of the test run. Although each person has his own standards of effective performance, the effectiveness ratio is a good tool to identify quickly the best performing parameter sets if you are comparing a number of them, such as after an optimization run. As a general rule of thumb, systems that yield effectiveness ratios over 100 are performing pretty well. Effectiveness ratios over 150 are very good. The very best performance produces effectiveness ratios over 200.

Effectiveness Ratio with Open Equity

When the test run produces a large amount of open equity, either plus or minus, the effectiveness ratio for closed trades will either understate or overstate system performance. In such cases, I use the effectiveness ratio that includes open equity in its computation. This also appears in all historical performance reports generated by my software.

While there are many different classifications of performance to consider, there is a strong correlation between the key measures when tested over the same time period in the same market. Those systems with the highest average profit per trade will also usually have the highest profit factor and the lowest drawdown. The important thing is to evaluate systems against criteria that are important to you because you are the one who is going to be trading the system. You are the one who will undergo the emotional ups and downs as the system makes profits and losses. You must have confidence that the system will be profitable over time. Without that confidence, you will not be able to keep trading the system when it takes losses.

In this chapter we have examined the challenges and choices facing the diligent trader who wants to backtest his trading ideas before risking any money in actual trading. There is one remaining question that is so controversial and so crucial to creating effective mechanical commodity systems that it deserves its own separate discussion. The next chapter will present a unique view of the perplexing problem of optimization.

6 Optimization

There is no subject more important to the commodity trading system creator than optimization. This is the process of refining the parameters of the system by testing various combinations on back data. The personal computer has made the process fast and accurate. However, there has been considerable debate among experts in the field on the value of optimization. To explain the various points of view, *Commodity Traders Consumer Report* assembled six prominent individuals with differing backgrounds and strong opinions on the subject. It created a simulated panel discussion, which is reproduced below.

Participants were Robert Pardo, Jack Schwager, Bo Thunman, Steven Kille, Robert Pelletier, and Thomas Hoffman. Robert Pardo is the owner of the Pardo Corporation, which develops and markets software packages for traders. His products include a number of expensive, optimizable systems including *Swing Trader, Calvin,* and *Max.* Before organizing his software company in 1980, Bob had a varied career with brokerage and investment banking firms. He has published numerous articles on trading systems. Jack Schwager is Director of Research at Prudential-Bache. He is the author of scores of articles on trading and *A Complete Guide to the Futures Markets,* which I have called the best commodity trading book ever written. Bo Thunman retired early from the machine tool business in 1977. He has been actively trading the markets and designing computer trading systems ever since. In 1982, he founded Club 3000, a group of traders who exchange ideas on all aspects of trading in the club's newsletter. Steve Kille owns Microvest, another company that creates and markets software for traders. One of his programs, *Back Trak,* allows users to create and optimize trading systems without any programming skill. *Back Trak* allows the user to combine a large collection of popular studies and approaches. Bob Pelletier owns Commodity Systems, Inc. (C.S.I.), the premier financial data base for futures traders. He has been heavily involved in financial software and systems development and has written a number of articles on his work. Tom Hoffman is a retired nuclear engineer. Since 1983 he has been a full-time commodity trading researcher and trader. He marketed a system called the *GM Trading System* in 1983. He currently trades his own account and manages accounts for others.

Optimization Roundtable

CTCR:

Before we begin, we should define some terms. Bob, what do we mean by mechanical trading systems and optimization?

PARDO:

A mechanical system is a trading method that produces objective buy/sell entry points, stop loss points, and long/short position exit points. A mechanical system involves no judgment. Everyone should always agree on what orders the system requires. To optimize a mechanical trading system means to determine how to use its set of trading rules most effectively. The optimization process involves empirically determining the most effective set of trading rules by a process of methodical testing of the range of possible system values. This may involve varying markets and time periods.

SCHWAGER:

The underlying premise of optimization is that parameter sets which worked best in the past have a greater probability of superior performance in the future.

THUNMAN:

Vilar Kelly tells a cute story which illustrates the problems with optimization. "Pete and Herb were good friends and liked to make large bets with one another. They decided the bets by flipping a penny. It had to be a penny. Herb always chose the coin and did the flipping. Pete always did the calling. Herb noticed that Pete invariably called heads, never tails. This gave Herb a brilliant idea. He went in search of a penny which would always turn up tails. He purchased one million newly created pennies. He managed to flip them all at once. He put all the pennies which turned up heads into a reject pile. He then tossed the remaining pennies, again eliminating all the heads. After twenty tosses, he had one remaining coin. He went back to his college statistics textbook and looked up the odds of tossing twenty consecutive tails. The book said it was miniscule. Eureka! He had successfully optimized the million pennies. Just wait until he sees Pete!"

Are we acting much differently when we take a set of data, say silver price history, and test numerous systems on that data? Sooner or later, we are bound to stumble across an algorithm which will show fabulous profits.

SCHWAGER:

I used a similar example in an article in June 1984 *Futures*. I called it the S.T.U.P.I.D. system, short for Sure Thing Unlimited Profit Ingenious Design system. I created a trading system optimized on a data base of 100 previous coin tosses. It produced $16 in profits for every $100 bet. Obviously, the system's results were favorable because it was based on hindsight.

The data I used to test the system was the same as I used to construct the rules. The silliness of this may be obvious with coin tosses, which we know are random, but it is incredible how frequently people commit the same error in constructing and testing futures trading systems. Astute traders may be able to find patterns in commodity prices which they can exploit. But it is ludicrous to assume that an optimized system—a system in which you fit the parameter values to past data—can gauge future performance.

CTCR:

Jack, you once did an experiment to see exactly what the correlation was between past performance and future profitability. Would you tell us about it?

SCHWAGER:

The question I was researching was whether a particular system's best performing parameter sets for a past period would outperform randomly selected parameter sets in a future period. If not, even theoretically elegant optimization procedures may be futile exercises in self-delusion.

I described the experiment in detail in an article in August 1984 *Futures*. I arbitrarily picked a trading system I had designed in the past and a portfolio of 10 varied markets. I selected a system representative of trend-following methods. It had average performance.

I found that in some instances, the best performing parameter sets for the future period were also near the top of the list in the prior period. But even more frequently the best performing sets of the past were the worst performing sets in the future. Similarly, although the worst performing parameter sets of the past were sometimes also near the bottom of the list in the future period, the reverse pattern was no less common. Overall, there seemed to be no consistent pattern that the best and worst parameter sets of a prior period would maintain their relative performance in a following period. Moreover, selecting the prior period's best performing parameters for trading would not have provided any improvement over selecting parameters at random. Ironically, in that particular experiment, choosing the worst performing parameters from the prior period actually would have been a better strategy for trading than selecting the best.

CTCR:

What do you conclude from those results?

SCHWAGER:

Although an optimization-based selection of parameter sets for trading may lead to improved results for some systems, the potential value of optimization is probably much smaller than generally believed. I would even go so far as saying that sophisticated optimization procedures are probably a waste of time.

CTCR:

Bob, we know you disagree with Jack on this.

PARDO:

Yes, I do. I was a bit annoyed after reading Jack's series of articles. Common sense will tell you that the only way to uncover and isolate the most effective values for a system's variables is to examine and test the performance of various ranges of combinations of these variables over a variety of price histories. Examining the results of such testing will show which combinations generate the most winning trades and the largest profit with the smallest risk. This is what the optimization process is all about—trial and error testing of specific trading rules in various combinations, under a variety of different markets and conditions.

Schwager's optimization test was on an unspecified system. We do not even know if the system chosen was effective under any circumstances. After all, profitable trading systems do not grow on trees. Nor did he describe the optimization and testing procedure he employed. As a result of these omissions, it is difficult to form any intelligent impressions as to the merit of what Jack has to say.

Apparently, he feels that some system creators have abused the optimization process by developing fraudulent optimizations with the only purpose in mind to sell ineffective systems at top dollars. While this may be true, it has little to do with the design and testing of the best methods for the optimization of a trading system. It has a great deal to do with unethical and fraudulent marketing practices. And this is an entirely different subject matter than the one Schwager set out to discuss.

I believe that many people were left with the inaccurate impression from reading Schwager's articles that optimization is a totally fraudulent practice. He concluded that because his unspecified trading system performed poorly under an unspecified and perhaps inappropriate optimization procedure, all optimization should be rejected. He would have served the trading public better if he had explained the proper methods to use in designing and optimizing a trading system.

SCHWAGER:

Bob talks about common sense. As Voltaire said, "Common sense is not so common." In the first place, my article did show that the system I chose was profitable in 9 of 10 markets, even with random parameter sets. But this misses the point entirely. The particular system's performance is not in question, but rather the relative value of optimization. What optimization tells you is the best combinations for trading the past. The link between past and future performance is far more tenuous than Bob Pardo and many others would like us to believe. Perhaps his sense of reason is colored by his obvious self-interest in perpetuating common misconceptions about the value of optimization.

These test results were the product of one particular trial based on a number of arbitrarily selected inputs. Changing the inputs would have changed the results (although not necessarily the conclusion). Time and patience permitting, many other trials using different systems, test periods, and market portfolios could have been performed. However, based on my experience, I do not think the results would have been radically different. The point is that this example represented a blind test of a typical trend-following system for a substantial time period and a broad selection of markets. Given these considerations, the fact that optimization proved to be worthless in improving trading performance certainly raises significant questions about its value. However, don't take my word for it. Choose your own favorite system, and preselect a parameter set list, market portfolio, and test period. Then repeat my experiment.

I have not proven categorically that optimization is worthless. No doubt it is helpful for some systems. Rather, my intention was to make system traders question the value of a procedure that so many take for granted as being meaningful—if not valuable—without ever having tested that assumption.

Finally, I did describe proper methodologies for testing trading systems in my *Futures* articles, and I would be happy to reiterate them now.

CTCR:

Perhaps it would be a good idea to back up first and discuss the broader question of the computer's place in a profitable trader's approach.

KILLE:

Before we do that, could I say that in my opinion the question of whether or not optimization works is irrelevant. The real issue concerns the effectiveness of technical analysis itself. In fact, the whole argument boils down to the same old debate over the random walk phenomenon. If markets are truly random in nature then neither optimization, technicals, fundamentals, intuition, nor any other analytical method will result in consistent profits. If, on the other hand, markets are not completely random, technical analysis will work. In that case, optimization will work even better.

As an example, assume that the markets are not completely random and technical analysis is an effective method of trading. Assume further that your chosen indicator interacts with the underlying cycles. Welles Wilder's Relative Strength Index is a perfect example. Wilder suggested a 14-day RSI because 14 days was the average half-cycle of all commodities. This does not mean that 14 days is the half-cycle length of all commodities. What happens if you employ the 14-day RSI in a market which has an actual half-cycle length of 22 days? It will not perform as well. The trick is to use a length which is sufficiently close to the actual half-cycle length of the commodity during the time you are trading it. The most effective method for determining the best RSI length is to optimize individual commodities.

For this example, I assumed that an underlying cycle does exist. I also assumed that RSI is an effective tool which can be used to profit from these cycles. These two assumptions should be in question, not the value of optimization. Optimization is simply a technique used to capitalize on the assumptions. If no underlying cycles exist or if RSI is an ineffective formula, optimization would be futile.

If we assume that markets are completely random, optimization is useless. So is any other trading technique. Under this hypothesis, it would be wrong to criticize optimization when the real culprit is random markets.

If you believe that markets are not completely random, then technical analysis will work and optimization will work even better. If you believe in the random walk theory, you should start throwing darts and quit wasting your time on market analysis.

PARDO:

I'd like to give you my conclusions about the character of market behavior based on my experience with commodity trading and system design.

CTCR:

Go ahead.

PARDO:

First, futures price action exhibits a large *non-random* component. Second, a certain portion of futures price action is predictable within limits. Third, futures prices exhibit characteristics and identifiable profiles that one can measure and use to make various types of predictions. Fourth, futures markets exhibit definite price cycles or periodicities. Fifth, those cycles are nonstable or elastic in time factor (period) and price height (amplitude). Sixth, futures markets are composed of a series of minimarkets or minitrends.

I should also add that I have seen many so-called trading systems, and I am appalled by their one-dimensional nature and by the fact that many are marketed without the benefit of actual computer testing and optimization. Among those few systems that do have merit, most would benefit from proper optimization.

CTCR:

Let's go back to the basic question of the importance of the computer to today's commodity trader.

PARDO:

There really is no substitute for rigorously testing a trading idea or system over a wide range of markets and market conditions. One of the most valuable services microcomputers provide is the ability to accurately evaluate trading concepts before risking any money. It is cheaper and easier on the psyche to invest paper and computing time than to field test an unproven idea with cash in the pits. Too many fabulous trading ideas fade away under remorseless computer testing.

It is practically impossible to maintain and follow the newest generation of trading models without a microcomputer. It won't be long before a trader without a number crunching PC and a state-of-the-art trading model will be unable to compete in the marketplace.

CTCR:

Bob, what is your argument in favor of optimization?

PARDO:

Any historical paper trading is a simple optimization process. It consists of a simulation or test of a set of prescribed actions against real-time market conditions. You must test your system in all the markets you intend to trade. You can take the process one step farther. Perhaps you observe that a slight change in one of the values involved in the system improves performance by some measure—increased net profit, improved win/lose ratio, or reduced drawdown. If you test the system's variable parameters over a range of values, you can determine a specific set of parameter values which allows the rules to operate most effectively. And, if you test a range of values in different commodities, you may find that different values generate optimum performance in different markets. Going even farther, you can perform this operation over various historical time periods to see how performance changes under different market conditions.

The real questions pertaining to optimization are: 1) In what way can we improve our ability to determine optimal values for system variables? 2) How does the optimization process, especially in relation to the increasing usage of the microcomputer, bear on the development of systems and strategies? 3) What type of objective, verifiable, and mutually agreeable tests can we apply to the optimization process so that some type of standardization can emerge? and 4) What type of standards and tests need to be applied to an optimized trading system performance record when evaluating a trading system?

Whether or not there are those who believe in optimization, I will continue to optimize my various *Swing Trader* models, and I will continue to let my optimized models produce winning trades. We will develop even more powerful programs and optimizable systems, and we will continue to sell *Swing Trader* to satisfied customers who are laughing all the way to the bank.

CTCR:

Before that commercial, Bob mentioned standards of testing. This brings up the question of how you determine whether a system is performing well in the first place.

THUNMAN:

When testing over time periods longer than a few months, you immediately run into the problem of expiring futures contracts. Louis Mendelsohn, who designed and sells the *ProfitTaker* software program, solved the problem right in his software. Here is how he explained it. "The lack of a rollover capability is one of the most blatant limitations in trading system software. Traders testing actual contract prices are restricted to model development based on single contracts, with testing limited to a brief time span (i.e., 30 to 90 days) involving too few trades and too narrow a range of market conditions to develop stable models. While more extensive testing is preferable, that is usually restricted to perpetual contracts or actual contracts extending over a longer time period. In the latter case the result is unstable models because low volume and open interest during a contract's early months distort price behavior.

"For example, if you want to develop a model for use on March 1986 T-bonds, it would be incorrect to base it on the March 1986 contract data going back to March 1985, since in real time, traders would not have been trading that contract prior to November 1985. They would have traded the March 1985, June 1985, September 1985, December 1985, and March 1986 sequence of contracts and rolled forward prior to each contract's expiration. If you want to design profitable and stable models, your historical testing procedure must be a mirror-image of real-time trading.

"In the early development of *ProfitTaker* I solved this problem by building an automatic rollover capability into the historical simulator itself. The user has the option of testing perpetuals or single contracts on up to 520 days of data. Or, he can test any number of actual contracts, rolling forward automatically just prior to expiration—as traders would have done in real-time trading."

CTCR:

Bob, your firm supplies Perpetual Contracts which automatically compensate for the rollover problem. Like stock prices, they never expire.

PELLETIER:

The Perpetual Contract is calculated as a weighted average of the two distinct futures contracts that surround a given period of time in the future. They avoid distortions caused by expiring contracts and the wild fluctuations which often occur as a market approaches delivery.

One of the reasons why C.S.I. encourages the use of Perpetual Contracts for evaluating markets is because they remove from consideration two key elements that may distort the analysis: interest rates and carrying charges. Since the Perpetual Contract looks at the market a fixed period forward, 91 days, for example, it removes some of the effects of interest rates and carrying charges which may contribute to accelerated or decelerated market movement during the final months before contract expiration. Simulations which use real contract data may be biased toward periods of higher interest rates, which can vary between 5 and 6 percent. The effects of changing interest rates may favor periods of high interest rates over periods of low interest rates, and you may not be simulating the market that you are studying. More than likely, you may be simulating the interest rates and carrying charges that are part of the U.S. economy.

SCHWAGER:

I agree that your Perpetual Contracts are useful for testing trading systems, but I prefer the Continuous Futures price. I described its construction in my book. You use the nearest futures prices, but adjust them upward by a constant which compensates for prevailing prices on successive rollover dates. It has several advantages. First, it will reflect the equity changes due to the evaporation of carrying charges over time. Second, it will exactly parallel equity fluctuations in a trading position. Third, you can use the same series for signal generation and equity change calculations.

CTCR:

Let's talk about how to measure system performance. Bob, why don't you start.

PARDO:

The primary consideration is net profit. But you must consider net profit in proportion to the potential risk you must weather while earning the net profit. I measure this risk potential by maximum drawdown—the largest dollar loss generated by a series of unfavorable trades.

The risk/reward ratio is another key model-evaluation concept. To calculate the risk/reward ratio, I divide net profit by maximum drawdown. The higher this ratio, the better the model's risk-performance profile.

Another key performance consideration is the dollar value of the average trade. Obviously, the higher the value of the average trade, the higher the quality of the model. Because you incur a risk of loss with every trade, the fewer number of trades necessary to arrive at the same profit, the better the model's performance.

The optimization process also involves evaluating factors such as stability and portability. Stability refers to the constancy of model performance over a range of variable values. Portability involves the constancy of model performance over different historical time periods.

It is also important to evaluate the consistency of trades, both in time and dollar value. You should avoid models which produce peculiar bunchings of losers or winners, especially at the beginning or end of a test period. You should also understand the impact of unusually big wins or losses on overall performance.

A simple way to avoid the impact of these irregularities is to examine trading model performance over a cross-section of historical time periods. This serves three purposes. It diminishes the impact of big wins or big losses. It substantiates the model's performance profile over a more statistically valid selection of data. And it displays a model's performance profile under varying market conditions.

If the model performs well over an historical cross-section containing a range of different market conditions—high and low volatility, trending and nontrending periods, etc.—then the chances are good for continuing favorable performance.

CTCR:

Jack, how do you identify favorable performance?

SCHWAGER:

Before I give my criteria, there is an important aspect of measuring performance I would like to touch on. Users of trading systems often discover that their real-time results are substantially worse than predicted by their paper trading. One cause is failure to include realistic assumptions in their testing.

To test a system without deducting commission costs would be an obvious error. But what is less obvious is that merely adjusting for actual commission costs is not enough. Commissions account for only a portion of transaction costs. You must also allow for the difference between the system's theoretical execution price and the actual fill price. For example, if you are testing a system which acts on the close, to assume you were filled at the midpoint of the closing range would not be realistic. In the real world, buys near the upper end of the closing range and sells near the lower end are far more common.

You can address this problem in two ways. First, use the worst possible fill price—for example, the high of the closing range to buy. Second, assume a transaction cost per trade greater than actual commission costs—for example, $50–100 per trade greater.

The second approach is more practical. Most data bases do not contain opening and closing ranges. And how would you decide the worst possible fill price for an intraday stop order? Moreover, assuming the worst possible fill on all trades is probably too extreme.

Failure to incorporate realistic transaction costs can be a particularly serious error when evaluating systems which generate frequent trading signals. Traders often choose an active trading system because it appears to exhibit the best performance. They don't notice that the performance is superior only because they failed to include proper transaction costs.

Unless programmed otherwise, a computerized trading system may permit executions on limit days or in the middle of gap openings. If so, the paper results will dramatically overstate actual performance.

Seemingly attractive trading systems can fall apart when you include such realistic assumptions. It is far better to make this discovery in the testing stage than in actual trading.

CTCR:

After you have incorporated those realistic assumptions, Jack, how do you decide when a system is performing well enough to trade?

SCHWAGER:

There is no end to the number of possible performance measures. Fortunately, there is no reason to look at a myriad of performance yardsticks, since they are almost invariably highly correlated. For example, if you were to test 50 trading systems or parameter sets and rank the results on the basis of 10 performance indicators, you could expect to find a surprising degree of similarity in the ranking order generated by each performance measure. I believe that anyone who performs such an experiment once will find the results so compelling that he or she will not bother using more than a handful of performance measures thereafter.

CTCR:

We agree wholeheartedly, although a broad variety of statistics can tell you a lot about how the system trades. This can be helpful in assessing how to improve a bad system.

SCHWAGER:

I use the following measures to evaluate trading system performance: 1) Percent return—the return relative to funds needed to trade the system.

This is insufficient by itself, but it is the natural starting point. Percent return figures should be viewed for intervals (e.g., years) as well as for the entire survey period. 2) Maximum and second maximum retracements. These figures give you an idea of the worst case possibilities. In addition to percent return, it is also important to employ some measure of equity fluctuation (e.g., variability in rate of gain, retracements in equity). Besides the obvious psychological reasons for wishing to avoid parameter sets and systems with high volatility, a risk measure is particularly significant because one might pick an unfavorable starting date for trading the system. 3) Sharpe ratio. This is the most widely used return/risk performance measure. 4) Gain-to-retracement ratio. This avoids some of the drawbacks of the Sharpe ratio. One major problem with the Sharpe ratio is that it does not distinguish between upside and downside fluctuations. Thus, the Sharpe ratio would penalize a system which has sporadic sharp increases in equity, even if equity retracements were small. Another problem with the Sharpe ratio is that it does not distinguish between intermittent losses and consecutive losses. Thus, assuming a constant account size, a system which alternated $8,000 monthly gains with $4,000 monthly losses over a two-year period would have the same Sharpe ratio as a system which lost $4,000 in each of the first 12 months and then gained $8,000 in each of the next 12 months. Few traders, however, would consider those systems equivalent.

Readers who are interested in a more detailed discussion of the Sharpe ratio and the gain-to-retracement ratio, as well as the formulas for their calculation, can read my article in the March 1985 issue of *Futures*. Please note that, due to an oversight, the sidebar in that article failed to explicitly state that the monthly standard deviation needs to be multiplied by the square root of 12 to derive an annualized standard deviation.

THUNMAN:

In my opinion, there are five performance criteria to look at when you are trying to form an opinion on a particular system, your own or somebody else's. The criteria are 1) Return on margin, 2) Sharpe ratio, 3) Profit/loss ratio, 4) Pessimistic return on margin, and 5) Consistency over different time periods. We could endlessly debate the relative merits of each of these criteria—do you go for maximum profit or maximum Sharpe ratio? I look at all five. As Jack said, they run together most of the time, but sometimes they do not. Then you have to make a judgment as to which you prefer.

Return on margin is a very simple value to compute. If the margin is $1,000 and your annual profit, after overhead, is $5,000, then your return on margin is 500 percent. The Sharpe ratio is defined as the annualized return, divided by the annualized standard deviation of return. The higher the return and the lower the standard deviation, the higher the Sharpe ratio. The math involved is moderately complex. I bought some books on statistical analysis and advanced programming to find out how to do standard deviation analysis [*Advanced BASIC* by James S. Coan is a good one]. The straighter your equity curve, the higher will be your Sharpe ratio. What is an acceptable Sharpe ratio? If you analyze weekly equity, anything below 1.0 is shaky. I have seen 10 plus, and for a complete portfolio, 6–7 is not impossible.

Should the Sharpe ratio be computed on open equity or closed positions only? Here again, you choose your own poison. It can be argued that closed profits are all that count. The flip side is that margin calls are on open, not closed positions. You better know where you have been before you closed out a trade. I use open equity.

What data points should you use to make the Sharpe ratio computation? You can use daily, weekly, or monthly equity amounts. I use weekly data since a month is a very long time in commodity trading. You compute the total closed profits and the open equity on the day of evaluation and see what return you had on your total margin for the period in question. Your margin can include any amount of reserve. That does not affect the Sharpe ratio. If you have a $50,000 account and you made $3,000 in a week (total closed profits plus open equity at the end of the week), then your annualized weekly profit would be 6 percent times 52 weeks, or 312 percent for that week. When you have a full year of these weekly data points, you have enough to do an evaluation.

The Sharpe ratio is not an ideal indicator of performance since it only measures a combination of two performance characteristics: return on margin and straightness of the equity curve. If the equity curve is nearly straight, the standard deviation is near zero and a high Sharpe ratio results for almost any rate of return. A savings account paying 5 percent annually would show a Sharpe ratio of infinity, but you wouldn't consider that a very good trading system.

The profit-loss ratio is easy to calculate. Some system vendors would have you believe that if a system has 10 winners and 1 loser, it has a 10:1 profit-loss ratio. But the winners are not the same dollar amount as the losers. The correct definition is the total dollar amount of the winners, divided by the total dollar amount of the losers. What is a good number to shoot for? Probably 2:1 if you like sleeping at night. A trading system that shows a profit-loss ratio of 3:1 or better would be most pleasant to use.

I am indebted to Rod Sharp (no relation to the Sharpe of the ratio) for the pessimistic return on margin (PROM) procedure. Rod is a professional mathematician, and he came up with something easy to program and quite accurate in its application. Jack and I have indicated that various performance measurements yield pretty consistent rankings. If you optimize your system on the basis of PROM, you will have a simple and reliable measure of performance.

You compute PROM by assuming you had one standard deviation fewer winners and one standard deviation more losers than you actually did. Then calculate the total profit using the system's average win and average loss. If, using that assumption, you still have a positive rate of return, chances are you have a pretty good system. PROM alerts you to the effects of having too few trades and to the interaction between winners and losers because of their relative number and size.

Now comes the bad part—long term consistency. Bad, because here is where most systems fall apart. The consistency within the test period, perhaps a year, is defined pretty well by the Sharpe ratio. However, when you have optimized your system over one time period, you must test it on another. If you optimized on 1985 data, you must test the system on 1984 and 1983 and any other years of data you have to see if it always performs acceptably.

The most severe test of all is the Monte Carlo test. You pick random starting dates and random test period lengths and run a large number of tests. If your system can handle that, it should be able to handle any market.

Before you get excited over all this evaluation technology, please remember that statisticians will point out that there are not enough data points in a reasonable time period in commodities to draw any statistical inferences at all.

CTCR:

Now that we know how to judge trading system performance, let's get to the actual optimization process. Assume we have a trading system with a number of variable parameters. Assume we have a computer, historical data, and a program which will allow us to test any permutations of the variable parameters on the historical data. How do we find the best values for the variable parameters to trade in the markets?

SCHWAGER:

Perhaps the most critical error made by users of commodity trading systems is the assumption that the performance of the optimized parameter sets during the test period provides an approximation of the potential performance of those sets in the future. Such assumptions will lead to grossly overstated evaluations of a system's true potential. It must be understood that commodity price fluctuations are subject to a great deal of randomness. Thus, the ugly truth is that the question of which parameter sets will perform best during any given period is largely a matter of chance. The laws of probability indicate that if enough parameter sets are tested, even a meaningless trading system will yield some sets with favorable past performance. Evaluating a system based on the optimized parameter sets (i.e., the best performing sets during the survey period) would be best described as fitting the system to past results rather than testing the system.

CTCR:

But, Jack, you certainly are not suggesting that picking system parameters at random is as good as no testing at all. When you do test, how do you do it?

SCHWAGER:

At least two testing methods can eliminate (or at least temper) the influence of hindsight: the blind simulation approach and the equal weight approach.

In the blind simulation approach, you test in a time period that deliberately excludes the most recent years. Based upon the results, you decide on the specific parameter sets and the number of contracts to be traded in each market. Then you simulate trading results for a subsequent period. This can be repeated, moving through time, until you reach the current date. Ideally, you should repeat the process several times.

This approach avoids hindsight. It also duplicates the decision process that would be used in actually trading the system. Although blind simulation may be the most theoretically sound method for testing systems, it has two practical drawbacks. First, in many markets the number of available years to use for simulation is limited. Many existing futures markets did not trade actively until 1975 or later (in some cases, such as petroleum products and stock indexes, much later). Second, even if sufficient past data is available, blind simulation is tedious.

The equal weight approach offers an alternative to blind simulation and avoids some of its drawbacks. In the equal weight approach the analyst designing the system should restrict himself to using either price data from only one or two markets or data from a larger number of markets over a shorter span of time, such as less than a year. Before running any simulations, you must decide the markets to be traded, the number of contracts to be traded in each market, and a common parameter set list to be tested in each market. You evaluate probable system performance by taking the average performance of all the parameter sets. In other words, the worst performing parameter set would receive equal weight to the best performing set. This is a more realistic assumption than using the best parameter set as the performance gauge.

Rather than using the average parameter set performance, you can use the median performing parameter set on a predetermined list. Thus, for example, if in 1978 the median parameter set realized a gain of $1,500 (i.e., half the sets on the list had higher gains and the other half had lower gains), you assume the system would have achieved a $1,500 gain in that year. The basic premise underlying the median parameter set approach is that, on balance, one should be able to do at least as well as the median set in actual trading. Even if empirical evidence suggested that optimization had no value, one could approximate the median parameter set results using a random selection process. Consequently, even though the representative parameter sets are selected on the basis of data concurrent with the performance evaluation period, this approach is entirely valid because it is based on a reasonably conservative assumption.

The blind simulation approach probably comes closest to duplicating real-life trading circumstances. However, the last two methods are as conservative and have the advantage of requiring far less calculation. All three approaches represent valid procedures for testing a system.

Avoiding hindsight is critical in constructing simulated results. Unfortunately, simulated results have acquired a bad name because they often represent optimized results—how the system would have performed using the best parameter sets tested. The problem is, in real life one does not know which parameter sets are best until after the trades are completed.

As a final note, in order for the above process to be valid, it is necessary to determine the criteria for optimizing your system prior to testing. Otherwise, the results can be biased.

CTCR:

What about systems which are designed specifically for, and work in, only one market?

SCHWAGER:

Although it is probably unrealistic to expect any single system to work in all markets, generally speaking, a good system should demonstrate profitability in a large majority (75 percent) of actively traded markets. In fact, the selection of a system to be traded in a given market should depend on the performance of that system over the broad range of markets as well as its performance in that market. There are some important exceptions. A system employing fundamental input would, by definition, be applicable only to a single market. In addition, the behavior of some markets is so atypical (e.g., pork bellies) that systems designed for trading such markets might well perform poorly over the broad range of markets.

Traders often forget that factors as broad as the market itself or as narrow as minute differences in price movement on a given day can make a significant difference in the performance of a trading system.

The kind of market in which a system trades may be a dominant factor in the system's performance. Sometimes poor results do not suggest inadequacies in the system. Rather, they are an unavoidable consequence of a particular sequence of price movements peculiar to that time.

Similarly, large gains do not always reflect an effective trading system. Consider the 1979–80 silver market. Given the record-breaking uptrend and downtrend exhibited by that market, any system which followed trends would have been profitable during that period.

While a big market can be the key to trading performance in some instances, so might a single tick or point be crucial in others. Systems trading, like baseball, is a game of inches. Given the right combinations of circumstances, even a minute difference in price movement on a single day could have an extraordinary impact on the profitability of a given system as it is defined by a specific parameter set.

The moral is, to a large extent, performance depends on luck. This has two important implications: First, diversification is critically important as "bad luck insurance." The most valuable kind of diversification is trading as many different markets as possible. But, if sufficient funds are available, the diversification concept can be extended to incorporate the simultaneous trading of several systems in each market and even several parameter sets in each system. By diversifying as much as possible, given the constraints of available funds, you can ease the impact of isolated, abnormally poor results.

Second, to be meaningful, testing systems and comparing their trading results must be based on an extended survey period and a broad list of markets and parameter sets. Otherwise, isolated instances of abnormally superior or inferior performance by selected parameter sets could be misleading in evaluating the merits of a trading system.

CTCR:

Once you've done all your testing and decided on a system or group of systems, how long can you trade without going through the whole testing process again?

PARDO:

We instruct users of *Swing Trader* to check their optimization values periodically. One of the fascinating things our work has pointed up is a phenomenon I call market drift. Market drift is the tendency of market price to shift its primary identifying characteristics over a period of time. As a consequence of market drift, we believe it is necessary to periodically check system values and reoptimize them as market conditions demand.

CTCR:

I promised the statistician types we would give them a chance to further complicate the problem. Bob, why don't you start.

PELLETIER:

Drawing from my experience as a statistician and researcher for General Electric for over 10 years, I can tell you that most traders make the error of ignoring the concept of freedom loss. Each parameter introduced into a system represents a measure of control which limits the reliability of the outcome. This is not to say that optimization (such as trying all combinations of three moving averages) does not have some merit. But the more control parameters your system uses (such as moving averages, stops, market ranges, R.S.I. percentages, stochastic levels of significance, etc.), the less likely it is that future trading will match your test results.

The best systems are ones which use a very low number of variables, two to five at the most. The historical data used for testing should be of sufficient length to generate at least 30 trades. This number comes from sampling theory, which requires 30 samples to approach normality. I would favor a system using only two parameters which simulated a $10,000 total profit in 30 or more trades over a system using seven parameters which generated a $1,000,000 profit in 20 trades. The future reliability of the former system would be much higher because of the large sample and the small control or minimum freedom loss.

You should be as suspicious of your own simulated results as you should be of the advertised claims of systems sellers who brag about unbelievable profits over short periods of time.

CTCR:

Bob, do you have any suggestions about reducing the number of parameters or control, as you call it?

PELLETIER:

I would start by examining each of my trading rules to determine whether any two or more parameters explain the same phenomenon. If two parameters are redundant, using both may improve the simulation results, but the reliability or predictability of the model will decrease.

For example, if two of the variable parameters were volume and price range, and volume and price range are highly correlated, then you will have consumed two degrees of freedom when only one was necessary. You should choose the variable with the best performance and discard the other.

Another good place to cut out user control is the entry point. Whether you enter on the open, the close, or in between is of little consequence. Giving the system user the opportunity to choose only prolongs computer churning with little effect on the result.

KILLE:

I agree with Bob on the importance of running historical tests on sufficiently long periods of time. He is not saying this just to sell more C.S.I. data. I suggest using at least five years.

I disagree with him on some other points, however. First, while it is true that there is loss of freedom when introducing another variable into a simulation, this is only relevant when dealing with smaller data sets. When conducting a simulation over 1,000 data points (approximately five years) or more, the addition of another parameter has a negligible effect. Therefore, I think you should include as many parameters as possible into a model, so long as each new parameter is adding information. If fewer parameters were desirable, the folks at Chase Econometrics would not use hundreds of variables in their econometric models.

I strongly disagree that whether the system enters its trades at the open, the close, or in between, is of little consequence. Common sense indicates that the method of entry and exit can significantly affect a trading system.

PELLETIER:

I'm familiar with what Chase Econometrics does because I have done similar work. There is a difference between what commodity traders do and what Chase does. The typical commodity trader looks at past prices. A few add volume and open interest. Chase looks at interest rates, freight car loadings, taxation levels, the balance of payments, GNP, unemployment, energy costs, currency values, raw material costs, etc., etc. Chase,

I hope, has the sense to verify that each input variable is not highly correlated with any of the others. There's a big difference between predicting future business activity from a long list of independent fundamentals and predicting future commodity price direction from past prices of the same commodity. We commodity traders don't have as much to work with, but there's no sense in manufacturing redundant parameters to improve simulation results.

HOFFMAN:

The statistical concept of "significance level" is useful in judging the correlation between simulated results from past data and future real-time trading results. I look at this whole question as being similar to evaluating any kind of future performance based on past testing of a random variable. For example, an engineer performs a series of tensile strength tests on a given alloy to determine its suitability for a specific application. The measured strength varies from test sample to test sample, but based on his previous testing the engineer can evaluate the future performance of his design. In particular, he can estimate the probability of failure. There is a small but finite probability that any bridge will fail. This probability can and must be estimated before building the bridge. Similar to commodity trading methods, bridges could have signs that read, "Past testing does not guarantee future integrity."

I do not mean to imply that attainable significance levels for commodity trading are the same as those for bridge building. But I do think it is important to realize that the problem of quantifying future performance based on the past testing of a random variable is not new. Furthermore, I think traders should use the techniques developed to deal with predictability in other contexts to evaluate commodity trading methods as well.

One could argue that the futures markets are continually changing, whereas the physical properties of materials stay the same over time. If that is really the case, then all commodity systems traders are kidding themselves. The goal of the system trader should be to find and exploit those market characteristics which do not change. The best tool he has to identify them is the significance level.

By significance level, I mean the probability that your results could not be duplicated by pure chance. If a system had a low significance level of, say 10 percent, it would mean there was a 90 percent probability that throwing darts or flipping a coin would lead to results as good as your system. This would obviously not be a very good system. If a system had a significance level of 50 percent, it would mean that there is a 50:50 chance you could flip a coin to make buy and sell decisions and do as well as the system. That's still not a very worthwhile system. As the significance level approaches 100 percent, it becomes more and more probable that the system will achieve good results in future trading.

Perhaps the mathematics of calculating a simplified significance level will help illustrate my point. To estimate the significance level, I need two parameters. The first parameter measures the actual performance of the system. The total profit produced by a system is a single sample of a random variable and therefore contains no information as to variability, a key factor in judging future performance. Taken by itself, the total profit has very limited value in the evaluation of a method. The same criticism can be made of judging systems by parameters such as maximum drawdown, number of consecutive losses, best and worst trade, etc. To overcome this problem, some people use the Sharpe ratio, which is the average yearly return divided by its standard deviation. It can be adjusted to use different time periods. I prefer to use the average profit per trade divided by its standard deviation. Let's call this the performance ratio.

The second parameter is the number of degrees of freedom. This is equal to the number of trades produced by the system during the test period less the number of restrictions it uses. The number of degrees of freedom is important because it will expose systems which are highly curve-fitted. Systems with many rules, parameters, and exceptions tend to work well on past data, but often fail when applied to future real-time trading. The reason for the failure is that the rules have been created to perform well with the back data. If you gave me data from a "random walk" market, I could set up 100 rules to trade that market which would produce 100 winning trades in a row. The system would have a great Sharpe ratio and a great performance ratio, but because of its low degrees of freedom, it would have a low significance level.

In evaluating a trading system, counting the number of restrictions is not always easy. What I do is read the trading rules carefully and count any statement, clause, or phrase that would change the number of resulting trades. Each condition for entering is counted. Each condition for exiting is counted. You must count rules for short position entries and exits separately, even if they are the reverse of long positions. If you are testing a portfolio of commodities and the system uses different parameters for different markets, they must all be counted separately. If a method only works on a few commodities, the market becomes a restriction and you must multiply the restrictions in the rules by the number of markets in the test. I recommend that you be conservative in assigning the number of restrictions. In other words, if in doubt about a restriction, count it. Once the number of degrees of freedom exceeds 120, increasing them further does not appreciably change the significance level. So you should strive to be sure that the number of total trades in the test exceeds the number of restrictions by at least 120. Then your test will have meaning in terms of predicting the likelihood that future results will have some relationship to past performance.

There is a standard statistical table which gives the significance level based on the performance ratio and the number of degrees of freedom. It is called a t-distribution table. You can find it in statistics books or books with mathematical tables. As an example, a system whose performance ratio was 0.7 and had 10 degrees of freedom would have a significance level of 75 percent. In order to increase the significance level to 90 percent, the performance ratio would have to rise to 1.372.

However, the performance ratio is much more important in influencing the significance level than the degrees of freedom. To use the previous example, to produce the same significance level of 75 percent, if you raised the degrees of freedom from 10 to infinity, the performance ratio required would drop only from 0.7 to 0.677. Using a significance level of 90 percent, if you raised the degrees of freedom from 10 to infinity, the performance ratio required would drop only from 1.372 to 1.289. In order to achieve a 99 percent significance level with 120 or more degrees of freedom, the performance ratio must be 2.358. To raise the significance level to 99.95 percent with 120 or more degrees of freedom, the performance ratio must be 3.373.

This simplified significance level approach is not perfect. The calculation of the performance ratio assumes that profits and losses are normally distributed. In actuality, most trading systems are skewed to the profit side because they have small losses and larger profits. This defect diminishes in importance as the number of degrees of freedom increases.

Ignoring the above problem, the significance level is the likelihood that you have found a method which is exploiting nonrandom, time-invariant characteristics of the market. A large significance level suggests that the probability of future profits using the method is high.

I once purchased a trading system called *Pool Operator.* I counted eight restrictions per commodity with variable rules for 14 commodities. The advertised track record for the portfolio had a total of only 81 trades. There were thus 112 restrictions—many more than trades. This means there were no degrees of freedom. *Pool Operator* may be a good method, but the track record had not demonstrated it was any better than flipping a coin. Although the performance value was high, the significance level was zero.

My current approach to system evaluation uses log-equity changes rather than per trade profits and losses. That means I use the logarithm of the total daily equity value of the system or portfolio being tested. My performance ratio is based on the difference in these daily logarithm values rather than the equity change in dollars. Log-equity change values have a nearly normal distribution for all trading methods. To compute the degrees of freedom using this method, I count the number of days the system is in the market rather than the number of trades.

PARDO:

If the truth be known, the very people who most stridently criticize the optimization process, namely statistically oriented people, are the very ones who have provided us with the rationale for optimization. When a statistician develops a regression model, he essentially tests, by a process of trial and error, the degree to which a set of variables correlate to each other. He examines a series of variables in turn and either rejects or integrates them into the model based upon the performance criteria of accepted statistical tests and measures. We students of optimization consider that statistical process to be an optimization process.

I agree with the basic statistical points made by Bob Pelletier and Tom Hoffman. However, determining the correct degrees of freedom is not as simple as just counting up the number of system restrictions and deducting the result from the number of trades. Our work suggests that different kinds of rules use greater or lesser degrees of freedom. Although the problem is complex, we are working toward incorporating statistical measures of confidence into our historical simulation test reports.

A big advantage statisticians have over commodity system developers is commonly accepted measures of validity. About the only test that futures traders have been applying to their optimized systems is the trading test. Namely, how well does the optimized system do in simulated trading? There is nothing intrinsically wrong with the trading test, but it does fail to address an important question. If a trading strategy has been simulated historically, at what point, if any, in the future will performance deteriorate or improve? And if performance will change, is the point at which this will occur predictable?

THUNMAN:

One of our members, Govinda Khalsa, thinks the emphasis should be on analyzing the market rather than fitting system rules to past data: "The usual perspective in developing trading models is to take a variation on moving averages and then optimize it. But if your model assumes a trending market and you get a trading-range market, you're in trouble. Or you optimize your model for a trading cycle of 30 days, and then it becomes 20 or 45 days.

"The model building process should really focus on measuring the market time series data, not optimizing some ad hoc mode such as a moving average or channel length. This suggests that the model should incorporate a statistical description of the data. It should update automatically whenever the measured characteristics change.

"There are tools for determining if there is some pattern in the market that we can count on with measurable probability. If there is no pattern of acceptable probability, the system should stay out of the market. For instance, the Box-Jenkins approach has demonstrated that you can create several types of dynamic responses. Such models include combinations of long-term trends, cyclical and seasonal patterns, simple short-term correlations between consecutive days, or no pattern at all (uncorrelated noise)."

PARDO:

I agree that more accurate measurement of price action will lead to better trading models. But all trading models and methods already analyze the underlying market time series data either directly or indirectly. Methods of integrating this analysis into the trading model have lagged behind.

I am very interested in Box-Jenkins techniques. A few years ago, we made use of a professional statistician and a major university main frame computer to analyze a massive amount of commodity price data. Our goal was to develop a statistical model that would project price forward with some degree of tradeability. A model developed by a statistician and considered sound by statistical methods is not necessarily tradeable. We determined that certain statistical relationships do hold in standard daily futures price data which are sufficient to build a model with some predictive capability. However, based on the error range these models exhibited, they would have been useless for trading. Consequently, we put the project on the back burner for reactivation when new insights might provide more fruitful results.

CTCR:

We appear to be on the horns of a dilemma. If we change our optimized parameter values frequently based on very recent market characteristics, there won't be enough data points to achieve acceptable statistical reliability. If we optimize over longer periods going far back into the past, there is less likelihood the markets will retain the same price characteristics in the future.

THUNMAN:

Rod Sharp proposed a possible answer: "The dynamic nature of our markets suggests that the best systems will be those which dynamically adapt themselves to changing market conditions. An example would be a channel breakout system where the width of the channel automatically varies with the recent volatility of the market."

CTCR:

Our thanks to all the participants for what we hope was an enlightening discussion on this crucial area.

I believe that some optimization is inevitable in creating a trading system, but that the developer must exercise extreme care if he wants his system to perform well in the future as well as the past. The powerful personal computer and new, sophisticated software make it easier than ever to create a seemingly profitable system. In reality, through the process of optimization, the computer has just curve-fitted the rules to the back data used in testing.

In order to prevent excessive curve-fitting, the careful system developer must do some or all of the following: 1) limit the number of optimizable rules, 2) optimize over broad ranges rather than choosing the very best values, 3) maximize the number of closed trades in the test, 4) test the same parameters over multiple markets, and 5) test the optimized system over data not used for the optimization.

I hope you were taking notes as your read the first six chapters because it is now time for a short test. Please read the following statement and decide whether it is true or false.

> Hypothetical or simulated performance results have certain inherent limitations. Unlike an actual performance record, simulated results do not represent actual trading. Also, since the trades have not actually been executed, the results may have under- or over-compensated for the impact, if any, of certain market factors, such as lack of liquidity. Simulated trading programs in general are also subject to the fact that they are designed with the benefit of hindsight. No representation can be made that any actual account will or is likely to achieve profits or losses similar to those shown in hypothetical performance results.

TRUE or FALSE?

If you said false, you better reread at least the last two chapters. Federal law, by the way, requires that statement to be included in any promotional material that includes hypothetical trading results. All of the statistical material in this book is hypothetical trading.

Now that we have examined the general theory of system trading and understand historical testing and evaluation, we are about ready to start creating some actual systems. Before we get to that serious work, I thought you might like to take an entertaining little detour through the wonderland of commercial system selling. The next chapter will show you how clever marketers have exploited traders' seemingly limitless appetite for the Holy Grail system that will guarantee their success as traders.

Chapter

7

A Short History of System Merchandising

In any activity where there is a great deal of money to be made, there are bound to be con men operating. The futures industry is no exception. Probably no segment of the industry typifies the sleaze involved more than system merchandising. Every effective con game involves a victim who is either totally dull-witted or trying to make an easy buck himself, often dishonestly. The commodity trader who falls prey to unscrupulous system sellers is hoping to buy a money machine. He may even expect to unwrap it and be able to retire with no further financial worries and a minimum of effort. This is no more possible in commodities than in any other easy-money endeavor. Why is it that it is always the other guy who made easy money? The only easy money I know is inherited. Even that comes at a price.

There are, to be sure, many honest trading system vendors mixed in with the opportunists and outright crooks. Because of the ignorance about historical testing and future performance, there are many honest vendors who are nevertheless making misleading claims and peddling ineffective products. They are not crooks; they just don't know any better. As we take this short journey through the fantasyland of trading system advertising, I leave it to you to decide which is which.

The first large display advertisement hawking an expensive trading system appeared in *Commodities* magazine (now *Futures*) in February 1977. This was perhaps the only high-priced trading system without a catchy name. In fact, there was no name at all. It was referred to only as a "trading method" with small letters. The vendor, located in Fresno, California, called himself Behavioral-Quantitative Studies. There was a track record presented in the ad which claimed 21 out of 24 profitable trades in February 1975 pork bellies over an eight-month period. The claimed net profit was $36,776, after deducting commissions. The price was $800. Careful readers were warned that "past performance is no guarantee of future performance and thus no method can guarantee a future profit." The system itself was a simple seasonal method that bought and sold on the basis of the day of the week.

The typical system seller has not traded the system himself, so he must establish credibility for it in some other way. One of the favorites is to allude to some other mysterious trader who invented the method and now wishes to share it with a select group of strangers. In this case the claim was that "the trading record was not hypothetical paper trades but actually based on the activities of an obscure professional trader. This trader has asked that his name not be revealed. He is a psychologist by profession and has used his talents as a scientist of mind and behavior to dissect the beginnings of trends in the belly market." Although the system's printed track record assumed trading one contract at a time, the ad claimed, "in actuality this psychologist trader started out with 15 contracts, never trading more than 15 contracts on any one signal and trading exactly as indicated in the above record. He ended the period with a net profit of $541,221. Since achieving his incredible fortune in the market, this trader has reverted back to his original profession of psychology, as well as enjoying his newly found fortune. He has consented to reveal to a small coterie of the public his insights into the market." The ad indicated that no more than 50 copies would be sold.

Another perceived problem of system sellers is restricting duplication and sharing of the system with nonpurchasers. This promotion handled the problem in a nebulous way: "Each copy will be registered in the name of its holder. Each purchaser of the method, upon purchase, automatically places himself in jeopardy if he chooses to reveal the method to anyone." This was a prophetic warning. Several years later this vendor himself was sued by Larry Williams for selling a Williams system under the fictitious name of Ray Palladino. Although Palladino never admitted wrongdoing, he settled the case for $10,000.

In the universe of commodity system selling, two stars shine more brightly than the rest, Larry Williams and J. Welles Wilder, Jr. I will come back to Wilder later. Williams started out writing a stock market newsletter in Carmel, California, in 1967. On the suggestion of his broker, he tried some of his stock market tools on the commodities markets and found they worked. He then started publishing a commodity letter as well. After a big killing in the 1973 bull markets for himself and others, he published a book called *How I Made One Million Dollars Last Year Trading Commodities*. This is an excellent book and is still in print.

Larry Williams pioneered the commodity seminar business. Although most of the systems he has sold over years were his own, he joined with Charles Lindsay in 1974 to promote Lindsay's "Trident" trading systems at seminars around the country. Both the Williams book and the Trident seminars caused Williams problems with the S.E.C. (Securities and Exchange Commission), which regulated the commodity industry before Congress established the Commodity Futures Trading Commission. The S.E.C. thought the advertisements for the book were too "promotional and flamboyant." Because Williams offered the seminars with a money-back guarantee, the S.E.C. made the absurd claim that he was selling a "security," which had to be registered. He ran up astronomical legal bills before a federal judge in Los Angeles threw the case out of court.

This was not the first time the S.E.C. had misconstrued the reality of commodity trading systems. In 1959, Ed Gotthelf started marketing an advisory service called *Commodex,* based on objective buy and sell rules generated from past changes in price, volume, and open interest. *Commodex* is a mechanical system just like those described in this book. Its rules are fully disclosed to subscribers. Traded over a broad spectrum of markets, it has been a consistently good performer, and the service is still available today. The S.E.C. thought that *Commodex* had enough subscribers to influence the markets in which it was making recommendations. They took the laughable position that the *Commodex* signals were "inside information," which Gotthelf himself could not trade.

Larry Williams was not deterred by his run-in with the S.E.C. He continued to promote a succession of systems with names such as "Triangulation," "Propulsion," "Sequential," "Floor Trader," "Striker," "Trend Catcher," and "Day Trader's Delight" at prices from $1,000 to $10,000. On the "Floor Trader Method" he offered double the $3,000 cost of the system back if it did not make money in three markets over a one-year period. He also invented the idea of charging part of the cost of an expensive system up front ($2,000) with the remainder to be paid later "out of profits from the system." This was truly a brilliant marketing ploy.

Because of his troubles with the regulatory bureaucracy, Larry developed a keen interest in politics. It became his first love. In the middle of these commodity promotions Williams took time out to run as a Republican for the United States Senate in Montana. Twice he lost by only about a 4 percent margin even though he had no previous political experience. "Commodity traders can start at the top," he explained.

Unlike most other system developers and promoters, Larry has been an active trader over the years. Although he no longer publishes a newsletter, he continues to do commodity research, give seminars, and trade accounts for himself and others. He holds the unofficial world's record for trading contests. In the 1987 World Cup of Futures Trading, Larry started with $10,000 in his account and traded it to the inconceivable amount of $2,300,000. He ended the year with over $1,100,000 in profits. Ironically, Williams was modest about his trading ability. He said he learned "how inadequate as a trader I am. It sounds funny, but I am a horrible trader," he told me. "I made my money by being a good system developer and a pretty good system follower. It's an old lesson I just keep relearning. I've got to follow the system. I also learned beyond a shadow of a doubt that systems do work." I should say!

Williams's accomplishment in that contest was beyond anything that seems possible by using the ideas discussed in this book. However, from my friendship and association with Williams, I am satisfied that he did not employ any revolutionary secrets that, if you knew, you could use to duplicate his performance. His systems use the same kinds of concepts you will learn here and from other commodity trading books. As I will explain in Chapter 15, having a winning trading system does not insure that you will profit from it.

Williams needed some luck at the beginning to increase his capital base rapidly. The stock market obliged by taking off in January 1987. Larry traded up to the limits of his account margin and consistently took huge risks that most people would not be able to match. Don't forget, the same system that made over $2 million in profits lost over $1 million during the course of the year. Those who would aspire to match Larry Williams' profitable trading should ask themselves if they could accept his losing trading as well. No one knows when a system's winning and losing periods will come. Nevertheless, Larry Williams' trading record will probably last as long as Joe DiMaggio's 56-consecutive-game hitting streak or the Los Angeles Lakers' 33 consecutive wins.

One of my favorite characters in the system vending business is a Florida operator who for many years could be identified by his distinctive writing style and trademark prices ending in 90, most often $290. He is still promoting, although he has finally realized that a different price might confuse people about who they are dealing with. His latest system was priced at $299.

In 1981, using the company name Market Dynamics in Lakeland, Florida, he advertised a system called "Market Dynamics Trading Method." The brochure said the inventor of the method was one Marvin Romley, who had set the price at $490. "Marvin Romley's interest in commodities goes back to the 1920s," it continued. "He is the author of the Market Dynamics Trading Manual, which received high grades from its readers. Dr. Alan A. Andrews, a man now in his eighties and who made his first million trading commodities while in his twenties, said of Mr. Romley's manual that it was the best of two ever written on commodity trading. And Dr. Andrews should know."

Indeed. The other was probably Andrews' own. Andrews was an actual person who also lived in Florida. He operated as a nonprofit foundation, selling a $500 trading course and an advisory newsletter. The newsletter had an eye-popping trading record. For example, his four October 1983 letters showed 39 profitable trades totalling $72,038 and but one $375 loss. He was later publicly accused of creating this record through "20/300 hindsight." He apparently rewrote his recommendations after the fact. Or, as Peter Aan once said in describing a famous advisory service's advertising, "The easy way to commodity trading profits is to make them up." Naturally, Andrews' newsletter's profits were an excellent advertisement for the $500 trading course.

Mr. Romley did offer a guarantee. This type of phantom guarantee is common. Unlike Larry Williams' double-your-money-back guarantee described above, which allowed the customer to paper-trade the system, Romley required the customer to trade the system for a one-year period to claim his $490 refund. He knew no one could afford to trade a losing system for a year to recoup a measly $490.

In 1984, under the name Market Concepts of Tampa, Florida, the same individual sold a system called "The Colt 88 Method." The brochure described its alleged inventor:

> Henry Colt has been into futures for more decades than he would care to count at this point in his life. It started in his early youth when a commodity trader neighbor bought flashy new cars and Henry and his father were hired to polish and fine tune them several times a month. When the family moved to a more rural area, again a neighbor in a beautiful home . . . the best in the area . . . turned out to be a commodity trader.

Henry was trained to be an engineer, the greatest career to pursue back in those days before World War II. But knowing where the real money was . . . commodity futures . . . that memory never left and Henry pursued commodity trading with a vengeance. Mr. Colt acquired a library of almost every stock and commodity trading method that has ever been published . . . some systems were a few dollars; other ran as high as $30,000. And during all of this intensive study, research and application, Mr. Colt discovered certain principles that he has been using very successfully. More so than any of the methods in his library. With accuracy of 88 percent and better, you can understand why this has to be the most profitable method available today.

We had a very serious discussion with Mr. Colt about the price. We felt that a method that makes this kind of money with this kind of certainty is worth at least $10,000. But Mr. Colt, an experienced hand in the markets and in life, felt he wanted others to have the benefit of his life's work. He didn't want to give it away because then no one would consider the value of it. Yet he didn't want to charge the price we felt its value should bring. He insisted, after a lot of days thinking about it, that the price should be set high enough so that the purchaser will apply himself and bring about the reality of Colt 88 profits. So he set the price at $290, less than a one-cent move in pork bellies. We tried to budge him higher, but he firmly set the price, and that's it for the time being. He agreed that if we offer it again the price will be $2,500. Mr. Colt, now moving on in years, wants others to benefit from his research and market concepts. He is for you, the common man, the average trader. With his method you no longer will be average.

While the Market Dynamics brochure referred to the system as "like a license to rob the bank, legally," the Market Concepts system was called "the key to the vault." Mr. Colt's guarantee was almost identical to Marvin Romley's. It required actual trading of the system for one year to obtain a refund.

Henry Colt was an engineer. This was a favorite occupation of the Florida operator. His first system offering in 1980 was "The Engineer's Trading Method," sold by Financial Research Ltd. in Clearwater, Florida. The advertisement said this method was "the result of an electrical engineer's study of price motion in commodities over many, many years. Familiar with wave form analysis, cycles, distortions, and the mathematical analysis of wave forms, the engineer developed a trading method with the following objectives: huge profits, accuracy, completely mechanical . . . no judgment, reliable and usable with all commodities." Its price, $290.

In 1983, the Florida operator used the name Market Research of St. Petersburg, Florida, to sell the "$100,000 Gann Trading Method" for $290. W. D. [William Delbert] Gann is a legendary commodity trader whose legend was created by people selling his purported trading methods. The brochure for this system claimed Gann traded the markets until age 76 and averaged $1,000,000 a year in profits. (The 1981 Market Dynamics ad had invoked the Gann name and said he amassed a fortune of over $50,000,000.) The brochure explained the $100,000 figure in the method's title by claiming that Gann had revealed it to a few select clients for that amount. Gullible bargain hunters could therefore brag about getting a colossal 99.71 percent discount! The brochure went on for pages describing the incredible trading feats of W. D. Gann, all no doubt invented by its author or copied from other fictional sources.

After his death in 1955, Gann's estate sold his papers to Billy Jones. Gann's papers were so voluminous that Jones needed a large moving van to transport them across the country. For many years thereafter Jones's Lambert-Gann Publishing Company sold Gann courses and books. From what has been published, it is obvious that Gann was a pack rat who saved every scrap of paper he ever doodled on. It is inconceivable that if he was making such immense profits, he would not have saved his account statements to prove it. Yet no Gann account statements have ever seen the light of day. Someone who had spoken to a Gann relative told me that Gann had no substantial estate when he died.

The most esoteric Gann trading approaches involve complicated numerology and geometry. Although proponents can give many superficially impressive examples of instances where they worked, there has never been any rigorous demonstration of their effectiveness. The "$100,000 Gann Trading Method" took 110 pages to explain that Gann's greatest secret was that he used astrology. It was up to the reader to figure out for himself how to apply astrology in his own trading. There was, however, one piece of information you may still be able to use. The manual said Gann predicted 1990 would be a bearish year for the stock market.

In 1985 the same person, using the name Eric Olsen in Orlando, Florida, sold the "Maximus System." The brochure went right to the soul of the struggling commodity trader: "What you really need is an advantage over other players . . . some strategy . . . some ingenious plan, some trading method that really works . . . works in all kinds of markets . . . trending markets, fast or slow; as well as on sideways markets. The Maximus Trading Method is that method. You want a concept that the crowds of losers are not using . . . a concept that really works. Things will be different in your home after you get your copy of Maximus. Why? Because you'll hit the floor running every morning. You'll know that terrific profits are waiting for you each trading day. You'll rush home feeling younger than you have in years. And why not. Money solves a lot of problems and opens lots of doors. It's exciting to be a winning trader, utilizing Maximus and seeing those $$$ pour in." The price of Maximus . . . $290.

After you plunked down your $290 and received the system, you would have found out why the track record in the brochure looked so good. It was riddled with inaccuracies. What would turn out to be losing signals were overlooked. Winning trades were made in conflict with system rules. The rules often resulted in buy and sell signals at the same time. Naturally, under such circumstances, the author chose the one that later turned out to be profitable.

While most commodity system promotions are perfectly legal, a few do appear to stray across the line into criminal fraud. The authorities seem powerless to stop commodity con artists. I know of no criminal fraud charges ever brought against a system promoter. One was convicted of fraud, but he was prosecuted not for his system selling, but for losing managed money trading the system and other commodity-related, fraudulent activities. His $850 "Lightning System" was featured in a full-page ad in the November 1982 *Commodities* magazine. It showed a seven-year track record totalling $1.8 million in profits. According to the charges, the system had never been tested at all, and the track record was a complete invention.

Commodity system selling joined with technology in 1981 when J. Gresham Northcott, Jr. sold "The Phasor Trading System." At a cost of $3,000, this was the most expensive commodity system product marketed to the general public up to that time. The brochure billed it as "A marriage of the most profitable, totally mechanical trading system ever devised with the simplicity of a system-dedicated pocket computer." This marriage, as it turned out however, was not made in heaven.

After detailing his long experience with commodity trading systems, Northcott bragged, "I know what makes a good system and I know the devastating flaws in most of the systems that are sold to the public. Having seen these, I'm going to be absolutely certain that my system is unflawed." The Radio Shack portable computer was to make system computations easy. The brochure told prospective purchasers: "Chart books, computer technicians, complex systems analysis, etc.— Throw Them Away!—they are simply not needed. Punch the Open, High, Low and Close into the Northcott Computer every day and take the trades it specifies. It really is as simple as that. The computer easily fits into your pocket—and can be operated anywhere. What goes on in the computer is highly complex. But for you the trader, the work is the utmost in simplicity—just punch in a few numbers each day for each commodity." Using a computer had the not-so-incidental benefit of allowing Northcott to hide the system rules in the software. The brochure went on for eight pages describing the "safe and steady stream of profits" the purchaser could expect and how easy it would be to make them.

Like many a marriage, the promised fantasy turned out to be distinctly different from the reality. In this case posterity has a written record of what happened after the system was sold. An enterprising individual, Bo Thunman, formed a Phasor Users Group, or as he facetiously called it, the Phasor Non-users Group, to share intelligence in an effort to recover some value from his $3,000 investment. He began publishing a newsletter containing his and others' comments, suggestions and experiences trying to use Phasor.

Northcott should have called it Murphy's System. Everything went wrong. The computer did not work properly. The manual was full of errors. The system generated signals so close together in price that the market had moved beyond the next signal before it could be executed. There was a flaw in the historical testing logic of the program, which resulted in omitting many losing trades. The manual introduced potentially variable parameters that held out hope of success if only the right parameter values could be discovered. They couldn't. One purchaser did not want to be bothered with running the program every day. He sent $50,000 to be managed by Northcott's firm and reported six consecutive losing months. The brochure had said that the system "demonstrated over more than four years that it can take profits of almost $5,000 per week." There was apparently not a single individual who was able to make a profit using the system as advertised. Thunman and the rest of the group eventually gave up on Phasor and "relegated the computer to use as a paper weight."

In the spring of 1982, the next major commodity system promotion hit the mails. Donald Mart was selling the "Paragon Trading System." Its 12-page brochure led off with the statement: "For the last four and a half years, the Paragon Trading System averaged over $10,000 per month net profit!" It continued on in about the same vein as the Phasor brochure, only Paragon traded 12 markets instead of Phasor's 11 and the performance figures were better. This system was locked in a Hewlitt-Packard programmable calculator.

In spite of the failure of the Phasor System, the users group newsletter reported that most of its members had purchased the $3,000 Paragon System. This led to changing the name of the users group to Club 3000. Thunman broadened its scope to include all technical trading systems, and it is still in existence today.

After some initial enthusiasm, the Paragon System failed to meet its purchasers' expectations as well. For example, the Club 3000 newsletter reported one purchaser who had 10 straight losses and others who briefly made money fading (trading opposite to) the system.

The failure of Paragon did not stop Mart from rolling out the "Matrix/Guardian System" in 1984. This brochure was 16 pages long, the system traded 21 markets, and the price was $3,250. It ran on a personal computer. The system rules again were not disclosed.

Although the Matrix/Guardian brochure went into some detail on Mr. Mart's commodity career, the only mention of his Paragon System promotion was the following oblique reference: "I got sidetracked by another major trading program development." Mart had called Paragon "the most profitable and unique trading system ever developed," but now Matrix/Guardian was "the most powerful trading system ever devised."

In order to allay the fears generated by previous similar system promotions, Mart came up with a new gimmick—"An Unprecedented Quadruple Guarantee," which included a performance guarantee. He enlisted Bo Thunman of Club 3000 to act as an impartial referee and paper-trade the system for one year. If the system did not show a profit trading its 21 markets over that period, purchasers would be entitled to their money back. The guarantee took up a full page using very small type and had a fancy diploma-like border. As imposing as it looked, there were several obvious deficiencies. After claiming historical profits of $210,561 per year for the last 11 years, Mart was pretty chintzy to guarantee only that the system would make *some* profit in the future. One would naturally wonder why, since Mart's Wilshire Trading Company was also offering to manage accounts with Matrix/Guardian, he did not just trade his own actual account to establish performance so slippage could be included. The brochure's explanation was double-talk: "We tried to figure a way to audit impartial, actual accounts to determine performance, but found it impossible due to many reasons, the main one being the variances people employ (even subconsciously) when trading a system with no way then of correlating these audited results with those of everyone else, and on and on. . . ."

Thunman was not being compensated for tracking the system and found that, even using a computer, it was too much work. He requested that Mart provide him access to a phone-up data base so he could obtain the data automatically, but Mart never did. Thunman quit after five months. At that time the system had generated 31 closed trades and $24,472 in losses. Thunman does not know what happened to people who tried to collect on their performance guarantee.

The title of World's Greatest Commodity System Promoter goes without question to Welles Wilder. Unlike Larry Williams, Wilder never demonstrated any trading prowess. What he did demonstrate was an unparalleled ability to get people to pay him money to learn his latest trading method.

The most worthwhile achievement of Wilder's career was his 1978 book, *New Concepts in Technical Trading Systems*. In it he described six complete trading systems and two unique trading tools. One of the latter, the Relative Strength Index, went on to become one of the most popular oscillators for measuring overbought and oversold markets. Many commercial chart services still use it as one of their indicators. Like all other similar authors, Wilder made no demonstration that any of his systems actually would produce significant trading profits. The real value of the book is its explanation of how to create a trading system. Wilder approached the problem logically and theoretically rather than just crunching numbers to see what worked. I have no respect for Wilder's later efforts, but I do strongly recommend this book, which is still available. Although later testing has shown that the systems did not work as well as theory suggested, Wilder presented many worthwhile concepts and approaches.

Wilder sold his first system in 1976. He called it "The Trend Reversal System," and priced it at $1,000, big money for a commodity system in those days. Although his later advertising referred to it as the "Ultimate System," Wilder was a long way from finished creating new and better mousetraps to sell to eager but disenchanted traders.

After his 1978 book, Wilder devoted his marketing efforts to other people's ideas. His next major promotion was the "Reverse Point Wave System," which he taught at a series of $500 seminars in 1980 and 1981. Although he touted it as his discovery, the Reverse Point Wave was actually the expanding top chart pattern described in Edwards and Magee's 1948 classic, *Technical Analysis of Stock Trends*. In this series of seminars Wilder introduced several other men to the trading public who later struck out on their own in the systems promotion business. One of these was J. Gresham Northcott, Jr., perpetrator of the Phasor Trading System.

In 1982, Wilder joint-ventured an advisory letter based on the Reverse Point Wave. It was a disaster. The recommendations lost over $100,000, and it was discontinued. This did not deter Wilder, however.

During the next several years, in conjunction with a different partner, he promoted the Reverse Point Wave as a $450 home-study stock market course. The brochure had the following headline: "The Most Accurate Trading Signal is Still Virtually Unknown."

In late 1981, Wilder joined forces with J. L. Patterson to promote the Wilder/Patterson Computer Graphics Gallery. This was a high-tech, computerized implementation of Patterson's "Cybercast" and "Curvilinear" systems and Wilder's Reverse Point Wave. Its most expensive configuration was referred to as "the big machine," which you could set up in your own office for a mere $370,000. You would be hooked into the exchanges and receive real-time quotes. The computer would use them to generate charts and trading signals. The big machine was a Hewlett-Packard minicomputer with coordinating printers, plotters, etc. If the big machine was too steep for your pocketbook, you could "go on line" and receive the information by wire for only $15,000 plus $2,000 per month. The Graphics Gallery brochure is vintage Wilder copywriting:

> Imagine yourself walking into a Wilder/Patterson Computer Graphics Gallery in your city. Imagine also that you know nothing about commodities. (In this case, that can even be an advantage!) You walked in off the sidewalk because you were intrigued when you looked through the display window and noticed what at first appeared to be an off-track betting parlor. Two dozen traders are seated behind tables watching several big movie screens. One of the screens shows strange symbols with prices. Two other screens show five minute bar charts with strange lines projected all over the charts. Every few minutes the charts change and new and different updated charts appear on the screens. The people sitting behind the tables are intently watching the charts and prices and are constantly making phone calls. Suddenly a cheer is heard and someone says, "T-bills just hit the target!"
>
> "What in the world is going on?" you ask yourself. You walk over to what looks like the manager's desk and voice the question out loud. The manager introduces himself and explains that this is a Commodity Trading Gallery. "Would you like to learn what it is all about?" You answer, "No thanks, I've heard about commodity trading . . . and on top of that most traders lose." He smiles and says, "That's the connotation that most people have, but the Gallery is a *new dimension* in commodity trading. You can learn this new dimension in two days and if you have the discipline to follow what you learn, you should be correct on a high percentage of the trades that you take. Would you like to learn more?" Naturally, you ask, "What does it cost?" He answers, "Nothing, except two days of your time. You then try it out here at the Gallery for a few days in hypothetical trading, and when you are confident that you are ready, you can open an account and call your trades directly to the floor utilizing the special brokerage arrangement set up here at the Gallery.
>
> For the next two days you sit in on a continuous training film (with supplementary personal instruction) which teaches you how to use R.P.W.–Cybercast indicators. You learn that the basis of the system is a coming together at a moment of coincidence of at least six of these indicators within a one-half hour time frame. You learn the point value of these indicators. When enough of the 23 indicators come together that you have accumulated six points, you can take the trade . . . eight points, and the trade becomes more sure . . . ten points, and the trade approaches

a "dead lock cinch." A week later, you are trading for real . . . and making money . . . consistently. You tell a friend about your success . . . and you finish by saying, "Just think, two weeks ago I couldn't even spell Cybercast."

Patterson was an ex-convict who candidly admitting dreaming up some of his commodity systems while doing time in prison. He was also quoted as saying in an unguarded moment that his methods did not help clients to profit but only to lose their money more slowly. The big machine was apparently the commodity version of the big sting.

In 1983, Wilder moved into the realm of the personal computer. Together with Stanley Kroll, he sold the Kroll-Wilder System for $2,850 (not including the computer). This was Kroll's long-term trading approach packaged for the Apple computer. Wilder went all-out on this promotion, creating a 16-page, full color brochure. Kroll continues to sell the software (now reduced to $2,450) and claims it has been profitable over the years. Although a number of purchasers have tried to unload their Kroll/Wilder software in the *Futures* magazine classifieds, Kroll says one person turned $19,000 into over $100,000 in the four years after he bought the product. According to Kroll, the system would have made nearly $250,000 trading its 15-market portfolio over that period. There was a drawdown, however, of over $50,000. It would thus have taken nerves of steel to keep trading the system to its ultimately profitable conclusion.

All of this was only a training ground, preparing Wilder for his most ambitious promotion and the biggest commodity system promotion ever—the Delta Society International, launched in 1984. This, too, Wilder described in a 16-page, full-color brochure. He now proposed to sell "the secret of the perfect order behind the markets." When you became a member of the Delta Society International, Wilder would send you yearly until the year 2000 a computer diskette, from which you could obtain long-term and intermediate-term turning point dates in 25 markets. The computer program did no calculating; it just contained the list of turning points. It could more conveniently have been printed on paper, but to the superficial reader, the computer made it seem more mysterious. The cost of membership was $3,500 plus $100 per year, adjusted for inflation. This entitled you to the turning points only. For $35,000 you could become a "director" in the Delta Society International and actually learn the secret formula itself.

The brochure is a fascinating study in marketing psychology. *Commodity Traders Consumer Report* (August 1984) published a special report that analyzed it in detail. The report also contained a rebuttal from Wilder. Here is a brief excerpt from the first Delta brochure which describes how Wilder discovered the "secret."

My name is Welles Wilder. I wish that I could say that I discovered this phenomenon, but I'm not that smart. It all began with a phone call. It was the second week in September 1983. The essence of the conversation went like this:

"Mr. Wilder, my name is Jim Sloman. I have discovered something about the markets that I want to present to you."

"What is it," I replied, "a trading system?"

"It's not a trading system, although it could be used to trade the markets. If you will come to Chicago, I will show it to you."

I replied that I had received phone calls of this nature before and had been on a number of wild-goose chases, and was not too interested in going on another one. Could he just tell me over the phone what it was he wanted to show me and why he wanted to show it to me.

Jim replied that he could only show it to me if I came to Chicago. He insisted that it would certainly be worth a day of my time. I asked a few questions as to the nature of the trading method.

"Does it follow or predict market action?"

"Predicts."

"Does it involve Fibonacci numbers?"

"No."

"Does it have anything to do with the works of Elliott or Gann?"

"No."

"Or Andrews or Dow or anybody else?"

"No."

"Is this a completely original discovery?"

"Yes."

At this point I was getting interested and the answer to my next two questions clinched it.

"Why do you want to show me your discovery?"

"I need a very large sum of money to begin another project."

"How will I know its value in order to make a decision?"

"Come to Chicago and I will show it to you. At that point you can decide whether or not you want to buy it."

Several days later I caught the 8:00 A.M. flight from Greensboro to Chicago, and Jim met me at the airport. On the way to his apartment, I directed the conversation toward learning something about him.

He is a very gifted person. His intellectual abilities were first recognized in high school when he placed among the top in the country in a national exam given to all senior math students. Subsequently, he was awarded a National Merit Scholarship to Princeton University, where he studied math and physics in special advanced classes.

Jim had done many different things since college, looking for an elusive fulfillment. He started out on the corporate ladder, became a high achiever but felt that something was missing. He wrote a novel and studied film directing at Columbia University. He had been a stock broker and briefly a commodity trader, but he left that profession because he felt that he did not have the right temperament for it. Lately Jim had been experimenting with manifesting things by visualizing them.

Jim turned into the parking lot of the only apartment building on the North shore of Lake Michigan with its own private beach. His beautiful apartment overlooked the lake. We could hear the surf rolling in.

"How did you ever get this apartment?" I asked.

Jim said, "I visualized that I was living in a beautiful apartment overlooking Lake Michigan. Shortly after, through a series of seemingly accidental circumstances, it happened."

We were sitting in the living room chatting and I was scheduled to catch the 5:30 flight back to Greensboro.

"How long will it take to show me your discovery?"

"Not long," said Jim, "but first if you wouldn't mind, I would like to tell you how this thing, Delta, came about."

"Is that what you call it, Delta?"

"Yes. Delta is a Greek letter derived from a word meaning 'door,' in this case a door to the unknown. It also means to me the word *diagnosis,* a diagnosis of the markets. A few months ago I began thinking about the markets in a way that was different for me. I attempted to find out if there was some kind of order in all markets. I visualized the markets as being a hologram. Do you know what a hologram is, Welles?"

"Yes, a hologram is a projection in three dimensions."

"Right. Do you know how one is made?"

"No."

"A hologram is made by projecting laser light through a holographic negative . . . much like a photographic negative. However, if one looks at the holographic negative with normal lighting, it looks like mass confusion. When laser light is projected through the negative, then the three-dimensional hologram appears . . . the confusion is replaced by perfect order.

"This was my approach to finding order in the markets. Suppose the holographic negative was the markets . . . mass confusion. If, so to speak, I could find the right laser to shine through that negative, if there was order there, it would be immediately obvious." He asked me to come into the kitchen and sit down at the table. "Here is a regular bar chart of the last nine months of the S&P's. It's mass confusion. Now look at the same chart with the projection on the chart. Just study it for a minute."

I looked at the chart. It was overlaid with colored lines and numbers. It took about five seconds for it to hit me . . . to comprehend what I was seeing. I simply could not believe the answer was that simple. I suddenly felt a sense of awe . . . like my eyes were opened and I was seeing something that no one else had ever seen. I felt like the person who had spent a lifetime searching for something and ended up finding it in his own back yard. Suddenly, Jim brought me back to reality with a question.

"Welles, where is the next turning point for the S&P's?"

"Why it's right here," I exclaimed, pointing to a place on the chart about two weeks in the future from the last daily bar. It was suddenly so clear why it had to be there.

"Right," said Jim, "and obviously it will be a top. Now where will the next bottom come after that top?"

"Right here," I answered, feeling a spine-tingling sense of wonder. It was obvious that I was shaken by what I was seeing. "Let's see some other charts."

For the next several hours Jim explained the discovery to me. I looked at 15 different bar charts of 15 different commodities under the projection of Jim's colored lines and numbers. It was obvious that there was an order that the markets followed. Each turning point did not necessarily come on the exact day that it should have, but it was incredibly close . . . within two or three days in most cases. I knew what this order was and I knew what was causing it. The realization slowly sank in that with this knowledge I would always know, with very high probability and as far in advance as I wanted to project it, where the intermediate turning points would occur.

"I'm quite sure that it will continue as you see it now in the past or in the future because **what causes it never changes,** but you will just have to prove this to yourself. There is one other aspect to this that will verify that for you. Delta also holds true in a long term perspective on either weekly or monthly charts. Here is a monthly chart of live hogs since 1962 with the projection on it."

I studied the monthly chart since 1962 and again was awed by the beauty of it. The significance of what I was not seeing did not escape me. The **long term** Delta gave the major direction and major turning points. Using this with the **intermediate term** Delta gave the complete picture.

It had been several hours since we arrived at Jim's apartment and I knew both the **long term** and **intermediate term** Delta. Jim sensed that we had come to the moment of truth.

"Well, Welles, is Delta worth what I am asking you to pay for it?"

I thought to myself, of course it is worth it, and what's more, I already know it.

"Jim," I answered, "let me see if I understand this deal. If I pay you this sum of money, does it mean that Delta is mine to do with as I choose? Does it mean that I could take credit for discovering it? Does it mean that you will tell no one else the secret?"

"Exactly," said Jim. "I would like you to know my feeling on two things. One is that I would like to think that this knowledge will not die with you. I would like you to make the fruits of it available somehow. The second is that you would give me credit for discovering it. However, Delta is yours . . . you do not have to do either of these things."

"Would you also agree to consult with me if I should have any questions in the future?"

"Yes," Jim replied.

I said, "Jim, you've got a deal."

I sat down and wrote Jim a check for a very large sum of money.

Handing Jim the check, I had another question. "Of all the people to whom you could have chosen to sell Delta, why me?"

"Welles, I read one of your brochures, and something said to me, this is the person that should have it. The only way I could sell it was to first reveal it to a buyer . . . then once he knew it, why would he buy it? This was my problem. Somehow, I knew you would pay for it even after you knew it."

"Jim, I'll have to admit, the thought flashed through my mind to make you a counteroffer for less money. Then I remembered that just two days ago I found out unexpectedly that I was going to receive this sum of money from an investment that I had made several years ago. I have learned that when things come together like that, you don't fool around with them. Too many good things have happened for me not to believe that there is a reason behind them. In the same way that you trusted me with Delta, I trust you when you tell me that you will tell no one else about it."

I packed the Delta charts in my briefcase and sat down to make some notes to myself about the Delta phenomenon. I could not think of anything to write down. Once you saw it, it was so incredibly simple . . . yet at the same time it was just as incredible that someone could set out to discover it and actually do so. I think only one other person may have discovered it. Of course, it can't be proved, but George Marechal must have discovered the long term part of this. It would explain the timing of the market turns shown in his 1933 stock market chart.

I still had a little while before I needed to leave for the airport, so Jim and I decided to walk to a restaurant nearby and have something to eat. Jim was somewhat shy to talk about himself, but I was persistent. I wanted to know more about a person who could conceptualize the Delta phenomenon. I learned that another area of Jim's interest was the phenomenon of the human mind. He has written and published a book on life and the mind which he titled *Nothing*.

Another thorny problem that system vendors must confront is how to explain why, if their system is so good, they just don't use it themselves. Why do they have to sell it others? Wilder's Delta brochure handled it this way: "During the last six months of research and study into Delta, a thought kept popping up in the back of my mind. The Delta discovery was too significant not to be shared in some way with others. The secret must be kept secret but the results and the capabilities of Delta should be shared. The secret also would have to be passed on to succeeding generations, but how could this be done? . . . I mulled this over for a couple of weeks and then one morning at 3:00 A.M. the solution came. The answer was that the Delta Society International would be the guardian and perpetuator of the secret." Thus, Wilder would not be selling a system, he would be sharing a secret and passing on an important discovery to future generations. This was to be a charitable effort.

The system itself was not really a system at all. It gave no buy or sell signals. The members received nothing but dates of projected market turning points and varied suggestions of possible entry and exit techniques. Since Wilder said the short-term dates were 81 percent accurate only within four days before or after a signal and the long-term dates were accurate only within four weeks before or after a signal, there was a wide band of indecision time for someone attempting to trade with the information. While Wilder attempted to predict whether the date would be a high or a low, he allowed himself the freedom to change his mind afterward and declare that there had been an "inversion." This is precisely what happened with a Deutschemark chart Wilder had used to illustrate the first brochure. The predicted bottom did not occur. Wilder later claimed in the second brochure that the Delta system was not at fault, only his interpretation.

Wilder added a new twist to the constant efforts of vendors to keep purchasers from sharing their systems. The Delta Society membership contract not only contained a vow of secrecy, it also required the prospective member to promise never to say anything bad about Delta. This was obviously intended to extend the life of the promotion by inhibiting negative comments from disenchanted members. Wilder backed it up with publicized threats of lawsuits. It worked incredibly well. Although *Commodity Traders Consumer Report* received a number of very negative communications, no one wanted his comments published, even anonymously, because they were afraid of being sued by Wilder. Ironically, one person, after excoriating the system, admitted he didn't want his comments aired because he was afraid Wilder would cancel his membership and he would lose access to future signals. Hope springs eternal.

Others were not so inhibited. Robert Pelletier, president of Commodity Systems, Inc. and a former statistician, pointed out that there are so many arguable turning points on a commodity chart that it was possible to obtain equally good results picking turning points by throwing darts at the chart. Larry Williams said he created a system that had better apparent results by using a group of people's birthdays. Wilder produced a second brochure with illustrative charts showing Delta turning points for the S&P and cattle. They appeared to be fairly accurate in calling the turns. *Commodity Traders Consumer Report* pointed out that if one used the S&P turning points to predict cattle and the cattle turning points to predict the S&P, the results would appear equally effective.

Wilder eventually cut off sales in early 1986. He said he sold over one thousand $3,500 memberships and forty-one $35,000 directorships. Wilder announced his retirement saying, "All I've really ever wanted to do for the last 13 years is finally find something and stay with it and trade for myself. I have no interest in developing anything else."

Fat chance. A year later Wilder was at it again, this time promoting a book called *The Adam Theory of Markets*. Although Wilder claimed he "paid $1,000,000 to learn the original concepts presented in the book," he was selling it for only $65. The brochure said he learned these concepts from Jim Sloman, the same person who taught him the Delta system. The brochure had to explain how anything could ever top Delta, billed as "the secret of the perfect order behind the markets." It said, "Both Delta and Adam are about market symmetry. Delta is the market's outer symmetry. Adam is the market's inner symmetry."

I wrote the following in a review of the Adam book published in *Commodity Traders Consumer Report:*

> Wilder claims he is selling in this book ideas for which he paid Jim Sloman $1,000,000. We hope for the sake of poetic justice he did. Our favorite Jim Sloman fact is that he spent a year writing a book called *Nothing.* This book could have been called *Nothing New.*
>
> There are really two parts to the book. The first part covers the general psychology of successful trading and money management. Stripped of all the silly Sloman stories, this is really quite good. But you should have read all of it before. Wilder admits, "When you finish reading this book you are going to think you already knew most of what was in it." We would go farther and say if that's so, what you didn't already know was probably not worth learning.
>
> Sloman has now convinced Wilder about a point we've been making for years. That is you shouldn't be so concerned about predicting the next market direction. Wilder actually recommends ignoring the indicators he described in his 1978 book, *New Concepts in Technical Trading Systems.* The same logic would also apply to the Delta turning points which he sold for a total of around $5 million.
>
> Let's see if we have this straight. Jim Sloman found the secret of the perfect order behind the markets and called it Delta. He showed Wilder how to predict major and minor turning points in any market many years in advance. Wilder decided, "The Delta discovery was too significant not to be shared with others." So he sold it to struggling traders for a total of $5 million plus another $100,000 or so a year until the year 2000. [Plus the inflation adjustment. Wilder didn't want to be *too* generous.] Then he paid Sloman a million dollars for another secret. This one was called the Adam Theory of markets. The Adam Theory says to forget about any method which tries to predict the markets. Wilder retired. Wilder unretired. Wilder is now selling the second secret in a book for $65 so he can "have the privilege of making this discovery available to others." Frankly, all this altruism is making us a little sick.

We don't like to disclose too much of the specifics of books and systems in our reviews. It's usually not necessary. We hope Mr. Wilder will forgive us for violating our rule this one time to reveal what he calls "the single most important statement ever made about trading." Are you sitting down? **"Cut your losses short and let your profits run."** The bold type is Wilder's. We would add to that, "Trade with the trend." Of course, that's in the Adam Theory, too. We wonder what percentage of the million dollars was allocated to those ideas.

There is one new trading method revealed in this book, which Wilder says is the subject of a pending patent application. "Such patent rights will be strictly enforced against violators." Big deal. This gimmick is one of the stupidest we have ever seen. Using it would directly contradict the essential principles of success advanced in the rest of the book. Of course, Wilder can show a couple of charts where it works. Although he will be happy to sell you a computer program to help apply it for $395, he offers no computer-test evidence that the method works. Can you imagine using a predicting mechanism that is by definition guaranteed to be wrong at all major turning points? Wilder even admits this.

With all the ridicule we have justifiably heaped upon Wilder and this book, we still recommend that you buy it. It is only $65. Wilder claims some of the profit will go to a trust supporting children's charities. We think it will be instructive for you to see where this supposed guru has ended up after so many years of peddling one secret after another about how to solve the mysteries of commodity trading. Whenever you are tempted to send a few thousand to the next huckster selling inside secrets, grab this book before you grab your checkbook.

I hope you enjoyed our little side-trip though commodity system fantasyland. Before I start discussing the specifics of trading system design, we need some benchmarks to judge system effectiveness. In the next chapter we will look at the performance of some well-known trading approaches and systems during the test period I will use for the systems and methods described in succeeding chapters.

8 How Well Do Popular Methods Perform—A Frame of Reference

I promised at the beginning of the book that I would show you the actual performance of various trading system approaches. For a comparison to have the most meaning, there should be a standardized evaluation plan. This means a consistent test period, common test markets, and the same performance standards. In addition, before you can judge the effectiveness of trading systems and methods, you must have a frame of reference to define what good performance is.

I want to emphasize that I do not intend this to be a definitive exegesis on what will work in the future and what will not. There are an infinite number of variations and parameters you could employ with each of the various system ideas. No book could ever hope to cover them all. There are also numerous other markets and test periods I could have employed. The future will certainly introduce some new variables, although over the long term I doubt this will have a substantial influence on the ideas presented in this book. As I have repeatedly stressed, you should consider this book as a starting point for your own research rather than a nicely wrapped package of ultimate truth. I am showing you the correct route to success and how pleasant the scenery will look when you get there. You will have to obtain or create your own transportation vehicle.

The Test Markets

For an example of the report format, look at Exhibit 8–1. I have chosen 10 markets to use in each test. This is a well-diversified selection of the most popular trading markets. They are the S&P 500, T-bonds, Eurodollars, Swiss francs, Japanese yen, gold, heating oil, soybeans, sugar, and live cattle. Even if I had taken the time and the space to include more markets, I doubt whether you would learn anything substantially different. You are free to test your systems in any market that attracts you. However, you will probably obtain better trading performance by concentrating on the most liquid markets. A

EXHIBIT 8-1   Performance Report, Two Moving Averages, 5 days and 20 days

	S&P 500	T-Bonds	Euro dollars	Swiss Francs	Japanese Yen	Comex Gold	Heating Oil	Soy beans	Sugar	Live Cattle	Average
Number of Closed Trades	91	68	64	68	72	68	53	74	67	56	68
Number of Profitable Trades	25	27	25	26	24	22	20	25	20	15	23
Percent Profitable	27%	40%	39%	38%	33%	32%	38%	34%	30%	27%	34%
Total Profit or Loss	-67,675	22,790	9,850	2,588	28,700	9,760	2,440	-7,238	-3,024	-9,144	-1,095
Average Profitable Trade	3,725	3,055	1,486	2,136	2,529	2,296	1,827	1,491	1,161	1,020	2,148
Average Losing Trade	-2,436	-1,455	-700	-1,260	-666	-886	-1,032	-908	-557	-596	-1,112
Maximum Drawdown	-77,725	-10,594	-8,500	-12,475	-8,800	-13,470	-11,647	-20,100	-5,062	-13,528	-18,190
Average Profit Per Trade	-744	335	154	38	399	144	46	-98	-45	-163	-16

more complete discussion of the various trading vehicles appears in Chapter 12.

I chose the S&P 500 as the most popular stock index future. I selected two interest rate markets. The T-bonds market is the most actively traded of all futures markets and represents long-term rates. I included Eurodollars rather than T-bills because in the last few years it has eclipsed T-bills as the market of choice for short-term interest rates. There are two interest rate markets because they are more popular than agricultural markets and respond well to system trading.

I chose two currencies for the same reason. The Swiss franc is the patriarch of the currencies, and although it has slightly less liquidity now than the Deutschemark, it is usually more volatile. It thus offers greater profit potential. Because of our increasing trade with Japan, the yen has taken over as the most liquid currency. It was especially profitable for systems during the five-year test period I employed. As you can see from the disparate results, these two currencies do not move together.

Gold is the king of the precious metals. Although silver has more volatility, it is a more difficult market to trade. In the energy group I chose heating oil over crude oil only because crude oil did not start trading until 1983. It would have been impossible to have parallel tests over the same five-year period in crude oil. Crude oil is a far more liquid market and is my primary energy market for trading. Systems should yield similar results trading heating oil and crude oil.

Although technically not a grain, the soybean and its products are usually grouped with the grains (corn, wheat, and oats) because of the similarities. Soybeans are second to corn in the grain market liquidity department, but corn is a comparatively slow mover and does not yield as good system results. Sugar is by far the most liquid and popular of the international food markets.

Live cattle is the most popular of the meats. The pork bellies market is perhaps more famous (or infamous), but I do not recommend it as a trading vehicle. The cattle market is a far better one to trade, although still difficult. Hogs would be my second choice. That market yields better system performance than the cattle market, but I did not want to cheat by picking it for that reason.

The Test Period and Data Type

Selecting a test period is always a difficult decision; I chose five years. If a system has worked well for the last five years, I don't care if it didn't work before that. I might be curious as to why, but it would not deter me from trading the system. One could use the same logic to argue for an even shorter test period. I rejected a shorter test period because I wanted even the long-term systems to generate enough trades so that the results would be statistically significant. In addition, five years has a comfortable ring to it that suggests greater validity than two or three years.

There are two reasons I chose to end the five-year period on June 30, 1987, rather than some later date. First and foremost, I did not want to include October 1987, the time of Blue Monday and the Great Crash of 1987. This event had a substantial effect on all the markets and would probably have skewed the results. It seemed better to stop the test at the year's halfway point to allay any suspicion that I chose the test period to affect the results. The second reason I stopped the tests in June 1987 was that it gave me a whole year to retest the best systems beyond that date. This retesting confirms the validity of the five-year tests and confutes any suggestion of inadvertent curve-fitting during the testing. The period also provides you a viable recent test period that does not include the data over which I ran the original tests.

For the reasons given in Chapter 5, I used the continuous contract data format for all tests. This provides as accurate a picture of likely future profitability as using actual contracts, and it makes the testing procedure faster and easier.

Performance Standards and Methodology

In Chapter 5 I discussed evaluating system performance at great length. I described 21 separate performance measures. One of the important points I made was that since the best systems seem to score better in every performance measure, to identify the best system it doesn't much matter which performance category you compare. I am including in the system performance tables the performance criteria that are necessary to create a complete picture of the system's trading personality.

The question arises as to what to do with a trade that remains open at the end of the test period. Some may argue that until a trade is closed out, it should not be counted in the profit column. I disagree. In actual trading your profits at the end of the day are placed in your account and you may draw them out, even without closing out the trade, so long as you do not violate minimum margin requirements. To ignore open profits at the end of the test period would unfairly penalize long-term systems that may have a very large trade going. I have included open profits and losses at the end of the test period and counted the trade as an additional closed trade. This gives the fairest comparative picture of system performance.

There are eight performance measures in each table. In combination they show how active the system was, how accurate it was, how well it cut losses short and let profits run, how bad its worst period was, and how profitable it was both in the aggregate and on average. All figures in each table include a deduction of $100 per trade for slippage and commissions. I placed the average profit per trade at the bottom of each column because that is the single most significant performance figure in determining system effectiveness.

From my experience I would not consider trading a system unless it returned an average profit per trade over $200 after slippage and commissions. A system that makes over $500 per trade is exceptional, and profits over $1,000 per trade seldom occur in a fair test of a non-curve-fitted system. (A day trading system must be rated on a different scale. I would consider a day trading system that traded every day exceptional if it averaged $75 after slippage and commissions. If it did not trade every day, I would raise the figure to $100. Such systems are hard to come by unless curve-fitted.)

It is also prudent to check the drawdown. Most traders have unrealistic expectations for drawdown. Like individual losses, drawdowns are a necessary evil in commodity trading. If you can't trade through them, you will never be successful. You must consider drawdown in relation to overall profits. If trading only one market, I would accept a maximum drawdown of up to 25 percent of total profits. A very low drawdown in relation to total profits is often an indication of a curve-fitted system. If you are well-capitalized and trading a diversified portfolio, the drawdown in each individual market is less important because all the maximum drawdowns will not occur at once.

I look at the percentage of profitable trades only as an afterthought. You will notice that even with the best systems this figure seldom goes over 50 percent. A profitable system can be right as infrequently as 30 percent of the time. Insisting on a high percentage of profitable trades is the product of an ego-need to be right. The best you can hope for in a system is about 60 percent in one market. This is infrequent. The trade-off for a high winning percentage is a lower ratio of average win to average loss. This reflects a system that is probably taking its profits too quickly. You should be satisfied with anything over 35 percent and pleased with anything over 40 percent.

The average column, on the far right, contains more than just the averages of the figures in the table. Its numbers are the overall averages of all trades generated in the particular test. That means a particular market that generates a proportionally higher number of trades will have a proportionally greater effect on the average results. Thus, one especially bad market can make the average performance look much worse than it would, considering just the other nine markets. One especially good market could have the opposite effect, but that did not occur as frequently.

Four Popular Systems

As a benchmark to compare the performance of the various approaches and systems, I want to begin with four well-known, popular systems. They have all been around for many years. The first two are moving-average systems.

Donchian's 5- and 20-Day Moving Averages

Richard Donchian is one of the true elder statesmen of commodities. He started using this system to manage money in 1961. A moving average is a way of smoothing data. It is most often used with raw price data, such as the close, but moving averages are also useful in constructing separate indicators, such as oscillators. You construct a simple five-day moving average of the close by taking an average of the last five closing prices. Every day the moving average changes as you add the latest price and drop off the earliest price from your average. The purpose of a moving average is to measure the trend over the time period you use to calculate it. A price above the moving average suggests an uptrend; a price below the moving average suggests a downtrend.

Although you could use a single moving average as the basis for a trading system, it does not work very well. Donchian selected two moving averages, one representing one week and the other representing four weeks. The system is always in the market. It goes long when the 5-day moving average is above the 20-day and reverses to short when the 5-day moving average is below the 20-day. Thus, the system goes long when the short-term trend is up, and by using the crossover as a signal, it tries to anticipate an intermediate-term trend change. Exhibit 8–2 illustrates how it looks with a bar chart. The system will be very profitable when the market is making good trending moves. When the market is dawdling around in a trading range, it generates losses as the moving averages whip back and forth.

Exhibit 8–1 shows the results using the 10-market evaluation scan. On average the system lost money, although it was profitable in six of the nine markets. Overall performance was dragged down by the horrendous results in the S&P 500. Even in the profitable markets the drawdown was usually large in relation to the cumulative profit.

Three Moving Averages—The 4-, 9-, and 18-Day

A popular three-moving-average system, which a number of commercial chart services publish along with their bar charts, is a combination of the 4-, 9-, and 18-day moving averages. The system uses the 9- and 18-day averages like the previously described 5- and 20-day system. The four-day average is added as a very-short-term filter to minimize whipsaws. You take no crossover signal until the four-day average is moving in the direction of the trade. Exhibit 8–3 shows a sample bar chart with the three moving averages underneath.

EXHIBIT 8-2   Daily Chart of Soybeans with 5- and 20-Day Moving Averages (November 1988 contract)

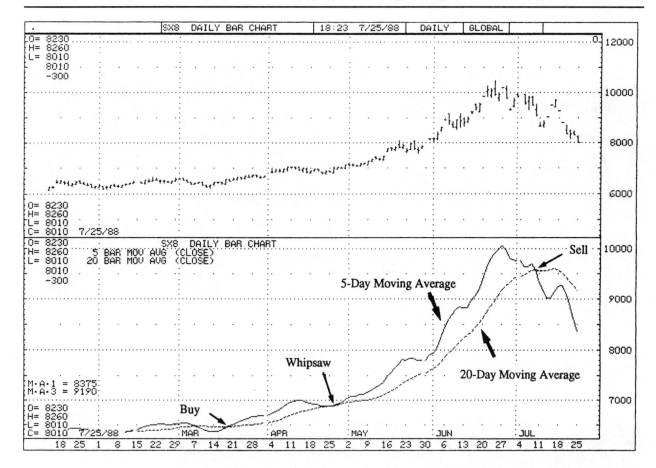

Exhibit 8–4 shows the trading results. The amount of trading decreases slightly and profits are generally better than with the two-moving-average approach. Still, there is nothing there to get excited about. Over the years, traders have tried various ways to improve moving average performance by refining the calculation. This has resulted in exponentially smoothed, linear-weighted, and step-weighted moving-average systems. These refinements have not made an appreciable difference in performance.

Moving Average Convergence Divergence (MACD)

MACD was an intriguing combination of moving-average oscillators proposed a number of years ago by Gerald Appel. He took the difference between the approximate exponential equivalents of 12- and 26–period moving averages and created an oscillator line. (The exponential equivalents are 0.15 and 0.075.) He created a second line by taking the approximate exponential equivalent of a nine-period moving average of the first line (0.20 exponential). I use the term "period" to cover any time interval—a week, a day, an hour, five-minutes, etc. The time period of the study should match the time period of the bar chart.

EXHIBIT 8-3   Daily Chart of T-Bonds with 4-, 9-, and 18-Day Moving Averages (September 1988 contract)

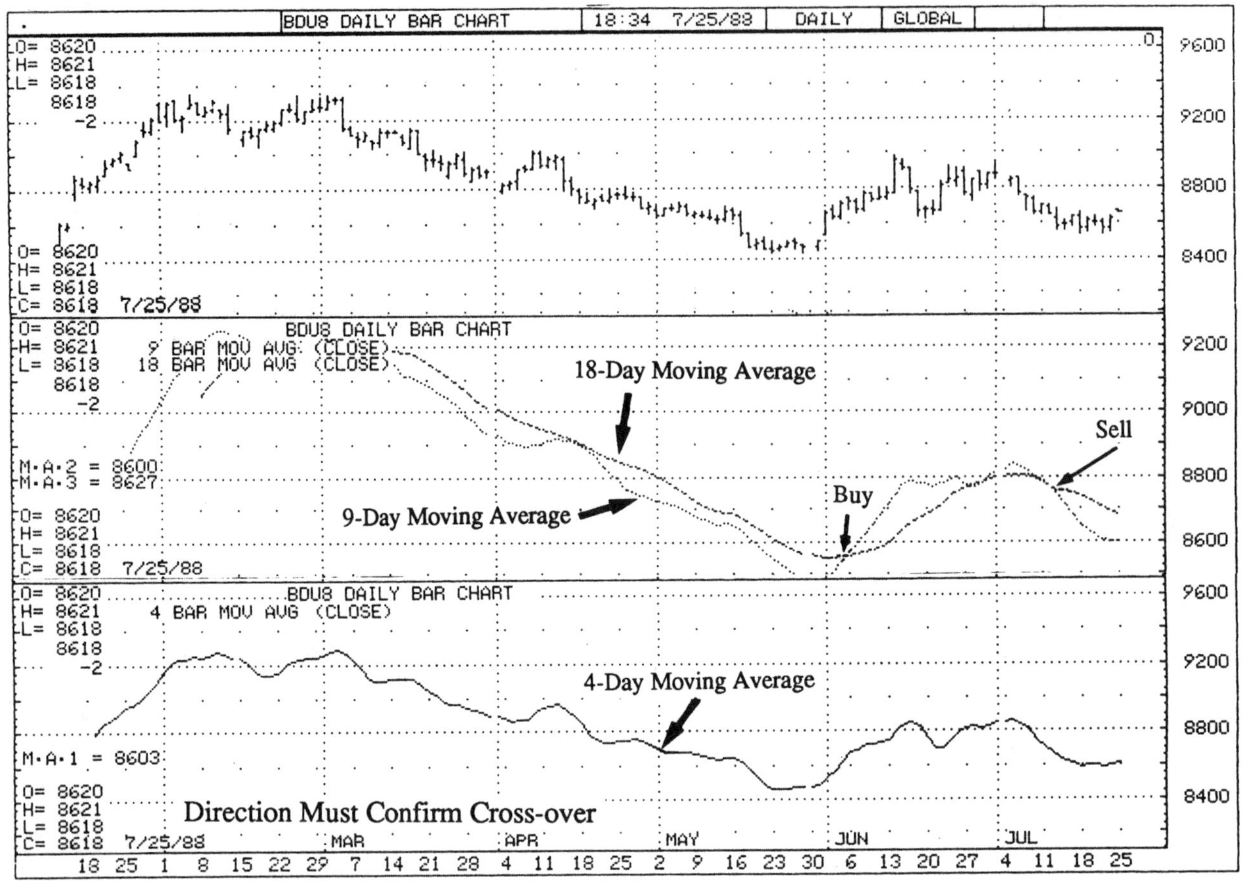

EXHIBIT 8-4   Performance Report, Three Moving Averages, 4, 9, and 18 Days

	S&P 500	T-Bonds	Euro dollars	Swiss Francs	Japanese Yen	Comex Gold	Heating Oil	Soy beans	Sugar	Live Cattle	Average
Number of Closed Trades	67	56	58	58	52	58	46	60	59	52	57
Number of Profitable Trades	20	21	22	22	26	19	12	22	20	13	20
Percent Profitable	30%	37%	38%	38%	50%	33%	26%	37%	34%	25%	35%
Total Profit or Loss	-75,650	16,440	14,775	4,763	34,625	13,920	-605	3,338	-3,147	-13,200	-474
Average Profitable Trade	3,179	3,404	1,794	2,088	2,241	2,415	3,086	1,676	1,108	1,060	2,206
Average Losing Trade	-2,962	-1,572	-686	-1,144	-910	-820	-1,106	-883	-648	-692	-1,190
Maximum Drawdown	-80,375	-15,619	-7,425	-12,050	-4,638	-11,520	-17,535	-12,000	-6,328	-15,344	-18,283
Average Profit Per Trade	-1,129	294	255	82	666	240	-13	56	-53	-254	-8

The two MACD lines operate like a two-moving-average crossover system. Exhibit 8–5 shows a sample chart with the indicator. It has been popular with traders because its signals often anticipate trend changes.

Exhibit 8–6 shows the five-year performance. Overall it is inferior to the two previous moving average methods. Exhibit 8–7 shows the results obtained by using simple moving averages—rather than the exponential moving averages originally proposed—to make calculation easier. They are generally not as good as those produced by exponential averages.

EXHIBIT 8-5 Daily Chart of Swiss Francs with MACD System

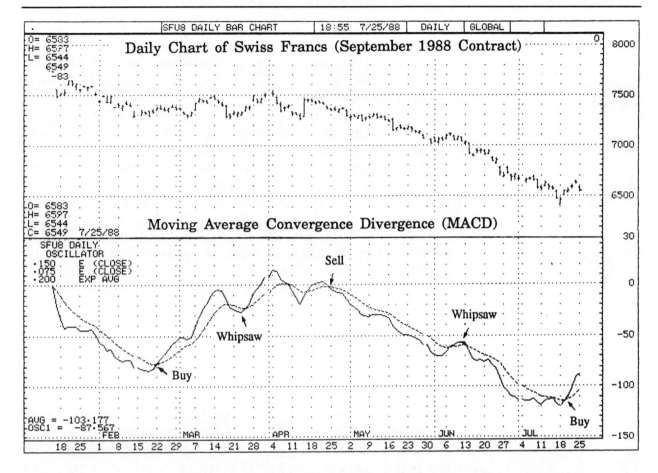

EXHIBIT 8-6 Performance Report, Moving Average Convergence Divergence (Exponential Moving Averages)

	S&P 500	T-Bonds	Euro dollars	Swiss Francs	Japanese Yen	Comex Gold	Heating Oil	Soy beans	Sugar	Live Cattle	Average
Number of Closed Trades	101	97	87	80	81	89	78	81	80	76	85
Number of Profitable Trades	25	40	34	31	28	32	25	30	25	25	30
Percent Profitable	25%	41%	39%	39%	35%	36%	32%	37%	31%	33%	35%
Total Profit or Loss	-42,650	480	1,675	26,950	17,525	7,440	-20,294	-450	-4,682	-13,532	-2,754
Average Profitable Trade	3,744	2,274	1,174	2,352	2,096	1,619	1,479	1,414	880	664	1,783
Average Losing Trade	-1,793	-1,587	-722	-938	-777	-778	-1,079	-841	-484	-591	-997
Maximum Drawdown	-49,400	-16,873	-8,575	-7,688	-7,687	-9,550	-26,880	-14,325	-7,403	-13,532	-16,191
Average Profit Per Trade	-422	5	19	337	216	84	-260	-6	-59	-178	-32

EXHIBIT 8-7 Performance Report, Moving Average Convergence Divergence (Simple Moving Averages)

	S&P 500	T-Bonds	Euro dollars	Swiss Francs	Japanese Yen	Comex Gold	Heating Oil	Soy beans	Sugar	Live Cattle	Average
Number of Closed Trades	81	83	81	88	79	84	65	76	84	72	79
Number of Profitable Trades	30	32	33	35	30	38	31	40	34	24	33
Percent Profitable	37%	39%	41%	40%	38%	45%	48%	53%	40%	33%	41%
Total Profit or Loss	-32,950	5,510	-4,800	9,713	11,400	5,500	-2,419	-7,588	-6,160	-12,264	-3,406
Average Profitable Trade	3,224	2,750	1,078	1,874	1,870	1,416	1,351	1,086	699	701	1,595
Average Losing Trade	-2,543	-1,617	-841	-1,054	-912	-1,050	-1,302	-1,417	-598	-606	-1,192
Maximum Drawdown	-41,950	-15,223	-12,675	-13,888	-10,863	-12,800	-13,041	-15,700	-9,520	-12,264	-15,792
Average Profit Per Trade	-407	66	-59	110	144	65	-37	-100	-73	-170	-43

Channel Breakout

Another trading approach popularized by Richard Donchian is the channel breakout. (He called it the "weekly rule.") The original system said to buy whenever price moves above the highest high of the last four weeks. You hold the position and then reverse and sell when price moves below the low of the last four weeks. It is a simple but surprisingly effective system. You are always in the market and guaranteed to participate in all big trending moves. Naturally, you can optimize the length of the time-channel for each market and improve performance in the past. You can also vary the system by requiring that the market close outside the channel before taking action.

Exhibit 8–8 shows the performance of the four-week channel breakout system using intraday entries. Overall performance was pretty good. It would have been even better if not dragged down by the S&P 500. I suspect that some markets would perform consistently better with a different channel length. Avoiding over-optimization would require careful work, however. Without including the S&P, the results would have been quite respectable.

The Two Percent System

In Chapter 4 I put forward as an example of a non-curve-fitted system a simple trend-following idea that used a 2 percent price change as an action trigger. Just for fun, I thought it might be interesting to compare the performance of that really primitive approach to the other famous systems in this chapter. To achieve comparability between the markets, rather than use 2 percent of the absolute price level, which has no independent significance, I used 2 percent of the value of the contract. You can obtain the value of the contract by multiplying the price times the contract size, which is the same as the value of a one-point move. In interest rate futures, the contract value does not fluctuate with the price. To produce equivalence in T-bonds, I multiplied the price by the value of a one-point move ($1,000). Using the same formula in Eurodollars produces such a large price change that it gen-

EXHIBIT 8-8   Performance Report, Channel Breakout, Four-Week Channel, Intraday Breakout

	S&P 500	T-Bonds	Euro dollars	Swiss Francs	Japanese Yen	Comex Gold	Heating Oil	Soy beans	Sugar	Live Cattle	Average
Number of Closed Trades	47	34	30	36	28	38	26	46	30	28	34
Number of Profitable Trades	16	12	12	17	14	13	10	12	13	8	13
Percent Profitable	34%	35%	40%	47%	50%	34%	38%	26%	43%	29%	37%
Total Profit or Loss	-43,425	18,410	16,025	5,875	36,413	920	15,847	-10,475	3,909	-216	4,328
Average Profitable Trade	3,770	4,976	2,425	2,611	4,063	2,377	3,365	1,864	1,478	1,970	2,931
Average Losing Trade	-3,347	-1,877	-726	-2,027	-1,462	-1,199	-1,111	-966	-899	-799	-1,523
Maximum Drawdown	-58,975	-10,455	-5,775	-11,125	-4,012	-15,480	-6,556	-23,638	-5,690	-7,176	-14,888
Average Profit Per Trade	-924	541	534	163	1,300	24	609	-228	130	-8	126

EXHIBIT 8-9 Performance Report, Two-Percent Reversal System (5-Day Window)

	S&P 500	T-Bonds	Euro dollars	Swiss Francs	Japanese Yen	Comex Gold	Heating Oil	Soy beans	Sugar	Live Cattle	Average
Number of Closed Trades	216	222	109	114	59	233	233	205	338	262	199
Number of Profitable Trades	84	98	45	48	18	87	118	73	133	79	78
Percent Profitable	39%	44%	41%	42%	31%	37%	51%	36%	39%	30%	39%
Total Profit or Loss	39,575	12,600	-13,221	27,363	-10,950	-4,680	-260	-37,896	-14,605	-41,028	-4,310
Average Profitable Trade	2,273	1,348	815	1,742	2,513	992	545	667	275	318	903
Average Losing Trade	-1,146	-964	-779	-852	-1,371	-623	-561	-656	-249	-362	-656
Maximum Drawdown	-27,613	-24,064	-21,226	-6,916	-26,111	-17,305	-17,192	-39,577	-14,602	-42,088	-23,669
Average Profit Per Trade	183	57	-121	240	-186	-20	-1	-185	-43	-157	-22

erates no trades. To generate a reasonable number of trades, I multiplied the Eurodollar price times $500, which is one-fifth the value of a one-point move.

Exhibit 8–9 shows the trading results. This is obviously no world-beater system, but it does do considerably better in the S&P 500 than all the moving average systems.

In case you hadn't noticed, every one of the well-known, popular systems we have looked at so far lost money on average except the channel breakout. Its overall average profit per trade of $126 was less than my initial $200 threshold of acceptability. Six different systems were tested on 10 markets each. Of these 60 tests, only 5 yielded profits over $500 per trade and only one resulted in more than $1,000 per trade. For every system that showed an overall average loss, the deduction of $100 per trade for slippage and commissions made the difference between a profitable and losing system. That is why it is so important to include a realistic deduction. Otherwise, many track records appear profitable when in reality, they are not. If I had deducted only $50, every system would have been profitable overall.

The Babcock Long-Term System

I will now teach you a simple, long-term system I devised specifically for this book. Its average profit per trade for all ten markets was $848. Eight of the ten markets returned more than $500 average profit per trade, and five markets had an average profit of over $1,000 per trade. It achieved these impressive results while trading over only the last 90 percent of the time period used for the other systems. This is because its rules require at least six months of data before trading can start.

The *Babcock Long-term System* takes action only after the market makes a 130-day high or low. That is the equivalent in market days of six months. It means that today's high is the highest price of the last 130 market days or today's low is the lowest price of the last 130 market days in that market. If that is the case, take the following steps to trade the system:

1. Wait until after the close the next day (the day after the 130-day high or low).
2. Measure the distance between the highest high of the last 20 market days and the lowest low of the last 20 market days.
3. Add the distance calculated in Step 2 to today's close (the day after the 130-day high or low). This point will be your buying threshold.
4. Subtract the distance calculated in Step 2 from today's close (the day after the 130-day high or low). This point will be your selling threshold.
5. Wait for the market to touch either the buying or selling threshold point. If the market hits your buying threshold point first, buy on the close that day. Keep the selling threshold point as a reversing stop. If the market hits your selling threshold point first, sell on the close that day. Keep the buying threshold point as a reversing stop.

If the market makes a new 130-day high before it reaches either of the initial threshold points, repeat Steps 1, 2, 3, and 4. Replace the previous selling threshold point with the new one if it is higher than the previous one. Replace the buying threshold point if it is lower than the previous one. Otherwise, maintain the current buying and selling threshold points.

If the market makes a new 130-day low before the market reaches either of the initial threshold points, repeat Steps 1, 2, 3, and 4. Replace the previous buying threshold point with the new one if it is lower than the previous one. Replace the previous selling threshold point with the new one if it is higher than the previous one. Otherwise, maintain the current buying and selling threshold points.

If the market makes a new 130-day high when you are already in a long position, repeat Steps 1, 2, 3, and 4. Replace the previous selling threshold point with the new one if it is higher than the previous one. If the new buying threshold point is at a price level different from the one that caused the current long entry, keep track of it in case you are stopped out with the $2,500 money management stop (see below) or reversed to short. It would then become a new buying threshold point. You never use the same threshold point twice in a row. This may leave you out of the market with no buying threshold point. In that case, monitor the current selling threshold point for a possible short entry, and wait for the market to generate a new buying threshold point.

If the market makes a new 130-day low when you are already in a short position, repeat Steps 1, 2, 3, and 4. Replace the previous buying threshold point with the new one if it is lower than the previous one. If the new selling threshold point is at a price level different from the one that caused the current short entry, keep track of it in case you are stopped out with the $2,500 money management stop or reversed to long. It would then become a new selling threshold point. You never use the same threshold point twice in a row. This may leave you out of the market with no selling threshold point. In that case, monitor the current buying threshold point for a possible long entry, and wait for the market to generate a new selling threshold point.

In the unlikely event that the market makes a new 130-day extreme opposite the one on which you are working before either threshold point has been hit, cancel the current threshold points and begin again with the new 130-day extreme. (This could happen only in a dead market where the six-month highs and lows were very close together.)

Once in a trade, set a stop-loss point to exit the market at the point that will result in a $2,500 loss before commissions. This money management stop is necessary because the rules do not guarantee an opposite signal if the market changes trend. Without a stop-loss order, a huge loss could result.

Hold the position until the market reaches the stop-loss point or generates an entry signal in the opposite direction by hitting an opposite threshold point. If the market hits your stop-loss point, exit the current position and continue to monitor any current buying and selling threshold points for a new entry. If an opposite entry signal occurs, exit the current position and enter the new position signaled. Then monitor any opposite threshold point for another possible stop and reverse, and set a new $2,500 money management stop. Each time a new 130-day high or low occurs, repeat Steps 1, 2, 3, and 4. (In real trading, if you are holding a position in an expiring contract, roll over to the contract with the highest open interest just before first notice day. This does not apply in our historical tests because we are using continuous contracts, which do not expire.)

You may be wondering why the system does not enter during the day as soon as the market hits a threshold point. Why does it wait until the close to enter? If actually trading the system, it would probably be better to enter during the day, using a stop order as soon as the market hits a threshold point. However, in historical testing, if we encounter a day in which the daily range includes both an entry and a stop-loss point, we have no way of knowing which price occurred first. This could have a significant effect on the results. By delaying action until the close, we know we can't be stopped out the same day. I discussed this historical testing quirk in Chapter 5. Because of the construction of the algorithm, it is extemely unlikely that both an unexecuted buy and sell threshold point would fall within the same day's range. If that did occur, we would execute first the one that fell closest to the open.

EXHIBIT 8-10   Performance Report, Babcock Long-Term System with $2,500 Stop

	S&P 500	T-Bonds	Euro dollars	Swiss Francs	Japanese Yen	Comex Gold	Heating Oil	Soy beans	Sugar	Live Cattle	Average
Number of Closed Trades	12	7	13	14	12	7	13	9	10	17	11
Number of Profitable Trades	3	4	6	6	6	3	6	4	7	6	5
Percent Profitable	25%	57%	46%	43%	50%	43%	46%	44%	70%	35%	45%
Total Profit or Loss	14,950	33,831	4,675	7,725	8,413	11,690	10,878	9,975	11,387	-16,844	9,668
Average Profitable Trade	11,208	10,064	2,887	4,685	3,698	7,507	4,038	5,131	2,188	868	4,496
Average Losing Trade	-2,075	-2,142	-1,807	-2,548	-2,296	-2,708	-1,906	-2,110	-1,310	-2,005	-2,105
Maximum Drawdown	-9,275	-2,600	-7,025	-6,112	-7,888	-8,230	-7,316	-6,325	-1,993	-18,172	-7,494
Average Profit Per Trade	1,246	4,833	360	552	701	1,670	837	1,108	1,139	-991	848

Exhibit 8–10 shows the trading results. The system does very well in every market but live cattle. You shouldn't be too harsh on it for that. Look through the book and try to find *any* system that makes money in cattle.

Now that you have seen the evaluation plan and examined the performance of some well-known trading systems and a brand new long-term system I devised, we are ready to break trading systems down into their component parts and explore each in detail. In the next chapter we will look at most traders' favorite analytical subject—entry methods. They are designed to help you trade with the trend, the first cardinal rule of commodity trading.

9

Entry Methods

To most traders this will be the most significant chapter in the book. Anyone who has examined the commodity trading problem in a cursory way will conclude that all you have to do to be successful is to take a position in the correct direction of the market. The key, therefore, is knowing when to buy and when to sell. If you enter at the right time, all the rest will take care of itself. Although obviously true, like almost everything connected with investing, what is most obvious is obviously wrong.

While the decision on when to enter trades is certainly the most interesting aspect of trading, it is less important and less difficult than deciding when to exit a trade. Looking for that edge that will result in profitable trading, beginners spend endless hours trying to learn how to define the trend and predict when the market will go up or down. The superstition is that the market speaks in some kind of code. If the trader can only break it, he will be able to predict the future. The more his analytical tools fail to work, the harder he looks for something better.

Although no one will ever be able to prove that predicting future market direction with precision is impossible, I am convinced that it is. The key to successful trading does not depend on exact predictions, however. It lies in using a consistent approach that trades with the trend and employing proper money management techniques.

In this chapter I will look at the overall problem of trade entry. There are so many possible ways to make this trading decision that whole books could be written on this aspect alone. I will cover the theory of picking entry points and provide several examples of each of the most popular approaches. You will see exactly what works and what does not. You should then be able to make some decisions about the personality of your own chosen trading system and research the ingredients that will match your preferred trading style.

In my book *Advanced Trading Principles and Systems,* I described what I call the two great dilemmas of commodity trading. The first is whether to enter a trade as price is moving in your favor or against you. (I will discuss the second in Chapter 10.) If you are going to buy a market, you have a choice of buying after price has been going up for a time or buying after price has been going down for a time. There are advantages and disadvantages to each approach. If you buy after price has been going up (called "buying strength"), the market is confirming the direction of your trade. The most bullish thing a market can do is go up. On the other hand, since the market moves in waves and up movements are followed by down movements, you will have to place your protective stop farther away when you trade this way. This increases the amount of risk if you are wrong. Because you have waited for at least some of the favorable move to occur before taking action, you also limit your profits to some extent. The same advantages and disadvantages apply to the opposite equivalent in short selling, which is called "selling weakness."

On the other hand, if you buy a market after it has been going down instead of up (called "buying weakness"), you solve some problems but create others. Since you are buying on the downwave, you can place your stop closer and risk less if you are wrong. If the market does turn up as you expect, you are in a position to catch the entire move instead of only part of it. On the other hand, you are anticipating a change of price direction rather than going with the market. This always increases the chance you will be wrong. The same advantages and disadvantages apply to the opposite equivalent in short selling, which is called "selling strength."

There is no correct solution to this dilemma. There are knowledgeable experts on both sides. You should adopt the style you prefer so long as you prove its effectiveness in historical testing.

Trend Indicators

As I indicated in Chapter 1, speaking of the trend is only relevant in connection with a particular time period. Any market can have conflicting trends over different time periods. Since the first cardinal rule of trading is to trade with the trend, you should expect that most systems will have some kind of trend indicator. This is not essential, however. Some methods try to predict an imminent change in trend and are therefore entering when the trend is against them at the moment. Other methods, such as moving averages, incorporate a trend indicator into the entry technique.

I will examine three kinds of trend indicators. All may be used on their own as entry triggers or as a filter to determine trend direction. When used as a filter, you would use a different entry trigger to signal actual entry in the direction of the trend as measured by the filter. The three indicators all use different combinations of price data (open, high, low, and close). We will be able to see which price data points do the best job of calling the future trend. That, after all, is the purpose of having a trend indicator in the first place.

I have chosen 10 days (two weeks) and 28 days (a popular number) as representative short and intermediate time lengths. Naturally, using different time lengths yields different results, depending on the market, but trying to optimize the length would probably not increase overall effectiveness.

Momentum

Momentum is the simplest form of trend indicator, but also one of the best. It looks at the direction of the closing price and uses only the closing price in its calculation. To calculate it, first determine the time period for the trend measurement. Then compare today's close with the close at the beginning of your chosen time period. If today's close is higher, the trend is up. If today's close is lower, the trend is down. If today's close is the same, the trend is the same as the momentum yesterday. Thus, if you want the 20-day trend (four market weeks), compare today's close with the close 20 market days ago. You would expect, wouldn't you, that if the trend were up, today's close would be higher than the close 20 days ago? That's what this indicator measures. You can use the same simple method over any time period and become an instant market expert.

Exhibits 9–1 and 9–2 show the results of trading solely with a momentum trend indicator using 10 days and 28 days to measure. The system goes long on the close when momentum is positive, reverses to short on the close when momentum is negative, and uses no stop.

Directional Movement

A method that determines the trend not by looking at the daily closing prices, but by looking at just the high and low prices each day, was created by Welles Wilder and described in his 1978 book, *New Concepts in Technical Trading Systems,* one of the best books ever on commodity trading systems.

EXHIBIT 9-1   Performance Report, Simple Momentum System, 10 Days

	S&P 500	T-Bonds	Euro dollars	Swiss Francs	Japanese Yen	Comex Gold	Heating Oil	Soy beans	Sugar	Live Cattle	Average
Number of Closed Trades	182	158	134	165	200	203	150	188	204	124	171
Number of Profitable Trades	51	60	48	59	53	52	40	56	46	33	50
Percent Profitable	28%	38%	36%	36%	26%	26%	27%	30%	23%	27%	29%
Total Profit or Loss	-55,250	44,730	21,925	1,938	20,775	-11,240	-16,666	-18,038	-25,144	-14,496	-5,147
Average Profitable Trade	2,421	2,055	1,226	1,358	1,446	1,349	1,306	1,004	619	624	1,235
Average Losing Trade	-1,364	-801	-429	-738	-380	-539	-625	-563	-338	-386	-613
Maximum Drawdown	-71,575	-10,891	-8,850	-11,412	-11,500	-25,060	-23,528	-33,050	-25,872	-15,792	-23,753
Average Profit Per Trade	-304	283	164	12	104	-55	-111	-96	-123	-117	-30

EXHIBIT 9-2   Performance Report, Simple Momentum System, 28 Days

	S&P 500	T-Bonds	Euro dollars	Swiss Francs	Japanese Yen	Comex Gold	Heating Oil	Soy beans	Sugar	Live Cattle	Average
Number of Closed Trades	118	99	77	91	101	116	67	113	95	79	96
Number of Profitable Trades	32	27	30	26	31	32	19	24	20	18	26
Percent Profitable	27%	27%	39%	29%	31%	28%	28%	21%	21%	23%	27%
Total Profit or Loss	-18,725	10,100	24,325	-3,100	18,700	-8,150	7,451	-19,938	-2,990	-15,364	-769
Average Profitable Trade	3,009	3,246	1,538	1,819	1,855	1,441	2,168	1,426	1,353	851	1,711
Average Losing Trade	-1,337	-1,077	-464	-775	-554	-646	-702	-608	-400	-503	-726
Maximum Drawdown	-40,475	-28,388	-6,950	-13,650	-7,763	-28,050	-17,510	-39,338	-8,075	-17,736	-20,793
Average Profit Per Trade	-159	102	316	-34	185	-70	111	-176	-31	-194	-8

If the trend is moving up, you would expect that today's high price would usually be higher than yesterday's. Contrarily, in a downtrending market, today's low is usually lower than yesterday's. The difference between today's high and yesterday's high is up directional movement; the difference between today's low and yesterday's low is down directional movement. Exhibit 9–3 illustrates the concept. If a day has both up and down directional movement, Wilder uses the larger of the two and ignores the other. It is possible to measure net directional movement mathematically over the time period you have chosen to measure the trend. This determines whether the trend is up or down over that period.

Exhibits 9–4 and 9–5 show the results of trading with the directional movement indicator using 10 days and 28 days to measure. The system goes long on the close when net directional movement is positive, reverses to short on the close when net directional movement is negative, and uses no stop.

Open/Close Indicator

This is an alternate trend indicator I created several years ago. It looks at the relationship between the opening price and the closing price on the same day. In an uptrending market, you will find that the

EXHIBIT 9-3   Wilder's Directional Movement Concept

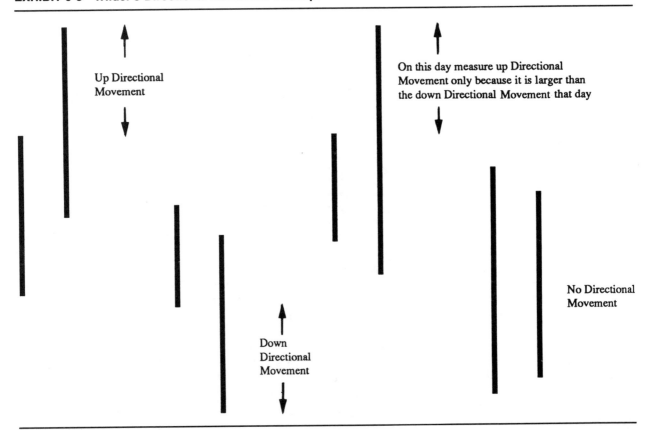

EXHIBIT 9-4   Performance Report, Directional Movement System, 10 Days

	S&P 500	T-Bonds	Euro dollars	Swiss Francs	Japanese Yen	Comex Gold	Heating Oil	Soy beans	Sugar	Live Cattle	Average
Number of Closed Trades	143	124	109	116	130	132	100	119	126	116	122
Number of Profitable Trades	47	56	33	41	47	37	37	40	41	34	41
Percent Profitable	33%	45%	30%	35%	36%	28%	37%	34%	33%	29%	34%
Total Profit or Loss	-39,200	30,210	11,125	-1,838	21,475	-11,580	-4,897	-14,513	2,901	-16,896	-2,321
Average Profitable Trade	2,363	1,675	1,378	1,581	1,356	1,339	1,361	1,101	733	562	1,234
Average Losing Trade	-1,565	-934	-452	-889	-509	-644	-876	-741	-318	-439	-742
Maximum Drawdown	-61,275	-20,278	-10,425	-14,138	-8,687	-22,770	-20,954	-25,213	-7,269	-19,040	-21,005
Average Profit Per Trade	-274	244	102	-16	165	-88	-49	-122	23	-146	-19

EXHIBIT 9-5   Performance Report, Directional Movement System, 28 Days

	S&P 500	T-Bonds	Euro dollars	Swiss Francs	Japanese Yen	Comex Gold	Heating Oil	Soy beans	Sugar	Live Cattle	Average
Number of Closed Trades	60	70	49	59	69	77	51	77	47	65	62
Number of Profitable Trades	24	23	24	24	27	21	14	28	15	17	22
Percent Profitable	40%	33%	49%	41%	39%	27%	27%	36%	32%	26%	35%
Total Profit or Loss	-1,275	38,410	26,975	20,000	15,625	630	6,527	-10,163	8,702	-8,700	9,673
Average Profitable Trade	3,355	3,346	1,777	2,265	1,874	1,807	2,710	1,059	1,573	924	1,849
Average Losing Trade	-2,272	-819	-627	-982	-833	-666	-848	-813	-464	-508	-867
Maximum Drawdown	-38,250	-13,784	-3,925	-9,113	-8,087	-18,230	-13,310	-22,500	-4,278	-14,384	-14,586
Average Profit Per Trade	-21	549	551	339	226	8	128	-132	185	-134	155

close is most often higher than the open. In a downtrending market, the opposite is true. Therefore, if you total the closes over the desired time period and compare it with the total of the opens over the same time period, you should get an indication of the trend. If the total of the closes is greater than the total of the opens, the trend should be up. If the total of the opens is greater than the total of the closes, the trend should be down. This trend indicator is the only one I know that incorporates the opening price. That is its only advantage. It allows you to use an important piece of data (25 percent of all the daily price data you have available) in determining the trend.

If you have computer software, you can use the moving average of the opens and closes instead of the total. The result is the same. If you are doing the calculations by hand, it is easier just to use the totals. By doing a little addition and subtraction, you can determine ahead of time where the market will have to close to make the trend be up or down.

Exhibits 9–6 and 9–7 show the results of trading with the open/close indicator using 10 days and 28 days to measure. The system goes long on the close when the total of the closes is greater than the opens, reverses to short on the close when the total of the opens is greater than the closes, and uses no stop.

Combination

Finally, we can see whether using all four available data points (open, high, low, and close) at once would increase overall effectiveness.

EXHIBIT 9-6   Performance Report, Open/Close Trend System, 10 Days

	S&P 500	T-Bonds	Euro dollars	Swiss Francs	Japanese Yen	Comex Gold	Heating Oil	Soy beans	Sugar	Live Cattle	Average
Number of Closed Trades	167	161	158	149	167	202	127	193	172	145	164
Number of Profitable Trades	53	49	47	50	58	64	42	58	50	33	50
Percent Profitable	32%	30%	30%	34%	35%	32%	33%	30%	29%	23%	31%
Total Profit or Loss	-43,000	80	1,150	1,713	21,013	-31,970	-16,443	-5,988	-17,853	-19,732	-11,103
Average Profitable Trade	2,439	2,185	1,078	1,561	1,348	978	1,128	1,003	550	681	1,312
Average Losing Trade	-1,511	-955	-446	-771	-524	-685	-750	-475	-371	-377	-679
Maximum Drawdown	-77,450	-31,680	-18,650	-15,938	-13,088	-41,900	-22,037	-25,338	-20,776	-20,728	-28,758
Average Profit Per Trade	-257	1	7	11	126	-158	-129	-31	-104	-136	-68

EXHIBIT 9-7   Performance Report, Open/Close Trend System, 28 Days

	S&P 500	T-Bonds	Euro dollars	Swiss Francs	Japanese Yen	Comex Gold	Heating Oil	Soy beans	Sugar	Live Cattle	Average
Number of Closed Trades	117	78	86	102	98	127	78	109	110	64	97
Number of Profitable Trades	37	31	29	37	29	45	26	25	29	15	30
Percent Profitable	32%	40%	34%	36%	30%	35%	33%	23%	26%	23%	31%
Total Profit or Loss	-44,900	50,600	4,050	3,213	16,900	-16,870	17	-17,450	-11,458	-4,464	-2,036
Average Profitable Trade	2,297	3,086	1,041	1,591	2,081	1,014	1,639	1,424	748	1,195	1,629
Average Losing Trade	-1,624	-959	-459	-856	-630	-762	-818	-632	-408	-457	-771
Maximum Drawdown	-50,350	-14,604	-16,275	-17,213	-13,050	-19,940	-19,778	-32,213	-16,251	-9,532	-20,920
Average Profit Per Trade	-384	649	47	32	172	-133	0	-160	-104	-70	-21

EXHIBIT 9-8   Performance Report, Combination Trend System, 10 Days

	S&P 500	T-Bonds	Euro dollars	Swiss Francs	Japanese Yen	Comex Gold	Heating Oil	Soy beans	Sugar	Live Cattle	Average
Number of Closed Trades	79	58	55	62	54	68	53	71	59	56	62
Number of Profitable Trades	19	21	18	21	18	19	14	24	25	13	19
Percent Profitable	24%	36%	33%	34%	33%	28%	26%	34%	42%	23%	31%
Total Profit or Loss	-41,350	15,250	18,825	-3,388	24,575	-10,940	-18,207	-5,700	5,253	-8,336	-2,402
Average Profitable Trade	4,471	3,855	2,497	2,420	3,078	2,017	2,428	1,551	1,023	1,380	2,176
Average Losing Trade	-2,105	-1,776	-706	-1,322	-857	-1,005	-1,337	-913	-596	-611	-1,168
Maximum Drawdown	-62,925	-20,218	-11,075	-16,188	-10,288	-19,580	-25,922	-21,238	-4,267	-14,592	-20,629
Average Profit Per Trade	-523	263	342	-55	455	-161	-344	-80	89	-149	-39

EXHIBIT 9-9   Performance Report, Combination Trend System, 28 Days

	S&P 500	T-Bonds	Euro dollars	Swiss Francs	Japanese Yen	Comex Gold	Heating Oil	Soy beans	Sugar	Live Cattle	Average
Number of Closed Trades	28	27	21	31	29	34	19	39	25	23	28
Number of Profitable Trades	9	8	10	13	9	9	7	13	10	8	10
Percent Profitable	32%	30%	48%	42%	31%	26%	37%	33%	40%	35%	35%
Total Profit or Loss	-16,375	19,060	23,775	-9,750	5,600	2,110	16,212	-12,263	11,659	-804	3,922
Average Profitable Trade	7,153	8,150	3,915	2,788	4,150	3,592	4,458	1,976	2,195	1,734	3,481
Average Losing Trade	-4,250	-2,427	-1,398	-2,556	-1,587	-1,209	-1,248	-1,460	-685	-978	-1,823
Maximum Drawdown	-36,075	-21,311	-10,275	-19,338	-13,713	-11,330	-12,214	-23,625	-3,405	-10,592	-16,188
Average Profit Per Trade	-585	706	1,132	-315	193	62	853	-314	466	-35	142

Exhibits 9–8 and 9–9 show the results of trading with the combination indicator using 10 days and 28 days to measure. The system goes long on the close when the all three trend indicators are positive, reverses to short on the close when all three trend indicators are negative, and uses no stop.

It appears from this limited test that Wilder's directional movement formula is better than the other two at signalling the correct trend. I have also found that to be true in other contexts. It is possible that using different time lengths would give different results, but I doubt it. It is reasonable to conclude, therefore, that highs and lows are more significant than opens and closes in judging the trend of the market.

Another observation is that, with only a few exceptions, the longer time period yielded more profits regardless of the indicator. This result is consistent with the widely accepted belief that long-term trading is usually more profitable than short-term trading.

Oscillators

Oscillators are the favorite tools for determining when price has moved up too far (the market is overbought) or down too far (oversold) and is ripe for a reaction in the opposite direction. The trader normally anticipates the change in trend by selling an overbought market or buying an oversold one. That is the use I will examine.

In the interest of completeness, I should mention that the values of most oscillators—in relation to the mathematical equilibrium point (usually 0 or 50 percent)—can function perfectly well as trend indicators. If the oscillator is above the equilibrium point, assume the trend is up; if below, assume the trend is down. Also, some systems do the opposite. They buy overbought and sell oversold markets when oscillator signals reach specified levels. An example is Jake Bernstein's *Stochastic Pop*.

The entry problem is a bit more complicated than just buying when the oscillator has an oversold reading and selling when it is overbought, although that is one way to do it. I will test both oscillators by buying or selling as soon as the oscillator reaches those trigger levels. Exhibit 9–10 illustrates this method. The problem with this approach is that sometimes the market will just continue in its trend after becoming overbought or oversold. In fact, a market often becomes highly overbought or oversold at the beginning of a sustained move in one direction.

To try to avoid those situations, you could wait for the oscillator to retrace a certain amount after first reaching its overbought or oversold trigger level. Exhibit 9–11 illustrates this concept. I will use this approach as well to test both oscillators.

Finally, perhaps the favorite oscillator method is not only to wait for an overbought or oversold market and then a retracement, but also to wait for a divergence. A divergence is an indication of slowing price momentum that takes place when price pushes to a new extreme high or low while the accompanying oscillator does not reach a new extreme reading of its own. Thus, there is a divergence between price and the oscillator. Exhibit 9–12 illustrates the concept of divergence. I will also test both oscillators by waiting for a divergence before acting. To eliminate catastrophic losses, I have added a $2,500 panic stop to these

EXHIBIT 9-10   Daily Chart of Live Cattle with Relative Strength Index Extreme-Only System
(August 1988 contract)

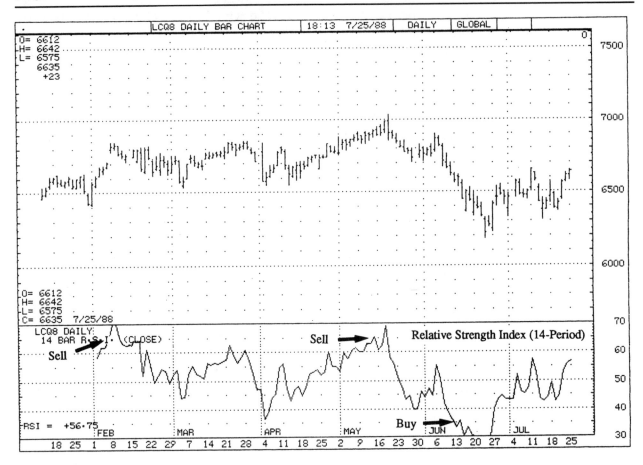

oscillator systems to minimize the damage that would occur if the market does not respond after a signal.

Traders employ a wide selection of oscillators. Some use only the closing prices, some use only highs and lows, and some use all three. I don't know of any that includes the open. While each has its adherents, the results tend to be the same since they are all measuring with the same limited universe of data points. Extending the time length of the oscillator results in fewer signals. This can be overcome by reducing the oscillator value required to act.

Mathematically speaking, the design of an oscillator will filter out cycles in the data that are less than twice its length. Thus, you should select an oscillator length equal to one half the length of the time cycle you want to trade. If you want to receive signals in tune with a 28-day cycle in the data, use an oscillator length of 14 days. If the cycle holds, you should expect to see the market in an upswing for about 14 days and a downswing for about 14 days, although the price movements over those time spans may be wildly unequal.

EXHIBIT 9-11   Daily Chart of Eurodollars with Relative Strength Index Oscillator Extreme and Retrace System (September 1988 contract)

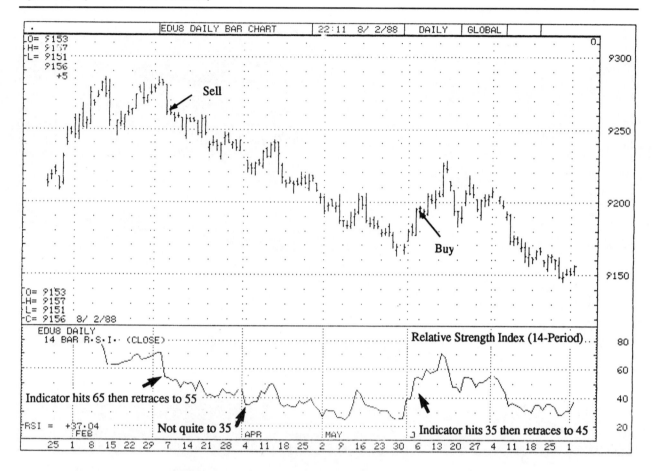

Relative Strength Index

Perhaps the most popular oscillator is Welles Wilder's Relative Strength Index, described in his book, *New Concepts in Technical Trading Systems*. It is part of every computer software charting package and appears in many commercial chart services. Wilder's contribution was to standardize its readings between 0 and 100 so that it works in the same general way regardless of market and regardless of price level. The calculation uses only closing prices as data points and mathematically combines the price differentials among up closes and down closes over the chosen time length. Readings of 100 represent pure up movement and readings of 0 represent pure down movement. Wilder's name for it often causes confusion in that relative strength in market analysis most often refers to a comparison of two or more markets or market groups, whereas this oscillator doesn't relate to anything but itself. To avoid this misunderstanding, Wilder's oscillator is usually called RSI.

Wilder suggested using a 14-day period for RSI regardless of market. Another popular time length used by several commercial chart

EXHIBIT 9-12　Daily Chart of Japanese Yen with Relative Strength Index Oscillator Divergence System
(September 1988 contract)

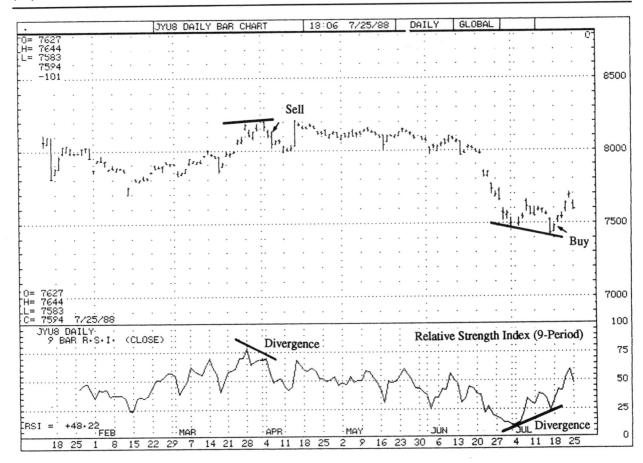

services is nine days. The longer the time length you apply, the more infrequent will be the trading signals. The level at which the market becomes overbought or oversold varies depending upon the time length. It decreases as the time length increases.

Exhibit 9–13 shows the results using a 9-day RSI. The system buys as soon as RSI drops to 30 and sells when it rises to 70. Unless stopped out, the system stays with a position until the market generates an opposite signal.

Exhibit 9–14 involves the same system except it uses a 14-day RSI. The threshold levels were reduced to 35 and 65 so that a reasonable number of signals were generated.

Exhibit 9–15 gives the results for the nine-day RSI when, in addition to the extreme reading, there must also be a retracement before a signal occurs. Using the nine-day RSI, the indicator must first hit 70 and then retrace to 60 for a buy signal; it must hit 30 and retrace to 40 for a sell signal.

Exhibit 9–16 shows what results from using the same system with the 14-day RSI and slightly lower signal levels. For a sell signal, the indicator must hit 65 and then retrace to 55; for a buy signal the indicator must hit 35 and then retrace to 45.

EXHIBIT 9-13   Performance Report, RSI Oscillator, 9 Days, Extreme-Only (70/30%), $2,500 Stop

	S&P 500	T-Bonds	Euro dollars	Swiss Francs	Japanese Yen	Comex Gold	Heating Oil	Soy beans	Sugar	Live Cattle	Average
Number of Closed Trades	43	42	33	38	30	38	26	32	25	21	33
Number of Profitable Trades	15	20	15	18	10	23	13	21	15	10	16
Percent Profitable	35%	48%	45%	47%	33%	61%	50%	66%	60%	48%	49%
Total Profit or Loss	2,100	15,081	-26,825	3,638	-30,937	4,310	-8,316	3,963	-10,082	-8,324	-5,539
Average Profitable Trade	5,032	3,728	935	2,926	2,136	2,010	1,712	1,489	750	1,071	2,249
Average Losing Trade	-2,621	-2,704	-2,269	-2,452	-2,615	-2,795	-2,352	-2,483	-2,133	-1,731	-2,472
Maximum Drawdown	-21,675	-15,694	-26,825	-9,800	-35,262	-10,710	-12,347	-7,963	-15,870	-9,064	-16,521
Average Profit Per Trade	49	359	-813	96	-1,031	113	-320	124	-403	-396	-169

EXHIBIT 9-14   Performance Report, RSI Oscillator, 14 Days, Extreme-Only (65/35%), $2,500 Stop

	S&P 500	T-Bonds	Euro dollars	Swiss Francs	Japanese Yen	Comex Gold	Heating Oil	Soy beans	Sugar	Live Cattle	Average
Number of Closed Trades	34	35	25	32	26	31	23	25	17	17	27
Number of Profitable Trades	7	14	10	16	10	19	14	16	7	9	12
Percent Profitable	21%	40%	40%	50%	38%	61%	61%	64%	41%	53%	46%
Total Profit or Loss	-26,050	-8,875	-19,800	537	-15,550	5,270	18,587	11,638	-14,748	-4,872	-5,386
Average Profitable Trade	6,346	3,302	1,260	2,715	2,510	2,173	2,955	2,195	1,098	1,221	2,527
Average Losing Trade	-2,610	-2,624	-2,160	-2,681	-2,541	-3,001	-2,532	-2,610	-2,244	-1,983	-2,532
Maximum Drawdown	-34,875	-16,894	-21,825	-11,038	-16,500	-11,770	-6,526	-7,688	-20,095	-8,808	-15,602
Average Profit Per Trade	-766	-254	-792	17	-598	170	808	466	-868	-287	-203

EXHIBIT 9-15   Performance Report, RSI Oscillator, 9 Days, Extreme and Retrace (70-60%/30-40%), $2,500 Stop

	S&P 500	T-Bonds	Euro dollars	Swiss Francs	Japanese Yen	Comex Gold	Heating Oil	Soy beans	Sugar	Live Cattle	Average
Number of Closed Trades	39	45	35	37	27	38	27	33	25	24	33
Number of Profitable Trades	14	19	18	17	11	22	13	18	13	10	16
Percent Profitable	36%	42%	51%	46%	41%	58%	48%	55%	52%	42%	47%
Total Profit or Loss	8,100	-21,781	-17,525	-4,588	-7,087	-10,390	-17,833	-14,163	-8,593	-18,920	-11,278
Average Profitable Trade	5,043	2,505	1,056	2,775	2,663	1,334	1,231	1,081	890	591	1,909
Average Losing Trade	-2,500	-2,669	-2,149	-2,588	-2,273	-2,484	-2,417	-2,241	-1,680	-1,773	-2,336
Maximum Drawdown	-18,800	-31,206	-22,525	-8,800	-15,775	-18,540	-22,068	-18,600	-12,288	-18,920	-18,752
Average Profit Per Trade	208	-484	-501	-124	-262	-273	-660	-429	-344	-788	-342

EXHIBIT 9-16   Performance Report, RSI Oscillator, 14 Days, Extreme and Retrace (65-55%/35-45%), $2,500 Stop

	S&P 500	T-Bonds	Euro dollars	Swiss Francs	Japanese Yen	Comex Gold	Heating Oil	Soy beans	Sugar	Live Cattle	Average
Number of Closed Trades	30	35	22	33	22	29	22	23	17	18	25
Number of Profitable Trades	7	16	11	16	12	15	13	13	9	8	12
Percent Profitable	23%	46%	50%	48%	55%	52%	59%	57%	53%	44%	48%
Total Profit or Loss	-26,525	-12,000	-4,300	-1,287	10,875	-1,950	6,313	4,438	-10,178	-11,160	-4,577
Average Profitable Trade	4,521	2,357	1,650	2,559	2,836	1,847	2,189	2,144	873	879	2,178
Average Losing Trade	-2,529	-2,616	-2,041	-2,484	-2,316	-2,118	-2,460	-2,344	-2,255	-1,819	-2,345
Maximum Drawdown	-33,250	-25,063	-10,725	-10,962	-5,450	-8,440	-11,141	-11,600	-12,773	-11,672	-14,108
Average Profit Per Trade	-884	-343	-195	-39	494	-67	287	193	-599	-620	-182

EXHIBIT 9-17 Performance Report, RSI Oscillator, 9 Days, Divergence (70/30% Initial Threshold), $2,500 Stop

	S&P 500	T-Bonds	Euro dollars	Swiss Francs	Japanese Yen	Comex Gold	Heating Oil	Soy beans	Sugar	Live Cattle	Average
Number of Closed Trades	8	7	6	6	9	12	5	10	9	6	8
Number of Profitable Trades	1	3	4	1	5	5	3	4	5	5	4
Percent Profitable	13%	43%	67%	17%	56%	42%	60%	40%	56%	83%	46%
Total Profit or Loss	-9,425	2,581	4,025	-12,850	12,763	-5,850	6,258	-8,125	-5,962	12,016	-457
Average Profitable Trade	8,925	4,452	2,325	213	4,775	2,710	3,862	2,016	408	2,923	2,931
Average Losing Trade	-2,621	-2,694	-2,637	-2,613	-2,778	-2,771	-2,664	-2,698	-2,001	-2,600	-2,621
Maximum Drawdown	-15,750	-6,750	-2,675	-13,063	-8,025	-13,280	-5,328	-10,988	-7,838	-2,600	-8,630
Average Profit Per Trade	-1,178	369	671	-2,142	1,418	-488	1,252	-813	-662	2,003	-59

EXHIBIT 9-18 Performance Report, RSI Oscillator, 14 Days, Divergence (65/35% Initial Threshold), $2,500 Stop

	S&P 500	T-Bonds	Euro dollars	Swiss Francs	Japanese Yen	Comex Gold	Heating Oil	Soy beans	Sugar	Live Cattle	Average
Number of Closed Trades	6	6	5	5	5	8	3	8	6	5	6
Number of Profitable Trades	1	2	2	1	3	3	1	1	3	4	2
Percent Profitable	17%	33%	40%	20%	60%	38%	33%	13%	50%	80%	37%
Total Profit or Loss	-8,775	-3,787	13,550	-10,188	9,588	180	2,611	-16,950	789	6,624	-636
Average Profitable Trade	4,375	3,494	10,725	213	5,000	4,393	7,939	1,800	1,207	2,306	3,990
Average Losing Trade	-2,630	-2,694	-2,633	-2,600	-2,706	-2,600	-2,664	-2,679	-944	-2,600	-2,504
Maximum Drawdown	-13,150	-7,800	-5,225	-10,400	-5,350	-10,400	-5,328	-18,750	-2,598	-2,600	-8,160
Average Profit Per Trade	-1,462	-631	2,710	-2,038	1,918	23	870	-2,119	131	1,325	-112

Exhibit 9–17 covers the third oscillator method, divergence. Using nine-day RSI, the system waits for a divergence after the indicator touches 70 for a sell signal or 30 for a buy signal. There were comparatively few trades.

Exhibit 9–18 completes the RSI systems by using 14-day RSI for the divergence variation. The indicator must touch 65 and then have a divergence for a sell signal, and it must touch 35 and then have a divergence for a buy signal. None of these RSI oscillator systems showed very impressive results. On average, they all lost money.

Stochastics

The grandfather of stochastics as applied to commodity trading is Dr. George C. Lane. He is well-known to seminar devotees for his exuberant speaking style. Sometimes you wonder whether you haven't stumbled into a revival meeting instead of an investment lecture. The idea was originated by a Czechoslovakian and perfected in the 1960s by Lane and his colleagues, surreptitiously using a University of Michigan computer in the dark of night.

The concept is based on the quirk that as prices trend higher, the close tends to fall on average closer and closer to the high of the daily range. The reverse holds true for downtrends. The study uses two lines instead of one. They are called %K and %D. The formula for %K is

$$\%K = 100 \times [(C - Lp) / (Hp - Lp)],$$

where

   C = today's close,
   Lp = the lowest low of the time period selected, and
   Hp = the highest high of the time period selected.

When today's close is equal to the highest high of the time period involved, %K is 100. When today's close is equal to the lowest low of the time period involved, %K is 0. There is a continuum in between. Some traders may recognize this as the inverse of the oscillator described in Larry Williams' 1975 book, *How I Made One Million Dollars Last Year Trading Commodities*. Williams called his oscillator %R.

The use of regular %K is called Fast Stochastics. The more popular version is Slow Stochastics, whose %K is a three-period moving average of regular %K, which damps the otherwise fairly violent action of the oscillator. (Period refers to whatever time increment you are using for the bars on the chart. It may be days, weeks, 60 minutes, 5 minutes, etc.) In either version, to get the complete indicator you add a second line, called %D, which is a three-period moving average of whatever %K line you happen to be using. This follows the %K line closely, and crossovers of the two lines provide potential trading signals, depending on the overall value of the indicators. If you have been following the mathematics, you will have realized that %D for Fast Stochastics is the same as %K for Slow Stochastics.

Exhibit 9–19 shows a price chart with a Fast Stochastics and several Slow Stochastics of various time periods. You can see why most traders use the slow version. I have also superimposed some RSI charts using similar time periods. These demonstrate the redundancy between the indicators. Even though stochastics uses high, low, and closing prices whereas RSI uses only closes, the results are remarkably similar. This similarity tends to hold for all oscillators and suggests that traders who use more than one oscillator at a time with the same time period are probably wasting their time. It should not be surprising that oscillators are closely correlated. After all, they are all supposed to measure the same thing—the overbought/oversold condition of the market. Even though stochastics uses high, low and closing prices whereas RSI uses only closes, the results are remarkably similar.

Exhibits 9–20 through 9–25 show the results of similar systems as those described above using Slow Stochastics instead of RSI. I adjusted the action levels slightly to allow for the different construction of the indicator, although the principles remain the same. My signals were generated by the %D line, although you could use the %K as well. The results were better than with RSI, especially using divergence. However, the relatively small number of trades raises a caution flag.

EXHIBIT 9-19   Daily Chart of S&P 500 With Assorted RSI and Stochastics Oscillators
(September 1988 contract)

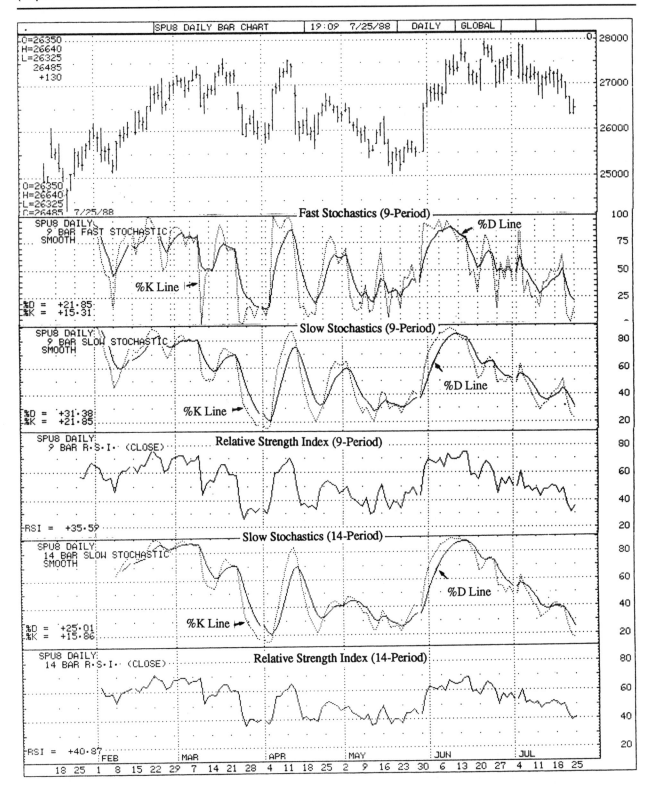

EXHIBIT 9-20   Performance Report, Slow Stochastics, 9 Days, Extreme Only (90/10%), $2,500 Stop

	S&P 500	T-Bonds	Euro dollars	Swiss Francs	Japanese Yen	Comex Gold	Heating Oil	Soy beans	Sugar	Live Cattle	Average
Number of Closed Trades	26	37	33	38	32	14	23	29	24	23	28
Number of Profitable Trades	9	19	17	19	14	7	11	19	14	12	14
Percent Profitable	35%	51%	52%	50%	44%	50%	48%	66%	58%	52%	51%
Total Profit or Loss	14,750	18,206	-13,550	-5,975	-21,937	4,790	-9,894	6,075	-4,819	-8,672	-2,103
Average Profitable Trade	6,572	3,431	1,135	2,334	1,545	3,391	1,700	1,616	1,035	840	2,180
Average Losing Trade	-2,612	-2,610	-2,053	-2,648	-2,420	-2,707	-2,383	-2,463	-1,931	-1,704	-2,379
Maximum Drawdown	-13,000	-14,900	-15,925	-18,350	-25,575	-13,560	-19,186	-8,388	-12,321	-12,080	-15,328
Average Profit Per Trade	567	492	-411	-157	-686	342	-430	209	-201	-377	-75

EXHIBIT 9-21   Performance Report, Slow Stochastics, 14 Days, Extreme Only (85/15%), $2,500 Stop

	S&P 500	T-Bonds	Euro dollars	Swiss Francs	Japanese Yen	Comex Gold	Heating Oil	Soy beans	Sugar	Live Cattle	Average
Number of Closed Trades	52	54	36	46	34	33	31	42	29	31	39
Number of Profitable Trades	28	27	16	24	13	18	16	26	17	19	20
Percent Profitable	54%	50%	44%	52%	38%	55%	52%	62%	59%	61%	53%
Total Profit or Loss	53,550	-2,088	-26,475	-1,025	-27,075	13,670	-15,015	14,963	-7,066	-5,780	-234
Average Profitable Trade	4,163	2,550	802	2,135	1,550	2,782	1,352	1,671	836	863	2,036
Average Losing Trade	-2,626	-2,628	-1,965	-2,376	-2,249	-2,427	-2,443	-1,780	-1,773	-1,848	-2,270
Maximum Drawdown	-13,000	-15,600	-27,975	-19,625	-30,750	-9,290	-19,281	-9,313	-13,072	-8,980	-16,689
Average Profit Per Trade	1,030	-39	-735	-22	-796	414	-484	356	-244	-186	-6

EXHIBIT 9-22   Performance Report, Slow Stochastics, 9 Days, Extreme and Retrace (90-80%/10-20%), $2,500 Stop

	S&P 500	T-Bonds	Euro dollars	Swiss Francs	Japanese Yen	Comex Gold	Heating Oil	Soy beans	Sugar	Live Cattle	Average
Number of Closed Trades	29	35	35	40	32	15	25	29	25	25	29
Number of Profitable Trades	8	18	16	16	15	6	11	14	13	11	13
Percent Profitable	28%	51%	46%	40%	47%	40%	44%	48%	52%	44%	44%
Total Profit or Loss	-2,750	22,125	-20,275	-34,638	-8,300	-900	-8,859	-2,000	-6,319	-19,248	-8,116
Average Profitable Trade	6,138	3,344	1,019	1,620	1,983	3,548	1,982	1,819	1,128	413	2,102
Average Losing Trade	-2,469	-2,240	-1,925	-2,523	-2,238	-2,466	-2,190	-1,831	-1,748	-1,699	-2,162
Maximum Drawdown	-30,625	-11,769	-23,400	-36,450	-17,400	-15,020	-16,232	-10,725	-12,485	-19,340	-19,345
Average Profit Per Trade	-95	632	-579	-866	-259	-60	-354	-69	-253	-770	-280

EXHIBIT 9-23   Performance Report, Slow Stochastics, 14 Days, Extreme and Retrace (85-75%/15-25%), $2,500 Stop

	S&P 500	T-Bonds	Euro dollars	Swiss Francs	Japanese Yen	Comex Gold	Heating Oil	Soy beans	Sugar	Live Cattle	Average
Number of Closed Trades	54	58	37	47	32	32	35	45	29	30	40
Number of Profitable Trades	22	22	20	21	16	16	17	24	15	16	19
Percent Profitable	41%	38%	54%	45%	50%	50%	49%	53%	52%	53%	47%
Total Profit or Loss	18,525	-21,488	-12,425	-10,000	1,550	3,700	-16,428	-7,850	-7,615	-7,652	-5,968
Average Profitable Trade	4,188	2,704	901	2,074	2,052	2,466	1,210	1,124	921	704	1,895
Average Losing Trade	-2,300	-2,249	-1,791	-2,060	-1,955	-2,234	-2,056	-1,659	-1,531	-1,351	-1,990
Maximum Drawdown	-20,800	-31,806	-18,625	-17,562	-12,688	-19,120	-20,366	-11,025	-11,700	-9,360	-17,305
Average Profit Per Trade	343	-370	-336	-213	48	116	-469	-174	-263	-255	-150

EXHIBIT 9-24   Performance Report, Slow Stochastics, 9 Days, Divergence (85/15% Initial Threshold), $2,500 Stop

	S&P 500	T-Bonds	Euro dollars	Swiss Francs	Japanese Yen	Comex Gold	Heating Oil	Soy beans	Sugar	Live Cattle	Average
Number of Closed Trades	5	12	8	8	7	7	2	8	9	8	7
Number of Profitable Trades	1	4	3	3	4	1	1	3	4	5	3
Percent Profitable	20%	33%	38%	38%	57%	14%	50%	38%	44%	63%	39%
Total Profit or Loss	-2,300	19,831	-1,775	9,138	8,363	-7,010	1,005	-5,525	-7,665	7,320	2,138
Average Profitable Trade	8,250	10,213	2,092	7,417	4,056	8,610	3,604	2,496	1,143	2,124	4,439
Average Losing Trade	-2,637	-2,627	-1,610	-2,623	-2,621	-2,603	-2,599	-2,603	-2,448	-1,100	-2,386
Maximum Drawdown	-7,950	-7,800	-5,200	-10,513	-5,262	-13,020	-2,599	-13,013	-10,792	-2,600	-7,875
Average Profit Per Trade	-460	1,653	-222	1,142	1,195	-1,001	503	-691	-852	915	289

EXHIBIT 9-25   Performance Report, Slow Stochastics, 14 Days, Divergence (80/20% Initial Threshold), $2,500 Stop

	S&P 500	T-Bonds	Euro dollars	Swiss Francs	Japanese Yen	Comex Gold	Heating Oil	Soy beans	Sugar	Live Cattle	Average
Number of Closed Trades	5	10	6	4	3	8	3	5	4	5	5
Number of Profitable Trades	2	4	2	0	1	3	1	3	1	3	2
Percent Profitable	40%	40%	33%	0%	33%	38%	33%	60%	25%	60%	38%
Total Profit or Loss	10,625	10,281	5,300	-10,463	14,088	-8,410	-2,753	7,275	-5,306	3,144	2,378
Average Profitable Trade	9,213	6,619	6,625	0	19,313	1,530	2,701	4,158	2,487	1,964	5,280
Average Losing Trade	-2,600	-2,699	-1,988	-2,616	-2,612	-2,600	-2,727	-2,600	-2,598	-1,374	-2,480
Maximum Drawdown	-2,600	-5,419	-5,200	-10,463	-2,625	-8,620	-5,454	-2,600	-5,306	-2,600	-5,089
Average Profit Per Trade	2,125	1,028	883	-2,616	4,696	-1,051	-918	1,455	-1,326	629	449

EXHIBIT 9-26   Performance Report, Directional Movement, 10 Days, Stochastics, 14 Days, Extreme and Retrace, $2,500 Stop

	S&P 500	T-Bonds	Euro dollars	Swiss Francs	Japanese Yen	Comex Gold	Heating Oil	Soy beans	Sugar	Live Cattle	Average
Number of Closed Trades	2	3	2	7	2	3	4	2	0	2	3
Number of Profitable Trades	1	2	2	2	0	2	0	2		0	1
Percent Profitable	50%	67%	100%	29%	0%	67%	0%	100%		0%	41%
Total Profit or Loss	42,350	54,638	7,125	-5,437	-5,800	7,340	-10,480	7,263		-5,200	9,180
Average Profitable Trade	44,950	27,447	3,562	3,781	0	4,970	0	3,631		0	11,976
Average Losing Trade	-2,600	-256	0	-2,600	-2,900	-2,600	-2,620	0		-2,600	-2,496
Maximum Drawdown	-2,600	-256	0	-13,000	-5,800	-2,600	-10,480	0		-5,200	-3,994
Average Profit Per Trade	21,175	18,213	3,562	-777	-2,900	2,447	-2,620	3,631		-2,600	3,400

You may be wondering what would happen if you combined several of the indicators we have examined so far. Exhibit 9–26 shows what happens if you combine 10-day directional movement and 14-day Slow Stochastics (using the retracement method) into a system. Both indicators must coincide in the direction of the trade to generate a signal. The results were in some cases spectacular, but there were very few trades.

Entry Triggers

Trend indicators help you identify the trend that should guide your overall trading strategy. Oscillators are tools to measure market strength within the overall trend as psychology pulls and pushes prices up and down in their characteristic wave patterns. Depending on your trading style, oscillators help you buy or sell when short-term price action is weak or strong. As we have seen, these two yardsticks can be used alone or in combination to produce a trading system. There is another common ingredient in many trading systems that provides a very-short-term action indicator. I call it an entry trigger. Often the construction of an entry trigger is such that it contains its own trend indicator, so that an entry signal can occur only in the direction of the projected trend. Other entry triggers require use of an additional trend indicator. You can combine these entry triggers with oscillators as further filters.

There are three popular types of entry triggers that contain their own trend indicators. They are moving averages, channels, and volatility envelopes. I have described and shown the performance of some moving average and channel systems in Chapter 8. They can be effective in the long term if you trade a large and diversified portfolio of markets. Small traders tend to shun them because they are slow-moving and usually have large drawdown periods when the markets are not trending. To trade with them takes more capital and patience than most traders possess.

Volatility Envelopes

A relatively new idea that has become very popular with systems traders is what I call a volatility envelope. It is a variation on the channel breakout concept described in Chapter 8. To the best of my knowledge Larry Williams developed the volatility envelope approach and first publicized it in 1983. The idea of this approach is to measure overall short-term volatility and then create a channel or envelope around the current closing price that reflects this volatility. When the market picks up enough short-term momentum to break out of this envelope, you follow the market. In the basic version you maintain your position until the market gives an opposite signal. At that point you exit the current trade and take a position in the opposite direction.

These systems measure the recent volatility every day so that the size of the envelope changes every day. They usually try to keep a position, either short or long, at all times, so as not to miss any good moves. Some variations attempt to exit the market entirely when short-term volatility exceeds a certain level that would cause violent intraday whipsaws. The potentially variable parameters are the number (most commonly two to four) of recent days to use in measuring volatility, whether to use actual range or true range (defined in Chap-

EXHIBIT 9-27   Volatility Envelope Concept

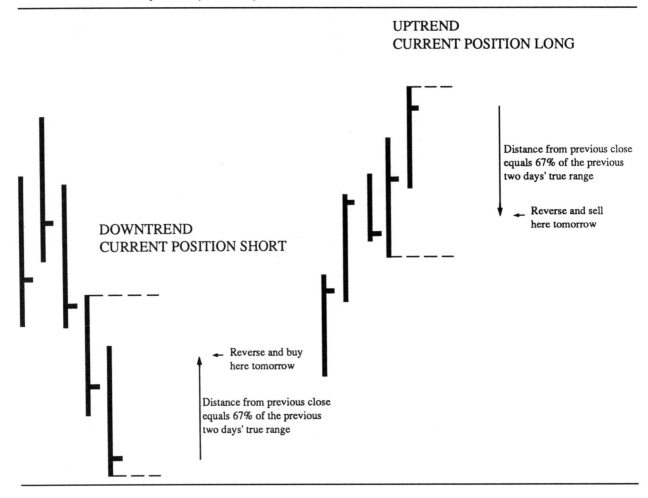

ter 10) to measure volatility, the percentage (usually 60–90) of overall volatility to use in computing the size of the envelope, and the centering point for computing the envelope boundaries for tomorrow (usually today's close, but sometimes some other benchmark). Exhibit 9–27 illustrates the idea.

Volatility envelopes are the basis for several software system packages currently selling for $3,000 and up. Larry Williams once sold a written variation of the idea at a seminar for $10,000 ($2,000 down and the rest from trading profits). Volatility systems like this are easy to optimize, and optimized values tend to test very well historically. The best market is stock index futures. They are also effective in other financial markets such as T-bonds, Eurodollars, T-bills, and continental currencies. They don't seem to work as well in the other markets. If you take care not to over-optimize, they can be very effective systems.

Exhibit 9–28 contains results from one version of a volatility envelope system. I used two days for the time period, 67 percent of the

EXHIBIT 9-28   Performance Report, Volatility Envelope, 67% of Last 2 Days' True Range, from Close

	S&P 500	T-Bonds	Euro dollars	Swiss Francs	Japanese Yen	Comex Gold	Heating Oil	Soy beans	Sugar	Live Cattle	Average
Number of Closed Trades	187	193	189	216	221	232	156	197	207	175	197
Number of Profitable Trades	94	90	78	88	71	82	56	80	69	58	77
Percent Profitable	50%	47%	41%	41%	32%	35%	36%	41%	33%	33%	39%
Total Profit or Loss	112,625	41,290	17,375	20,600	12,925	1,759	-920	13,600	-930	-14,360	20,396
Average Profitable Trade	2,157	1,569	811	1,196	1,187	1,079	1,215	855	552	530	1,162
Average Losing Trade	-969	-970	-415	-661	-476	-578	-689	-468	-283	-385	-569
Maximum Drawdown	-7,667	-13,418	-8,542	-11,640	-13,118	-16,770	-17,767	-15,418	-5,661	-14,361	-12,436
Average Profit Per Trade	602	214	92	95	58	8	-6	69	-4	-82	103

true range for the envelope size, and no stop. The results in the S&P 500 were extraordinary, but not uncommon for this kind of system. T-bonds were quite profitable but had a large drawdown. The other markets made less than $100 per trade or showed losses. I could have improved performance substantially by varying the parameters separately for each market and adding a reversing stop. Note that this is a very active system. It generated the highest number of trades of any basic system shown in this book. This should make it popular with brokers.

The Babcock Long-term System described in Chapter 8 is a variation of the volatility envelope idea. It is a very long-term system, and its envelope adjusts in an asymmetrical way.

Price Patterns

One of the most popular entry triggers for trading systems is price patterns. There are four key prices each day, and since you can use a fair number of previous days to create the patterns, the number of possible price patterns is staggering. Price patterns are attractive also because they comport with the common superstition that there is a repeating logic to market action that can be exploited if only it can be deciphered. An example might be to buy on the close after two down closes followed by a day whose open is lower than the previous low but whose close is higher than the open. The reverse order for sells in this system would be to sell on the close after two up closes followed by a day whose open is higher than the previous low but whose close is lower than the open.

I want to distinguish such short-term price patterns from intermediate-term, classical chart patterns such as head and shoulders tops, triangles, wedges, flags, and pennants. The short-term entry triggers I am now describing use relationships involving individual open, high, low, and closing prices. Classical patterns on bar charts describe an overall picture that depends mostly on high and low prices.

I have not found any compelling evidence that short-term price patterns are separately effective other than when they are merely confirming a short-term trend. An example would be three up closes in a row as a buy signal. They may be useful, however, as an action trigger in a larger system that comports with the three cardinal rules of trading. I have chosen to test three such patterns.

Key Reversal

The key reversal is a common pattern that has been known and used for many years. It refers generally to a situation where, for a buy signal, the market makes a lower low than the day before but closes higher. A top reversal would be the opposite. It has become fashionable lately to debunk the significance of key reversal days. However, the debunkers usually leave out one essential ingredient of the pattern. That is, for buy signals, the low that occurs must be significantly lower, not just fractionally lower, than the previous low. For sell signals the higher high must be significantly higher than the previous high followed by a lower close that day. Exhibit

EXHIBIT 9-29 Two Price Patterns, Key Reversal and Breakout from Inside Day

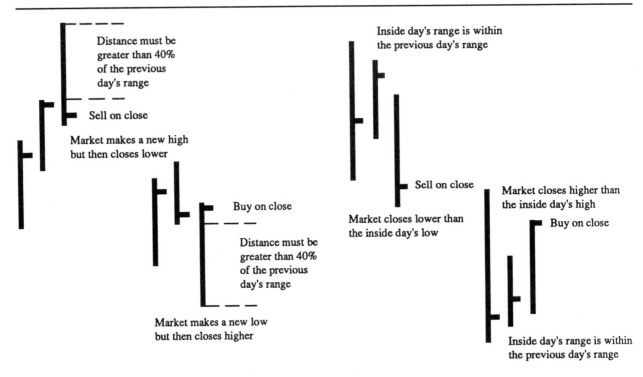

KEY REVERSAL   **BREAKOUT FROM INSIDE DAY**

EXHIBIT 9-30   Performance Report, Key Reversal Pattern (Extreme 40% of Range from Previous Extreme), $2,500 Stop

	S&P 500	T-Bonds	Euro dollars	Swiss Francs	Japanese Yen	Comex Gold	Heating Oil	Soy beans	Sugar	Live Cattle	Average
Number of Closed Trades	39	46	34	30	26	37	46	35	50	30	37
Number of Profitable Trades	13	15	15	14	11	16	24	14	22	18	16
Percent Profitable	33%	33%	44%	47%	42%	43%	52%	40%	44%	60%	43%
Total Profit or Loss	3,325	-13,131	6,325	28,812	25,625	-14,740	10,394	-13,400	-10,376	4,852	2,769
Average Profitable Trade	4,785	3,262	1,977	3,803	4,424	1,779	1,756	1,071	793	948	2,240
Average Losing Trade	-2,264	-2,002	-1,228	-1,527	-1,536	-2,058	-1,443	-1,352	-994	-1,017	-1,588
Maximum Drawdown	-20,925	-38,581	-9,700	-5,200	-17,075	-14,960	-8,185	-18,788	-13,931	-4,108	-15,145
Average Profit Per Trade	85	-285	186	960	986	-398	226	-383	-208	162	74

9–29 illustrates my definition of a key reversal. The problem is that it doesn't occur very often, so it is a problematical tool to use in a trading system.

Exhibit 9–30 shows the results of trading the key reversal pattern. I required that the extreme price on the day of the signal be at least as far from the previous extreme as 40 percent of the previous day's range. This eliminates the common pattern where, for instance, the market makes a slightly lower low than the day before and then closes higher. Most people would call this a key reversal. This system requires that the lower low be as far from the previous day's low as 40 percent of the previous day's range. Because of the possibility that the market might just keep going in the wrong direction, I added a $2,500 panic stop.

A String of Favorable Closes in a Row

Several consecutive closes in the same direction form an easily understood pattern whose effectiveness would result from its confirmation of the short-term trend, rather than from any mysterious combination of price events. It makes sense as an entry confirmation for other filters, especially a system that used an oscillator to buy after detecting an oversold condition and to sell after detecting an overbought condi-

EXHIBIT 9-31   Performance Report, Three Favorable Closes in a Row, Enter on Third Close, $2,500 Stop

	S&P 500	T-Bonds	Euro dollars	Swiss Francs	Japanese Yen	Comex Gold	Heating Oil	Soy beans	Sugar	Live Cattle	Average
Number of Closed Trades	94	84	69	74	77	57	70	84	67	60	74
Number of Profitable Trades	28	28	36	32	31	26	26	25	23	20	28
Percent Profitable	30%	33%	52%	43%	40%	46%	37%	30%	34%	33%	37%
Total Profit or Loss	-48,600	-5,619	27,800	19,975	34,963	27,600	-4,278	-32,975	-9,791	-5,596	348
Average Profitable Trade	3,038	2,873	1,432	2,100	2,288	2,221	1,659	1,353	1,005	985	1,937
Average Losing Trade	-2,025	-1,537	-720	-1,125	-782	-973	-1,077	-1,132	-748	-633	-1,148
Maximum Drawdown	-64,850	-30,337	-3,325	-8,937	-4,937	-8,810	-15,363	-40,050	-9,791	-11,000	-19,740
Average Profit Per Trade	-517	-67	403	270	454	484	-61	-393	-146	-93	5

tion. In such cases, you would want to see the market move in the direction of the overall trend before taking action. The system says to buy on the close of the third day which results in three up closes in a row. It sells on the close of the third day which results in three down closes in a row. There is a $2,500 panic stop. Exhibit 9–31 shows the trading results.

Inside Day, Then Favorable Movement

Inside days and outside days have always fascinated traders. An inside day is a day whose high is lower and whose low is higher than the day before. An outside day is just the opposite. Its high is higher and its low is lower than the day before. Inside days, especially those with narrow range and low volume, often precede changes in trend. I have chosen to test the inside day in combination with another significant pattern, a close that falls beyond the previous day's range. Thus, this pattern will signal a buy on the close of a day that follows an inside day and on which the close is above the high of the inside day. Conversely, we will sell on the close of a day that follows an inside day if the close is below the low of the inside day. Exhibit 9–29 illustrates the pattern.

Exhibit 9–32 shows the trading results. Again, I added a $2,500 panic stop in case the signal does not work and no reverse signal occurs.

Combinations of Entry Concepts

Naturally, we will want to combine the best of the various entry approaches to see whether we can make a better system than one based on any of them alone. Traders have the idea that if they combine a great number of useful indicators into one giant system, they will have a supersystem that will be better than its individual components. This

EXHIBIT 9-32 Performance Report, Inside Day Pattern, then Close Beyond Either Extreme, $2,500 Stop

	S&P 500	T-Bonds	Euro dollars	Swiss Francs	Japanese Yen	Comex Gold	Heating Oil	Soy beans	Sugar	Live Cattle	Average
Number of Closed Trades	54	39	27	48	65	55	26	43	36	41	43
Number of Profitable Trades	13	12	13	16	19	24	11	13	13	14	15
Percent Profitable	24%	31%	48%	33%	29%	44%	42%	30%	36%	34%	34%
Total Profit or Loss	-40,200	17,788	7,675	-12,625	-27,937	3,960	9,353	3,013	-733	-11,528	-5,123
Average Profitable Trade	3,290	5,874	2,308	2,766	1,574	1,700	2,447	2,939	1,186	708	2,356
Average Losing Trade	-2,024	-1,952	-1,595	-1,778	-1,258	-1,188	-1,171	-1,173	-702	-794	-1,398
Maximum Drawdown	-52,025	-13,444	-5,475	-19,962	-29,887	-7,810	-5,867	-12,788	-11,773	-14,660	-17,369
Average Profit Per Trade	-744	456	284	-263	-430	72	360	70	-20	-281	-118

EXHIBIT 9-33   Performance Report, Directional Movement, 10 Days, Three Favorable Closes, $2,500 Stop

	S&P 500	T-Bonds	Euro dollars	Swiss Francs	Japanese Yen	Comex Gold	Heating Oil	Soy beans	Sugar	Live Cattle	Average
Number of Closed Trades	36	44	37	43	38	32	34	41	30	31	37
Number of Profitable Trades	12	12	14	18	16	11	11	13	11	7	13
Percent Profitable	33%	27%	38%	42%	42%	34%	32%	32%	37%	23%	34%
Total Profit or Loss	11,225	20,475	24,600	5,625	24,563	-390	2,383	-738	2,208	-5,216	8,474
Average Profitable Trade	5,683	6,395	2,846	2,525	3,144	2,658	2,898	1,890	1,721	2,203	3,205
Average Losing Trade	-2,374	-1,758	-663	-1,593	-1,170	-1,411	-1,282	-904	-880	-860	-1,311
Maximum Drawdown	-20,550	-14,419	-4,925	-10,450	-4,138	-15,420	-23,796	-12,550	-4,799	-11,316	-12,236
Average Profit Per Trade	312	465	665	131	646	-12	70	-18	74	-168	232

approach is overrated. If all the separate indicators depend upon the same price data, it is unlikely that combining their results will improve matters.

Indicators may be sensibly combined if they represent different sets of data, such as different time lengths of the same price series or different data series entirely. For instance, if it worked, it would be preferable to have a silver indicator that examined gold prices rather than some redundant silver indicator. I do not recall seeing a single commodity trading system constructed this way, perhaps because such extraneous indicators do not work. However, it does not seem redundant to combine a longer-term trend indicator and a shorter-term oscillator with a very-short-term entry trigger. Or you could combine a trend indicator and an entry trigger. These analyze different time periods in the same data set.

Exhibits 9–33 and 9–34 show that combining a trend indicator with the previously described price patterns improves the results considerably. Compared to the other results we have seen, both of these systems performed quite well.

One of my favorite system filters is an eight-day high or low. This has been a component in a number of commercial systems, both my own and others'. The idea is that you require an eight-day low to precede a buy signal and an eight-day high to precede a sell signal. An eight-day low is a day on which the low was the lowest price of eight consecutive days (that day and the seven previous days). An eight-day

EXHIBIT 9-34   Performance Report, Directional Movement, 10 Days, Inside Day Pattern, $2,500 Stop

	S&P 500	T-Bonds	Euro dollars	Swiss Francs	Japanese Yen	Comex Gold	Heating Oil	Soy beans	Sugar	Live Cattle	Average
Number of Closed Trades	21	18	16	15	21	22	13	16	12	12	17
Number of Profitable Trades	2	7	8	7	7	7	4	4	7	6	6
Percent Profitable	10%	39%	50%	47%	33%	32%	31%	25%	58%	50%	36%
Total Profit or Loss	-27,625	18,481	9,100	21,338	7,525	-12,450	-2,648	-13,325	13,114	4,296	1,781
Average Profitable Trade	8,912	5,663	2,816	6,236	4,886	1,947	4,097	2,100	2,607	1,925	3,832
Average Losing Trade	-2,392	-1,924	-1,678	-2,789	-1,905	-1,739	-2,115	-1,810	-1,027	-1,209	-1,946
Maximum Drawdown	-39,725	-13,244	-5,300	-5,537	-9,512	-12,530	-13,250	-16,388	-2,954	-2,688	-12,113
Average Profit Per Trade	-1,315	1,027	569	1,423	358	-566	-204	-833	1,093	358	107

EXHIBIT 9-35   Performance Report, Directional Movement, 10 Days, 4-Day Extreme, Three Favorable Closes, $2,500 Stop

	S&P 500	T-Bonds	Euro dollars	Swiss Francs	Japanese Yen	Comex Gold	Heating Oil	Soy beans	Sugar	Live Cattle	Average
Number of Closed Trades	27	41	31	37	34	29	29	37	21	25	31
Number of Profitable Trades	8	11	14	18	14	10	9	11	10	7	11
Percent Profitable	30%	27%	45%	49%	41%	34%	31%	30%	48%	28%	36%
Total Profit or Loss	18,275	13,181	29,000	9,175	20,225	-7,920	1,896	-75	8,058	-2,672	8,914
Average Profitable Trade	7,663	6,639	2,900	2,451	3,154	2,576	2,731	2,282	2,108	2,079	3,342
Average Losing Trade	-2,264	-1,995	-682	-1,839	-1,196	-1,773	-1,134	-968	-1,183	-957	-1,433
Maximum Drawdown	-19,900	-16,256	-3,975	-8,800	-4,038	-16,890	-14,699	-11,350	-4,846	-9,992	-11,075
Average Profit Per Trade	677	321	935	248	595	-273	65	-2	384	-107	287

EXHIBIT 9-36   Performance Report, Directional Movement, 10 Days, 3-Day Extreme, Inside Day Pattern, $2,500 Stop

	S&P 500	T-Bonds	Euro dollars	Swiss Francs	Japanese Yen	Comex Gold	Heating Oil	Soy beans	Sugar	Live Cattle	Average
Number of Closed Trades	19	18	15	15	21	22	12	13	10	12	16
Number of Profitable Trades	2	6	7	7	7	6	3	4	5	4	5
Percent Profitable	11%	33%	47%	47%	33%	27%	25%	31%	50%	33%	32%
Total Profit or Loss	-22,425	3,388	8,500	21,338	7,525	-17,150	-4,043	-7,213	11,477	-1,200	20
Average Profitable Trade	8,912	5,041	3,132	6,236	4,886	1,942	5,167	2,347	3,206	1,946	4,082
Average Losing Trade	-2,368	-2,238	-1,678	-2,789	-1,905	-1,800	-2,172	-1,844	-911	-1,123	-1,962
Maximum Drawdown	-34,525	-13,300	-5,300	-5,537	-9,512	-17,150	-13,759	-11,888	-3,323	-3,836	-11,813
Average Profit Per Trade	-1,180	188	567	1,423	358	-780	-337	-555	1,148	-100	1

high is a day on which the high was the highest price of eight consecutive days (that day and the seven previous days). This works like a simple oscillator to filter out situations where the market has already made a big move in the desired direction and therefore is likely to react and stop you out. I don't know why eight is the best number of days. It seems to work well. It is long enough to be meaningful but short enough to generate a reasonable number of trades.

Because the previously described price patterns do not occur very often, it was impossible to generate enough trades by combining them with an eight-day high or low filter. To keep the same concept but generate a reasonable number of trades, I cut the number of days for the high or low. Because the inside-day pattern occurred less often than three consecutive closes in the same direction, I used a three-day low with the three consecutive close pattern and a four-day low with the inside-day pattern. I combined these two ideas with a 10-day directional movement trend indicator. The results in Exhibits 9–35 and 9–36 improved on the three-close pattern (compare with Exhibit 9–33) but not the inside-day pattern (compare with Exhibit 9–34). This is intended as an example of how to combine various complementary ideas into a system, rather than a definitive statement on what may or may not work. You can see that the possible system combinations are as limitless as your imagination.

There you have a good selection of entry tactics to help you comply with the first cardinal rule of commodity trading. We are therefore ready to move on to the second cardinal rule. The next chapter will explore various ways of cutting losses short, preferably without interfering with a trade otherwise destined to be profitable.

10 Stop-Loss Methods

The second cardinal rule of commodity trading is to cut losses short. Since most traders will have more losing trades than profitable trades, it is important to keep the losing trades smaller than the profitable ones. This sounds simple enough. Who wants to take big losses? The problem is that while no one wants to take big losses, most people don't want to take *any* losses. To take a small loss is certainly better than taking a big loss, but it is still not acceptable. As a trade progresses, there are a million rationalizations about why it is not necessary to take a loss at this time. The result is that small losses turn into big losses. The most important tool for risk control is the stop-loss order. This is an order that you place to exit a trade automatically when it goes against you.

It is easy to become paranoid about placing stop-loss orders. The market has a habit of going just to your stop before turning around and moving in the right direction. In hindsight it often appears that your stop point was actually the perfect place to add to your position instead of abandoning it. The usual reaction is to assume there is a conspiracy in the trading pit to find your stops. The trader decides to outwit the evil floor traders by not placing stops in the market. He will use "mental" stops. This means he has an exit point in mind, but he will wait for the market to hit it before getting out. Thus, the floor traders will not know in advance where the stop point is located. But for some reason, when the market finds his mental stops, the trader is slow to act or he changes his mind. The result—big losses. The market never seems to turn around at your stop point if you fail to get out.

Even experienced traders are not immune from paranoid delusions. I remember a professional trader, money manager, and newsletter writer who responded this way: When the market would move within a tick or two of his stop and then rebound, he would brag on his hotline about his "well-placed stop." When the market took out his stop, he would complain that the floor traders had been gunning for his stops. While an excessive ego certainly played a role in his contradictory explanations, these emotions are common. Resist them. The market is not gunning for your stops. It is much bigger than you. You tend to remember the unfortunate times when your stops were hit prematurely but quickly forget the times when being stopped out avoided an even bigger loss.

One advantage of a mechanical system is that it gives you unemotional stop-loss points. You must have the discipline to place the orders, however, or they will do you no good. That means your broker calls the stop to the exchange floor as an "open stop." It stays in the floor broker's book until you cancel it. The floor broker automatically executes the order without any further input from you if the price reaches your stop point. Barring excessive slippage (which does occasionally occur), you will take a loss of predetermined size when you are wrong. This is part of your plan and part of trading. You cannot avoid it. The more you try to avoid losses, the more you will deny yourself success.

I recommend that you place an open stop in the market as soon as your entry order is filled. Most brokers will allow you to place a stop order at the same time as your entry order. The stop order is a conditional order, to be entered if and when your entry order is filled. Using the conditional order is even better than waiting for a fill because it requires you to decide where your stop-loss will be before you place your entry order. This is an essential part of the thought process of entering a position, but you would be surprised how many traders get into a trade without any idea of where they will get out if it goes against them. Here is an example of such a conditional order:

> Day only, buy one September Japanese yen at seventy-five forty-six stop. If filled, enter an open order to sell one September Japanese yen at seventy-four forty-six stop.

"Day only" means your entry order expires at today's close if not filled. Your conditional stop order is an "open order," which means it remains in effect until you cancel it or the contract expires. This is also called a "good 'til canceled" order. If you are using an open stop order, be sure to cancel it if you exit your position without the stop having been triggered. Some brokerage firms have time limits on open orders. Be sure in such a case that your broker informs you when the order expires so you can replace it.

Taking quick losses automatically is so important that you often hear it said that good traders actually like losses. What they like are small losses because it means they have avoided a big loss. The profits will come. But you will attain long-term *net* profits only if you can avoid the big losses that will invariably outbalance any profits you may make. One of the hallmarks of an unsuccessful trader is those big losses that somehow always manage to creep into his account.

When beginning traders start to appreciate the importance of cutting losses and have some unpleasant experiences with stops, they begin to perceive stop placement as having the same mystical aura as predicting the market. They assume that professionals have some inside knowledge of precisely where to place stops so that they are stopped out only if the market is eventually going to go against them. That is silly. There is no science to it. Just as no one knows in advance exactly where the market is going, no one knows exactly where to place a stop. Remember that much of short-term market action is random. The important thing is that you use appropriately sized stop-loss orders consistently. *Exactly* where you place them is not particularly significant in the long run.

Although I do not believe in magic stop points, there is one recognized rule for placing stops that has merit. That is to avoid placing stops at even numbers. Since people tend to place entry orders at these numbers, the market has a habit of turning around at such points. It is best to place your stop just beyond the even numbers. Thus, instead of placing a sell-stop in sugar at 6.00, place it at 5.99 or 5.95. Instead of placing a soybean buy-stop at 7.92, place it at 7.92¼ or 7.93. Never place a stop-loss order at a price ending in two zeros. You should also apply the same principle to entry orders. If your mechanical system says to take action at such an even number, I suggest changing the order by one or two ticks to avoid the even number.

The principal purpose of the stop-loss order is to avoid catastrophic losses. In a system without a trend indicator as part of its entry rules, there is also another purpose. That is to allow you to exit (and optimally reverse your position) if the market changes its trend. Once you enter a position, the theoretical goal is to hold that position—in spite of short-term, random price action against you—so long as the trend remains in your favor and the potential loss remains within acceptable limits.

In Chapter 9 I described the first of two great dilemmas for commodity traders. The second involves stop placement. Like the first, there is no obvious solution. The problem is the proper size of your protective stops. If you use a wide stop, there is less chance that short-term random activity will take you out of your position before the market has a chance to move in your favor. However, if the market does hit your wide stop, the loss is relatively big. If you use a smaller stop to minimize the size of the loss, there is a greater chance that random market action will stop you out prematurely (before a change in trend). You will have to determine the best size for your stops through testing and self-analysis. If you use stops that are bigger than you feel comfortable with, the extra risk will interfere with proper decision making. Added fear of large losses will cause you to deviate from your trading plan. I have found through testing that almost all trading systems work better with stops wider than I would like to use. In a majority of markets the most effective stops seem to be between $1,500 and $2,000 in size.

Price (Volatility) Stops

One way to compute a stop point is to use a mathematical operation using price data. Since the range of prices from high to low represents market volatility, the underlying theory of these methods is to take some measurement of recent market volatility and use it to compute a stop distance. The supposition is that if volatility remains about the same and you place your stop beyond the limits of recent volatility, you will not be stopped out by market meanderings within the trend. If the market hits your stop, it will be because there was an uncontrollable increase in volatility or a change in trend.

The distance between today's high and today's low is one measure of today's volatility. It is called the day's range. When yesterday's close lies outside today's range, today's volatility should also include the distance between the previous close and today's range. That is commonly called the true range. You can measure volatility for as many days back as you like and then compute a stop based on the overall volatility or the average volatility. To obtain the stop point, you would then subtract this volatility amount from the entry point (or the entry-day low) for long positions or add it to the entry point (or the entry-day high) for short positions.

In order to compare the effectiveness of different stop strategies, I have taken one of the more profitable entry methods and tested it in combination with the various stop-placement methods. The original system is the one associated with Exhibit 9–35. For ease of comparison, I have reproduced its results in this chapter as Exhibit 10–1. The new system uses the alternate stop when it would result in a smaller loss than the $2,500 panic stop included in the original system. The idea is to test the effectiveness of making losses smaller by using a smaller stop constructed in various ways.

Exhibit 10–2 shows the results of using a volatility stop constructed by taking 80 percent of the average true range over the last 10 days and subtracting it from long entry points or adding it to short

EXHIBIT 10–1   Performance Report, Directional Movement, 10 Days, 4-Day Extreme, Three Favorable Closes, $2,500 stop

	S&P 500	T-Bonds	Euro dollars	Swiss Francs	Japanese Yen	Comex Gold	Heating Oil	Soy beans	Sugar	Live Cattle	Average
Number of Closed Trades	27	41	31	37	34	29	29	37	21	25	31
Number of Profitable Trades	8	11	14	18	14	10	9	11	10	7	11
Percent Profitable	30%	27%	45%	49%	41%	34%	31%	30%	48%	28%	36%
Total Profit or Loss	18,275	13,181	29,000	9,175	20,225	-7,920	1,896	-75	8,058	-2,672	8,914
Average Profitable Trade	7,663	6,639	2,900	2,451	3,154	2,576	2,731	2,282	2,108	2,079	3,342
Average Losing Trade	-2,264	-1,995	-682	-1,839	-1,196	-1,773	-1,134	-968	-1,183	-957	-1,433
Maximum Drawdown	-19,900	-16,256	-3,975	-8,800	-4,038	-16,890	-14,699	-11,350	-4,846	-9,992	-11,075
Average Profit Per Trade	677	321	935	248	595	-273	65	-2	384	-107	287

EXHIBIT 10–2   Performance Report, Exhibit 9-35 System Plus Volatility Stop, 80% of 10-Day Average True Range

	S&P 500	T-Bonds	Euro dollars	Swiss Francs	Japanese Yen	Comex Gold	Heating Oil	Soy beans	Sugar	Live Cattle	Average
Number of Closed Trades	33	53	54	52	52	45	40	57	35	45	47
Number of Profitable Trades	7	10	10	14	14	7	9	8	7	5	9
Percent Profitable	21%	19%	19%	27%	27%	16%	23%	14%	20%	11%	20%
Total Profit or Loss	30,030	22,331	13,167	9,340	20,000	-2,639	6,473	-6,850	8,663	-7,341	9,317
Average Profitable Trade	8,286	5,834	3,142	2,575	2,860	2,593	2,480	2,030	2,561	1,423	3,358
Average Losing Trade	-1,076	-837	-415	-703	-527	-547	-511	-471	-331	-361	-566
Maximum Drawdown	-15,200	-10,131	-6,245	-7,813	-4,138	-10,150	-8,549	-10,521	-2,836	-9,357	-8,494
Average Profit Per Trade	910	421	244	180	385	-59	162	-120	248	-163	200

EXHIBIT 10–3   Performance Report, Exhibit 9-35 System Plus Volatility Stop, 50% of 5-Day Total True Range

	S&P 500	T-Bonds	Euro dollars	Swiss Francs	Japanese Yen	Comex Gold	Heating Oil	Soy beans	Sugar	Live Cattle	Average
Number of Closed Trades	27	42	34	39	38	32	30	40	24	31	34
Number of Profitable Trades	8	11	14	18	14	10	9	11	10	7	11
Percent Profitable	30%	26%	41%	46%	37%	31%	30%	28%	42%	23%	33%
Total Profit or Loss	20,750	16,737	23,825	8,625	15,294	-5,520	2,410	1,306	10,161	-4,562	8,903
Average Profitable Trade	7,663	6,624	2,718	2,427	3,113	2,226	2,731	2,239	2,081	2,014	3,267
Average Losing Trade	-2,134	-1,811	-711	-1,670	-1,179	-1,263	-1,056	-804	-760	-778	-1,230
Maximum Drawdown	-17,600	-15,413	-5,625	-8,494	-5,606	-12,220	-12,947	-9,900	-2,938	-9,346	-10,009
Average Profit Per Trade	769	399	701	221	402	-172	80	33	423	-147	264

entry points. Exhibit 10–3 shows the results of using a volatility stop constructed by taking 50 percent of the total true range over the last five days. Deciding which is the best performing system is not always simple. There are a number of figures you can compare. Although the average profit per trade goes down using these two stop techniques, the total profits go up and the average drawdown and average losing trade decrease.

One popular method for calculating a close stop is to use the price relationships on the day of entry to establish the stop. For example, on a long position you could first subtract the close from the high and then place the stop that distance below the low. Reverse the process for shorts. Subtract the low from the close and place the stop that distance above the high. Since you do not know these relationships on the day of entry until after the close, if you enter intraday, you can use the prices from the day before entry to establish a temporary stop. Then, after the close on the day of entry, you can recalculate the stop for the next day based on entry-day prices. From then on you can keep the same initial protective stop or recalculate it every day.

If you recalculate the stop periodically, you will have to decide whether to move it farther away from the market (the current market price) if the new calculation so indicates. Most people prefer never to move a protective stop farther away from the market. If they are re-calculating the stop, they actually move it only if the calculation means moving the stop closer to the market.

Stop methods that require waiting until the day after entry to calculate the stop result in having no stop on the day of an intraday entry. If you are trading a volatile market, this could occasionally result in a larger-than-desired loss. At the least, having no stop could cause some anxious moments, and it is not recommended. To avoid this, you could use some alternate panic stop on the day of entry such as a money management stop (described below), and then revert to the system stop the next day.

Exhibit 10–4 shows that while this stop, used with this entry method, cut the average loss and the average drawdown substantially, it also cut profitability. Because the decrease in profits was minimal, it may be worth the tradeoff. This stop method may work better with other entry methods.

EXHIBIT 10–4   Performance Report, Exhibit 9-35 System Plus Day-of-Entry-Price-Relationships Stop

	S&P 500	T-Bonds	Euro dollars	Swiss Francs	Japanese Yen	Comex Gold	Heating Oil	Soy beans	Sugar	Live Cattle	Average
Number of Closed Trades	34	51	48	56	50	43	40	55	30	42	45
Number of Profitable Trades	7	10	12	14	13	6	9	8	9	6	9
Percent Profitable	21%	20%	25%	25%	26%	14%	23%	15%	30%	14%	21%
Total Profit or Loss	27,300	21,181	16,650	3,900	17,638	-5,610	2,875	-7,475	11,997	-5,224	8,323
Average Profitable Trade	8,286	5,991	2,773	2,460	3,060	3,217	2,468	2,264	2,236	1,484	3,341
Average Losing Trade	-1,137	-945	-462	-727	-598	-673	-624	-544	-387	-392	-650
Maximum Drawdown	-15,950	-13,388	-4,750	-13,125	-4,113	-12,090	-12,339	-12,800	-2,391	-8,848	-9,979
Average Profit Per Trade	803	415	347	70	353	-130	72	-136	400	-124	185

Time Stops

Instead of concentrating on recent volatility for guidelines to placing stops, you can place the emphasis on time parameters. You can place a stop beyond the price extreme over a recent increment of time such as the lowest low for the last week or the last four weeks; the highest high for the last 3 days or 12 days; or the low on the day of entry. These kinds of stops are more closely related to the concept of support and resistance than to volatility. The idea is that if price has not traded beyond a certain point for the last so-many days, it is not likely to do so in the future, absent a change in trend.

Exhibits 10–5 and 10–6 show what happens with two different time periods, 5 days and 10 days. These stop methods have the same

EXHIBIT 10–5   Performance Report, Exhibit 9-35 System Plus 5-Day Extreme-Price Stop

	S&P 500	T-Bonds	Euro dollars	Swiss Francs	Japanese Yen	Comex Gold	Heating Oil	Soy beans	Sugar	Live Cattle	Average
Number of Closed Trades	28	41	32	38	39	34	30	40	24	29	34
Number of Profitable Trades	8	11	14	17	14	10	9	11	10	7	11
Percent Profitable	29%	27%	44%	45%	36%	29%	30%	28%	42%	24%	33%
Total Profit or Loss	18,825	17,119	29,475	10,613	15,375	-6,920	1,343	550	9,517	-3,112	9,278
Average Profitable Trade	7,700	6,639	2,900	2,574	3,069	2,182	2,731	2,239	2,081	1,998	3,313
Average Losing Trade	-2,139	-1,864	-618	-1,578	-1,104	-1,198	-1,107	-830	-806	-777	-1,228
Maximum Drawdown	-19,650	-15,663	-3,900	-7,300	-5,588	-12,050	-14,174	-10,288	-3,493	-8,592	-10,070
Average Profit Per Trade	672	418	921	279	394	-204	45	14	397	-107	277

EXHIBIT 10–6   Performance Report, Exhibit 9-35 System Plus 10-Day Extreme-Price Stop

	S&P 500	T-Bonds	Euro dollars	Swiss Francs	Japanese Yen	Comex Gold	Heating Oil	Soy beans	Sugar	Live Cattle	Average
Number of Closed Trades	28	41	32	37	36	31	30	40	22	28	33
Number of Profitable Trades	8	11	14	18	14	10	9	11	10	7	11
Percent Profitable	29%	27%	44%	49%	39%	32%	30%	28%	45%	25%	34%
Total Profit or Loss	17,350	16,056	28,550	10,075	18,900	-4,510	1,271	-1,200	10,142	-3,608	9,303
Average Profitable Trade	7,700	6,639	2,900	2,451	3,114	2,532	2,731	2,239	2,103	1,998	3,326
Average Losing Trade	-2,213	-1,899	-669	-1,792	-1,123	-1,420	-1,110	-891	-907	-838	-1,312
Maximum Drawdown	-21,125	-15,663	-4,825	-8,550	-5,238	-12,500	-13,867	-11,075	-3,927	-8,996	-10,577
Average Profit Per Trade	620	392	892	272	525	-145	42	-30	461	-129	286

general effect as the previous stop methods. They appear to be a slight improvement. Using different time lengths may yield better results.

Those who trade with chart patterns often have a natural place for their stops based on the pattern involved. This is similar to a time stop because the pattern extreme is an important support or resistance point. The theory of the pattern is that the stop will not be violated without a change in trend.

A slight variation on the time theme is what I call a "prove-it-or-lose-it" stop. This means you exit a trade anytime it is not profitable after a certain initial period of time, for example, five days. You must always use this in combination with some other initial stop-loss, in case the market moves against you during the initial waiting period. If you are still in the trade at the end of the waiting period, you exit after that whenever the trade is unprofitable on the close. The theory of this tactic is that good trades should move in your direction fairly quickly. If they don't, then it is best to exit the trade and wait for another opportunity.

Exhibit 10–7 shows the effect of using a five-day prove-it-or-lose-it stop. Overall profits are increased, drawdown is decreased substantially, the winning percentage and average profit per trade decrease.

The ultimate prove-it-or-lose-it stop would be one day long. You would exit a trade anytime it was not profitable at the close. This would result in a great many small losses, but there would be good profits as well because good traders will tell you that many of their best trades were profitable right from the start and stayed that way.

Exhibit 10–8 shows the results. As you might expect, the winning percentage drops from 36 percent all the way down to 17 percent. That

EXHIBIT 10–7   Performance Report, Exhibit 9-35 System Plus 5-Day Prove-It-or-Lose-It Stop

	S&P 500	T-Bonds	Euro dollars	Swiss Francs	Japanese Yen	Comex Gold	Heating Oil	Soy beans	Sugar	Live Cattle	Average
Number of Closed Trades	31	50	44	48	44	40	36	52	33	35	41
Number of Profitable Trades	8	11	13	15	14	9	9	11	8	7	11
Percent Profitable	26%	22%	30%	31%	32%	23%	25%	21%	24%	20%	25%
Total Profit or Loss	32,525	18,500	19,000	3,650	22,850	-3,000	4,598	-788	6,903	640	10,488
Average Profitable Trade	7,700	6,173	2,504	2,446	3,091	1,924	2,490	1,927	2,300	1,630	3,169
Average Losing Trade	-1,264	-1,267	-437	-1,001	-681	-655	-660	-536	-460	-385	-740
Maximum Drawdown	-12,425	-14,919	-4,075	-11,200	-4,375	-7,500	-9,922	-7,050	-3,833	-5,096	-8,039
Average Profit Per Trade	1,049	370	432	76	519	-75	128	-15	209	18	254

EXHIBIT 10–8   Performance Report, Exhibit 9-35 System Plus 1-Day Prove-It-or-Lose-It Stop

	S&P 500	T-Bonds	Euro dollars	Swiss Francs	Japanese Yen	Comex Gold	Heating Oil	Soy beans	Sugar	Live Cattle	Average
Number of Closed Trades	32	57	55	56	51	48	41	59	44	44	49
Number of Profitable Trades	8	8	9	12	14	5	9	8	5	5	8
Percent Profitable	25%	14%	16%	21%	27%	10%	22%	14%	11%	11%	17%
Total Profit or Loss	45,200	15,331	14,150	4,525	24,413	-6,440	5,115	-6,213	1,872	-3,184	9,477
Average Profitable Trade	7,700	6,232	3,194	2,786	2,860	2,438	2,392	1,923	2,624	1,511	3,415
Average Losing Trade	-683	-705	-317	-657	-422	-433	-513	-424	-288	-275	-467
Maximum Drawdown	-5,875	-12,925	-6,450	-7,800	-2,512	-8,980	-9,197	-11,738	-4,302	-5,200	-7,498
Average Profit Per Trade	1,413	269	257	81	479	-134	125	-105	43	-72	195

means only one out of every six trades made money. Nevertheless, cumulative profits went up 6 percent and drawdown went down 32 percent. The average losing trade decreased an incredible 67 percent.

Money Management Stops

The money management stop is a simple but effective idea. You budget an amount for losses based on the volatility of the market you are trading and the overall size of your account. You place your stop at the point that will result in a loss equal to your budget, including commissions and a reasonable amount for slippage. Thus, in the S&P 500, if your budget was $1,000 per loss and you calculated slippage and commissions to be about $100 per trade, you would place your stops $900 (or 180 points) from your entry points. This is called a money management stop.

Some people argue that money management stops are bad because they have no relationship to market activity. This is true. However, it may be an advantage precisely because their placement is random in relation to price action. If you are using a money management stop, your stop order will probably not be located at some significant chart point where many other stop orders are bunched. The market has a habit of turning around after filling those groups of stops. By using money management stops, you avoid the crowd. Volatility stops also avoid those predictable chart points.

Exhibits 10–9, 10–10, and 10–11, show the effect of adding three different money management stops—$500, $1,000, and $2,000. All three increase cumulative profitability and lower drawdown. The larger two also increase the average profit per trade.

Since different markets have different volatilities, it is counterproductive to use the same money management stop for all markets. One way to adhere to the same general principle but adjust for market volatility is to use a stop based on a percentage of the exchange minimum margin required for that market. The exchanges base margins to some extent on recent volatility, so this is an automatic way to adjust your stop to the market. The biggest problem with this approach is that it is very difficult to test historically. Margins change periodically,

EXHIBIT 10–9   Performance Report, Exhibit 9-35 System Plus $500 Money Management Stop

	S&P 500	T-Bonds	Euro dollars	Swiss Francs	Japanese Yen	Comex Gold	Heating Oil	Soy beans	Sugar	Live Cattle	Average
Number of Closed Trades	40	58	41	56	45	44	38	49	25	31	43
Number of Profitable Trades	7	8	13	13	14	7	9	8	10	7	10
Percent Profitable	18%	14%	32%	23%	31%	16%	24%	16%	40%	23%	22%
Total Profit or Loss	38,000	24,012	19,700	5,100	21,875	-7,390	5,855	-3,038	12,478	1,248	11,784
Average Profitable Trade	8,286	6,837	2,662	2,638	3,044	2,454	2,557	2,495	2,081	2,014	3,326
Average Losing Trade	-606	-614	-532	-679	-669	-664	-592	-561	-555	-535	-609
Maximum Drawdown	-12,200	-11,725	-4,675	-11,875	-3,550	-11,370	-9,033	-10,250	-2,891	-4,588	-8,216
Average Profit Per Trade	950	414	480	91	486	-168	154	-62	499	40	276

EXHIBIT 10–10   Performance Report, Exhibit 9-35 System Plus $1,000 Money Management Stop

	S&P 500	T-Bonds	Euro dollars	Swiss Francs	Japanese Yen	Comex Gold	Heating Oil	Soy beans	Sugar	Live Cattle	Average
Number of Closed Trades	30	50	35	44	40	31	34	43	21	30	36
Number of Profitable Trades	8	11	14	17	14	9	9	10	10	7	11
Percent Profitable	27%	22%	40%	39%	35%	29%	26%	23%	48%	23%	30%
Total Profit or Loss	38,050	25,031	21,000	10,713	18,525	4,050	-2,472	-8,563	11,436	-4,144	11,363
Average Profitable Trade	7,700	6,173	2,562	2,387	3,141	2,850	2,567	2,036	2,108	2,077	3,254
Average Losing Trade	-1,070	-1,099	-708	-1,106	-979	-982	-1,023	-877	-876	-812	-968
Maximum Drawdown	-11,150	-9,463	-5,025	-9,287	-4,300	-7,960	-16,980	-15,875	-3,721	-8,928	-9,269
Average Profit Per Trade	1,268	501	600	243	463	131	-73	-199	545	-138	317

EXHIBIT 10–11   Performance Report, Exhibit 9-35 System Plus $2,000 Money Management Stop

	S&P 500	T-Bonds	Euro dollars	Swiss Francs	Japanese Yen	Comex Gold	Heating Oil	Soy beans	Sugar	Live Cattle	Average
Number of Closed Trades	28	41	31	37	34	29	30	38	21	25	31
Number of Profitable Trades	8	11	14	18	14	10	9	11	10	7	11
Percent Profitable	29%	27%	45%	49%	41%	34%	30%	29%	48%	28%	36%
Total Profit or Loss	23,725	20,431	29,000	11,825	21,125	-3,380	-172	-1,663	8,214	-2,432	10,667
Average Profitable Trade	7,663	6,639	2,900	2,451	3,154	2,576	2,731	2,323	2,108	2,079	3,346
Average Losing Trade	-1,879	-1,753	-682	-1,700	-1,151	-1,534	-1,179	-1,008	-1,169	-944	-1,327
Maximum Drawdown	-17,975	-13,663	-3,975	-7,812	-4,038	-12,890	-14,520	-12,288	-4,774	-9,752	-10,169
Average Profit Per Trade	847	498	935	320	621	-117	-6	-44	391	-97	340

EXHIBIT 10–12   Performance Report, Exhibit 9-35 System Plus Average-Margin Stop

	S&P 500	T-Bonds	Euro dollars	Swiss Francs	Japanese Yen	Comex Gold	Heating Oil	Soy beans	Sugar	Live Cattle	Average
Number of Closed Trades	27	41	35	37	34	29	30	39	21	30	32
Number of Profitable Trades	8	11	14	18	14	10	9	11	10	7	11
Percent Profitable	30%	27%	40%	49%	41%	34%	30%	28%	48%	23%	35%
Total Profit or Loss	18,275	13,181	21,000	11,825	21,125	-3,380	-172	-988	11,436	-4,144	8,816
Average Profitable Trade	7,663	6,639	2,562	2,451	3,154	2,576	2,731	2,323	2,108	2,077	3,303
Average Losing Trade	-2,264	-1,995	-708	-1,700	-1,151	-1,534	-1,179	-948	-876	-812	-1,336
Maximum Drawdown	-19,900	-16,256	-5,025	-7,812	-4,038	-12,890	-14,520	-11,188	-3,721	-8,928	-10,428
Average Profit Per Trade	677	321	600	320	621	-117	-6	-25	545	-138	273

and there is no readily available record of historical margin levels. A solution is to take an average margin level for the particular market and use a percentage (or multiple) of that as a money management stop.

Exhibit 10–12 shows the result of incorporating the following stops based on 100 percent of the average margin: T-bonds ($2,500), Eurodollars ($1,000), Swiss francs ($2,000), Japanese yen ($2,000), gold ($2,000), heating oil ($2,000), soybeans ($1,500), sugar ($1,000), and cattle ($1,000). The margin in the S&P 500 has been $6,000 or greater, and that is not a realistic size for a stop. I would set a $2,500 maximum. This was identical to the original panic stop, so it would not have changed the system results. This stop method had little effect on the profitability of this system.

Intraday or Close-Only Stops

When placing a stop, you have a choice to make it an intraday stop or a close-only stop. The floor broker will execute an intraday stop anytime price touches your stop point during the day. If it is a close-only stop, he will execute it only if the market is trading at or beyond your stop point as the market settles near the close. Some people argue that the closing price is the key price of the day, and they do not want to be stopped out by volatile or random market action during the day if it is not confirmed by the closing price. It is certainly true that using a close-only stop can keep you in a market when emotional trading at some point during the day would otherwise have resulted in a premature stop-out. The negative feature of a close-only stop is that you have no control over where the price may end up at the close. Your close-only stop could be positioned at a point that will result in approximately a $1,000 loss. By the time it is executed on the close, the market may have gone much farther against you, resulting in a $3,000 loss. Since the purpose of a stop-loss order is to control risk, I favor the intraday stop, which does a better job of keeping losses small. I am willing to suffer some premature stop-outs to be more certain I will not suffer too big a loss.

Exhibit 10–13 shows the results of a system identical to that described in connection with Exhibit 10–2, except I used close-only stops instead of intraday stops. For this particular system, using close-only stops resulted in slightly worse performance in all categories except profitable trade percentage. Other systems may tell a different story.

Reversing Stops

The normal tactic when stopped out of a position by a stop-loss rule is to wait on the sidelines for a new entry signal to take a new position. Some systems may perform better if you reverse your position when the market hits your stop-loss point as well as when you get an opposite entry signal. To reverse means to exit the current position and simultaneously enter a new position in the opposite direction. Exhibit

EXHIBIT 10–13   Performance Report, Exhibit 9-35 System Plus Close-Only Volatility Stop, 80% of 10-Day Average True Range

	S&P 500	T-Bonds	Euro dollars	Swiss Francs	Japanese Yen	Comex Gold	Heating Oil	Soy beans	Sugar	Live Cattle	Average
Number of Closed Trades	29	50	46	49	46	39	37	51	30	37	41
Number of Profitable Trades	8	11	13	15	14	9	9	9	9	6	10
Percent Profitable	28%	22%	28%	31%	30%	23%	24%	18%	30%	16%	25%
Total Profit or Loss	22,925	21,031	15,300	1,700	16,538	990	3,028	-7,338	10,518	-3,908	8,078
Average Profitable Trade	7,700	5,613	2,571	2,478	2,974	2,412	2,561	2,032	2,236	1,701	3,194
Average Losing Trade	-1,842	-1,044	-549	-1,043	-784	-691	-715	-610	-457	-455	-798
Maximum Drawdown	-13,725	-10,919	-5,900	-10,425	-4,212	-7,720	-12,612	-12,825	-2,705	-7,532	-8,858
Average Profit Per Trade	791	421	333	35	360	25	82	-144	351	-106	195

EXHIBIT 10–14   Performance Report, Exhibit 9-35 System Plus Reversing Volatility Stop, 50% of 5-Day Total True Range

	S&P 500	T-Bonds	Euro dollars	Swiss Francs	Japanese Yen	Comex Gold	Heating Oil	Soy beans	Sugar	Live Cattle	Average
Number of Closed Trades	36	47	37	40	40	43	31	43	25	34	38
Number of Profitable Trades	10	14	14	20	14	13	10	13	11	8	13
Percent Profitable	28%	30%	38%	50%	35%	30%	32%	30%	44%	24%	34%
Total Profit or Loss	15,500	14,737	23,425	12,438	21,825	-16,860	2,740	2,438	12,553	-3,124	8,567
Average Profitable Trade	7,828	5,412	2,925	2,409	3,538	2,169	2,492	2,248	2,040	2,095	3,262
Average Losing Trade	-2,414	-1,850	-762	-1,787	-1,066	-1,502	-1,056	-893	-706	-765	-1,320
Maximum Drawdown	-26,825	-16,769	-6,550	-6,712	-5,731	-25,750	-11,236	-12,138	-2,518	-7,908	-12,214
Average Profit Per Trade	431	314	633	311	546	-392	88	57	502	-92	228

EXHIBIT 10–15   Performance Report, Exhibit 9-2 System (Simple Momentum, 28 Days) Plus $1,000 Money Management Stop

	S&P 500	T-Bonds	Euro dollars	Swiss Francs	Japanese Yen	Comex Gold	Heating Oil	Soy beans	Sugar	Live Cattle	Average
Number of Closed Trades	118	100	77	91	101	116	67	112	95	77	95
Number of Profitable Trades	29	28	29	24	31	31	18	24	20	17	25
Percent Profitable	25%	28%	38%	26%	31%	27%	27%	21%	21%	22%	26%
Total Profit or Loss	14,125	28,406	23,550	-2,275	21,288	-4,710	4,921	-13,650	-2,450	-14,812	5,439
Average Profitable Trade	3,082	3,154	1,528	1,881	1,855	1,442	2,125	1,426	1,353	827	1,924
Average Losing Trade	-846	-832	-433	-708	-517	-581	-680	-544	-393	-481	-610
Maximum Drawdown	-24,925	-17,075	-5,000	-9,875	-8,912	-23,850	-16,556	-33,050	-7,814	-17,184	-16,424
Average Profit Per Trade	120	284	306	-25	211	-41	73	-122	-26	-192	57

10–14 illustrates the result of this kind of reversing rule when applied to the system described in connection with Exhibit 10–3. Although the average performance is slightly worse with the reversing rule, it improves performance in 6 of the 10 individual markets.

This chapter has shown you the effect of adding various stop-loss rules to a profitable system. In most cases they improved at least some overall performance categories. To show you what might happen when a stop-loss rule was added to a marginal system, we combined a simple $1,000 money management stop with the 28-day simple momentum system described in Chapter 9 (see Exhibit 9–2). Adding the one simple rule resulted in improved performance overall and in 8 of the 10 individual markets (see Exhibit 10–15). It was not enough, however, to make the resulting system tradeable except in a few of the markets. That system still needs work. Perhaps we can improve it still more with a better profit-taking mechanism.

If your system has cleverly chosen a good entry spot and the trade has avoided being stopped out at your judiciously placed initial stop-loss point, you are ready to face perhaps the most difficult decision in trading. The next chapter examines various ways to exit a trade with a profit. This is where you find out how to let your profits run, the third cardinal rule of commodity trading.

11 Exit Methods

The third cardinal rule of commodity trading is to let profits run. While novices are struggling with the problems of whether and when to buy or sell, the experts concede that knowing how to exit trades is actually more difficult than knowing how to enter. Kelly Angle publishes *The Timing Device* newsletter and trades accounts for others. Although he has often led the performance rankings in *Commodity Traders Consumer Report,* perhaps his greatest claim to fame is how he became interested in trading in the first place. His father amassed over $100 million in profits on his very first commodity trade. It was in the 1979–80 gold market, and he finally closed out the trade for $54 million. "That," Kelly says with a wink, "made me appreciate the potential of leveraged markets." When he started trading himself, Kelly lost money for several years. He credits his big turnaround to learning how to let profits run. "This is the hardest thing for any trader to do regardless of experience," Kelly counsels. "But it is also the most important. Traders get good at cutting losses because that's usually what they see first. You either learn to take losses or you go broke. Since you get fewer good trades, it takes longer to learn how to handle them."

It is easy to understand why letting profits run is such a problem psychologically. Many trades start out with a bang and then fizzle out. Traders become used to seeing relatively good profits suddenly disappear or even turn into losses. They can rationalize taking a profit before it gets away. They hear their broker say, "You never go broke taking a profit." The market seems to do everything possible to shake your confidence in a profitable trade. Scary news stories appear. There are sudden reactions attributed to profit-taking. There are always contrary expert opinions to worry about.

One of the best books a speculator can read for insight into the psychology of trading is *Reminiscences of a Stock Operator,* by Edwin Lefevre. This book is commonly thought to have been written by—or based on the career of—Jesse Livermore, one of the greatest speculators of all time. Lefevre says, "It never was my thinking that made the big money for me. It was always my sitting. It is no trick at all to be right on the market. Men who can both be right and sit tight are uncommon. I found it one of the hardest things to learn. But it is only

159

after a stock operator has firmly grasped this that he can make big money."

A properly designed mechanical system can help you immensely by relieving you of the responsibility for deciding when enough is enough. You just need the patience to follow the system. Compared to entry and stop-loss tactics, the trade-exiting options are more limited. The simplest option is to omit any special profit-taking rules and just wait for your system to issue an opposite entry signal. At that time you take profits on your current trade and initiate the new one in the opposite direction. This is a common and effective way to handle the problem. Other possible alternatives are the breakeven stop, trailing stop, fixed or variable profit objective, and oscillator objective.

In order to compare the effectiveness of different profit-taking strategies, I have begun with the profitable entry method used in the last chapter for testing stops and combined it with one of the better stop strategies—the $2,000 money management stop. The original system is the one associated with Exhibit 9–35. The complete basic system for this chapter is the one associated with Exhibit 10–11. For ease of comparison, I have reproduced its results in this chapter as Exhibit 11–1. The idea is to test the effectiveness of various exit strategies compared to simply waiting for a reverse entry signal.

Breakeven Stops

As you might imagine, one of the most frustrating things in commodity trading is making a good profit on a trade and then seeing it wither away. It is really awful when, after imagining how you are going to spend all those profits, you end up actually taking a loss on the trade. There is a trading axiom that warns about this: "Never let a profitable trade turn into a loss."

The tactic to accomplish this is the breakeven stop. This means that when a trade shows a certain amount of profit, the trader cancels his initial stop-loss order and places a new stop-loss order at a point that guarantees no loss on the trade. The amount of profit you require before moving the stop is the breakeven profit target. Once you move

EXHIBIT 11–1 Performance Report, Directional Movement, 10 Days, 4-Day Extreme, Three Favorable Closes, Plus $2,000 Money Management Stop

	S&P 500	T-Bonds	Euro dollars	Swiss Francs	Japanese Yen	Comex Gold	Heating Oil	Soy beans	Sugar	Live Cattle	Average
Number of Closed Trades	28	41	31	37	34	29	30	38	21	25	31
Number of Profitable Trades	8	11	14	18	14	10	9	11	10	7	11
Percent Profitable	29%	27%	45%	49%	41%	34%	30%	29%	48%	28%	36%
Total Profit or Loss	23,725	20,431	29,000	11,825	21,125	-3,380	-172	-1,663	8,214	-2,432	10,667
Average Profitable Trade	7,663	6,639	2,900	2,451	3,154	2,576	2,731	2,323	2,108	2,079	3,346
Average Losing Trade	-1,879	-1,753	-682	-1,700	-1,151	-1,534	-1,179	-1,008	-1,169	-944	-1,327
Maximum Drawdown	-17,975	-13,663	-3,975	-7,812	-4,038	-12,890	-14,520	-12,288	-4,774	-9,752	-10,169
Average Profit Per Trade	847	498	935	320	621	-117	-6	-44	391	-97	340

your stop, barring excessive slippage or a nasty gap opening, no loss
can occur. The trader has the best of all possible worlds. He can wait
patiently for his profits to increase while knowing he cannot sustain a
loss. He is playing, as they say in the casinos, with the house's money.

As rational as this strategy appears, my experience in testing trading systems over the years has convinced me it is fatally flawed. The
problem is that while it does protect you against some losses, it more
often snuffs out a good trade too soon. After all, nothing says that a
profitable trade that turns into a loss must eventually hit your initial
stop-loss point. It may first turn into a profit again—a big profit—that
you can miss if you use a small breakeven profit target and move your
stop to the breakeven point too soon. If you use a very large breakeven
profit target, the process becomes irrelevant because you invariably
receive a reverse entry signal before the breakeven stop can be
executed. The best of all possible worlds turns out to be not so hot
after all.

Exhibits 11–2 and 11–3 show the results of using a $1,000 break-
even stop and a $2,000 breakeven stop. Just to demonstrate that I don't
know what I'm talking about, the $1,000 breakeven stop works very
effectively with this system, improving results overall in 6 of the 10
individual markets. Perhaps this is another situation where the exception proves the rule. The $2,000 breakeven stop made things worse. I
still stand by my statement that the breakeven stop usually does not
help results.

While the breakeven stop is a worthwhile tactic to test as a possible
addition to your system, don't be surprised if it doesn't work as well

EXHIBIT 11–2 Performance Report, Exhibit 10–11 System Plus $1,000 Break-Even Stop

	S&P 500	T-Bonds	Euro dollars	Swiss Francs	Japanese Yen	Comex Gold	Heating Oil	Soy beans	Sugar	Live Cattle	Average
Number of Closed Trades	34	45	31	38	35	31	31	38	22	26	33
Number of Profitable Trades	8	10	14	17	13	10	9	11	10	7	11
Percent Profitable	24%	22%	45%	45%	37%	32%	29%	29%	45%	27%	33%
Total Profit or Loss	21,100	28,625	30,625	21,550	21,688	-3,440	6,705	3,388	7,072	-1,556	13,576
Average Profitable Trade	6,363	6,962	2,900	2,539	3,286	2,512	2,567	2,323	2,003	2,016	3,256
Average Losing Trade	-1,146	-1,171	-587	-1,029	-956	-1,360	-745	-821	-1,080	-825	-987
Maximum Drawdown	-15,850	-12,831	-3,975	-7,462	-4,188	-12,310	-10,282	-12,288	-4,774	-9,492	-9,345
Average Profit Per Trade	621	636	988	567	620	-111	216	89	321	-60	410

EXHIBIT 11–3 Performance Report, Exhibit 10–11 System Plus $2,000 Break-Even Stop

	S&P 500	T-Bonds	Euro dollars	Swiss Francs	Japanese Yen	Comex Gold	Heating Oil	Soy beans	Sugar	Live Cattle	Average
Number of Closed Trades	33	44	31	38	34	31	30	38	21	25	33
Number of Profitable Trades	8	10	14	17	13	10	9	11	10	7	11
Percent Profitable	24%	23%	45%	45%	38%	32%	30%	29%	48%	28%	34%
Total Profit or Loss	15,475	15,881	29,000	10,538	20,775	-6,380	-172	-1,725	8,214	-2,432	8,917
Average Profitable Trade	6,363	6,962	2,900	2,539	3,382	2,512	2,731	2,323	2,108	2,079	3,295
Average Losing Trade	-1,417	-1,581	-682	-1,554	-1,104	-1,500	-1,179	-1,010	-1,169	-944	-1,250
Maximum Drawdown	-21,475	-17,925	-3,975	-7,462	-4,038	-15,250	-14,520	-12,288	-4,774	-9,752	-11,146
Average Profit Per Trade	469	361	935	277	611	-206	-6	-45	391	-97	274

as theory suggests. My guess is your system will perform better if you leave your initial protective stop in place until you are ready to protect a portion of profit, not just insure a breakeven trade.

Trailing Stops

Trailing stops also can be used to protect profits. The idea is to adjust your stop-loss as profits accumulate in the trade. You keep it far enough away so that reactions within the trend cannot reach it, but close enough so that if the trend does reverse without a system opposite-entry signal, you will protect as much profit as possible. The trick, of course, is to know where that magic dividing line is.

The trailing stop is such a sensible idea that a whole system can consist of just a trailing stop rule. Perhaps the most effective system in Welles Wilder's classic book, *New Concepts in Technical Trading Systems,* worked exactly that way. Refer back to Exhibits 4–2 and 4–3 in Chapter 4, which illustrate his *Parabolic Time/Price System.* As the market begins a move, the stop-and-reverse point is its maximum distance from the current price. This gives the market the necessary leeway while it commences its move. Once the trend is under way, the trailing stop moves mathematically closer and closer to the current price. The longer the move continues, the more likely becomes a trend reversal and the closer the stop follows the closing price. Theoretically, when the market reverses enough to hit the stop, it signals a change in trend. You exit your current profitable position and establish an opposite one.

There are a myriad of ways to calculate a trailing stop in an effort to maximize its contribution. You can base it on chart pivot points, distance, time, geometric angles—you name it. Let your imagination run wild.

Exhibits 11–4 and 11–5 show what happens when you combine two different sized trailing stops with the basic system. In each case, you would exit a long trade when the closing price was $1,000 or $2,000, respectively, below the highest close of the move. You would exit a

EXHIBIT 11–4   Performance Report, Exhibit 10–11 System Plus $1,000 Trailing Stop

	S&P 500	T-Bonds	Euro dollars	Swiss Francs	Japanese Yen	Comex Gold	Heating Oil	Soy beans	Sugar	Live Cattle	Average
Number of Closed Trades	66	75	44	66	56	51	47	57	25	35	52
Number of Profitable Trades	20	30	20	28	22	21	21	15	11	12	20
Percent Profitable	30%	40%	45%	42%	39%	41%	45%	26%	44%	34%	38%
Total Profit or Loss	-3,800	-8,469	17,275	5,413	13,700	2,340	-1,126	-15,738	9,266	-3,112	1,575
Average Profitable Trade	1,985	1,435	1,739	1,349	1,831	1,320	1,140	1,173	1,620	835	1,464
Average Losing Trade	-946	-1,145	-729	-852	-782	-846	-964	-794	-611	-571	-860
Maximum Drawdown	-16,125	-18,563	-4,975	-11,475	-4,112	-10,960	-11,705	-19,838	-3,066	-5,748	-10,657
Average Profit Per Trade	-58	-113	393	82	245	46	-24	-276	371	-89	30

EXHIBIT 11–5 Performance Report, Exhibit 10–11 System Plus $2,000 Trailing Stop

	S&P 500	T-Bonds	Euro dollars	Swiss Francs	Japanese Yen	Comex Gold	Heating Oil	Soy beans	Sugar	Live Cattle	Average
Number of Closed Trades	55	55	32	43	36	40	36	45	21	25	39
Number of Profitable Trades	18	16	15	21	14	13	10	13	10	7	14
Percent Profitable	33%	29%	47%	49%	39%	33%	28%	29%	48%	28%	35%
Total Profit or Loss	-9,650	12,312	28,700	24,075	24,288	-8,150	-5,879	-7,425	10,538	-2,004	6,681
Average Profitable Trade	2,712	4,156	2,647	2,477	3,465	1,905	1,926	2,086	2,274	2,079	2,657
Average Losing Trade	-1,580	-1,389	-647	-1,270	-1,101	-1,219	-967	-1,079	-1,110	-920	-1,184
Maximum Drawdown	-26,625	-14,119	-3,975	-5,700	-5,013	-16,010	-16,319	-18,038	-4,628	-9,332	-11,976
Average Profit Per Trade	-175	224	897	560	675	-204	-163	-165	502	-80	172

EXHIBIT 11–6 Performance Report, Exhibit 10–11 System Plus Recent Pivot Point Trailing Stop

	S&P 500	T-Bonds	Euro dollars	Swiss Francs	Japanese Yen	Comex Gold	Heating Oil	Soy beans	Sugar	Live Cattle	Average
Number of Closed Trades	61	74	64	71	64	54	51	64	46	44	59
Number of Profitable Trades	19	27	33	26	25	17	25	25	20	13	23
Percent Profitable	31%	36%	52%	37%	39%	31%	49%	39%	43%	30%	39%
Total Profit or Loss	-8850	-15275	14825	-475	19225	3150	1686	-3738	-1475	-4920	415
Average Profitable Trade	2262	1437	900	1277	1765	1668	942	957	494	716	1234
Average Losing Trade	-1234	-1151	-480	-749	-638	-681	-841	-709	-437	-459	-770
Maximum Drawdown	-16400	-22181	-4000	-10662	-5713	-9160	-6459	-12800	-3265	-7640	-9828
Average Profit Per Trade	-145	-206	232	-7	300	58	33	-58	-32	-112	7

short trade when the closing price was $1,000 or $2,000, respectively, above the lowest close of the move. The $1,000 trailing stop is obviously much too tight and results in worse performance in every market but one. The $2,000 trailing stop improved performance in 4 of the 10 markets, although overall performance was worse than without it. I would not abandon this strategy on the basis of these two limited tests.

Exhibit 11–6 shows the results of using a trailing stop below the most recent pivot point. A pivot point low is a day with a low that is lower than the low of both the previous and following day. A pivot point high is a day with a high that is higher than the high of both the previous and following day. Pivots points tend be important support and resistance points that mark the outer boundaries of extended moves. You keep your stop just outside the most recent pivot point and move it closer to the market when a new pivot point occurs. Combined with this particular system, this type of trailing stop was a disaster. I would not dismiss it from consideration, however, since it has performed well for me in the past combined with other system rules.

One of the necessary evils of a trailing stop is that it is guaranteed to leave some potential profits on the table. You must always sacrifice the amount of profit between the move's highest profit level and the trailing stop. This can be a considerable amount. There are three potential ways to avoid losing so much potential profit: the fixed profit objective, the variable profit objective, and the oscillator profit objective.

Fixed and Variable Profit Objectives

It is surprising that the idea of profit objectives took so long in coming. It was not until the 1980s that a system appeared whose preferred method of exiting trades was just to shoot for a fixed amount of profit, say $1,000. In 1981, I sold a popular system called *Serial Analysis I,* created by Larry Hirabedian, which did just that. Several years later, Bob Dennis incorporated a similar rule into his *Dennis S&P System.* Research suggested that for some markets a fixed profit objective yielded results superior to those of the traditional trailing stop methods. This was especially true in the volatile stock index markets, where profits could appear and disappear amazingly quickly.

Naturally, the amount of fixed profit that you set for your target should have some relationship to the volatility in the particular market you are trading. You would not want to have the same profit objective in hogs or corn as you did in T-bonds. This leads to optimization in an effort to find the best profit objective. There is an especially great danger of curve-fitting when profit objectives are involved. The computer will be able to tell you with precision exactly what profit target worked best in the past. It is often a fairly high number that corresponds to the biggest move made in that commodity during the test period. It is highly unlikely that this target will work well in the future. If you do decide to incorporate a fixed profit target into your system, keep it relatively small to avoid this curve-fitting trap. If a small fixed profit target does not work as well as other profit-taking methods, don't use it at all.

Exhibits 11–7, 11–8, 11–9, 11–10 and 11–11 show the effect of incorporating five different profit targets with the basic system: $500, $1,000, $2,500, $5,000, and $10,000. None of them appeared to be of much value because, rather than letting profits run, they cut profits short. As you can see from comparing the tables, profit targets can drastically increase the percentage of winning trades. You can curve-fit a system this way to show a very high percentage of winning trades, maybe even 100 percent winners if you make the target small enough. In order to do this, you drastically reduce your average profit on winning trades without decreasing your average loss on losing trades. The

EXHIBIT 11–7   Performance Report, Exhibit 10–11 System Plus $500 Profit Target

	S&P 500	T-Bonds	Euro dollars	Swiss Francs	Japanese Yen	Comex Gold	Heating Oil	Soy beans	Sugar	Live Cattle	Average
Number of Closed Trades	114	131	102	119	119	80	86	88	50	54	94
Number of Profitable Trades	93	107	80	96	94	63	65	60	38	38	73
Percent Profitable	82%	82%	78%	81%	79%	79%	76%	68%	76%	70%	78%
Total Profit or Loss	-3,250	4,650	10,775	3,188	9,313	-50	-3,574	-9,313	486	-448	1,178
Average Profitable Trade	439	520	446	463	482	507	486	494	422	416	473
Average Losing Trade	-2,100	-2,126	-1,133	-1,795	-1,440	-1,882	-1,675	-1,392	-1,297	-1,016	-1,604
Maximum Drawdown	-11,050	-14,163	-3,700	-4,975	-4,912	-6,370	-9,356	-18,113	-5,178	-7,912	-8,573
Average Profit Per Trade	-29	35	106	27	78	-1	-42	-106	10	-8	12

EXHIBIT 11–8   Performance Report, Exhibit 10–11 System Plus $1,000 Profit Target

	S&P 500	T-Bonds	Euro dollars	Swiss Francs	Japanese Yen	Comex Gold	Heating Oil	Soy beans	Sugar	Live Cattle	Average
Number of Closed Trades	90	104	73	93	85	65	66	71	38	40	73
Number of Profitable Trades	62	75	46	65	58	41	37	38	22	22	47
Percent Profitable	69%	72%	63%	70%	68%	63%	56%	54%	58%	55%	64%
Total Profit or Loss	-450	13,569	16,100	13,575	19,613	-3,650	-10,971	-7,550	1,496	2,736	4,447
Average Profitable Trade	939	1,010	939	933	999	999	961	921	866	882	956
Average Losing Trade	-2,095	-2,144	-1,003	-1,682	-1,420	-1,859	-1,604	-1,290	-1,097	-926	-1,549
Maximum Drawdown	-18,150	-13,419	-5,075	-7,150	-4,650	-12,890	-18,212	-17,900	-6,148	-7,580	-11,117
Average Profit Per Trade	-5	130	221	146	231	-56	-166	-106	39	68	61

EXHIBIT 11–9   Performance Report, Exhibit 10–11 System Plus $2,500 Profit Target

	S&P 500	T-Bonds	Euro dollars	Swiss Francs	Japanese Yen	Comex Gold	Heating Oil	Soy beans	Sugar	Live Cattle	Average
Number of Closed Trades	65	74	48	58	55	47	45	54	26	29	50
Number of Profitable Trades	27	33	22	29	25	20	16	18	12	9	21
Percent Profitable	42%	45%	46%	50%	45%	43%	36%	33%	46%	31%	42%
Total Profit or Loss	-13,825	-369	19,900	11,250	23,663	-1,570	-10,384	-6,088	6,686	-2,628	2,664
Average Profitable Trade	2,404	2,313	1,874	2,078	2,378	2,241	2,228	2,060	1,877	1,677	2,167
Average Losing Trade	-2,072	-1,871	-820	-1,690	-1,193	-1,718	-1,587	-1,199	-1,131	-886	-1,485
Maximum Drawdown	-28,225	-20,075	-4,550	-9,225	-5,588	-14,290	-19,577	-16,450	-6,148	-9,912	-13,404
Average Profit Per Trade	-213	-5	415	194	430	-33	-231	-113	257	-91	53

EXHIBIT 11–10   Performance Report, Exhibit 10–11 System Plus $5,000 Profit Target

	S&P 500	T-Bonds	Euro dollars	Swiss Francs	Japanese Yen	Comex Gold	Heating Oil	Soy beans	Sugar	Live Cattle	Average
Number of Closed Trades	52	59	37	45	41	37	36	44	23	27	40
Number of Profitable Trades	12	19	17	19	16	13	10	12	11	7	14
Percent Profitable	23%	32%	46%	42%	39%	35%	28%	27%	48%	26%	34%
Total Profit or Loss	-25,675	15,850	23,525	14,213	23,525	3,140	-4,361	-3,550	8,303	-2,560	5,241
Average Profitable Trade	4,556	4,490	2,290	3,116	3,357	3,252	2,985	2,677	2,115	2,157	3,194
Average Losing Trade	-2,009	-1,737	-770	-1,730	-1,208	-1,631	-1,316	-1,115	-1,247	-883	-1,442
Maximum Drawdown	-31,450	-19,844	-4,550	-9,475	-4,825	-16,390	-16,077	-14,200	-6,148	-9,912	-13,287
Average Profit Per Trade	-494	269	636	316	574	85	-121	-81	361	-95	131

EXHIBIT 11–11   Performance Report, Exhibit 10–11 System Plus $10,000 Profit Target

	S&P 500	T-Bonds	Euro dollars	Swiss Francs	Japanese Yen	Comex Gold	Heating Oil	Soy beans	Sugar	Live Cattle	Average
Number of Closed Trades	43	46	33	37	35	31	32	41	21	25	34
Number of Profitable Trades	10	13	16	18	15	10	9	11	10	7	12
Percent Profitable	23%	28%	48%	49%	43%	32%	28%	27%	48%	28%	35%
Total Profit or Loss	4,475	30,556	28,875	11,825	20,450	-2,090	-5,277	-4,788	8,214	-2,432	8,981
Average Profitable Trade	6,935	6,749	2,530	2,451	2,898	3,261	2,665	2,670	2,108	2,079	3,418
Average Losing Trade	-1,966	-1,733	-682	-1,700	-1,151	-1,652	-1,272	-1,139	-1,169	-944	-1,409
Maximum Drawdown	-13,775	-16,544	-3,975	-7,812	-4,038	-18,450	-19,033	-15,413	-4,774	-9,752	-11,357
Average Profit Per Trade	104	664	875	320	584	-67	-165	-117	391	-97	261

EXHIBIT 11–12   Performance Report, Exhibit 10–11 System Plus Variable Target (20-Day Range at Entry)

	S&P 500	T-Bonds	Euro dollars	Swiss Francs	Japanese Yen	Comex Gold	Heating Oil	Soy beans	Sugar	Live Cattle	Average
Number of Closed Trades	51	59	47	53	52	43	42	50	32	33	46
Number of Profitable Trades	13	21	25	24	26	20	14	21	18	16	20
Percent Profitable	25%	36%	53%	45%	50%	47%	33%	42%	56%	48%	43%
Total Profit or Loss	-9,100	4,444	26,900	5,763	21,975	480	-4,612	-2,225	4,195	1,048	4,887
Average Profitable Trade	5,067	3,385	1,775	2,352	2,097	2,094	2,539	1,518	1,065	1,147	2,218
Average Losing Trade	-1,973	-1,754	-794	-1,748	-1,252	-1,800	-1,434	-1,176	-1,069	-1,017	-1,478
Maximum Drawdown	-30,000	-21,375	-4,050	-9,487	-4,513	-14,640	-17,934	-11,725	-6,148	-9,752	-12,962
Average Profit Per Trade	-178	75	572	109	423	11	-110	-45	131	32	106

long-term result is a poor system. The few relatively big losses will kill you because the small profits are not large enough to overcome them.

Another method of handling the profit target approach is to make the target vary with the market's current volatility at the time of entry. Exhibit 11–12 shows the results of using such a profit target based on the 20-day total range at the time of entry. You would calculate the difference between the highest high and lowest low of the last 20 days at the time of entry. When the market reached that amount of profit, you would exit the trade. Note that in every market the average profit was lower with the profit target than without. This means the basic system rules were doing a better job of letting profits run and explains the superior performance of the basic system. Although the results in this particular case were not an improvement, a parameter other than 20 days might have worked better.

I have had success designing systems with another kind of variable profit objective, based on a multiple of a variable initial protective stop. The initial stop changed with the volatility of the market at the time of entry. The profit target was two or three times the distance of the initial protective stop. This is a reasonable multiple but is not inviolate. A normal goal in trading is to shoot for profits that are much bigger than the potential losses. If your approach is profitable less than 50 percent of the time, as most are, it is necessary to have bigger profitable trades than losers to end up with overall profits. A 2:1 ratio is usually the least that good traders will accept when considering a trade. Many aim for profits of five or more times the potential loss. You can build this concept into your mechanical system by setting a profit target that is a multiple of whatever initial risk has been defined by your system rules. If you have not already exited the position by the time the market reaches your target, you take profits there and wait for the next entry signal. Ideally, the profits you lose, in situations where the market continues much farther in your favor, are more than offset by the profits you gain by exiting at a better level than you would have if using a trailing stop or waiting for an opposite entry signal.

Since the basic system for this chapter has a fixed rather than a variable stop, I could not use it with this type of target. Instead, Exhibit 11–13 shows the results of combining this kind of target with the variable stop rule connected to Exhibit 10–6. This was the highest

EXHIBIT 11–13 Performance Report, Exhibit 10–6 System Plus Variable Target (3 Times Initial Risk)

	S&P 500	T-Bonds	Euro dollars	Swiss Francs	Japanese Yen	Comex Gold	Heating Oil	Soy beans	Sugar	Live Cattle	Average
Number of Closed Trades	40	49	39	44	43	38	36	45	29	30	39
Number of Profitable Trades	10	16	17	19	15	11	9	13	12	9	13
Percent Profitable	25%	33%	44%	43%	35%	29%	25%	29%	41%	30%	33%
Total Profit or Loss	14,525	9,944	27,200	14,438	17,288	-6,510	3,536	-875	5,399	-2,496	8,245
Average Profitable Trade	8,435	4,507	2,562	2,987	3,149	3,199	4,179	2,388	1,568	1,677	3,372
Average Losing Trade	-2,328	-1,884	-743	-1,693	-1,070	-1,544	-1,262	-998	-789	-838	-1,371
Maximum Drawdown	-20,300	-19,156	-4,825	-6,912	-6,788	-17,580	-16,445	-11,075	-4,444	-8,996	-11,652
Average Profit Per Trade	363	203	697	328	402	-171	98	-19	186	-83	210

high (for shorts) or lowest low (for longs) for the last 10 days. The target was three times the initial risk for each particular trade. The profit target resulted in a slight improvement in four of the markets, but overall performance was worse. Even though the profit target did its job by increasing the average profitable trade by $46, it caused the system to exit trades sooner. Thus, the system was able to take more trades, but the overall performance decreased. You may find this kind of profit target to be more useful with a different system.

Oscillator Profit Objectives

You have already seen in Chapter 9 how an oscillator can identify an overbought or oversold condition that is favorable for entering a trade. Just as an overbought condition can set up a good short entry, in some systems it can be a good place to take profits on a current long position. Conversely, an oversold condition can be a good place to take profits on a short position. Whether or not an oscillator works as a profit-taking indicator depends on the particular oscillator rule. The danger is that markets tend to become overbought or oversold quite quickly at the beginning of a good move. It is thus difficult to let profits run if you are using an oscillator as a profit-taking signal. The ends of long moves are more likely to take place when there is a divergence in the oscillator. That means the oscillator level is less overbought or oversold at the end of the move than it was at a less profitable point in the move. Oscillator profit objectives are not my preference for exit signals.

Exhibits 11–14 and 11–15 show the results of two different oscillator targets combined with the basic system. The Exhibit 11–14 system would take profits whenever the nine-day RSI reached 70 percent for long positions or 30 percent for short positions. The Exhibit 11–15 system would take profits whenever the 14-day RSI reached 80 percent for long positions or 20 percent for short positions. Neither offered an improvement over the basic system.

Compare the average profitable trades among the systems to see which was doing a better job of letting profits run. In almost every case, the system with the highest average profitable trade turned in

EXHIBIT 11–14   Performance Report, Exhibit 10–11 System Plus Oscillator Target (RSI, 9-Day, 70/30%)

	S&P 500	T-Bonds	Euro dollars	Swiss Francs	Japanese Yen	Comex Gold	Heating Oil	Soy beans	Sugar	Live Cattle	Average
Number of Closed Trades	101	124	143	127	144	85	101	102	90	75	109
Number of Profitable Trades	56	61	76	71	77	46	53	51	43	40	57
Percent Profitable	55%	49%	53%	56%	53%	54%	52%	50%	48%	53%	53%
Total Profit or Loss	6,775	-4,556	7,550	6,125	-6,550	1,180	-14,091	-9,525	-10,848	-9,824	-3,376
Average Profitable Trade	1,221	893	332	632	462	837	465	567	226	280	595
Average Losing Trade	-1,368	-937	-263	-692	-629	-957	-807	-753	-438	-601	-724
Maximum Drawdown	-18,325	-15,181	-4,650	-9,775	-9,787	-10,600	-16,609	-17,288	-13,082	-12,876	-12,817
Average Profit Per Trade	67	-37	53	48	-45	14	-140	-93	-121	-131	-31

EXHIBIT 11–15   Performance Report, Exhibit 10–11 System Plus Oscillator Target (RSI, 14-Day, 80/20%)

	S&P 500	T-Bonds	Euro dollars	Swiss Francs	Japanese Yen	Comex Gold	Heating Oil	Soy beans	Sugar	Live Cattle	Average
Number of Closed Trades	35	60	53	40	63	46	41	46	29	25	44
Number of Profitable Trades	10	19	25	19	31	18	13	14	15	7	17
Percent Profitable	29%	32%	47%	48%	49%	39%	32%	30%	52%	28%	39%
Total Profit or Loss	8,800	8,781	22,575	13,850	17,675	-14,760	-14,826	-4,488	5,174	-2,432	4,035
Average Profitable Trade	5,688	4,346	1,695	2,551	1,567	1,647	1,661	2,280	1,360	2,079	2,322
Average Losing Trade	-1,923	-1,800	-707	-1,648	-966	-1,586	-1,301	-1,138	-1,088	-944	-1,336
Maximum Drawdown	-17,975	-18,644	-4,075	-8,350	-5,000	-21,670	-19,033	-13,413	-6,220	-9,752	-12,413
Average Profit Per Trade	251	146	426	346	281	-321	-362	-98	178	-97	92

the most profitable performance. Thus, when you incorporate alternate profit-taking rules into your system, implement tactics that will increase the profit of the average profitable trade. That is the essence of letting profits run. Don't fall into the trap of cutting the size of average profits in exchange for increasing the percentage of winning trades. In the long run, it is a losing exchange.

At the end of the last chapter, I showed the results of combining the best-performing stop rule with a system that began with only marginal profits (see Exhibit 10–15). The Exhibit 11–16 system builds on that by adding the most successful exit rule from this chapter, the $1,000 break-even stop. This caused an additional improvement in performance, but I would still not trade the system in its present form. The end result is consistent with my experience that entry rules are

EXHIBIT 11–16   Performance Report, Exhibit 10–15 System Plus $1,000 Break-Even Stop

	S&P 500	T-Bonds	Euro dollars	Swiss Francs	Japanese Yen	Comex Gold	Heating Oil	Soy beans	Sugar	Live Cattle	Average
Number of Closed Trades	118	101	77	91	101	116	67	112	95	77	96
Number of Profitable Trades	24	26	28	20	31	28	18	24	20	15	23
Percent Profitable	20%	26%	36%	22%	31%	24%	27%	21%	21%	19%	25%
Total Profit or Loss	3,425	34,619	23,575	6,525	22,513	-3,010	9,492	-11,313	-1,182	-15,284	6,936
Average Profitable Trade	2,844	3,369	1,580	2,125	1,855	1,455	2,125	1,426	1,353	919	1,941
Average Losing Trade	-690	-706	-422	-507	-500	-497	-587	-517	-376	-469	-534
Maximum Drawdown	-25,925	-14,169	-5,000	-5,162	-8,687	-21,210	-13,074	-31,000	-7,814	-17,656	-14,970
Average Profit Per Trade	29	343	306	72	223	-26	142	-101	-12	-198	73

the most significant in determining overall profitability. The additional refinements discussed in the last two chapters can improve performance, but not dramatically.

This completes a description of the various system ingredients that help you trade with the trend, cut losses short, and let profits run. To be profitable, your system must comply with those three essential trading principles. Up until now I have concentrated on generic rules of system design. The next chapter will discuss the variables that different markets introduce in system trading.

Chapter

12 Systems and Markets

System Specialization

The most popular trend in the last five years has been to create systems for one particular market only. In creating these systems you can start from scratch and create all the rules with a view toward performance in one market, or you can start with a basic framework and optimize the rules separately for each market.

The rationale is that each market has its own trading personality, and it is not reasonable to expect a system designed for, say, stock index futures, to work also in corn or hogs. While this theory sounds unassailable, I think it is more of a rationalization to hide curve-fitting than a deep theoretical truth. The overall volatility and trendiness of a market are the most significant variables. They determine whether a system can overcome the costs of trading. Those factors vary over time.

Here is a little experiment. Examine Exhibits 12–1, 12–2, 12–3, and 12–4. Each shows three daily charts of three different commodities. As you can see from the scale at the bottom, I copied them all on the same date. I have obliterated all other identifying information. I arranged each group of three so that they appear to have similar trading personalities. Each market in the group is tracing out a similar pattern. For those with some experience, it will be interesting to see if you can identify the markets by their supposed trading characteristics. Although this is not necessarily their correct order, either by number or within the illustrations, here are the groups:

1. Orange juice, crude oil, Japanese yen
2. Soybeans, Canadian dollar, live cattle
3. Cocoa, silver, cotton
4. Wheat, S&P 500, sugar

The members of each group are about as disparate as they could be, yet the market action appears quite similar. Unless somebody could recall the chart pattern, I think it would be impossible to tell one from another. (The correct answers appear at the end of the chapter.)

EXHIBIT 12-1   Three Daily Charts—Guess the Markets

Although it is difficult to identify markets on the basis of price action alone, there are distinct differences between the markets in terms of liquidity and fundamental influences. Those broad participation markets with the greatest psychological influences, such as gold and the stock market, are most apt to respond to technical analysis. Illiquid markets with dominant fundamental influence, like orange juice or oats, are more likely to respond to fundamental news and less reliable from a technical point of view. However, there are trends in all markets. Trend-following systems should work in the long run in any market that shows good trends.

While I am certainly not opposed to trading different systems in different markets, if you design a system for one market, there is a great danger of inadvertent curve-fitting. There is no magic test you can perform on the rules of a system that will measure its curve-fittedness. One good way to insure that a profitable system is not curve-fitted is to test it as is on several nonrelated markets. If it is profitable on the other markets as well, it is likely that the system is not curve-fitted. The more markets it works in, the better. If it is not profitable in other markets, watch out! That does not mean it definitely won't work in real-time trading, but it does suggest caution.

EXHIBIT 12-2   Three Daily Charts—Guess the Markets

The Effect of Price Action on System Performance

You may have noticed that some markets performed generally better than others when we tested various trading approaches and systems in Chapters 8 through 11. For example, the Japanese yen and T-bonds usually performed better than the other markets, regardless of the approach. This is a reflection of the price action in the markets during the time period tested. A low-volatility, highly trending market should always yield better results for a trend-following system than a high-volatility, non-trending market. A day-trading system should always do better in a market with a large average daily range than in one with a small average daily range because the average daily range is a measure of a day-trading system's potential profit.

So that you can evaluate the systems market by market, Exhibits 12–5 through 12–14 reorganize the performance by market instead of by system. On the individual system tables in Chapters 8 through 11, the average column represents the overall average of all trades rather than the average of each column. With three exceptions, this is also true of the average at the bottom of the summary tables in this chapter. The exceptions are average profitable trade, average losing trade,

EXHIBIT 12–3   Three Daily Charts—Guess the Markets

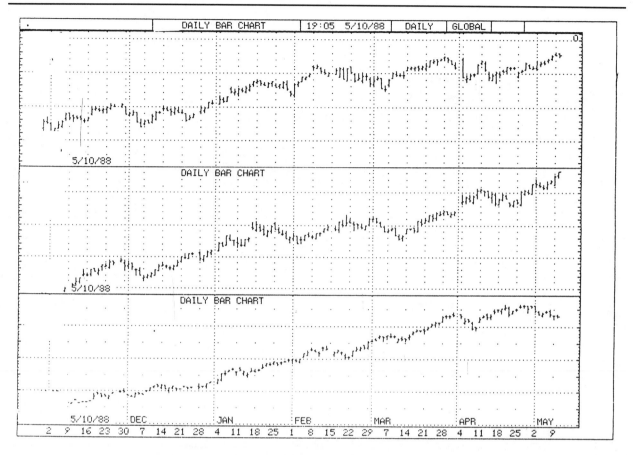

and maximum drawdown, where the averages represent the average of all systems instead of the average of all trades.

Exhibit 12–15 shows a summary of the overall average performance of each system. Even though I made no particular effort to pick the best performing parameters for the various examples, and even though the same parameters were tested on each of 10 markets with no individual optimization, the overall performance showed a profit. This demonstrates the power of system trading in the commodity markets. With more care in creating your system, you should be able to produce considerably better profits than this average. Note the exceptional performance of the Babcock Long-Term System (Exhibit 8–10) in comparison with all the others. The only one which beat it (Exhibit 9–26) had too few closed trades to be a reliable test. Nothing else came close.

When evaluating trading system performance, remember the importance of market price action during the test period. Don't be too elated over a system that performed well during an easy market period. For instance, any trend-following system should knock 'em dead in gold and silver during 1979–80. Don't eliminate a particular trend-following system from consideration just because it had a large drawdown if the particular test period would have been death on any such system. Check a more favorable test period to see whether perform-

EXHIBIT 12-4   Three Daily Charts—Guess the Markets

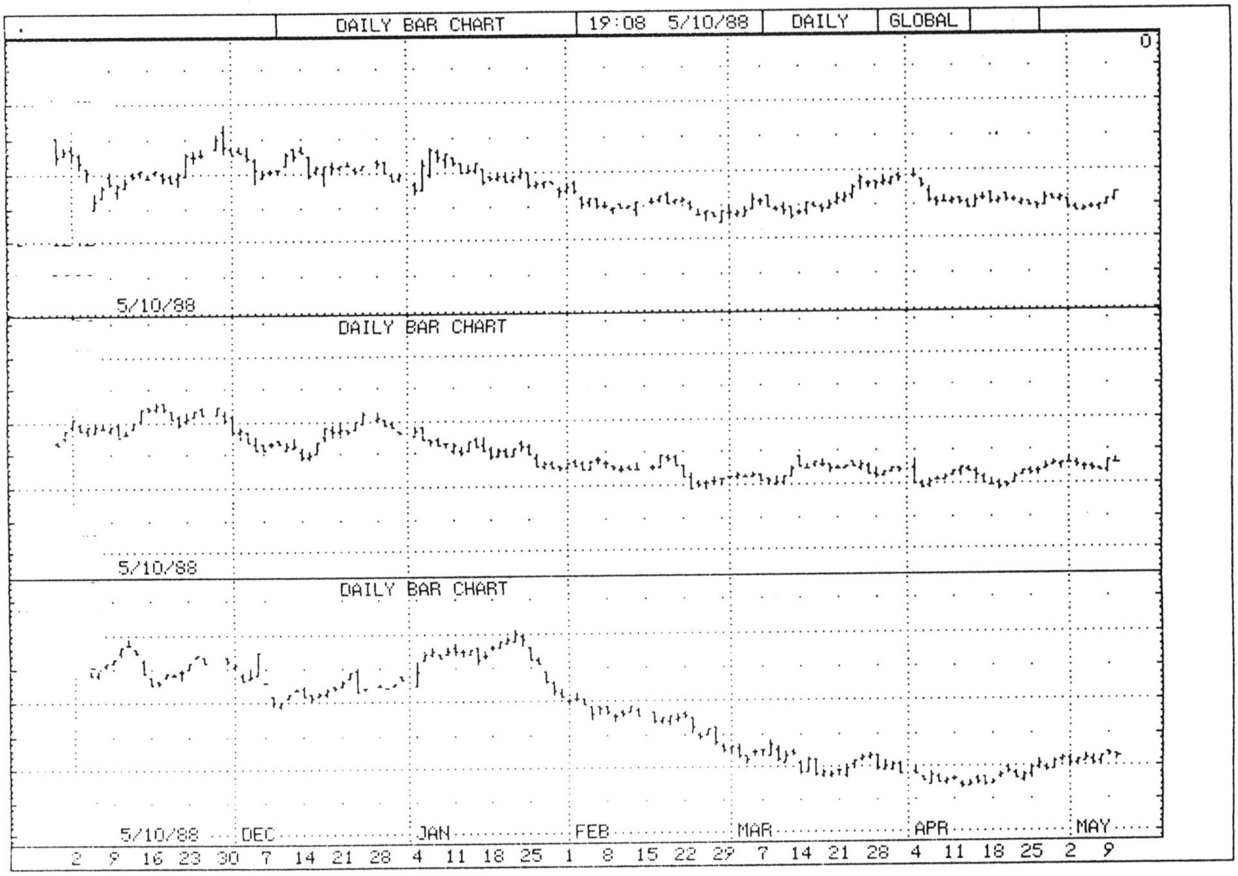

ance improves. To get a good overall picture of your system's performance, try to pick test periods long enough to encompass both trending and non-trending phases and both bull-market and bear-market segments.

I strongly recommend against systems that have different rules for long and short trades. These will be skewed to either bull or bear markets. They may perform better in the past than a symmetrical system because the data reflects the bull or bear trend favorable to the system. However, if the future shows the opposite trend, you are liable to get killed trading such a system. Don't fall for such seemingly sensible rationalizations as that markets tend to fall faster than they rise or perform differently in bear markets and bull markets. While these statements may be true, it is too difficult to create a testing procedure that will avoid curve-fitting such asymmetrical systems to back data. The best solution is to insist that your systems have symmetrical rules for long and short positions.

I have included in the Appendix weekly charts of the various markets included in tests in this book. They cover the years from 1978 to 1988. I have marked on them the test period I used—July 1, 1982 to June 30, 1987. Examine the price action in the various markets during this period as you evaluate each system's performance. There are also

EXHIBIT 12-5 Performance Report, Summary of Performance for All S&P 500 Systems

		Closed Trades	Profitable Trades	Percent Profitable	Total Profit or Loss	Average Profitable Trade	Average Losing Trade	Maximum Drawdown	Average Trade
EXHIBIT	8-2	91	25	27%	-67,675	3,725	-2,436	-77,725	-744
EXHIBIT	8-4	67	20	30%	-75,650	3,179	-2,962	-80,375	-1,129
EXHIBIT	8-6	101	25	25%	-42,650	3,744	-1,793	-49,400	-422
EXHIBIT	8-7	81	30	37%	-32,950	3,224	-2,543	-41,950	-407
EXHIBIT	8-8	47	16	34%	-43,425	3,770	-3,347	-58,975	-924
EXHIBIT	8-9	216	84	39%	39,575	2,273	-1,146	-27,613	183
EXHIBIT	8-10	12	3	25%	14,950	11,208	-2,075	-9,275	1,246
EXHIBIT	9-1	182	51	28%	-55,250	2,421	-1,364	-71,575	-304
EXHIBIT	9-2	118	32	27%	-18,725	3,009	-1,337	-40,475	-159
EXHIBIT	9-4	143	47	33%	-39,200	2,363	-1,565	-61,275	-274
EXHIBIT	9-5	60	24	40%	-1,275	3,355	-2,272	-38,250	-21
EXHIBIT	9-6	167	53	32%	-43,000	2,439	-1,511	-77,450	-257
EXHIBIT	9-7	117	37	32%	-44,900	2,297	-1,624	-50,350	-384
EXHIBIT	9-8	79	19	24%	-41,350	4,471	-2,105	-62,925	-523
EXHIBIT	9-9	28	9	32%	-16,375	7,153	-4,250	-36,075	-585
EXHIBIT	9-13	43	15	35%	2,100	5,032	-2,621	-21,675	49
EXHIBIT	9-14	34	7	21%	-26,050	6,346	-2,610	-34,875	-766
EXHIBIT	9-15	39	14	36%	8,100	5,043	-2,500	-18,800	208
EXHIBIT	9-16	30	7	23%	-26,525	4,521	-2,529	-33,250	-884
EXHIBIT	9-17	8	1	13%	-9,425	8,925	-2,621	-15,750	-1,178
EXHIBIT	9-18	6	1	17%	-8,775	4,375	-2,630	-13,150	-1,462
EXHIBIT	9-20	26	9	35%	14,750	6,572	-2,612	-13,000	567
EXHIBIT	9-21	52	28	54%	53,550	4,163	-2,626	-13,000	1,030
EXHIBIT	9-22	29	8	28%	-2,750	6,138	-2,469	-30,625	-95
EXHIBIT	9-23	54	22	41%	18,525	4,188	-2,300	-20,800	343
EXHIBIT	9-24	5	1	20%	-2,300	8,250	-2,637	-7,950	-460
EXHIBIT	9-25	5	2	40%	10,625	9,213	-2,600	-2,600	2,125
EXHIBIT	9-26	2	1	50%	42,350	44,950	-2,600	-2,600	21,175
EXHIBIT	9-28	187	94	50%	112,625	2,157	-969	-7,667	602
EXHIBIT	9-30	39	13	33%	3,325	4,785	-2,264	-20,925	85
EXHIBIT	9-31	94	28	30%	-48,600	3,038	-2,025	-64,850	-517
EXHIBIT	9-32	54	13	24%	-40,200	3,290	-2,024	-52,025	-744
EXHIBIT	9-33	36	12	33%	11,225	5,683	-2,374	-20,550	312
EXHIBIT	9-34	21	2	10%	-27,625	8,912	-2,392	-39,725	-1,315
EXHIBIT	9-35	27	8	30%	18,275	7,663	-2,264	-19,900	677
EXHIBIT	9-36	19	2	11%	-22,425	8,912	-2,368	-34,525	-1,180
EXHIBIT	10-2	33	7	21%	30,030	8,286	-1,076	-15,200	910
EXHIBIT	10-3	27	8	30%	20,750	7,663	-2,134	-17,600	769
EXHIBIT	10-4	34	7	21%	27,300	8,286	-1,137	-15,950	803
EXHIBIT	10-5	28	8	29%	18,825	7,700	-2,139	-19,650	672
EXHIBIT	10-6	28	8	29%	17,350	7,700	-2,213	-21,125	620
EXHIBIT	10-7	31	8	26%	32,525	7,700	-1,264	-12,425	1,049
EXHIBIT	10-8	32	8	25%	45,200	7,700	-683	-5,875	1,413
EXHIBIT	10-9	40	7	18%	38,000	8,286	-606	-12,200	950
EXHIBIT	10-10	30	8	27%	38,050	7,700	-1,070	-11,150	1,268
EXHIBIT	10-11	28	8	29%	23,725	7,663	-1,879	-17,975	847
EXHIBIT	10-12	27	8	30%	18,275	7,663	-2,264	-19,900	677
EXHIBIT	10-13	29	8	28%	22,925	7,700	-1,842	-13,725	791
EXHIBIT	10-14	36	10	28%	15,500	7,828	-2,414	-26,825	431
EXHIBIT	10-15	118	29	25%	14,125	3,082	-846	-24,925	120
EXHIBIT	11-2	34	8	24%	21,100	6,363	-1,146	-15,850	621
EXHIBIT	11-3	33	8	24%	15,475	6,363	-1,417	-21,475	469
EXHIBIT	11-4	66	20	30%	-3,800	1,985	-946	-16,125	-58
EXHIBIT	11-5	55	18	33%	-9,650	2,712	-1,580	-26,625	-175
EXHIBIT	11-6	61	19	31%	-8,850	2,262	-1,234	-16,400	-145
EXHIBIT	11-7	114	93	82%	-3,250	439	-2,100	-11,050	-29
EXHIBIT	11-8	90	62	69%	-450	939	-2,095	-18,150	-5
EXHIBIT	11-9	65	27	42%	-13,825	2,404	-2,072	-28,225	-213
EXHIBIT	11-10	52	12	23%	-25,675	4,556	-2,009	-31,450	-494
EXHIBIT	11-11	43	10	23%	4,475	6,935	-1,966	-13,775	104
EXHIBIT	11-12	51	13	25%	-9,100	5,067	-1,973	-30,000	-178
EXHIBIT	11-13	40	10	25%	14,525	8,435	-2,328	-20,300	363
EXHIBIT	11-14	101	56	55%	6,775	1,221	-1,368	-18,325	67
EXHIBIT	11-15	35	10	29%	8,800	5,688	-1,923	-17,975	251
EXHIBIT	11-16	118	24	20%	3,425	2,844	-690	-25,925	29
AVERAGE		58	20	34%	-378	5,907	-1,981	-27,971	-6

EXHIBIT 12-6   Performance Report, Summary of Performance for All T-Bond Systems

		Closed Trades	Profitable Trades	Percent Profitable	Total Profit or Loss	Average Profitable Trade	Average Losing Trade	Maximum Drawdown	Average Trade
EXHIBIT	8-2	68	27	40%	22,790	3,055	-1,455	-10,594	335
EXHIBIT	8-4	56	21	37%	16,440	3,404	-1,572	-15,619	294
EXHIBIT	8-6	97	40	41%	480	2,274	-1,587	-16,873	5
EXHIBIT	8-7	83	32	39%	5,510	2,750	-1,617	-15,223	66
EXHIBIT	8-8	34	12	35%	18,410	4,976	-1,877	-10,455	541
EXHIBIT	8-9	222	98	44%	12,600	1,348	-964	-24,064	57
EXHIBIT	8-10	7	4	57%	33,831	10,064	-2,142	-2,600	4,833
EXHIBIT	9-1	158	60	38%	44,730	2,055	-801	-10,891	283
EXHIBIT	9-2	99	27	27%	10,100	3,246	-1,077	-28,388	102
EXHIBIT	9-4	124	56	45%	30,210	1,675	-934	-20,278	244
EXHIBIT	9-5	70	23	33%	38,410	3,346	-819	-13,784	549
EXHIBIT	9-6	161	49	30%	80	2,185	-955	-31,680	1
EXHIBIT	9-7	78	31	40%	50,600	3,086	-959	-14,604	649
EXHIBIT	9-8	58	21	36%	15,250	3,855	-1,776	-20,218	263
EXHIBIT	9-9	27	8	30%	19,060	8,150	-2,427	-21,311	706
EXHIBIT	9-13	42	20	48%	15,081	3,728	-2,704	-15,694	359
EXHIBIT	9-14	35	14	40%	-8,875	3,302	-2,624	-16,894	-254
EXHIBIT	9-15	45	19	42%	-21,781	2,505	-2,669	-31,206	-484
EXHIBIT	9-16	35	16	46%	-12,000	2,357	-2,616	-25,063	-343
EXHIBIT	9-17	7	3	43%	2,581	4,452	-2,694	-6,750	369
EXHIBIT	9-18	6	2	33%	-3,787	3,494	-2,694	-7,800	-631
EXHIBIT	9-20	37	19	51%	18,206	3,431	-2,610	-14,900	492
EXHIBIT	9-21	54	27	50%	-2,088	2,550	-2,628	-15,600	-39
EXHIBIT	9-22	35	18	51%	22,125	3,344	-2,240	-11,769	632
EXHIBIT	9-23	58	22	38%	-21,488	2,704	-2,249	-31,806	-370
EXHIBIT	9-24	12	4	33%	19,831	10,213	-2,627	-7,800	1,653
EXHIBIT	9-25	10	4	40%	10,281	6,619	-2,699	-5,419	1,028
EXHIBIT	9-26	3	2	67%	54,638	27,447	-256	-256	18,213
EXHIBIT	9-28	193	90	47%	41,290	1,569	-970	-13,418	214
EXHIBIT	9-30	46	15	33%	-13,131	3,262	-2,002	-38,581	-285
EXHIBIT	9-31	84	28	33%	-5,619	2,873	-1,537	-30,337	-67
EXHIBIT	9-32	39	12	31%	17,788	5,874	-1,952	-13,444	456
EXHIBIT	9-33	44	12	27%	20,475	6,395	-1,758	-14,419	465
EXHIBIT	9-34	18	7	39%	18,481	5,663	-1,924	-13,244	1,027
EXHIBIT	9-35	41	11	27%	13,181	6,639	-1,995	-16,256	321
EXHIBIT	9-36	18	6	33%	3,388	5,041	-2,238	-13,300	188
EXHIBIT	10-2	53	10	19%	22,331	5,834	-837	-10,131	421
EXHIBIT	10-3	42	11	26%	16,737	6,624	-1,811	-15,413	399
EXHIBIT	10-4	51	10	20%	21,181	5,991	-945	-13,388	415
EXHIBIT	10-5	41	11	27%	17,119	6,639	-1,864	-15,663	418
EXHIBIT	10-6	41	11	27%	16,056	6,639	-1,899	-15,663	392
EXHIBIT	10-7	50	11	22%	18,500	6,173	-1,267	-14,919	370
EXHIBIT	10-8	57	8	14%	15,331	6,232	-705	-12,925	269
EXHIBIT	10-9	58	8	14%	24,012	6,837	-614	-11,725	414
EXHIBIT	10-10	50	11	22%	25,031	6,173	-1,099	-9,463	501
EXHIBIT	10-11	41	11	27%	20,431	6,639	-1,753	-13,663	498
EXHIBIT	10-12	41	11	27%	13,181	6,639	-1,995	-16,256	321
EXHIBIT	10-13	50	11	22%	21,031	5,613	-1,044	-10,919	421
EXHIBIT	10-14	47	14	30%	14,737	5,412	-1,850	-16,769	314
EXHIBIT	10-15	100	28	28%	28,406	3,154	-832	-17,075	284
EXHIBIT	11-2	45	10	22%	28,625	6,962	-1,171	-12,831	636
EXHIBIT	11-3	44	10	23%	15,881	6,962	-1,581	-17,925	361
EXHIBIT	11-4	75	30	40%	-8,469	1,435	-1,145	-18,563	-113
EXHIBIT	11-5	55	16	29%	12,312	4,156	-1,389	-14,119	224
EXHIBIT	11-6	74	27	36%	-15,275	1,437	-1,151	-22,181	-206
EXHIBIT	11-7	131	107	82%	4,650	520	-2,126	-14,163	35
EXHIBIT	11-8	104	75	72%	13,569	1,010	-2,144	-13,419	130
EXHIBIT	11-9	74	33	45%	-369	2,313	-1,871	-20,075	-5
EXHIBIT	11-10	59	19	32%	15,850	4,490	-1,737	-19,844	269
EXHIBIT	11-11	46	13	28%	30,556	6,749	-1,733	-16,544	664
EXHIBIT	11-12	59	21	36%	4,444	3,385	-1,754	-21,375	75
EXHIBIT	11-13	49	16	33%	9,944	4,507	-1,884	-19,156	203
EXHIBIT	11-14	124	61	49%	-4,556	893	-937	-15,181	-37
EXHIBIT	11-15	60	19	32%	8,781	4,346	-1,800	-18,644	146
EXHIBIT	11-16	101	26	26%	34,619	3,369	-706	-14,169	343
AVERAGE		62	23	37%	14,027	4,709	-1,666	-16,195	226

EXHIBIT 12-7   Performance Report, Summary of Performance for All Eurodollar Systems

	Closed Trades	Profitable Trades	Percent Profitable	Total Profit or Loss	Average Profitable Trade	Average Losing Trade	Maximum Drawdown	Average Trade
EXHIBIT 8-2	64	25	39%	9,850	1,486	-700	-8,500	154
EXHIBIT 8-4	58	22	38%	14,775	1,794	-686	-7,425	255
EXHIBIT 8-6	87	34	39%	1,675	1,174	-722	-8,575	19
EXHIBIT 8-7	81	33	41%	-4,800	1,078	-841	-12,675	-59
EXHIBIT 8-8	30	12	40%	16,025	2,425	-726	-5,775	534
EXHIBIT 8-9	109	45	41%	-13,221	815	-779	-21,226	-121
EXHIBIT 8-10	13	6	46%	4,675	2,887	-1,807	-7,025	360
EXHIBIT 9-1	134	48	36%	21,925	1,226	-429	-8,850	164
EXHIBIT 9-2	77	30	39%	24,325	1,538	-464	-6,950	316
EXHIBIT 9-4	109	33	30%	11,125	1,378	-452	-10,425	102
EXHIBIT 9-5	49	24	49%	26,975	1,777	-627	-3,925	551
EXHIBIT 9-6	158	47	30%	1,150	1,078	-446	-18,650	7
EXHIBIT 9-7	86	29	34%	4,050	1,041	-459	-16,275	47
EXHIBIT 9-8	55	18	33%	18,825	2,497	-706	-11,075	342
EXHIBIT 9-9	21	10	48%	23,775	3,915	-1,398	-10,275	1,132
EXHIBIT 9-13	33	15	45%	-26,825	935	-2,269	-26,825	-813
EXHIBIT 9-14	25	10	40%	-19,800	1,260	-2,160	-21,825	-792
EXHIBIT 9-15	35	18	51%	-17,525	1,056	-2,149	-22,525	-501
EXHIBIT 9-16	22	11	50%	-4,300	1,650	-2,041	-10,725	-195
EXHIBIT 9-17	6	4	67%	4,025	2,325	-2,637	-2,675	671
EXHIBIT 9-18	5	2	40%	13,550	10,725	-2,633	-5,225	2,710
EXHIBIT 9-20	33	17	52%	-13,550	1,135	-2,053	-15,925	-411
EXHIBIT 9-21	36	16	44%	-26,475	802	-1,965	-27,975	-735
EXHIBIT 9-22	35	16	46%	-20,275	1,019	-1,925	-23,400	-579
EXHIBIT 9-23	37	20	54%	-12,425	901	-1,791	-18,625	-336
EXHIBIT 9-24	8	3	38%	-1,775	2,092	-1,610	-5,200	-222
EXHIBIT 9-25	6	2	33%	5,300	6,625	-1,988	-5,200	883
EXHIBIT 9-26	2	2	100%	7,125	3,562	0	0	3,562
EXHIBIT 9-28	189	78	41%	17,375	811	-415	-8,542	92
EXHIBIT 9-30	34	15	44%	6,325	1,977	-1,228	-9,700	186
EXHIBIT 9-31	69	36	52%	27,800	1,432	-720	-3,325	403
EXHIBIT 9-32	27	13	48%	7,675	2,308	-1,595	-5,475	284
EXHIBIT 9-33	37	14	38%	24,600	2,846	-663	-4,925	665
EXHIBIT 9-34	16	8	50%	9,100	2,816	-1,678	-5,300	569
EXHIBIT 9-35	31	14	45%	29,000	2,900	-682	-3,975	935
EXHIBIT 9-36	15	7	47%	8,500	3,132	-1,678	-5,300	567
EXHIBIT 10-2	54	10	19%	13,167	3,142	-415	-6,245	244
EXHIBIT 10-3	34	14	41%	23,825	2,718	-711	-5,625	701
EXHIBIT 10-4	48	12	25%	16,650	2,773	-462	-4,750	347
EXHIBIT 10-5	32	14	44%	29,475	2,900	-618	-3,900	921
EXHIBIT 10-6	32	14	44%	28,550	2,900	-669	-4,825	892
EXHIBIT 10-7	44	13	30%	19,000	2,504	-437	-4,075	432
EXHIBIT 10-8	55	9	16%	14,150	3,194	-317	-6,450	257
EXHIBIT 10-9	41	13	32%	19,700	2,662	-532	-4,675	480
EXHIBIT 10-10	35	14	40%	21,000	2,562	-708	-5,025	600
EXHIBIT 10-11	31	14	45%	29,000	2,900	-682	-3,975	935
EXHIBIT 10-12	35	14	40%	21,000	2,562	-708	-5,025	600
EXHIBIT 10-13	46	13	28%	15,300	2,571	-549	-5,900	333
EXHIBIT 10-14	37	14	38%	23,425	2,925	-762	-6,550	633
EXHIBIT 10-15	77	29	38%	23,550	1,528	-433	-5,000	306
EXHIBIT 11-2	31	14	45%	30,625	2,900	-587	-3,975	988
EXHIBIT 11-3	31	14	45%	29,000	2,900	-682	-3,975	935
EXHIBIT 11-4	44	20	45%	17,275	1,739	-729	-4,975	393
EXHIBIT 11-5	32	15	47%	28,700	2,647	-647	-3,975	897
EXHIBIT 11-6	64	33	52%	14,825	900	-480	-4,000	232
EXHIBIT 11-7	102	80	78%	10,775	446	-1,133	-3,700	106
EXHIBIT 11-8	73	46	63%	16,100	939	-1,003	-5,075	221
EXHIBIT 11-9	48	22	46%	19,900	1,874	-820	-4,550	415
EXHIBIT 11-10	37	17	46%	23,525	2,290	-770	-4,550	636
EXHIBIT 11-11	33	16	48%	28,875	2,530	-682	-3,975	875
EXHIBIT 11-12	47	25	53%	26,900	1,775	-794	-4,050	572
EXHIBIT 11-13	39	17	44%	27,200	2,562	-743	-4,825	697
EXHIBIT 11-14	143	76	53%	7,550	332	-263	-4,650	53
EXHIBIT 11-15	53	25	47%	22,575	1,695	-707	-4,075	426
EXHIBIT 11-16	77	28	36%	23,575	1,580	-422	-5,000	306
AVERAGE	51	21	42%	12,365	2,206	-978	-8,118	245

EXHIBIT 12-8   Performance Report, Summary of Performance for All Swiss Franc Systems

		Closed Trades	Profitable Trades	Percent Profitable	Total Profit or Loss	Average Profitable Trade	Average Losing Trade	Maximum Drawdown	Average Trade
EXHIBIT	8-2	68	26	38%	2,588	2,136	-1,260	-12,475	38
EXHIBIT	8-4	58	22	38%	4,763	2,088	-1,144	-12,050	82
EXHIBIT	8-6	80	31	39%	26,950	2,352	-938	-7,688	337
EXHIBIT	8-7	88	35	40%	9,713	1,874	-1,054	-13,888	110
EXHIBIT	8-8	36	17	47%	5,875	2,611	-2,027	-11,125	163
EXHIBIT	8-9	114	48	42%	27,363	1,742	-852	-6,916	240
EXHIBIT	8-10	14	6	43%	7,725	4,685	-2,548	-6,112	552
EXHIBIT	9-1	165	59	36%	1,938	1,358	-738	-11,412	12
EXHIBIT	9-2	91	26	29%	-3,100	1,819	-775	-13,650	-34
EXHIBIT	9-4	116	41	35%	-1,838	1,581	-889	-14,138	-16
EXHIBIT	9-5	59	24	41%	20,000	2,265	-982	-9,113	339
EXHIBIT	9-6	149	50	34%	1,713	1,561	-771	-15,938	11
EXHIBIT	9-7	102	37	36%	3,213	1,591	-856	-17,213	32
EXHIBIT	9-8	62	21	34%	-3,388	2,420	-1,322	-16,188	-55
EXHIBIT	9-9	31	13	42%	-9,750	2,788	-2,556	-19,338	-315
EXHIBIT	9-13	38	18	47%	3,638	2,926	-2,452	-9,800	96
EXHIBIT	9-14	32	16	50%	537	2,715	-2,681	-11,038	17
EXHIBIT	9-15	37	17	46%	-4,588	2,775	-2,588	-8,800	-124
EXHIBIT	9-16	33	16	48%	-1,287	2,559	-2,484	-10,962	-39
EXHIBIT	9-17	6	1	17%	-12,850	213	-2,613	-13,063	-2,142
EXHIBIT	9-18	5	1	20%	-10,188	213	-2,600	-10,400	-2,038
EXHIBIT	9-20	38	19	50%	-5,975	2,334	-2,648	-18,350	-157
EXHIBIT	9-21	46	24	52%	-1,025	2,135	-2,376	-19,625	-22
EXHIBIT	9-22	40	16	40%	-34,638	1,620	-2,523	-36,450	-866
EXHIBIT	9-23	47	21	45%	-10,000	2,074	-2,060	-17,562	-213
EXHIBIT	9-24	8	3	38%	9,138	7,417	-2,623	-10,513	1,142
EXHIBIT	9-25	4	0	0%	-10,463	0	-2,616	-10,463	-2,616
EXHIBIT	9-26	7	2	29%	-5,437	3,781	-2,600	-13,000	-777
EXHIBIT	9-28	216	88	41%	20,600	1,196	-661	-11,640	95
EXHIBIT	9-30	30	14	47%	28,812	3,803	-1,527	-5,200	960
EXHIBIT	9-31	74	32	43%	19,975	2,100	-1,125	-8,937	270
EXHIBIT	9-32	48	16	33%	-12,625	2,766	-1,778	-19,962	-263
EXHIBIT	9-33	43	18	42%	5,625	2,525	-1,593	-10,450	131
EXHIBIT	9-34	15	7	47%	21,338	6,236	-2,789	-5,537	1,423
EXHIBIT	9-35	37	18	49%	9,175	2,451	-1,839	-8,800	248
EXHIBIT	9-36	15	7	47%	21,338	6,236	-2,789	-5,537	1,423
EXHIBIT	10-2	52	14	27%	9,340	2,575	-703	-7,813	180
EXHIBIT	10-3	39	18	46%	8,625	2,427	-1,670	-8,494	221
EXHIBIT	10-4	56	14	25%	3,900	2,460	-727	-13,125	70
EXHIBIT	10-5	38	17	45%	10,613	2,574	-1,578	-7,300	279
EXHIBIT	10-6	37	18	49%	10,075	2,451	-1,792	-8,550	272
EXHIBIT	10-7	48	15	31%	3,650	2,446	-1,001	-11,200	76
EXHIBIT	10-8	56	12	21%	4,525	2,786	-657	-7,800	81
EXHIBIT	10-9	56	13	23%	5,100	2,638	-679	-11,875	91
EXHIBIT	10-10	44	17	39%	10,713	2,387	-1,106	-9,287	243
EXHIBIT	10-11	37	18	49%	11,825	2,451	-1,700	-7,812	320
EXHIBIT	10-12	37	18	49%	11,825	2,451	-1,700	-7,812	320
EXHIBIT	10-13	49	15	31%	1,700	2,478	-1,043	-10,425	35
EXHIBIT	10-14	40	20	50%	12,438	2,409	-1,787	-6,712	311
EXHIBIT	10-15	91	24	26%	-2,275	1,881	-708	-9,875	-25
EXHIBIT	11-2	38	17	45%	21,550	2,539	-1,029	-7,462	567
EXHIBIT	11-3	38	17	45%	10,538	2,539	-1,554	-7,462	277
EXHIBIT	11-4	66	28	42%	5,413	1,349	-852	-11,475	82
EXHIBIT	11-5	43	21	49%	24,075	2,477	-1,270	-5,700	560
EXHIBIT	11-6	71	26	37%	-475	1,277	-749	-10,662	-7
EXHIBIT	11-7	119	96	81%	3,188	463	-1,795	-4,975	27
EXHIBIT	11-8	93	65	70%	13,575	933	-1,682	-7,150	146
EXHIBIT	11-9	58	29	50%	11,250	2,078	-1,690	-9,225	194
EXHIBIT	11-10	45	19	42%	14,213	3,116	-1,730	-9,475	316
EXHIBIT	11-11	37	18	49%	11,825	2,451	-1,700	-7,812	320
EXHIBIT	11-12	53	24	45%	5,763	2,352	-1,748	-9,487	109
EXHIBIT	11-13	44	19	43%	14,438	2,987	-1,693	-6,912	328
EXHIBIT	11-14	127	71	56%	6,125	632	-692	-9,775	48
EXHIBIT	11-15	40	19	48%	13,850	2,551	-1,648	-8,350	346
EXHIBIT	11-16	91	20	22%	6,525	2,125	-507	-5,162	72
AVERAGE		57	24	41%	5,981	2,388	-1,583	-10,808	105

EXHIBIT 12-9 Performance Report, Summary of Performance for All Japanese Yen Systems

		Closed Trades	Profitable Trades	Percent Profitable	Total Profit or Loss	Average Profitable Trade	Average Losing Trade	Maximum Drawdown	Average Trade
EXHIBIT	8-2	72	24	33%	28,700	2,529	-666	-8,800	399
EXHIBIT	8-4	52	26	50%	34,625	2,241	-910	-4,638	666
EXHIBIT	8-6	81	28	35%	17,525	2,096	-777	-7,687	216
EXHIBIT	8-7	79	30	38%	11,400	1,870	-912	-10,863	144
EXHIBIT	8-8	28	14	50%	36,413	4,063	-1,462	-4,012	1,300
EXHIBIT	8-9	59	18	31%	-10,950	2,513	-1,371	-26,111	-186
EXHIBIT	8-10	12	6	50%	8,413	3,698	-2,296	-7,888	701
EXHIBIT	9-1	200	53	26%	20,775	1,446	-380	-11,500	104
EXHIBIT	9-2	101	31	31%	18,700	1,855	-554	-7,763	185
EXHIBIT	9-4	130	47	36%	21,475	1,356	-509	-8,687	165
EXHIBIT	9-5	69	27	39%	15,625	1,874	-833	-8,087	226
EXHIBIT	9-6	167	58	35%	21,013	1,348	-524	-13,088	126
EXHIBIT	9-7	98	29	30%	16,900	2,081	-630	-13,050	172
EXHIBIT	9-8	54	18	33%	24,575	3,078	-857	-10,288	455
EXHIBIT	9-9	29	9	31%	5,600	4,150	-1,587	-13,713	193
EXHIBIT	9-13	30	10	33%	-30,937	2,136	-2,615	-35,262	-1,031
EXHIBIT	9-14	26	10	38%	-15,550	2,510	-2,541	-16,500	-598
EXHIBIT	9-15	27	11	41%	-7,087	2,663	-2,273	-15,775	-262
EXHIBIT	9-16	22	12	55%	10,875	2,836	-2,316	-5,450	494
EXHIBIT	9-17	9	5	56%	12,763	4,775	-2,778	-8,025	1,418
EXHIBIT	9-18	5	3	60%	9,588	5,000	-2,706	-5,350	1,918
EXHIBIT	9-20	32	14	44%	-21,937	1,545	-2,420	-25,575	-686
EXHIBIT	9-21	34	13	38%	-27,075	1,550	-2,249	-30,750	-796
EXHIBIT	9-22	32	15	47%	-8,300	1,983	-2,238	-17,400	-259
EXHIBIT	9-23	32	16	50%	1,550	2,052	-1,955	-12,688	48
EXHIBIT	9-24	7	4	57%	8,363	4,056	-2,621	-5,262	1,195
EXHIBIT	9-25	3	1	33%	14,088	19,313	-2,612	-2,625	4,696
EXHIBIT	9-26	2	0	0%	-5,800	0	-2,900	-5,800	-2,900
EXHIBIT	9-28	221	71	32%	12,925	1,187	-476	-13,118	58
EXHIBIT	9-30	26	11	42%	25,625	4,424	-1,536	-17,075	986
EXHIBIT	9-31	77	31	40%	34,963	2,288	-782	-4,937	454
EXHIBIT	9-32	65	19	29%	-27,937	1,574	-1,258	-29,887	-430
EXHIBIT	9-33	38	16	42%	24,563	3,144	-1,170	-4,138	646
EXHIBIT	9-34	21	7	33%	7,525	4,886	-1,905	-9,512	358
EXHIBIT	9-35	34	14	41%	20,225	3,154	-1,196	-4,038	595
EXHIBIT	9-36	21	7	33%	7,525	4,886	-1,905	-9,512	358
EXHIBIT	10-2	52	14	27%	20,000	2,860	-527	-4,138	385
EXHIBIT	10-3	38	14	37%	15,294	3,113	-1,179	-5,606	402
EXHIBIT	10-4	50	13	26%	17,638	3,060	-598	-4,113	353
EXHIBIT	10-5	39	14	36%	15,375	3,069	-1,104	-5,588	394
EXHIBIT	10-6	36	14	39%	18,900	3,114	-1,123	-5,238	525
EXHIBIT	10-7	44	14	32%	22,850	3,091	-681	-4,375	519
EXHIBIT	10-8	51	14	27%	24,413	2,860	-422	-2,512	479
EXHIBIT	10-9	45	14	31%	21,875	3,044	-669	-3,550	486
EXHIBIT	10-10	40	14	35%	18,525	3,141	-979	-4,300	463
EXHIBIT	10-11	34	14	41%	21,125	3,154	-1,151	-4,038	621
EXHIBIT	10-12	34	14	41%	21,125	3,154	-1,151	-4,038	621
EXHIBIT	10-13	46	14	30%	16,538	2,974	-784	-4,212	360
EXHIBIT	10-14	40	14	35%	21,825	3,538	-1,066	-5,731	546
EXHIBIT	10-15	101	31	31%	21,288	1,855	-517	-8,912	211
EXHIBIT	11-2	35	13	37%	21,688	3,286	-956	-4,188	620
EXHIBIT	11-3	34	13	38%	20,775	3,382	-1,104	-4,038	611
EXHIBIT	11-4	56	22	39%	13,700	1,831	-782	-4,112	245
EXHIBIT	11-5	36	14	39%	24,288	3,465	-1,101	-5,013	675
EXHIBIT	11-6	64	25	39%	19,225	1,765	-638	-5,713	300
EXHIBIT	11-7	119	94	79%	9,313	482	-1,440	-4,912	78
EXHIBIT	11-8	85	58	68%	19,613	999	-1,420	-4,650	231
EXHIBIT	11-9	55	25	45%	23,663	2,378	-1,193	-5,588	430
EXHIBIT	11-10	41	16	39%	23,525	3,357	-1,208	-4,825	574
EXHIBIT	11-11	35	15	43%	20,450	2,898	-1,151	-4,038	584
EXHIBIT	11-12	52	26	50%	21,975	2,097	-1,252	-4,513	423
EXHIBIT	11-13	43	15	35%	17,288	3,149	-1,070	-6,788	402
EXHIBIT	11-14	144	77	53%	-6,550	462	-629	-9,787	-45
EXHIBIT	11-15	63	31	49%	17,675	1,567	-966	-5,000	281
EXHIBIT	11-16	101	31	31%	22,513	1,855	-500	-8,687	223
AVERAGE		56	21	39%	13,271	2,879	-1,294	-8,970	239

179

EXHIBIT 12-10   Performance Report, Summary of Performance for All Gold Systems

		Closed Trades	Profitable Trades	Percent Profitable	Total Profit or Loss	Average Pro-fitable Trade	Average Losing Trade	Maximum Drawdown	Average Trade
EXHIBIT	8-2	68	22	32%	9,760	2,296	-886	-13,470	144
EXHIBIT	8-4	58	19	33%	13,920	2,415	-820	-11,520	240
EXHIBIT	8-6	89	32	36%	7,440	1,619	-778	-9,550	84
EXHIBIT	8-7	84	38	45%	5,500	1,416	-1,050	-12,800	65
EXHIBIT	8-8	38	13	34%	920	2,377	-1,199	-15,480	24
EXHIBIT	8-9	233	87	37%	-4,680	992	-623	-17,305	-20
EXHIBIT	8-10	7	3	43%	11,690	7,507	-2,708	-8,230	1,670
EXHIBIT	9-1	203	52	26%	-11,240	1,349	-539	-25,060	-55
EXHIBIT	9-2	116	32	28%	-8,150	1,441	-646	-28,050	-70
EXHIBIT	9-4	132	37	28%	-11,580	1,339	-644	-22,770	-88
EXHIBIT	9-5	77	21	27%	630	1,807	-666	-18,230	8
EXHIBIT	9-6	202	64	32%	-31,970	978	-685	-41,900	-158
EXHIBIT	9-7	127	45	35%	-16,870	1,014	-762	-19,940	-133
EXHIBIT	9-8	68	19	28%	-10,940	2,017	-1,005	-19,580	-161
EXHIBIT	9-9	34	9	26%	2,110	3,592	-1,209	-11,330	62
EXHIBIT	9-13	38	23	61%	4,310	2,010	-2,795	-10,710	113
EXHIBIT	9-14	31	19	61%	5,270	2,173	-3,001	-11,770	170
EXHIBIT	9-15	38	22	58%	-10,390	1,334	-2,484	-18,540	-273
EXHIBIT	9-16	29	15	52%	-1,950	1,847	-2,118	-8,440	-67
EXHIBIT	9-17	12	5	42%	-5,850	2,710	-2,771	-13,280	-488
EXHIBIT	9-18	8	3	38%	180	4,393	-2,600	-10,400	23
EXHIBIT	9-20	14	7	50%	4,790	3,391	-2,707	-13,560	342
EXHIBIT	9-21	33	18	55%	13,670	2,782	-2,427	-9,290	414
EXHIBIT	9-22	15	6	40%	-900	3,548	-2,466	-15,020	-60
EXHIBIT	9-23	32	16	50%	3,700	2,466	-2,234	-19,120	116
EXHIBIT	9-24	7	1	14%	-7,010	8,610	-2,603	-13,020	-1,001
EXHIBIT	9-25	8	3	38%	-8,410	1,530	-2,600	-8,620	-1,051
EXHIBIT	9-26	3	2	67%	7,340	4,970	-2,600	-2,600	2,447
EXHIBIT	9-28	232	82	35%	1,759	1,079	-578	-16,770	8
EXHIBIT	9-30	37	16	43%	-14,740	1,779	-2,058	-14,960	-398
EXHIBIT	9-31	57	26	46%	27,600	2,221	-973	-8,810	484
EXHIBIT	9-32	55	24	44%	3,960	1,700	-1,188	-7,810	72
EXHIBIT	9-33	32	11	34%	-390	2,658	-1,411	-15,420	-12
EXHIBIT	9-34	22	7	32%	-12,450	1,947	-1,739	-12,530	-566
EXHIBIT	9-35	29	10	34%	-7,920	2,576	-1,773	-16,890	-273
EXHIBIT	9-36	22	6	27%	-17,150	1,942	-1,800	-17,150	-780
EXHIBIT	10-2	45	7	16%	-2,639	2,593	-547	-10,150	-59
EXHIBIT	10-3	32	10	31%	-5,520	2,226	-1,263	-12,220	-172
EXHIBIT	10-4	43	6	14%	-5,610	3,217	-673	-12,090	-130
EXHIBIT	10-5	34	10	29%	-6,920	2,182	-1,198	-12,050	-204
EXHIBIT	10-6	31	10	32%	-4,510	2,532	-1,420	-12,500	-145
EXHIBIT	10-7	40	9	23%	-3,000	1,924	-655	-7,500	-75
EXHIBIT	10-8	48	5	10%	-6,440	2,438	-433	-8,980	-134
EXHIBIT	10-9	44	7	16%	-7,390	2,454	-664	-11,370	-168
EXHIBIT	10-10	31	9	29%	4,050	2,850	-982	-7,960	131
EXHIBIT	10-11	29	10	34%	-3,380	2,576	-1,534	-12,890	-117
EXHIBIT	10-12	29	10	34%	-3,380	2,576	-1,534	-12,890	-117
EXHIBIT	10-13	39	9	23%	990	2,412	-691	-7,720	25
EXHIBIT	10-14	43	13	30%	-16,860	2,169	-1,502	-25,750	-392
EXHIBIT	10-15	116	31	27%	-4,710	1,442	-581	-23,850	-41
EXHIBIT	11-2	31	10	32%	-3,440	2,512	-1,360	-12,310	-111
EXHIBIT	11-3	31	10	32%	-6,380	2,512	-1,500	-15,250	-206
EXHIBIT	11-4	51	21	41%	2,340	1,320	-846	-10,960	46
EXHIBIT	11-5	40	13	33%	-8,150	1,905	-1,219	-16,010	-204
EXHIBIT	11-6	54	17	31%	3,150	1,668	-681	-9,160	58
EXHIBIT	11-7	80	63	79%	-50	507	-1,882	-6,370	-1
EXHIBIT	11-8	65	41	63%	-3,650	999	-1,859	-12,890	-56
EXHIBIT	11-9	47	20	43%	-1,570	2,241	-1,718	-14,290	-33
EXHIBIT	11-10	37	13	35%	3,140	3,252	-1,631	-16,390	85
EXHIBIT	11-11	31	10	32%	-2,090	3,261	-1,652	-18,450	-67
EXHIBIT	11-12	43	20	47%	480	2,094	-1,800	-14,640	11
EXHIBIT	11-13	38	11	29%	-6,510	3,199	-1,544	-17,580	-171
EXHIBIT	11-14	85	46	54%	1,180	837	-957	-10,600	14
EXHIBIT	11-15	46	18	39%	-14,760	1,647	-1,586	-21,670	-321
EXHIBIT	11-16	116	28	24%	-3,010	1,455	-497	-21,210	-26
AVERAGE		57	20	35%	-2,503	2,351	-1,439	-14,394	-44

EXHIBIT 12-11   Performance Report, Summary of Performance for All Heating Oil Systems

		Closed Trades	Profitable Trades	Percent Profitable	Total Profit or Loss	Average Profitable Trade	Average Losing Trade	Maximum Drawdown	Average Trade
EXHIBIT	8-2	53	20	38%	2,440	1,827	-1,032	-11,647	46
EXHIBIT	8-4	46	12	26%	-605	3,086	-1,106	-17,535	-13
EXHIBIT	8-6	78	25	32%	-20,294	1,479	-1,079	-26,880	-260
EXHIBIT	8-7	65	31	48%	-2,419	1,351	-1,302	-13,041	-37
EXHIBIT	8-8	26	10	38%	15,847	3,365	-1,111	-6,556	609
EXHIBIT	8-9	233	118	51%	-260	545	-561	-17,192	-1
EXHIBIT	8-10	13	6	46%	10,878	4,038	-1,906	-7,316	837
EXHIBIT	9-1	150	40	27%	-16,666	1,306	-625	-23,528	-111
EXHIBIT	9-2	67	19	28%	7,451	2,168	-702	-17,510	111
EXHIBIT	9-4	100	37	37%	-4,897	1,361	-876	-20,954	-49
EXHIBIT	9-5	51	14	27%	6,527	2,710	-848	-13,310	128
EXHIBIT	9-6	127	42	33%	-16,443	1,128	-750	-22,037	-129
EXHIBIT	9-7	78	26	33%	17	1,639	-818	-19,778	0
EXHIBIT	9-8	53	14	26%	-18,207	2,428	-1,337	-25,922	-344
EXHIBIT	9-9	19	7	37%	16,212	4,458	-1,248	-12,214	853
EXHIBIT	9-13	26	13	50%	-8,316	1,712	-2,352	-12,347	-320
EXHIBIT	9-14	23	14	61%	18,587	2,955	-2,532	-6,526	808
EXHIBIT	9-15	27	13	48%	-17,833	1,231	-2,417	-22,068	-660
EXHIBIT	9-16	22	13	59%	6,313	2,189	-2,460	-11,141	287
EXHIBIT	9-17	5	3	60%	6,258	3,862	-2,664	-5,328	1,252
EXHIBIT	9-18	3	1	33%	2,611	7,939	-2,664	-5,328	870
EXHIBIT	9-20	23	11	48%	-9,894	1,700	-2,383	-19,186	-430
EXHIBIT	9-21	31	16	52%	-15,015	1,352	-2,443	-19,281	-484
EXHIBIT	9-22	25	11	44%	-8,859	1,982	-2,190	-16,232	-354
EXHIBIT	9-23	35	17	49%	-16,428	1,210	-2,056	-20,366	-469
EXHIBIT	9-24	2	1	50%	1,005	3,604	-2,599	-2,599	503
EXHIBIT	9-25	3	1	33%	-2,753	2,701	-2,727	-5,454	-918
EXHIBIT	9-26	4	0	0%	-10,480	0	-2,620	-10,480	-2,620
EXHIBIT	9-28	156	56	36%	-920	1,215	-689	-17,767	-6
EXHIBIT	9-30	46	24	52%	10,394	1,756	-1,443	-8,185	226
EXHIBIT	9-31	70	26	37%	-4,278	1,659	-1,077	-15,363	-61
EXHIBIT	9-32	26	11	42%	9,353	2,447	-1,171	-5,867	360
EXHIBIT	9-33	34	11	32%	2,383	2,898	-1,282	-23,796	70
EXHIBIT	9-34	13	4	31%	-2,648	4,097	-2,115	-13,250	-204
EXHIBIT	9-35	29	9	31%	1,896	2,731	-1,134	-14,699	65
EXHIBIT	9-36	12	3	25%	-4,043	5,167	-2,172	-13,759	-337
EXHIBIT	10-2	40	9	23%	6,473	2,480	-511	-8,549	162
EXHIBIT	10-3	30	9	30%	2,410	2,731	-1,056	-12,947	80
EXHIBIT	10-4	40	9	23%	2,875	2,468	-624	-12,339	72
EXHIBIT	10-5	30	9	30%	1,343	2,731	-1,107	-14,174	45
EXHIBIT	10-6	30	9	30%	1,271	2,731	-1,110	-13,867	42
EXHIBIT	10-7	36	9	25%	4,598	2,490	-660	-9,922	128
EXHIBIT	10-8	41	9	22%	5,115	2,392	-513	-9,197	125
EXHIBIT	10-9	38	9	24%	5,855	2,557	-592	-9,033	154
EXHIBIT	10-10	34	9	26%	-2,472	2,567	-1,023	-16,980	-73
EXHIBIT	10-11	30	9	30%	-172	2,731	-1,179	-14,520	-6
EXHIBIT	10-12	30	9	30%	-172	2,731	-1,179	-14,520	-6
EXHIBIT	10-13	37	9	24%	3,028	2,561	-715	-12,612	82
EXHIBIT	10-14	31	10	32%	2,740	2,492	-1,056	-11,236	88
EXHIBIT	10-15	67	18	27%	4,921	2,125	-680	-16,556	73
EXHIBIT	11-2	31	9	29%	6,705	2,567	-745	-10,282	216
EXHIBIT	11-3	30	9	30%	-172	2,731	-1,179	-14,520	-6
EXHIBIT	11-4	47	21	45%	-1,126	1,140	-964	-11,705	-24
EXHIBIT	11-5	36	10	28%	-5,879	1,926	-967	-16,319	-163
EXHIBIT	11-6	51	25	49%	1,686	942	-841	-6,459	33
EXHIBIT	11-7	86	65	76%	-3,574	486	-1,675	-9,356	-42
EXHIBIT	11-8	66	37	56%	-10,971	961	-1,604	-18,212	-166
EXHIBIT	11-9	45	16	36%	-10,384	2,228	-1,587	-19,577	-231
EXHIBIT	11-10	36	10	28%	-4,361	2,985	-1,316	-16,077	-121
EXHIBIT	11-11	32	9	28%	-5,277	2,665	-1,272	-19,033	-165
EXHIBIT	11-12	42	14	33%	-4,612	2,539	-1,434	-17,934	-110
EXHIBIT	11-13	36	9	25%	3,536	4,179	-1,262	-16,445	98
EXHIBIT	11-14	101	53	52%	-14,091	465	-807	-16,609	-140
EXHIBIT	11-15	41	13	32%	-14,826	1,661	-1,301	-19,033	-362
EXHIBIT	11-16	67	18	27%	9,492	2,125	-587	-13,074	142
AVERAGE		47	17	37%	-1,217	2,349	-1,354	-14,239	-26

181

EXHIBIT 12-12   Performance Report, Summary of Performance for All Soybean Systems

		Closed Trades	Profitable Trades	Percent Profitable	Total Profit or Loss	Average Profitable Trade	Average Losing Trade	Maximum Drawdown	Average Trade
EXHIBIT	8-2	74	25	34%	-7,238	1,491	-908	-20,100	-98
EXHIBIT	8-4	60	22	37%	3,338	1,676	-883	-12,000	56
EXHIBIT	8-6	81	30	37%	-450	1,414	-841	-14,325	-6
EXHIBIT	8-7	76	40	53%	-7,588	1,086	-1,417	-15,700	-100
EXHIBIT	8-8	46	12	26%	-10,475	1,864	-966	-23,638	-228
EXHIBIT	8-9	205	73	36%	-37,896	667	-656	-39,577	-185
EXHIBIT	8-10	9	4	44%	9,975	5,131	-2,110	-6,325	1,108
EXHIBIT	9-1	188	56	30%	-18,038	1,004	-563	-33,050	-96
EXHIBIT	9-2	113	24	21%	-19,938	1,426	-608	-39,338	-176
EXHIBIT	9-4	119	40	34%	-14,513	1,101	-741	-25,213	-122
EXHIBIT	9-5	77	28	36%	-10,163	1,059	-813	-22,500	-132
EXHIBIT	9-6	193	58	30%	-5,988	1,003	-475	-25,338	-31
EXHIBIT	9-7	109	25	23%	-17,450	1,424	-632	-32,213	-160
EXHIBIT	9-8	71	24	34%	-5,700	1,551	-913	-21,238	-80
EXHIBIT	9-9	39	13	33%	-12,263	1,976	-1,460	-23,625	-314
EXHIBIT	9-13	32	21	66%	3,963	1,489	-2,483	-7,963	124
EXHIBIT	9-14	25	16	64%	11,638	2,195	-2,610	-7,688	466
EXHIBIT	9-15	33	18	55%	-14,163	1,081	-2,241	-18,600	-429
EXHIBIT	9-16	23	13	57%	4,438	2,144	-2,344	-11,600	193
EXHIBIT	9-17	10	4	40%	-8,125	2,016	-2,698	-10,988	-813
EXHIBIT	9-18	8	1	13%	-16,950	1,800	-2,679	-18,750	-2,119
EXHIBIT	9-20	29	19	66%	6,075	1,616	-2,463	-8,388	209
EXHIBIT	9-21	42	26	62%	14,963	1,671	-1,780	-9,313	356
EXHIBIT	9-22	29	14	48%	-2,000	1,819	-1,831	-10,725	-69
EXHIBIT	9-23	45	24	53%	-7,850	1,124	-1,659	-11,025	-174
EXHIBIT	9-24	8	3	38%	-5,525	2,496	-2,603	-13,013	-691
EXHIBIT	9-25	5	3	60%	7,275	4,158	-2,600	-2,600	1,455
EXHIBIT	9-26	2	2	100%	7,263	3,631	0	0	3,631
EXHIBIT	9-28	197	80	41%	13,600	855	-468	-15,418	69
EXHIBIT	9-30	35	14	40%	-13,400	1,071	-1,352	-18,788	-383
EXHIBIT	9-31	84	25	30%	-32,975	1,353	-1,132	-40,050	-393
EXHIBIT	9-32	43	13	30%	3,013	2,939	-1,173	-12,788	70
EXHIBIT	9-33	41	13	32%	-738	1,890	-904	-12,550	-18
EXHIBIT	9-34	16	4	25%	-13,325	2,100	-1,810	-16,388	-833
EXHIBIT	9-35	37	11	30%	-75	2,282	-968	-11,350	-2
EXHIBIT	9-36	13	4	31%	-7,213	2,347	-1,844	-11,888	-555
EXHIBIT	10-2	57	8	14%	-6,850	2,030	-471	-10,521	-120
EXHIBIT	10-3	40	11	28%	1,306	2,239	-804	-9,900	33
EXHIBIT	10-4	55	8	15%	-7,475	2,264	-544	-12,800	-136
EXHIBIT	10-5	40	11	28%	550	2,239	-830	-10,288	14
EXHIBIT	10-6	40	11	28%	-1,200	2,239	-891	-11,075	-30
EXHIBIT	10-7	52	11	21%	-788	1,927	-536	-7,050	-15
EXHIBIT	10-8	59	8	14%	-6,213	1,923	-424	-11,738	-105
EXHIBIT	10-9	49	8	16%	-3,038	2,495	-561	-10,250	-62
EXHIBIT	10-10	43	10	23%	-8,563	2,036	-877	-15,875	-199
EXHIBIT	10-11	38	11	29%	-1,663	2,323	-1,008	-12,288	-44
EXHIBIT	10-12	39	11	28%	-988	2,323	-948	-11,188	-25
EXHIBIT	10-13	51	9	18%	-7,338	2,032	-610	-12,825	-144
EXHIBIT	10-14	43	13	30%	2,438	2,248	-893	-12,138	57
EXHIBIT	10-15	112	24	21%	-13,650	1,426	-544	-33,050	-122
EXHIBIT	11-2	38	11	29%	3,388	2,323	-821	-12,288	89
EXHIBIT	11-3	38	11	29%	-1,725	2,323	-1,010	-12,288	-45
EXHIBIT	11-4	57	15	26%	-15,738	1,173	-794	-19,838	-276
EXHIBIT	11-5	45	13	29%	-7,425	2,086	-1,079	-18,038	-165
EXHIBIT	11-6	64	25	39%	-3,738	957	-709	-12,800	-58
EXHIBIT	11-7	88	60	68%	-9,313	494	-1,392	-18,113	-106
EXHIBIT	11-8	71	38	54%	-7,550	921	-1,290	-17,900	-106
EXHIBIT	11-9	54	18	33%	-6,088	2,060	-1,199	-16,450	-113
EXHIBIT	11-10	44	12	27%	-3,550	2,677	-1,115	-14,200	-81
EXHIBIT	11-11	41	11	27%	-4,788	2,670	-1,139	-15,413	-117
EXHIBIT	11-12	50	21	42%	-2,225	1,518	-1,176	-11,725	-45
EXHIBIT	11-13	45	13	29%	-875	2,388	-998	-11,075	-19
EXHIBIT	11-14	102	51	50%	-9,525	567	-753	-17,288	-93
EXHIBIT	11-15	46	14	30%	-4,488	2,280	-1,138	-13,413	-98
EXHIBIT	11-16	112	24	21%	-11,313	1,426	-517	-31,000	-101
AVERAGE		59	20	34%	-5,276	1,870	-1,180	-16,105	-90

EXHIBIT 12-13 Performance Report, Summary of Performance for All Sugar Systems

		Closed Trades	Profitable Trades	Percent Profitable	Total Profit or Loss	Average Profitable Trade	Average Losing Trade	Maximum Drawdown	Average Trade
EXHIBIT	8-2	67	20	30%	-3,024	1,161	-557	-5,062	-45
EXHIBIT	8-4	59	20	34%	-3,147	1,108	-648	-6,328	-53
EXHIBIT	8-6	80	25	31%	-4,682	880	-484	-7,403	-59
EXHIBIT	8-7	84	34	40%	-6,160	699	-598	-9,520	-73
EXHIBIT	8-8	30	13	43%	3,909	1,478	-899	-5,690	130
EXHIBIT	8-9	338	133	39%	-14,605	275	-249	-14,602	-43
EXHIBIT	8-10	10	7	70%	11,387	2,188	-1,310	-1,993	1,139
EXHIBIT	9-1	204	46	23%	-25,144	619	-338	-25,872	-123
EXHIBIT	9-2	95	20	21%	-2,990	1,353	-400	-8,075	-31
EXHIBIT	9-4	126	41	33%	2,901	733	-318	-7,269	23
EXHIBIT	9-5	47	15	32%	8,702	1,573	-464	-4,278	185
EXHIBIT	9-6	172	50	29%	-17,853	550	-371	-20,776	-104
EXHIBIT	9-7	110	29	26%	-11,458	748	-408	-16,251	-104
EXHIBIT	9-8	59	25	42%	5,253	1,023	-596	-4,267	89
EXHIBIT	9-9	25	10	40%	11,659	2,195	-685	-3,405	466
EXHIBIT	9-13	25	15	60%	-10,082	750	-2,133	-15,870	-403
EXHIBIT	9-14	17	7	41%	-14,748	1,098	-2,244	-20,095	-868
EXHIBIT	9-15	25	13	52%	-8,593	890	-1,680	-12,288	-344
EXHIBIT	9-16	17	9	53%	-10,178	873	-2,255	-12,773	-599
EXHIBIT	9-17	9	5	56%	-5,962	408	-2,001	-7,838	-662
EXHIBIT	9-18	6	3	50%	789	1,207	-944	-2,598	131
EXHIBIT	9-20	24	14	58%	-4,819	1,035	-1,931	-12,321	-201
EXHIBIT	9-21	29	17	59%	-7,066	836	-1,773	-13,072	-244
EXHIBIT	9-22	25	13	52%	-6,319	1,128	-1,748	-12,485	-253
EXHIBIT	9-23	29	15	52%	-7,615	921	-1,531	-11,700	-263
EXHIBIT	9-24	9	4	44%	-7,665	1,143	-2,448	-10,792	-852
EXHIBIT	9-25	4	1	25%	-5,306	2,487	-2,598	-5,306	-1,326
EXHIBIT	9-26	0							
EXHIBIT	9-28	207	69	33%	-930	552	-283	-5,661	-4
EXHIBIT	9-30	50	22	44%	-10,376	793	-994	-13,931	-208
EXHIBIT	9-31	67	23	34%	-9,791	1,005	-748	-9,791	-146
EXHIBIT	9-32	36	13	36%	-733	1,186	-702	-11,773	-20
EXHIBIT	9-33	30	11	37%	2,208	1,721	-880	-4,799	74
EXHIBIT	9-34	12	7	58%	13,114	2,607	-1,027	-2,954	1,093
EXHIBIT	9-35	21	10	48%	8,058	2,108	-1,183	-4,846	384
EXHIBIT	9-36	10	5	50%	11,477	3,206	-911	-3,323	1,148
EXHIBIT	10-2	35	7	20%	8,663	2,561	-331	-2,836	248
EXHIBIT	10-3	24	10	42%	10,161	2,081	-760	-2,938	423
EXHIBIT	10-4	30	9	30%	11,997	2,236	-387	-2,391	400
EXHIBIT	10-5	24	10	42%	9,517	2,081	-806	-3,493	397
EXHIBIT	10-6	22	10	45%	10,142	2,103	-907	-3,927	461
EXHIBIT	10-7	33	8	24%	6,903	2,300	-460	-3,833	209
EXHIBIT	10-8	44	5	11%	1,872	2,624	-288	-4,302	43
EXHIBIT	10-9	25	10	40%	12,478	2,081	-555	-2,891	499
EXHIBIT	10-10	21	10	48%	11,436	2,108	-876	-3,721	545
EXHIBIT	10-11	21	10	48%	8,214	2,108	-1,169	-4,774	391
EXHIBIT	10-12	21	10	48%	11,436	2,108	-876	-3,721	545
EXHIBIT	10-13	30	9	30%	10,518	2,236	-457	-2,705	351
EXHIBIT	10-14	25	11	44%	12,553	2,040	-706	-2,518	502
EXHIBIT	10-15	95	20	21%	-2,450	1,353	-393	-7,814	-26
EXHIBIT	11-2	22	10	45%	7,072	2,003	-1,080	-4,774	321
EXHIBIT	11-3	21	10	48%	8,214	2,108	-1,169	-4,774	391
EXHIBIT	11-4	25	11	44%	9,266	1,620	-611	-3,066	371
EXHIBIT	11-5	21	10	48%	10,538	2,274	-1,110	-4,628	502
EXHIBIT	11-6	46	20	43%	-1,475	494	-437	-3,265	-32
EXHIBIT	11-7	50	38	76%	486	422	-1,297	-5,178	10
EXHIBIT	11-8	38	22	58%	1,496	866	-1,097	-6,148	39
EXHIBIT	11-9	26	12	46%	6,686	1,877	-1,131	-6,148	257
EXHIBIT	11-10	23	11	48%	8,303	2,115	-1,247	-6,148	361
EXHIBIT	11-11	21	10	48%	8,214	2,108	-1,169	-4,774	391
EXHIBIT	11-12	32	18	56%	4,195	1,065	-1,069	-6,148	131
EXHIBIT	11-13	29	12	41%	5,399	1,568	-789	-4,444	186
EXHIBIT	11-14	90	43	48%	-10,848	226	-438	-13,082	-121
EXHIBIT	11-15	29	15	52%	5,174	1,360	-1,088	-6,220	178
EXHIBIT	11-16	95	20	21%	-1,182	1,353	-376	-7,814	-12
AVERAGE		49	18	37%	1,019	1,469	-960	-7,398	21

EXHIBIT 12-14   Performance Report, Summary of Performance for All Live Cattle Systems

		Closed Trades	Profitable Trades	Percent Profitable	Total Profit or Loss	Average Profitable Trade	Average Losing Trade	Maximum Drawdown	Average Trade
EXHIBIT	8-2	56	15	27%	-9,144	1,020	-596	-13,528	-163
EXHIBIT	8-4	52	13	25%	-13,200	1,060	-692	-15,344	-254
EXHIBIT	8-6	76	25	33%	-13,532	664	-591	-13,532	-178
EXHIBIT	8-7	72	24	33%	-12,264	701	-606	-12,264	-170
EXHIBIT	8-8	28	8	29%	-216	1,970	-799	-7,176	-8
EXHIBIT	8-9	262	79	30%	-41,028	318	-362	-42,088	-157
EXHIBIT	8-10	17	6	35%	-16,844	868	-2,005	-18,172	-991
EXHIBIT	9-1	124	33	27%	-14,496	624	-386	-15,792	-117
EXHIBIT	9-2	79	18	23%	-15,364	851	-503	-17,736	-194
EXHIBIT	9-4	116	34	29%	-16,896	562	-439	-19,040	-146
EXHIBIT	9-5	65	17	26%	-8,700	924	-508	-14,384	-134
EXHIBIT	9-6	145	33	23%	-19,732	681	-377	-20,728	-136
EXHIBIT	9-7	64	15	23%	-4,464	1,195	-457	-9,532	-70
EXHIBIT	9-8	56	13	23%	-8,336	1,380	-611	-14,592	-149
EXHIBIT	9-9	23	8	35%	-804	1,734	-978	-10,592	-35
EXHIBIT	9-13	21	10	48%	-8,324	1,071	-1,731	-9,064	-396
EXHIBIT	9-14	17	9	53%	-4,872	1,221	-1,983	-8,808	-287
EXHIBIT	9-15	24	10	42%	-18,920	591	-1,773	-18,920	-788
EXHIBIT	9-16	18	8	44%	-11,160	879	-1,819	-11,672	-620
EXHIBIT	9-17	6	5	83%	12,016	2,923	-2,600	-2,600	2,003
EXHIBIT	9-18	5	4	80%	6,624	2,306	-2,600	-2,600	1,325
EXHIBIT	9-20	23	12	52%	-8,672	840	-1,704	-12,080	-377
EXHIBIT	9-21	31	19	61%	-5,780	863	-1,848	-8,980	-186
EXHIBIT	9-22	25	11	44%	-19,248	413	-1,699	-19,340	-770
EXHIBIT	9-23	30	16	53%	-7,652	704	-1,351	-9,360	-255
EXHIBIT	9-24	8	5	63%	7,320	2,124	-1,100	-2,600	915
EXHIBIT	9-25	5	3	60%	3,144	1,964	-1,374	-2,600	629
EXHIBIT	9-26	2	0	0%	-5,200	0	-2,600	-5,200	-2,600
EXHIBIT	9-28	175	58	33%	-14,360	530	-385	-14,361	-82
EXHIBIT	9-30	30	18	60%	4,852	948	-1,017	-4,108	162
EXHIBIT	9-31	60	20	33%	-5,596	985	-633	-11,000	-93
EXHIBIT	9-32	41	14	34%	-11,528	708	-794	-14,660	-281
EXHIBIT	9-33	31	7	23%	-5,216	2,203	-860	-11,316	-168
EXHIBIT	9-34	12	6	50%	4,296	1,925	-1,209	-2,688	358
EXHIBIT	9-35	25	7	28%	-2,672	2,079	-957	-9,992	-107
EXHIBIT	9-36	12	4	33%	-1,200	1,946	-1,123	-3,836	-100
EXHIBIT	10-2	45	5	11%	-7,341	1,423	-361	-9,357	-163
EXHIBIT	10-3	31	7	23%	-4,562	2,014	-778	-9,346	-147
EXHIBIT	10-4	42	6	14%	-5,224	1,484	-392	-8,848	-124
EXHIBIT	10-5	29	7	24%	-3,112	1,998	-777	-8,592	-107
EXHIBIT	10-6	28	7	25%	-3,608	1,998	-838	-8,996	-129
EXHIBIT	10-7	35	7	20%	640	1,630	-385	-5,096	18
EXHIBIT	10-8	44	5	11%	-3,184	1,511	-275	-5,200	-72
EXHIBIT	10-9	31	7	23%	1,248	2,014	-535	-4,588	40
EXHIBIT	10-10	30	7	23%	-4,144	2,077	-812	-8,928	-138
EXHIBIT	10-11	25	7	28%	-2,432	2,079	-944	-9,752	-97
EXHIBIT	10-12	30	7	23%	-4,144	2,077	-812	-8,928	-138
EXHIBIT	10-13	37	6	16%	-3,908	1,701	-455	-7,532	-106
EXHIBIT	10-14	34	8	24%	-3,124	2,095	-765	-7,908	-92
EXHIBIT	10-15	77	17	22%	-14,812	827	-481	-17,184	-192
EXHIBIT	11-2	26	7	27%	-1,556	2,016	-825	-9,492	-60
EXHIBIT	11-3	25	7	28%	-2,432	2,079	-944	-9,752	-97
EXHIBIT	11-4	35	12	34%	-3,112	835	-571	-5,748	-89
EXHIBIT	11-5	25	7	28%	-2,004	2,079	-920	-9,332	-80
EXHIBIT	11-6	44	13	30%	-4,920	716	-459	-7,640	-112
EXHIBIT	11-7	54	38	70%	-448	416	-1,016	-7,912	-8
EXHIBIT	11-8	40	22	55%	2,736	882	-926	-7,580	68
EXHIBIT	11-9	29	9	31%	-2,628	1,677	-886	-9,912	-91
EXHIBIT	11-10	27	7	26%	-2,560	2,157	-883	-9,912	-95
EXHIBIT	11-11	25	7	28%	-2,432	2,079	-944	-9,752	-97
EXHIBIT	11-12	33	16	48%	1,048	1,147	-1,017	-9,752	32
EXHIBIT	11-13	30	9	30%	-2,496	1,677	-838	-8,996	-83
EXHIBIT	11-14	75	40	53%	-9,824	280	-601	-12,876	-131
EXHIBIT	11-15	25	7	28%	-2,432	2,079	-944	-9,752	-97
EXHIBIT	11-16	77	15	19%	-15,284	919	-469	-17,656	-198
AVERAGE		45	14	31%	-6,050	1,350	-953	-10,717	-134

184

EXHIBIT 12-15   Performance Report, Summary of Performance for the Average of Each System

		Closed Trades	Profitable Trades	Percent Profitable	Total Profit or Loss	Average Profitable Trade	Average Losing Trade	Maximum Drawdown	Average Trade
EXHIBIT	8-2	68	23	34%	-1,095	2,148	-1,112	-18,190	-16
EXHIBIT	8-4	57	20	35%	-474	2,206	-1,190	-18,283	-8
EXHIBIT	8-6	85	30	35%	-2,754	1,783	-997	-16,191	-32
EXHIBIT	8-7	79	33	41%	-3,406	1,595	-1,192	-15,792	-43
EXHIBIT	8-8	34	13	37%	4,328	2,931	-1,523	-14,888	126
EXHIBIT	8-9	199	78	39%	-4,310	903	-656	-23,669	-22
EXHIBIT	8-10	11	5	45%	9,668	4,496	-2,105	-7,494	848
EXHIBIT	9-1	171	50	29%	-5,147	1,235	-613	-23,753	-30
EXHIBIT	9-2	96	26	27%	-769	1,711	-726	-20,793	-8
EXHIBIT	9-4	122	41	34%	-2,321	1,234	-742	-21,005	-19
EXHIBIT	9-5	62	22	35%	9,673	1,849	-867	-14,586	155
EXHIBIT	9-6	164	50	31%	-11,103	1,312	-679	-28,758	-68
EXHIBIT	9-7	97	30	31%	-2,036	1,629	-771	-20,920	-21
EXHIBIT	9-8	62	19	31%	-2,402	2,176	-1,168	-20,629	-39
EXHIBIT	9-9	28	10	35%	3,922	3,481	-1,823	-16,188	142
EXHIBIT	9-13	33	16	49%	-5,539	2,249	-2,472	-16,521	-169
EXHIBIT	9-14	27	12	46%	-5,386	2,527	-2,532	-15,602	-203
EXHIBIT	9-15	33	16	47%	-11,278	1,909	-2,336	-18,752	-342
EXHIBIT	9-16	25	12	48%	-4,577	2,178	-2,345	-14,108	-182
EXHIBIT	9-17	8	4	46%	-457	2,931	-2,621	-8,630	-59
EXHIBIT	9-18	6	2	37%	-636	3,990	-2,504	-8,160	-112
EXHIBIT	9-20	28	14	51%	-2,103	2,180	-2,379	-15,328	-75
EXHIBIT	9-21	39	20	53%	-234	2,036	-2,270	-16,689	-6
EXHIBIT	9-22	29	13	44%	-8,116	2,102	-2,162	-19,345	-280
EXHIBIT	9-23	40	19	47%	-5,968	1,895	-1,990	-17,305	-150
EXHIBIT	9-24	7	3	39%	2,138	4,439	-2,386	-7,875	289
EXHIBIT	9-25	5	2	38%	2,378	5,280	-2,480	-5,089	449
EXHIBIT	9-26	3	1	41%	9,180	11,976	-2,496	-3,994	3,400
EXHIBIT	9-28	197	77	39%	20,396	1,162	-569	-12,436	103
EXHIBIT	9-30	37	16	43%	2,769	2,240	-1,588	-15,145	74
EXHIBIT	9-31	74	28	37%	348	1,937	-1,148	-19,740	5
EXHIBIT	9-32	43	15	34%	-5,123	2,356	-1,398	-17,369	-118
EXHIBIT	9-33	37	13	34%	8,474	3,205	-1,311	-12,236	232
EXHIBIT	9-34	17	6	36%	1,781	3,832	-1,946	-12,113	107
EXHIBIT	9-35	31	11	36%	8,914	3,342	-1,433	-11,075	287
EXHIBIT	9-36	16	5	32%	20	4,082	-1,962	-11,813	1
EXHIBIT	10-2	47	9	20%	9,317	3,358	-566	-8,494	200
EXHIBIT	10-3	34	11	33%	8,903	3,267	-1,230	-10,009	264
EXHIBIT	10-4	45	9	21%	8,323	3,341	-650	-9,979	185
EXHIBIT	10-5	34	11	33%	9,278	3,313	-1,228	-10,070	277
EXHIBIT	10-6	33	11	34%	9,303	3,326	-1,312	-10,577	286
EXHIBIT	10-7	41	11	25%	10,488	3,169	-740	-8,039	254
EXHIBIT	10-8	49	8	17%	9,477	3,415	-467	-7,498	195
EXHIBIT	10-9	43	10	22%	11,784	3,326	-609	-8,216	276
EXHIBIT	10-10	36	11	30%	11,363	3,254	-968	-9,269	317
EXHIBIT	10-11	31	11	36%	10,667	3,346	-1,327	-10,169	340
EXHIBIT	10-12	32	11	35%	8,816	3,303	-1,336	-10,428	273
EXHIBIT	10-13	41	10	25%	8,078	3,194	-798	-8,858	195
EXHIBIT	10-14	38	13	34%	8,567	3,262	-1,320	-12,214	228
EXHIBIT	10-15	95	25	26%	5,439	1,924	-610	-16,424	57
EXHIBIT	11-2	33	11	33%	13,576	3,256	-987	-9,345	410
EXHIBIT	11-3	33	11	34%	8,917	3,295	-1,250	-11,146	274
EXHIBIT	11-4	52	20	38%	1,575	1,464	-860	-10,657	30
EXHIBIT	11-5	39	14	35%	6,681	2,657	-1,184	-11,976	172
EXHIBIT	11-6	59	23	39%	415	1,234	-770	-9,828	7
EXHIBIT	11-7	94	73	78%	1,178	473	-1,604	-8,573	12
EXHIBIT	11-8	73	47	64%	4,447	956	-1,549	-11,117	61
EXHIBIT	11-9	50	21	42%	2,664	2,167	-1,485	-13,404	53
EXHIBIT	11-10	40	14	34%	5,241	3,194	-1,442	-13,287	131
EXHIBIT	11-11	34	12	35%	8,981	3,418	-1,409	-11,357	261
EXHIBIT	11-12	46	20	43%	4,887	2,218	-1,478	-12,962	106
EXHIBIT	11-13	39	13	33%	8,245	3,372	-1,371	-11,652	210
EXHIBIT	11-14	109	57	53%	-3,376	595	-724	-12,817	-31
EXHIBIT	11-15	44	17	39%	4,035	2,322	-1,336	-12,413	92
EXHIBIT	11-16	96	23	25%	6,936	1,941	-534	-14,970	73
AVERAGE		54	20	37%	3,122	2,706	-1,379	-13,480	58

charts of most other popular trading markets. Use these weekly charts or daily charts for reference when you create and test your own systems or when you evaluate the performance of systems for sale.

Trading a Portfolio of Markets

The most important reason to consider trading different markets is diversification. Since commodity trading profits primarily accrue from big trending moves and since no one knows in which markets those moves will occur, the more markets you trade, the more big moves you are likely to catch. Since fundamental factors for different market groups are usually not synchronized, you will increase the diversification advantage if you trade markets from as many different groups as possible. Exhibit 12–16 lists the various general market groups.

There are also distinctions within each group. For instance, in the meats there are two cattle markets and two hog markets. Cattle and hogs do not always move together. In the financials, long- and short-term interest rates do not always move together. In the currencies, the Japanese yen and British pound will often diverge from each other and from the continental currencies. Corn and wheat have different harvest cycles and often move differently because of seasonal considerations.

If you choose your markets with an eye toward this kind of diversification, you can help damp the drawdowns in your trading. With a well-chosen portfolio of markets, some will be profitable while others are losing; over time you will earn profits from each market, but seldom all at the same time.

Just as you can diversify by trading a number of different markets in different groups, with enough capital you can further diversify by trading multiple systems in each market. This is a part of money management that I will discuss in Chapter 16. Although there is less likelihood of curve-fitting if the same parameters of the same system are

EXHIBIT 12-16   Commodity Groups and Markets

GRAINS	FOODS	MEATS	METALS	ENERGY
Corn	Sugar	Live Cattle	Copper	Crude Oil
Wheat, Chicago	Cocoa	Feeder Cattle	Gold	Heating Oil
Wheat, Kansas City	Coffee	Live Hogs	Silver	Unleaded Gas
Wheat, Minneapolis	Orange Juice	Pork Bellies	Platinum	
Oats			Palladium	**MISCELLANEOUS**
Soybeans	**CURRENCIES**	**FINANCIALS**	Aluminum	CRB Index
Soybean Meal	British Pound	T-Bonds		
Soybean Oil	Canadian Dollar	T-Bills	**STOCK INDEXES**	**CANADIAN**
	Swiss Franc	Eurodollars	S&P 500	Rapeseed
WOOD AND FIBER	Deutsche Mark	Municipal Bonds	New York Composite	Barley
Lumber	Japanese Yen	T-Notes	Major Market Maxi	Flaxseed
Cotton	U.S. Dollar Index		Value Line	Rye

profitable in a number of markets, there is no reason why you must *trade* the same system in all markets. For example, since intermediate-term systems (such as the volatility-envelope) work best in the financial markets, you could trade one of those systems in stock indexes, interest rate, and currency markets. You could use long-term systems in the agricultural markets. There is no reason you couldn't use a different system in every market. Just be sure each system was not overoptimized and be sure each system works in a variety of markets. If forced to choose between trading additional markets and additional systems, assuming the systems were about equally effective, I would opt for additional non-correlated markets so long as the additional markets were active and liquid.

Here are some comments about the trading characteristics of the most popular markets.

Stock Indexes

Long-term, trend-following systems do not perform well in these markets, although their very high volatility offers the potential for quick profits. For this reason, they are the best day-trading vehicles. Volatility-envelope systems seem to exploit their market action the best. Except during times of economic shock, intraday fills are good. (That means slippage is only a tick or two on stop orders.) Fills can be worse if you act on the open or close. There are often large gaps on the open, which can cause bigger-than-expected losses and destroy your money management strategy.

The S&P 500 is the most popular stock index market. Since the October 1987 crash, the margin has increased from $6,000 to the current $19,000. This increase was supposed to curb "excessive" speculation and obviate strict government regulation or even closing the stock futures markets entirely. Futures trading was not the cause of the crash, and regulating futures to death will not prevent another one. It only makes the market inaccessible to small traders, who add needed liquidity.

Those with accounts between $10,000 and $25,000 can still trade the New York Futures Exchange Composite Index. This contract is referred to as the NYFE (pronounced *knife*). Its index is based on a broader group of stocks, so that it is less volatile than the S&P. Its margin is currently only $6,000. You will definitely get more bang for the buck trading three NYFE's than one S&P. Fills are slightly worse than the S&P.

The Kansas City Value Line contract tracks the most broadly based stock index. It used to be a good alternative until the 1986–87 bull market, when its volatility decreased below the S&P. The Value Line's liquidity has now dropped to such low levels that I would not recommend it. The Chicago Board of Trade has a contract called the Major Market Index, which is intended to mirror action in the Dow Jones Industrials. Its liquidity is only slightly less than the NYFE. To gain a competitive edge, it opens 15 minutes earlier than the New York Stock Exchange and the other stock index futures contracts.

Financials

These are the interest rate futures first introduced in the late 1970s. Because of participation by the banking and savings and loan industries, they have become the most actively traded futures contracts. Since the long-term-rate instruments tend to move together and the short-term-rate instruments tend to move together, it is sufficient for a speculator to trade one market in each area.

Representing long-term rates, T-bonds is perhaps the best trading market of all. There are good trends, and the fills are excellent. T-bonds is one of the best day-trading markets because it has such good fills and a respectable daily range.

For T-bond traders, one fly in the ointment is the Board of Trade's decision to introduce evening trading. There is a special trading session between 4:00 and 7:00 P.M., Central time. The idea was to steal some business from exchanges in the Far East. The pit is manned by second-string floor traders, most of whom have other jobs.

The evening session has caused real problems for T-bond system traders. How do you treat the price history established during this orphan session? The Board of Trade considers the session a part of the next day's trading and publishes the 6:00 P.M. opening price as the opening price for the next day. Do you trade your system during the evening session? Do you take an entry signal during the evening session or wait to see if it is confirmed the next day? What if you would have been stopped out during the evening session, but not during the daytime session? If you trade the evening session, there are now two gaps to worry about: That between the afternoon close and the evening session and that between the evening session and the next morning.

Every trader I know ignores the evening session because of its low liquidity and seeming irrelevance to what happens the next day. That means the opening price for them is the opening price in the morning, just as it used to be. This price is no longer available in the *The Wall Street Journal,* which lists the evening open as its opening price. To keep your testing data base consistent with prices before the evening session started, you must obtain and use the morning's opening price and the daytime high and low.

The evening session acts more like a pipsqueak extension of the previous day's trading than a prelude to the next day. There is very low range and limited liquidity. I hope the idea shrivels up and dies like a worm on a hot sidewalk. There is talk about eventually making trading a 24-hour-a-day proposition. Whoever is responsible should be required to stand in the pits as long as trading continues.

T-bills was the original short-term rate market. As the U.S. deficit has swelled in the 1980s, it has been supplanted by Eurodollars which now equals T-bonds in open interest. Eurodollars has lower volatility than T-bonds, and although not as good a trading vehicle as T-bonds, Eurodollars is a good market for system traders. I recommend ignoring the other markets like municipal bonds and Treasury notes. They are redundant.

Currencies

Currencies are great trending markets. Their biggest problem is a propensity for large gaps between the afternoon's close and the next morning's opening. If the gap goes against you, the market can blow right through your stop and create a much larger loss than expected. When big economic news breaks during the night, the gaps can be huge. Nevertheless, because of the sustained trends, these are good markets for system traders. One way to compensate for the frequent gaps is to allow for greater slippage in your historical testing.

In terms of liquidity, the largest market is now the Japanese yen, followed by the Deutschemark, Swiss franc, British pound, and Canadian dollar. The Australian dollar has recently begun trading and may soon become a viable system market.

If you want to speculate on the value of the dollar, you usually take the opposite position in one of the major world currencies. There is a relatively new Dollar Index contract, which allows you to play the dollar against a basket of foreign currencies. This dilutes the risk of sudden fundamental developments in a particular foreign country. The Dollar Index is still building participation, but it bears watching as a good potential system trading vehicle for the future. As I will explain in a moment, its New York location must be considered a strike against it.

Metals

The metals are the inflation markets. They are also all New York markets. As a former New Yorker who lived nine years in Manhattan and nine years in Rochester, it pains me to have to say this, but watch out in the New York markets. It is common knowledge among traders that the fills in New York markets are not as good as those in Chicago's. A word often used to describe New York floor traders is *rapacious*. On entry orders you can try to protect yourself by using limits. This is dangerous for system traders, however, because you run the risk of missing the trade entirely. You certainly don't have the luxury of using limits on stop-loss orders. Just as the notorious grouchiness and bad manners of New Yorkers should not prevent you from visiting that miraculous city, inferior fills should not deter you from trading New York markets. Just prepare yourself. Consider it an extra tax on your trading to help balance the city budget.

When inflation returns, fortunes will be made in gold and silver, just as in 1979–80. Have your systems ready. Copper is a less liquid market, but when it comes to life, the moves are awesome. I avoid platinum and palladium because of low liquidity. Platinum is affected by South African politics. Palladium may eventually explode because of fundamentals—limited supply and important industrial usage. Aluminum had a brief fling with popularity, but it has since receded into oblivion with propane, rough rice, and iced broilers.

Grains

Corn, wheat, and oats are not good system markets. They do not have enough overall volatility to overcome the costs of trading. This limitation can disappear in drought markets, such as those we had in 1973–74 and 1988. When weather becomes an important factor, you might consider applying your favorite trend-following system to these markets. The Kansas City and Minneapolis wheat markets should be left to spread traders.

By the way, I recommend you avoid spreads as a low-risk substitute for a net futures position. A speculator trading spreads is like a golfer playing miniature golf. The risk may in many cases be lower, but so are the rewards. The commissions are higher. You cannot use intraday stop-loss orders. You must gauge not only the direction of the market but also the action of your spread. Like options, it is not unusual to have the market move in the desired direction only to have your spread react the wrong way. I look at spread relationships to help assess the bullishness of the market, but I never trade them. Seasonal spread trades taken regardless of the direction of the market are an exception.

Soybean Complex

Soybeans, soybean oil, and soybean meal usually suffer from the same lack of volatility as the grains. With the possible exception of soybeans, they are not good system markets except when fundamental conditions suspend the usual rules of behavior.

All the agricultural markets have strong seasonal influences caused by the harvest cycle. Although not invariable, they are helpful guidelines. Although I have never seen one, perhaps you could create a system that exploited this seasonal behavior.

Wood, Fiber, and Foods

These are all New York markets except lumber, which might as well be. I do not recommend trading lumber. It has low participation, and there are rumors of manipulation in the pit. Systems work in cotton. I place it in the lowest rank of acceptable markets. Sugar is the biggest market of the international foods. It is a good system market even during times of low volatility. Every six years or so, it goes (can I use the term?) bananas. Coffee and orange juice trading is dominated by their freeze seasons. Being located in South America, coffee country freezes during our summer, while Florida orange groves freeze in January and February. Even though massive freezes are infrequent, system trading during freeze season is impossible unless your system takes only long positions. The risk of being caught short is too great.

SYSTEMS AND MARKETS   **191**

Be careful of weather experts who have all called 20 of the last 2 freezes. They subscribe to the famous maxim, "If you're going to predict, predict often." Most traders are afraid of the coffee and cocoa markets, but I like them. They have long, sustained trends that can be very profitable. I never trade orange juice, although I do occasionally think about it.

Meats

There are two cattle markets, live and feeder cattle, and two pig markets, live hogs and pork bellies. These are perhaps the most difficult markets to trade, but I have never been able to understand why. Most professional traders won't touch them with a 10-foot lasso. The long-term charts do look a bit choppier than the other markets, but there are some good moves. Like the agricultural markets, the meats are strongly influenced by the breeding cycle. This could be part of a meat system design. Watch out for Department of Agriculture crop reports if you trade the meats. They usually result in explosive, multiday limit moves. Cattle can react to pig crop reports and vice versa. Being in the meat markets at the time of a report is gambling.

As you can see from the trading results in this book, the usual systems do not perform well in cattle. Omega Research's Bill Cruz sold computerized pork belly and live cattle systems in 1983 and 1984. They had impressive historical records at the time they were sold, and as I understand they have had respectable performance since.

Energy and Miscellaneous

Crude oil, heating oil, and unleaded gasoline are all large-participation, New York markets. Crude oil has more than twice the liquidity of heating oil, with gasoline a distant third. Crude is thus the market of choice and responds well to systems. This is an excellent market for diversification as it does not seem to be closely correlated with the other markets.

The Commodity Research Bureau (CRB) Index is a broad index of commodity prices that has been around for many years. Its related futures contract is relatively new. Its liquidity is currently too low for consideration, but I hope it gains broader acceptance. It could be a good vehicle for participating in very strong moves in one complex or another without worrying about limit moves. I would become interested in trading the CRB when its open interest climbs over 10,000 contracts.

Canadian markets are best left to the Canadians. They don't have to make currency conversions. Being grain markets, they are not good system candidates. For non–system traders, they can occasionally be helpful as early warning indicators for American grain and soybean markets.

Trading All the Markets at Once with the Dennis Commodity Rating Technique

The normal system approach is to operate with one market at a time and have the system decide when to buy, when to sell, and when to have no position in that market. The system treats each market in its own particular vacuum and pays no attention to what may be happening in other markets. The trader tries to be positioned in as many markets as capital will allow to increase the chances of catching big moves. Since any particular market makes a good tradeable move only infrequently, a great deal of effort can be wasted (and losses incurred) waiting for those profitable spurts.

Several years ago I began research on a system that would trade all the markets at once. The theory is that it is better to concentrate all your efforts on the markets that are likely to make a tradeable move right now. The trick is to know when a market is ready to move. The best way to identify markets that are likely to make a profitable surge is to choose those markets that are exhibiting the greatest current strength or weakness in relation to the universe of markets. In other words, buy the currently strongest markets and sell the currently weakest markets.

The research and computer programming involved in testing such a system was difficult. Other projects had priority. I have still not perfected my system, but I expect to continue the research when time allows. In the meantime, across the country in Massachusetts, my friend and trading system authority, Bob Dennis, was pursuing the same idea. He was so confident in the approach that rather than create a computer program to test his concept historically, in early 1987, he decided just to start trading it. While he has been refining the trading rules in light of his experience, the actual trading results were excellent. His algorithm ranks a universe of markets by relative strength during the last eight days. It looks at strength of price movement rather than direction. He trades the top five markets in the direction of their trend. Bob follows 27 markets, but you can include as many as you want so long as you have the daily data. I watch 30.

With Bob's encouragement, I created a software package that does all the Dennis calculations and generates a number of different useful reports both for current trading and historical research. It allows you to vary the number of previous days to use in ranking the markets as well as examine the historical progression of the rankings over the last 12 trading days. Exhibit 12–17 is an example of a six-day chronological report. It shows for the last six days the daily ranking and direction (short or long) of each market using the last eight days to compute relative strength. The program will generate reports for any prior date in your data base, but it cannot do hypothetical testing of various trading strategies to see how profitable the strategy was in historical trading.

The only negative aspect to this approach is that you will be receiving signals to trade markets that have already made a substantial

EXHIBIT 12-17   Dennis Commodity Rating Technique, Chronological Report

PORTFOLIO: CTCR

COMPUTED FROM: 880516
USE MARGINS IN COMPUTATIONS: .... NO
NUMBER OF DAYS FOR REGRESSION CALCULATIONS: 8
NUMBER OF SIGNAL DAYS REQUESTED: 6

CHRONOLOGICAL RANKINGS

COMMODITY..........	880516 RANKING		880513 RANKING		880512 RANKING		880511 RANKING		880510 RANKING		880509 RANKING	
SOYBEANS	L	1	L	4	L	4	L	4	L	6	L	7
COTTON	L	2	L	3	L	14	L	25	S	28	S	20
SOYBEAN MEAL	L	3	L	10	L	9	L	7	L	9	L	9
BRITISH POUND	L	4	L	2	L	7	L	9	L	10	S	30
PLATINUM	L	5	L	7	L	6	L	5	L	5	L	10
COFFEE	S	6	S	26	L	17	L	8	L	4	L	4
PORK BELLIES	L	7	L	6	L	8	L	19	L	30	L	26
SILVER NY	L	8	L	5	L	5	L	6	L	12	S	24
COPPER	L	9	L	8	L	3	L	3	L	2	L	3
GOLD NY	L	10	L	13	L	15	L	16	L	26	S	14
SUGAR	L	11	L	11	L	10	L	10	L	13	L	23
WHEAT	L	12	L	23	L	26	L	26	S	27	S	18
HOGS	L	13	L	12	L	11	L	12	L	7	L	5
LIVE CATTLE	L	14	L	14	L	12	L	11	L	8	L	6
SOYBEAN OIL	L	15	L	17	L	18	L	18	L	17	L	17
ORANGE JUICE	L	16	L	24	S	30	S	30	S	29	L	27
D-MARK	S	17	S	25	S	25	S	24	S	21	S	16
HEATING OIL	L	18	L	18	L	22	L	14	L	19	S	22
S&P 500	S	19	S	1	S	1	S	1	S	1	S	1
T-BONDS	S	20	S	15	S	13	S	17	S	16	S	15
SWISS FRANC	S	21	S	27	S	28	S	27	S	24	S	8
CANADIAN DOLLAR	L	22	L	20	L	24	S	29	S	15	S	13
COCOA	S	23	S	19	S	21	L	28	L	20	L	21
EURODOLLAR	L	24	L	29	S	29	S	23	S	23	S	25
LUMBER	S	25	S	22	S	16	S	13	S	14	S	12
T-BILLS	S	26	S	21	S	20	S	15	S	11	S	11
JAPANESE YEN	S	27	L	30	L	23	L	20	L	18	S	29
NY COMPOSITE	S	28	S	9	S	2	S	2	S	3	S	2
CRUDE OIL	L	29	L	28	L	27	L	22	S	25	S	19
CORN	S	30	S	16	S	19	S	21	S	22	S	28

move. After all, they are currently the very strongest or weakest of all the markets. This makes entering such markets appear quite dangerous and risky. While strong moves often precede even stronger moves in the future, they are also frequently followed by stiff reactions that will probably result in losses. In order to be successful, you must be prepared to trade a diversified group of these situations on a regular basis. While entering these trades is like jumping out of an airplane, your ability to cut losses short and let profits run is your parachute. If you trade this approach consistently and courageously, you should make a soft and profitable landing.

Using Trading Systems on Common Stocks

Mechanical trading systems work best in the commodity markets where there is greater volatility, greater leverage, and a far lower cost of trading. I hope I have convinced you that trading commodities need not be more risky in terms of the potential return than trading common stocks. Therefore, there should be no reason that you should want to trade systems in stocks rather than commodities. However, if you insist, you can use a mechanical approach such as I have described on stocks. Profitability will depend on the volatility of the particular market and the system you choose. In general, the higher the volatility of the market and the longer term your system is, the better will be your chance for success. Exhibit 12–18 shows the performance of four different systems on four different popular trading stocks. Each test assumes you traded 500-share lots with slippage and commissions of $500 per trade. The test period is the same five-year period used for all previous commodity tests.

Now you have covered the information you'll need to know before choosing and testing a system. But before you do, you should know about some extraordinary tools available to make the process quicker and easier. In the next chapter I'll describe the latest computer software designed for system traders.

EXHIBIT 12-18   Performance Report, Trading Systems Applied to Common Stocks

	IBM - Slow Stochastics, 9 days, divergence (70/30% initial threshold), $2,500 stop	TELEDYNE - Slow Stochastics, 9 days, divergence (70/30% initial threshold), $2,500 stop	MERCK - Three moving averages (60 days, 40 days and 20 days), $2,500 stop	DIGITAL EQUIPMENT Babcock Long-term System, $2,500 stop
Number of Closed Trades	5	6	12	12
Number of Profitable Trades	2	4	3	4
Percent Profitable	40%	67%	25%	33%
Total Profit or Loss	24,875	86,188	5,984	24,913
Average Profitable Trade	16,938	23,188	5,099	10,339
Average Losing Trade	-3,000	-3,281	-1,035	-2,055
Maximum Drawdown	-6,000	-6,563	-3,961	-10,050
Average Profit Per Trade	4,975	14,365	499	2,076

Answers to the Market Identification Quiz

Exhibit 12–1   S&P 500, wheat, sugar
Exhibit 12–2   Crude oil, Japanese yen, orange juice
Exhibit 12–3   Live cattle, soybeans, Canadian dollar
Exhibit 12–4   Silver, cotton, cocoa

13 Commodity System Software

The principal change in futures trading in the last 10 years has been the availability of powerful computers. Any trader who has sufficient capital to trade can afford one. Trading software has made such strides during this time that it is mind-boggling to imagine what the next 10 years may bring.

In light of the analytical capabilities of today's software, it is natural to suppose that anyone trying to trade without a computer is at a severe competitive disadvantage. This is certainly the picture that the software vendors portray in advertisement headlines like, "The Other Side of Your Trade Is Probably Using a Computer . . . They have a strong advantage!" Is this true? Not necessarily.

One of the most knowledgeable computer traders I know is Manning Stoller. He is a retired broker and brokerage firm executive who has all the popular software. The last I heard he had 9 computers and 12 monitors in his suburban Boston office, all devoted to futures trading. He lays it on the line: "If you can't make money trading without a computer, you won't make money with a computer. It will help you follow more markets and do everything very quickly. But by itself, it won't make money. The interpretation, the discipline, the money management do not come from the computer. Before buying a computer, learn how to make money without one."

Someone who wants to trade during the day based on intraday price action must certainly have a computer to track the market. One who makes all his decisions after the markets close may not need a computer at all. It depends on his trading approach.

There are a number of perfectly good trading methods, mostly chart-based, that do not require a computer. If you are successfully using one of those, there is no need to worry whether you are missing even greater profits by not having a computer. There is a tendency when things are going well to want more. Traders end up discarding profitable strategies in the search for ever higher and more unrealistic returns.

If you want to pursue mathematical analysis, a computer is probably worth the investment. It is silly to spend hours punching a calculator when a computer could do all the work for you with much less chance of a mistake.

To the extent that you find market analysis fun, a computer can really expand your enjoyment. There are so many exciting programs available today, and they are getting better every year, even as the cost of the hardware goes down. If you are in this for fun, I strongly suggest making the investment.

If you have less than $10,000 available for trading, you should probably put your limited capital into your trading account rather than use it to buy a computer. It is easy to spend money on souping up your system and on new software, but you will increase your chance of success more by having a larger trading account. However, everyone has his utility-of-money values, and you should do what will give you the most pleasure.

Computer software for futures trading would be an excellent topic for an entire book of its own. I cannot hope to cover the subject completely in one chapter. However, computers and systems trading are so inexorably intertwined that I want to include at least a sampler of system-related products in the various software categories.

Buying Hardware

Before looking at software, let me give you a few pointers on buying hardware. The average person first buys a computer, then he buys some software to run on it. Finally, he tries to figure out what to do with the software now that he has spent all this money! This is precisely the opposite of the correct approach.

Start by defining the tasks you want your computer system to perform. When you know exactly what you want your computer to do for you, look for the software that will accomplish those tasks in the most effective way considering your budget, abilities, and experience. The essential thing is not to buy the most complicated or expensive program just because it may be "the best." The best may not be necessary to accomplish what you need to help you trade. Why pay for features you will never use? Finally, when you know what software you will use, buy the computer hardware needed to run the software efficiently.

For futures traders this means invariably some type of IBM computer or IBM clone. All the best programs are available strictly for IBM-type machines. There are a few Macintosh programs now, but it is unlikely that Macintosh will ever catch up in this arena. The clones are better values, but I would stick to a name-brand clone rather than those that are assembled in the back of your local computer store. A good source for comparative information is popular magazines such as *PC, PC World,* and *InfoWorld.*

I strongly recommend that you buy your computer from a local dealer rather than by mail, even though you may be able to obtain the same machine at substantial savings by mail. There are invariably initial problems with computer hardware. It is so much easier to take it back to a dealer than have to make arrangements with a mail-order house halfway across the country. The extra money is well-spent. Software is just the opposite. It is always better to buy it cheaper by mail since you will depend on the manufacturer for support rather than the dealer.

Because there is a great deal of number crunching involved in futures trading analysis, buy the fastest computer you can afford. The 386 processor is the current standard, but it is still significantly more expensive than the last-generation 286. A fast 286 is quite acceptable. Be sure to buy a machine with a hard disk (30 or 40 megabytes) for storage. This makes your work much faster and more automatic. Some of the latest programs will not even run with floppy drives. A color monitor is prettier and I prefer it, but it is really not necessary for this kind of work. If you want to save a little money, choose a high-resolution monochrome system rather than color. If you do decide on color, get EGA or VGA high-resolution graphics.

Finally, don't succumb to the temptation to wait a few months for the next advance in technology because you don't want to be behind the times. If you do, you will never be able to buy. There is always new technology waiting in the wings. The newest changes are always expensive, and it is better to wait for the inevitable bugs to be ironed out before you buy. You can never hope to have the latest and best, but in the real world it isn't necessary. Even last year's technology is pretty mind-boggling.

Commodity Trading Software

I divide commodity trading programs into six categories. This is not intended as an exhaustive survey but rather an introduction to the field. I am including what I consider to be the best and most advanced programs currently available. There are many more choices that may fill your needs more precisely. *Commodity Traders Consumer Report* reviews new software in each issue and is an excellent source of up-to-date information on this rapidly changing universe. None of these programs will actually trade for you, so be sure to weigh their utility in actually making money in your trading account.

Toolboxes

A toolbox is a program whose basic function is to display price charts and charts of analytic studies. Many allow you to draw trend lines and other geometric lines on the charts as well. Some have limited ability to test the effectiveness of simple trading signals based on the studies. They should be used by a trader who wants to apply his judgment to trading decisions but who wants the assistance of mathematical or geometric indicators. Here are descriptions of two such toolbox programs.

Advanced Chartist by Robert Pardo. Pardo Corporation, 950 Skokie Boulevard, Suite 310, Northbrook, IL 60062. (312)-564-9903. For IBM PC/XT/AT compatibles. Price: $495. Not copyprotected.

This program has made great strides in its most recent release. It has added very-high-resolution color (VGA) and is now compatible with ASCII data as well as other common formats including tick data. The *Advanced Chartist* is everything you would want in a computer charting package. It has a large variety of indicators and geometric analysis tools. It automatically converts daily data to weekly or monthly. The best analysts emphasize longer-term charts, so this is a key feature. You can load daily data, convert it to weekly or monthly, and then run indicators and analyze the longer-term charts. One of my favorite features is an ability to calculate and display indicators of indicators. Thus, for instance, you could do a momentum of the Relative Strength Index (RSI).

There are 15 graphics tools, such as trend lines, angles, and parallel lines. There are fifteen support and resistance studies, such as ellipses, speed resistance lines, and MLR lines. There are 20 indicators, such as moving averages, Stochastics, and the Commodity Channel Index. If you have your own proprietary indicator, you may be able to create it, too, using the user-defined capabilities.

The user interface is easy and efficient. You can set it up to keep a number of windows in memory simultaneously. With a keystroke you can switch from one to another. You can scroll back through previous data that originally did not fit on the screen. You can work with pull-down menus or instant command keys. The manual is professionally done. If you have a math co-processor chip on your motherboard, the program will use it to speed calculations. You can create an automated charting routine with the macro feature. If a chart is too big to fit on one sheet of paper, you can print it sideways over several sheets of continuous paper.

All in all, this is a comprehensive, easy-to-use toolbox package that makes excellent use of the latest hardware advances.

Quickstudy, the analysis subsystem of QUICKTRIEVE, by Commodity Systems, Inc., 200 West Palmetto Park Road, Boca Raton, FL 33432. (800)-327-0175 or (305)-392-8663. For IBM PC/XT/AT or compatibles. Price: $295. Not copyprotected.

Commodity Systems, Inc. (CSI) has always been the predominant data base service for commodity traders. Naturally, they have a comprehensive data base management software package to assist subscribers in accessing and manipulating their data. It is called *Quicktrieve*.

The president of CSI, Bob Pelletier, is an innovator. In the last few years he has been adding charting and technical analysis functions to the *Quicktrieve* software. The charting section of the program is called *Quickplot*. It is the fastest at reading and plotting data I have seen. It contains moving averages, trend lines, a relative strength index, and a price-difference oscillator.

The advanced technical analysis section of the program is called *Quickstudy*. It has been slowly growing into a formidable technical analysis program. It now contains Stochastics, the Commodity Channel Index, Exponential and Weighted Moving Averages, On-balance

Volume, Appel's MACD, Detrend, Momentum, Spread/Ratio, and Williams %R. There is also a unique study called Non-seasonal Volume. Non-seasonal Volume is calculated by subtracting today's volume from the absolute value of today's open interest minus yesterday's open interest.

Pelletier has recently added three brand-new, proprietary studies to the *Quickstudy* subsystem. They are the Probable Direction Index (PDI), enhanced PDI, CSI Stop, and CSI Trend. PDI is a new adaptive oscillator incorporating price, volume, and open interest at the same time. CSI Stop is a statistically derived envelope around price, designed to help you set stops. CSI Trend is an index that measures whether recent prices are statistically random or not. It is another way of determining whether the market is in a trending phase and suitable for trading.

The most intriguing of the three is the Probable Direction Index. Although the formula for PDI is not disclosed, I do know that it uses Non-seasonal Volume as an input. In contrast to other oscillators, the PDI is intended to be more sensitive and generally earlier to warn of an impending market turning point.

Pelletier suggests that before you factor volume into an indicator, you can remove certain biases by also including the effect of open interest. This is the purpose of Non-seasonal Volume. PDI incorporates some adaptive logic that dynamically changes the weighting between Non-seasonal Volume and price. As one factor or the other becomes more predictive, the algorithm automatically increases the weight assigned to that factor.

Unfortunately, as with all other volume and open interest indicators, the user is hampered by their unavailability until the next day. Today's PDI must be calculated using estimated volume and open interest because that is all that is available. Pelletier claims this has not resulted in any appreciable distortion of the signals, however.

CSI Stop statistically predicts tomorrow's high, low, and close and displays the output numerically and graphically. In the graphics mode it displays the stop as an envelope. The technique is based on Pelletier's 10 years of radar signal processing experience at General Electric. The user inputs a "fit factor" between 0.01 and 1 and selects whether the output should be the predicted high and low or the stop. The stop is a close one, making it ideal for use with PDI.

CSI Trend tells you whether the current price activity is random or serially correlated. It does not tell direction nor does it have predictive qualities like PDI. CSI Trend requires the user to input the full cycle period and a smoothing constant. The output is a number ranging from 1 to 100. Readings under 45 identify trending markets, and readings over 65 identify random markets. Pelletier says high readings are rare because market movement tends not to be random. Expect randomness readings only about 25 percent of the time.

The only caveat I see to these unique analytical tools is that Pelletier has not published any historical testing data to demonstrate their true effectiveness.

Optimizable Systems and Black Boxes

A black box is a program that uses trading logic not disclosed to the user. Because of their earlier incarnations, they have a bad reputation among some traders, which in many cases is undeserved. Some of these, such as *Phasor and Paragon* (discussed in Chapter 7), were expensive, heavily marketed flops. The original black box systems did no more than generate trading signals based on the current data file. They had no historical testing capabilities. Unless you wanted to build a data file day by day and run the program after inputting each new day's data, you had to take the word of the vendor regarding its historical performance. Not knowing anything about how it worked, you had no way to determine if it was simply curve-fitted to back data.

There are a number of current programs available that do not reveal the complete details of all their trading rules, but that have alleviated the inherent problems of the original black boxes. I am definitely prejudiced on this subject because I have designed and sell a number of these programs myself.

There are two important differences between true black boxes and these new programs. First, the new programs have comprehensive historical testing capabilities that allow you to change the variable parameters and test the systems in any market over any time period. This allows you to determine for yourself how effective the systems are. Secondly, although the vendor does not disclose all the mathematical formulas, he does disclose enough about how the system works to allow intelligent optimization and use of the system. For example, suppose one of these was a sophisticated moving average system that calculated the moving averages in a revolutionary new way. If the buyer could vary the length of the moving averages and test the system historically, I suggest that it would not be important to successful use of the software for the user to know the details of the signal computation. Because all is not mysterious any more, these programs are now sometimes referred to as "gray boxes."

The significance of such software is that it allows a disciplined, objective approach to the market. The trader does not depend on his own emotional interpretion of market action to dictate his trades. The computer tells him exactly what to do on the basis of actual market action. The user can have confidence in the effectiveness of the system because he has been able to test it himself on historical data. He knows the characteristics of its historical performance. When the market starts to move up and the program tells him to buy at a certain price, it is not important that he knows exactly how the program calculated the trend-following indicator. What is important is that he knows that in the past, following such signals has, on balance, been quite profitable. He knows this not because the seller told him in a slick brochure, but because he has spent some considerable time testing the system himself with the help of the program.

There are no true black boxes being sold any more. I call all such programs optimizable systems. They have either fully or partially disclosed trading logic. If enough is disclosed to test and trade the system intelligently, I don't think it is important whether some secrets remain. It is far more important that such programs not have copy protection because that can interfere with unrestricted use of the program on your computer.

ProfitTaker by Louis B. Mendelsohn. Investment Growth Corporation, 1430 West Busch Boulevard, Suite 4, Tampa, FL 33612. (800)-282-4198 or (813)-933-1164. Requirements for IBM version: PC/XT/AT or compatibles, 256k, color graphics card, 2 floppy drives or hard disk, printer. Price: $995.

ProfitTaker is a series of programs that allow you to create a mechanical trading system, test it historically, optimize its parameters, and then generate real-time signals for actual trading. *ProfitTaker's* system is fully disclosed. First sold for the Apple computer in 1984, it is the original optimizable system program.

The program has three modules: ProfitAnalyst, ProfitTaker, and ProfitUtilities. The utilities are for maintaining a data base. You can create your own by hand or use CSI-formatted files. You can also use CSI's *Quicktrieve* program for automatic data updates. The manual is excellent and extensive, with a glossary and an index.

While the program's system is fully disclosed, it is nothing esoteric. It consists of a long-term moving average (3 to 50 days), a short-term moving average (2 to 35 days), and a timing filter (a one-day momentum of a 1- to 15-day moving average). You may add stops based on an optimizable oscillator formula. This feature attempts to overcome one of the biggest disadvantages of moving average systems—their inability to protect large profits. Stop values may be different for shorts and longs at the same time. Finally, you can enter and exit on any combination of the open and close. But you cannot test intraday entries or exits—a curious limitation. Owners who are too lazy to optimize on their own may subscribe to *ProfitTuner,* a monthly report listing profitable parameters for actively traded commodities.

As you test, you generate detailed printed reports. You have three choices: the Trading History Report, which shows the day-by-day action of the system; the Trading Signals Report, which prints only the days when there is a position change; and the Summary Report, which covers a full page and specifies over 30 measurements of your system's performance. When you find a combination you want to trade real-time, *ProfitTaker* will generate the signals for your entire portfolio with its Trading Position Report and Summary Analysis Report.

Mendelsohn provides free technical support and consultation, but there is no money-back guarantee.

The Volatility Breakout System by Doug Bry and Phil Spertus. Technical Trading Strategies, 4877 South Everett Street, Littleton, CO 80123. (800)-648-2232 or (303)-972-1433. For IBM PC/XT/AT or compatibles. Price: $3,000. Copyprotected with Softguard.

This fully-disclosed system made a big splash with full-page ads in *Futures* magazine, lots of direct mail, and glowing endorsements from various reviewers (including me). It brought to mind all the expensive systems that have been sold over the years (see Chapter 7). They all started with the same kind of fantastic track records and media hoopla. Almost none lived up to its promotional promise. Is this system going to be the one that makes millionaires out of its customers instead of just the promoter? Possibly.

I know the authors of the program, and they are honest and believe sincerely in their system. I don't find it suspicious that they are selling the system because I have never subscribed to the theory that a good system will self-destruct if sold to the public. I doubt that a huge number of people will buy this system for $3,000, and most of the ones who will actually trade it for any length of time will probably trade with different parameters anyway.

Although the authors publish different sets of historically successful parameters for stock indexes, T-bonds, and currencies, they don't necessarily recommend that the purchaser trade with their parameters. Being able, even encouraged, to create your own system will benefit those who want the ego satisfaction of being successful with their own creation rather than someone else's. The parameters provided will accommodate someone who doesn't want to be bothered with creating his own system.

The logic of this system is fully disclosed in the 62-page manual. This is a nice advantage over some other expensive software systems currently being sold for about the same price. The ideas are not revolutionary, but they are sound. The approach is similar to systems sold in the past by Larry Williams. The authors have added some very ingenious refinements that probably help account for the excellent historical trading performance.

There are some significant disadvantages to the system, however. It does not seem to work very well in nonfinancial markets. That leaves many markets unavailable for better diversification. This could be cured by trading other systems in those markets.

You must watch the market at the open and the close. The orders change every day, and you don't know the day's orders until the market opens. If you use a full-service broker, you could give him instructions before the opening to implement thereafter. However, if you use a discount broker and live on the West Coast, to trade the currencies you'll have to get up every morning at 5:15 A.M. In other parts of the country, commuting or a regular job could interfere with being available for the various market openings and closings.

The authors have continued to refine the software since its introduction. They have cured all the obvious deficiencies that originally existed. They continue research on the system and publish their results for customers. It is comforting to know that the vendor intends to continue supporting and improving its product.

Although the program is copyprotected, it allows a generous three hard disk installs and two floppy backups. I don't like to install protected software on my hard disk, but I had no trouble working from a floppy system disk with data on the hard disk.

An interesting problem has arisen for T-bond system traders since the Board of Trade instituted evening trading. How do you handle the new trading period? The Board of Trade considers the evening session to be part of the next day. However, historical testing (before the new evening trading began) involves only trading during the day. Should system traders ignore the evening session or incorporate its prices and trading into their system? The authors of the *Volatility Breakout System* suggest ignoring it. They look at only the daytime session in setting the open, high, and low prices to input into the computer. They do not trade during the night session. I have adopted the same approach for my own T-bond system testing and trading.

Historical profitability is not an issue with *VBS*. You can generate historical simulations with as much profit as anyone could reasonably expect. There are relatively low drawdowns as well. Compared to some other programs, *VBS* does well with fewer optimizable parameters. There are five, but two are closely related. A lot depends on how you create your version of the *Volatility Breakout System*. There is still plenty of opportunity to over-optimize. The manual alludes to this: "Fine tuning for the final few dollars of profit may not be as important as it appears. It is likely that the final tweaking of the system will not be significant. You will probably be better off selecting a parameter value which is in the middle of a range of superior performance."

The Professional Trading System by Bruce Babcock, Jr. CTCR Products, 1731 Howe Avenue, Suite 149, Sacramento, CA 95825. (916)-677-7562. For IBM PC/ XT/AT or compatibles, 256k, printer recommended. Price: $295. Guaranteed.

I have designed all my optimizable system programs to be competitive in quality with the expensive programs while being priced within the reach of every trader's budget. This program utilizes a long-term, trend-following algorithm with a little-known protective stop rule favored by a successful professional trader. I included fewer optimizable parameters than most systems have, in an effort to inhibit accidental curve-fitting. The system works well using only one changeable parameter. Holding that parameter the same, the system is profitable over a wide range of markets. It does increase profitability considerably, however, to vary that parameter for some markets. The trading logic of the system is not fully disclosed; however, as explained above, that is not necessary to use the program comfortably and successfully.

The Professional Trading System proved itself in a unique optimization contest *Commodity Traders Consumer Report* sponsored several years ago. Using *The Professional Trading System* software, the entrants determined system parameter sets for a portfolio of their choice of 12 markets. They were to test and optimize on identical 1981–85 data. There was a $1,000 prize for the best optimizer, but we awarded the big prizes ($20,000, $10,000, and $5,000) based on the entrants' portfolios' hypothetical performance *in the future*—July 1, 1986 to June 30, 1987. The entry deadline was December 31, 1986.

I was a little concerned about how well the contest entrants would do trading the future after doing their ultra-best to squeeze optimum performance out of past data. The one-year contest trading period was short enough so that good trends might not appear. It was certainly possible that the prize winners (although the best of all entrants) would actually lose money trading the future. That would prove embarrassing for me and my system. I held my breath for six months waiting for the contest trading period to end.

Considering the nature of the contest, the trading results were excellent. I think they prove the superiority of *The Professional Trading System*. Trading their chosen portfolio of 12 markets over the one-year period ending June 30, 1987, the top 20 optimizers *all* made good hypothetical profits, even after deducting $100 per trade for slippage and commissions. The first-place winner made $76,355. The second-place winner made $73,356. The third-place winner made $67,666. The 20th place performer made $16,498. Eleven out of the top 20 made more than $40,000 trading in 12 markets.

The Professional Trading System was the only major optimizable system program at the time that published hypothetical performance figures in its advertising. The initial 1986 ads contained detailed performance results for an unoptimized version using the same simple rules for each of 12 markets. No other software system had ever demonstrated profitability using the same parameters in all markets. During the one-year contest period, the system made $38,883 hypothetically trading that parameter set on those 12 markets.

I don't know if the contest results proved that optimization was helpful or not. It may have been luck. The portfolio of the winner of the best optimizer prize made $37,984 during the contest period and finished 13th in the contest. During the five-year optimization period (1981–85), his portfolio made $573,000, while the first-prize winner's optimized total was only $311,000. Draw your own conclusions.

Remember that hypothetical or simulated performance results have certain inherent limitations. Unlike an actual performance record, simulated results do not represent actual trading. Also, since the trades have not actually been executed, the results may have under- or over-compensated for the impact, if any, of certain market factors, such as lack of liquidity. Simulated trading programs in general are also subject to the fact that they are designed with the benefit of hindsight. No representation is being made that any account will or is likely to achieve profits or losses similar to those shown.

New Generation Optimizable Software Systems by Bruce Babcock, Jr. CTCR Products, 1731 Howe Avenue, Suite 149, Sacramento, CA 95825. (916)-677-7562. For IBM PC/XT/AT or compatibles, 256k, printer recommended. Price: $195 each or $795 for all 14 programs. Guaranteed.

My programmer, Stephen Winter, and I designed each of these programs with a similar user interface. They are intuitive and easy to use. Each program employs an entirely different trading system with different optimizable parameters, but the operational command structure is the same. There is a sophisticated historical testing and optimization module. When you decide on a tradeable parameter set, the program will generate real-time trading signals.

Each system comes with default parameters that I selected with a minimum of optimization. To maximize the integrity of the trading systems, I required that each work well over the same five-year period on two unrelated markets using the same parameters for long and short trades (dollar-adjusted to match the markets). The hypothetical trading results appear in the advertising. Other than *The Professional Trading System,* no other system being sold can make that claim. Nevertheless, when purchased as a group, the price is so low in comparison to other commodity system software as to be almost unbelievable.

Each of the systems comes with five years of historical data for its primary market along with suggested parameters for two markets. This is not to say that each system works only with the markets specified. The user is free to test and optimize any system in any market. Each also includes its own data management capability for creating, editing, and manually updating ASCII data files.

The first eleven *New Generation* systems are:

1. *Financial Genius* for the S&P and T-bonds. We designed this system for the volatile price action of the financial futures. It identifies trades with a unique pattern recognition algorithm.

2. *Silver Bullet* for silver and crude oil. This is a long-term system designed to exploit the tricky silver market. It employs a unique entry method based on reaction from a recent price extreme.

3. *Reversal Thrust* for the Swiss franc and crude oil. This is an excellent intermediate-term system that identifies trend changes by the unique interplay of two price pattern ratios.

4. *Protraction* for the British pound and T-bonds. If you look at the vertical price moves, they seem to make big profits before any reactions. This system takes advantage of that property by staying with a move as long as it continues, but exiting when it pauses.

5. *Channel No. 5* for Eurodollars and the Deutschemark. This is an ultra-modern version of the hoary but effective channel breakout system.

6. *Hot Pursuit* for cotton and Eurodollars. This is an extraordinary trailing stop-type system that incorporates momentum.

7. *Retracement* for the Japanese yen and the S&P. One of the most popular trading methods is to position with the major trend after a minor reaction against the major trend. This system is a mechanical implementation of that strategy.

8. *Super Slinky* for the Deutschemark and Eurodollars. This is the latest advanced incarnation of a system I wrote several years ago called Slinky. It has an uncanny ability to pick significant tops and bottoms.

9. *Equilibrium* for sugar and the Swiss franc. Rather than look for a trend or price pattern to signal a trade, this system looks for a mathematical price equilibrium. It then follows the next substantial market move.

10. *Oasis* for crude oil and the Japanese yen. We call this system *Oasis* because we originally designed it for the crude oil market. It is simple in concept but refreshingly effective. It seems to work even better in other markets.

11. *Warp Factor* for T-bonds and the Swiss franc. This system is a cousin of the *Protraction* system. Its triggering mechanism is rapidity of price movement. You set the threshold speed required before entering a position.

System Creators

Prudent traders should always test their trading plan before risking real money. Many ideas that may appear promising when you look at a few charts turn into disasters when tested with a computer over a longer period of time. If you know a programming language and want to spend the time, you can create your own testing software. What do you do if you are not a programmer? Until a few years ago, your only recourse was to hire a professional programmer. It seemed impossible to create a piece of software that would allow a nonprogrammer to create and test trading systems. However, a number of programs now exist that offer nonprogrammers wide flexibility to test trading ideas.

System Writer by William Cruz. Omega Research, Inc., 3900 N.W. 79th Avenue, Suite 520, Miami, FL 33166. (305)-594-7664. For IBM PC/XT/AT or compatibles with 640k memory. Hard disk strongly recommended. Price: $1,975. Copyprotected. 15-day money-back guarantee.

In a 1986 software review in *Commodity Traders Consumer Report*, I said a program that would allow the user to formulate his own unrestricted system and then test it historically without programming language ability would be "the financial trading software equivalent of putting men on the moon." Much to my surprise, just such a program is now available.

In December 1987, Bill Cruz flew to Sacramento to show me his *System Writer* program. I knew the claims he had been making, but I was very skeptical. I figured there would be important limitations on the systems you could create with it. After spending an entire day watching Bill demonstrate it and using it myself, he convinced me that he had in fact made a quantum leap in commodity trading software design.

Bill had three programmers working full-time on the project for four years. All the effort was worth it. There are not enough superlatives to do justice to the finished product. Considering what it can do and comparing it to other commodity software products, even at $1,975 it is grossly underpriced. The true comparative value is so high, almost no one would be able to afford it.

Although there were some limitations in that first edition, many of them have been eliminated in subsequent updates. Now the most significant one is that you cannot use more than one commodity data file at a time to generate signals. Thus, you can't trade spreads or use T-bond data to generate S&P trading signals. The only other practical limitation is your own ability to correctly describe your trading rules in *System Writer's* programming language, which Cruz optimistically calls "Easy Language." How "easy" it is will depend on you.

Bill likes to use the example of going to a seminar and hearing Larry Williams or Jake Bernstein describe a new system or indicator. "Now," promises Cruz, "you can go home and use *System Writer* to test its effectiveness. All you have to do is describe the entry and exit rules in plain, everyday English." But will you be able to translate the system accurately into Easy Language? The brochure gives the following example of a Key Reversal Buy signal translated into proper syntax: "If low of today is < low of yesterday and close of today is > than close of yesterday then buy tomorrow at market." That's fine for simple ideas, but systems as simple as that probably won't be very effective. Here's another example from the manual: "If @WeightedMA(Close,VarA,0) > @WeightedMA(Close,VarB,0) then sell tomorrow at market." That English maybe isn't so plain and everyday after all. Nor are True/False Functions, Else Clauses, or For, While, Repeat, and Chained or Nested If-Statements.

The program helps you get the syntax right by quickly flagging errors and explaining what you did wrong. But it can't guarantee you'll faithfully describe the system taught at the seminar. Easy Language may use mostly plain English, but advanced trading concepts are not so simply reduced to plain English. The manual won't be much help here. Although the program makes things as easy as it could, a package as powerful as this necessarily requires a certain amount of intelligence and sophistication to plumb its full capabilities.

A good analogy is the *Lotus 1–2–3* spreadsheet program. Most people can learn fairly easily to do simple spreadsheets with it. But they will never learn enough to take advantage of its real power. For instance, an expert can use its macro language to create complicated turn-key accounting or income tax applications, but could you ever hope to accomplish that?

System Writer can test your systems historically, but it can't help you decide which rules to combine to achieve satisfactory results. I suspect most people will have a hard time creating non-curve-fitted systems that can generate exceptional profits over long periods in more than one market. Yet that is the only kind of system that has a strong likelihood of generating profits in real-time trading. At least you should be able to identify methods and indicators that don't work.

In order to assist less knowledgeable users, the program allows the exporting and importing of trading rules. Thus, you could acquire others' ready-made indicators or whole systems and use or modify them on your computer. Cruz plans to encourage this kind of secondary market. Some will be free and some will be for purchase. With enough effort, you should eventually become skilled enough to create complicated systems.

To help you get started, the program comes with 23 indicators you can use as they are or modify. Some examples are Wilder's Relative Strength, Williams' %R, Momentum Oscillator, Runaway Gap, Key Reversal, Island Reversal, Outside Day Breakout, Simple Moving Average Crossover, Weighted Moving Average Crossover, Swing Index, Price Channel Breakout, Stochastic Crossover, and Bull/Bear Hooks. You can combine these any way you want or use them as a core and add additional rules or conditions. There are also some prewritten stop and profit-taking rules, but you are free to write your own if you can. A useful aspect of these canned signals is that you can see exactly how they are constructed in Easy Language.

My biggest gripe is that you must separately state and test entry and exit rules for long and short positions. To prevent curve-fitting, I prefer my systems to have identical rules for long and short trades. But in order to optimize an indicator length in *System Writer,* you have to test all the possible combinations for long and short trades rather than just those where the indicator length is the same for both. This is a waste of time. Cruz promises to remedy the problem in a future release. Also, I see no reason that a system cannot take action on today's close when the system gives a predictable signal on the close. *System Writer,* however, requires that all entries occur "tomorrow." The program's design favors those who want to create a system for a single market. It is more cumbersome for those who expect a system to work in multiple markets.

System Writer comes with its own data management program and can use many data formats including CSI, CompuTrac, ASCII, CompuServe, I.P. Sharp, and even Tick Data, Inc. for intraday system testing. When you find a system you want to trade, the Auto Run mode will generate daily signals after you update your data.

A hardware attachment between your parallel port and printer cable provides the foolproof copy-protection. This is transparent to other programs. I have had no trouble with mine.

This is truly the program of the future for testing and trading mechanical approaches in stocks and commodities. The investment of money and time required to acquire, learn, and use the program should be well rewarded.

Back Trak by Steven Kille. Microvest, P.O. Box 272, Macomb, IL 61455. (309)-837-4512. For IBM PC/XT/AT or compatibles with 512k and a printer. Hard disk recommended. No graphics card required. Price: $695.

Until *System Writer* came along, this was the best program for testing trading ideas. The difference between it and *System Writer* is that *Back Trak* limits you to systems that incorporate specific indicators and trading rules, while *System Writer* allows you to create virtually anything under the sun. *Back Trak* gives you so many different indicators and methods, however, that it still a worthwhile program. It does cost considerably less than *System Writer,* and requires no mathematical translation of system rules. You make all choices via menus.

Back Trak's available rules consist of analytical algorithms (studies) and exit and profit-stop techniques. There are 51 analytical algorithms, which can be divided into trend identifiers and overbought/oversold oscillators. Kille could have added more, but he ran out of ideas. No doubt as users suggest worthwhile additions to the list, Steve will add them to future updates. Although you can't create your own from thin air, there are so many variations here, maybe you won't need to. Your testing can involve optimizing the parameters of any variable algorithms.

When designing your system you can combine any five different studies at once. You also have complete freedom to use them for long or short trades only and for entry or exit only. An interesting twist is the ability to use oscillators to buy on weakness (say buying when RSI goes below 25) or to buy on strength (buying when RSI goes below 25 and then comes back above 25). Vice versa for shorts. The possibilities are so endless, you could not test them all in your lifetime. But that's only the beginning.

Next is your entry, exit, and profit-stop strategy. You can choose from 15 different stop-loss and profit-taking strategies or use reverse signals with no stops. There are, in addition, 10 ways to enter your positions after a signal.

If all this isn't enough, you can also add additional contracts as often as you want when the market moves against you by a certain amount or choose one of three pyramiding strategies to add positions as the market moves in your favor.

You can run optimizations on as many data files as your computer's memory will allow without re-entering the parameters. This permits chaining contracts together to simulate roll-overs. A new feature is called "Realtime Testing." This permits you to select some files for optimization and some others for testing the optimum parameters on data not involved in the optimization. This is an important concept in testing systems to prevent curve-fitted systems. *Back Trak* does it for you all at the same time.

The reporting capabilities are no less comprehensive than the system-creating features. You can choose from eight possible formats that range from printing only the optimum parameters for the entire test to printing every possible statistic available for each contract on a day-to-day basis. You can print any combination or all eight kinds of reports at the same time. You can also automatically graph your hypothetical results to assist in evaluating them. You get performance statistics in 26 categories, and you can include slippage and commissions.

Once your testing is finished, the program will run your system and give you a daily report for tomorrow's trading signals. If your printer can use the Graphics.com program in DOS, this option allows you to print a daily bar chart with volume and open interest with the signals. You can also see your system's up-to-the-minute results on the contract you are trading, the last five orders placed, and a record of the last five days of trading.

In addition to all the above, *Back Trak* contains a complete data management program that will allow you to create, manually update and edit your own data files. One major disadvantage is that it is limited to the CSI data format.

All this power comes in a menu-driven setup that is remarkably easy to use. Although it doesn't have the flexibility of *System Writer,* it is an excellent value for the price.

Advanced Toolboxes with Testing Capability

There are two programs that combine the toolbox concept with the ability to test the historical effectiveness of the indicators, either alone or in combination.

Computrac, Technical Analysis Group, 1017 Pleasant Street, New Orleans, LA 70115. (800)-535-7990 or (504)-895-1474. For IBM PC/XT/AT or compatibles. Price: $1,900 plus a $300 yearly update fee. Copyprotected.

Buying *CompuTrac* software is more than just receiving some new programs in the mail. You will be joining a group of traders (the Technical Analysis Group) who got together in 1978 to create a commodity trading software package. Their efforts evolved into the standard for the industry, and they now number over 6,000 worldwide. *CompuTrac* is the most complete package available for analyzing the markets on a daily, weekly, and monthly basis. They spend a great deal of effort in supporting their members. This is important when the package is as broad in scope as this is.

Buying *CompuTrac* software is a major investment of money and time. Learning how to use it and using it daily will be time-consuming. Purchasing it should not be taken lightly. You must consider the cost of all necessary hardware and software, the cost of obtaining the necessary data, the time it will take to learn and use the system, and the time it will take to use it on a daily basis. These costs must be balanced against the personal enjoyment and how it will benefit your trading effectiveness.

No software package has as many or better analytical tools than *CompuTrac*. There are over 40 studies or indicators and many additional chart analysis tools. Some of the best are available nowhere else. If you are not satisfied with all that is there, you can create your own indicators. Then *CompuTrac* will chart and test your indicator just like it was one of its own.

To serve the needs of its many thousands of users, the Group has made their software as flexible as computer memory will allow. There are user-defined options for just about everything. This is invaluable for customizing the studies for each commodity and obtaining just the presentation style you like.

The price you pay for such comprehensiveness and flexibility is complexity. Even though it is menu-driven, learning to use this software is truly like learning a foreign language. The manual is 433 pages long. You receive help from audio learning tapes that take you through a hands-on demonstration of most features. To learn the system thoroughly enough to benefit from all its sophisticated capabilities will be a lengthy process. The manual makes only a limited attempt to show you how the various studies can be used. I would suggest purchasing a manual first ($30), if possible, to give yourself a better idea of the software's possibilities and limitations.

One of the most important capabilities is automatic operation. Once you decide on a set pattern of analysis routines, you can program the computer to run them automatically on all your data files. You can start the operation and leave. When you return, you will find a whole batch of up-to-date charts printed just the way you like them. This can save hours of time, but setting up these "Master Procedures" is a complicated process.

One of the most crucial elements of *CompuTrac* is its capability to test historically a trading plan you create with its indicators. This has developed over the years into a very sophisticated component. Depending on your sophistication in setting up the tests, the program will handle most typical trading approaches.

CompuTrac is not for novices. It should not be the first computer program you buy. For those who want the ultimate in toolbox software and are willing to pay the price in money and time, this is the package to buy.

Market Research Language from Futures Software Associates, P.O. Box 263, Lima, PA 19037. (215)-872-4512. For IBM and compatibles with 512k memory. CGA/EGA or Hercules graphics. IBM or Epson-compatible printer optional. Works only with ASCII data. Price: $695. Demo disk and audio tape: $20.

Market Research Language (MRL) is the latest innovation in commodity trading software. It combines three separate functions into one package: data charting and manipulation; analytical study creation and charting; and indicator and system hypothetical testing. It is similar to combination packages in other software areas in that it does not do as good a job on the individual functions as dedicated packages. But you could pay almost $4,000 to buy the best dedicated charting, analysis, and system-testing software packages. *MRL* costs only a fraction. Before you whip out your checkbook, though, there are some important drawbacks you should understand.

MRL came into being in the late 1970s on a mainframe computer, designed by computer experts for computer experts. Now, 10 years later, they are marketing it to the trading public for use on a personal computer. They have not redesigned it for ease of use, however. The most important thing to understand is that it is not menu-driven. That means when you boot it up, it presents you with nothing but a blank line. It is just like DOS. If you insist on using a DOS shell program because you don't like typing all those arcane DOS commands, *MRL* is not for you. *MRL* requires more program expertise from users than any other program I know. If that does not intimidate you, read on.

MRL is an evolving program sold by a small company without the resources to improve it rapidly or support it intensively. For instance, to get technical support, you must leave a message and wait for a call back. The company is committed, however, to support its customers, improve the program, and stay with it for many years to come. We are confident that *MRL* will evolve into a fantastic piece of software usable by almost everyone, but we don't know how long it will take. Because the commodity software market is so small, it is unlikely that the company will generate the kind of profits that would accelerate the process. You must be prepared, therefore, to accept the current limitations and overcome them through your own effort. *MRL* does have some capability to ease your task with canned studies, editing, macros, and other structural features. The manual is currently on the bare-bones side, especially for a command-line program. However, we expect periodic supplements and improvements.

As of this writing the program includes 26 canned studies. No doubt, more will come later. These are all in ASCII files, so you can build on them and study their construction to help learn how to use the program. You can create any studies or indicators you can express mathematically, and then chart them with bar charts or incorporate them into trading systems. You can hypothetically test any indicator or system on your data. You can manipulate data in any way imaginable to create different data points than the usual price, volume, and open interest. For instance, you could incorporate T-bond data into an S&P system or study. A unique feature is a mathematical cycle-finder.

With some diligent effort on your part, you can create your own personalized analysis system with *MRL*. You will be able to enjoy the growth of the program in the years to come. If you have doubts about whether you can handle its complexities, I suggest you obtain the demo and perhaps buy the manual before committing to the program.

Simulators

These are clever programs that attempt to simulate what it is like to watch the market and trade during the day. They use actual intraday data files so the market action is realistically accurate. They allow you to practice trading using tick-by-tick data. The programs replay a day's price activity on your computer screen at the speed you choose. At any time you can stop the action and place orders. The programs then keep track of how your trading comes out. You can test your ability to react quickly to changing conditions, and you can test the effectiveness of a particular approach. Each of these two programs is a monument to the programmer's art. They are both brilliantly executed and look great in color.

Before buying either program, there are some threshold questions you need to answer. First, are you interested in intraday trading? Do you really want to watch the market during the day and do you have the time available? Second, are you going to use the program for its entertainment value or as a serious training tool? If you are primarily after entertainment, both programs will give you lots of fun, and I can definitely recommend them as ultrarealistic commodity trading games. They are light-years ahead of any available games, although considerably more expensive.

If you are after training for the real thing, you must consider whether this kind of "make believe" is valuable or not. One school of thought says, "Yes, paper-trading is a way to test your trading plan without risking precious capital." The other school of thought says, "No, the only thing you learn from paper-trading is how to paper-trade." No simulation can match the emotional roller coaster of real trading, and it may give you a false sense of ability. You will probably not react the same when real money is on the line. There is merit in both arguments, and I have no strong opinion one way or the other.

Trading Simulator by Doug Bry and Phil Spertus. Technical Trading Strategies, Inc., 4877 South Everett Street, Littleton, CO 80123. (800)-648-2232 or (303)-972-1433. For IBM PC/XT/AT or compatibles. Price: $395. Copyprotected. Free demo disk available.

Trading Simulator displays the intraday price activity only in the Chicago Board of Trade's Market Profile® format, invented by Peter Steidlmayer. Because the Market Profile chart method is inherently less flexible than bar charting, *Trading Simulator* is less complicated and much easier to use than the program that follows.

You enter the market and the date, and you are ready to begin. As the market opens, the prices begin to form the familiar profile on the screen. At the bottom of the screen you see the current time of day and the daily open, high, low, tick volume, and TPO (Time-Price-Opportunity) count. You can see up to 15 days of previous price action to ascertain the trend. The previous days' price action is shown as traditional price bars and value areas rather than a full-blown profile. The program also keeps track of tick volume. The user selects the price scaling and the speed with which the day's price activity unfolds. You can stop the action at any time to reflect on tactics or place an order. The program handles market, stop, limit, and close-only orders. You can trade any number of contracts. The program pauses at the end of the day, but you can hold positions overnight. You can even roll over to the next contract. At any time you can see a recapitulation of your trading and its profitability. You can vary the commission rate and the time delay before execution of your orders. One of the most interesting variables is the TPO time length. Steidlmayer always uses 30 minutes, but with *Trading Simulator,* you can experiment with other lengths. The program comes with tick data for the S&P, soybeans and T-bonds.

GUTS by Eric Scott Hunsader. Codeworks, Inc., P.O. Box 9581, Pensacola, FL 32513. (904)-435-6897. For IBM PC/XT/AT or compatibles. Price: $195. Not copyprotected. 15-day return privilege less $10 and shipping.

GUTS uses the traditional bar chart approach. Because the problems of simulating trading with intraday bar charts is inherently more complicated than with using Market Profiles, *GUTS* has much broader capability. Concomitantly, it is harder to learn. Although not the easiest program to learn, it does have a nice help facility, which at any time shows you all the available commands and what they do.

GUTS works in units of one day. At the end of a day's trading, you must stop and load more data for the next day. However, during the day you can trade up to 15 markets at once if you have the available tick data. (The program comes with data for four markets and five cash indexes.) Just as in real trading, you can switch back and forth among markets and trade them all. You can even watch them all at once on a simulated quote board.

The program allows all the standard kinds of orders, and you can trade multiple contracts. There is a programmable time delay for executing orders and variable commissions. It keeps detailed track of your trading record in relation to a starting account size and shows your entry and exit points on the charts. The trading record can span up to 255 trades over as many trading days as you want, so you can get a realistic picture of how you are doing over time. It will even give you margin calls!

GUTS goes farther than you would expect from such a program by building in analysis tools you can use on your intraday bar charts. You can draw trend lines and Gann Angle lines. It even has something called an Elliott Wave Ruler, which allows you to measure time in Fibonacci increments. A simple trend-line approach looks very attractive when you examine intraday charts. Here is a great way to test its true effectiveness over an extended time period and to see whether you have the discipline to follow it.

If you use either of these products in a realistic way, you should begin to appreciate the difficulty of intraday trading. But perhaps you are the exceptional person who will thrive on it. Since intraday trading equipment, software, and data are expensive, either or both of these programs would make an excellent preliminary investment for someone considering the purchase of intraday trading equipment.

Intraday Trading Graphics and Quote Systems

These are the real Cadillac programs, and their cost reflects it. They actually connect you to the exchanges by satellite dish, FM transmission, or dedicated telephone line. You can watch prices change and display price charts and analytic studies within seconds of the actual trades on the floor. Your ability to watch all the markets at once gives you an advantage over floor traders in that respect.

I always advise people considering this kind of equipment to look at it in operation. You can't buy it from a brochure. You must watch it in action to see how it works and judge whether it will mesh with your trading approach. Have the company direct you to a nearby user for a demonstration if at all possible.

System One from Commodity Quotegraphics, P.O. Box 758, Glenwood Springs, CO 81602. (800)-525-7082 or (303)-945-8686. Hardware and software for an all-in-one commodity workstation with quotes, charts, and news. Price: $475 to $597 per month, depending on features, plus $44 to $192 for exchange fees, depending on the exchanges you choose.

I have used the previous-generation Commodity Quotegraphics *TQ 20/20* system for quotes and charts since June 1983. I have written extensively about using its features to trade the markets. I am thus somewhat biased. It is not the bias, however, that can arise from receiving something free. I am a paying customer, and equipment like this does not come cheap. It is a bias that comes from a long relationship with one of the very best companies in the futures industry. Quote equipment is the most expensive investment a trader makes. Therefore, it is a good idea to examine the company as well as the product. The folks at CQG know what they're doing. They have a technically advanced yet reliable product, and they take care of their customers. I can truly say that dealing with CQG is like dealing with your favorite uncle. For example, if you have a hardware problem that requires service, they will send you another unit overnight before you even return the old one. The best comparison is Federal Express, an organization so competent it takes your breath away.

Back in 1982, the *TQ 20/20* system originally used a Radio Shack computer. Then, to increase its capability, CQG moved up to the Epson QX/10. Although not IBM-compatible, the Epson has served its needs well. Eventually the software grew to the limits allowed by the Epson machine, and in 1987, Epson stopped manufacturing the computer. Thus, CQG had to look for another computer to run its next-generation system. They decided to build their own. The result is the *System One*. I have been using a *System One* right alongside my original *TQ 20/20* system for several years now. It has matured into a magnificent commodity trading workstation.

Having seen the growth in capability of these systems over the last six years, the latest machines are truly amazing. The new computer is far more powerful with more memory, but it takes up only half the desk space of the old Epson. Since CQG makes its own keyboard, all the function keys are correctly labeled. This makes it a snap to learn. It uses 3.5-inch diskettes, which are easier to handle, although you seldom need to handle them. The new monitor screen is slightly smaller, but the displayed chart size is over 20 percent larger. If you want to see quotes or news and charts at the same time, you can have two monitors ($50 per month extra), but you can't have color. For hyperactive traders the *System One* can show up to 10 charts at once in separate windows on one screen.

Those who have experience maintaining their own data files can attest to how time-consuming it is, even if you collect daily data by modem. The *TQ 20/20* is mostly automatic, but you do have to maintain a list of 96 intraday charts and update the list as the various contracts expire. You also have to correct bad ticks on intraday charts on your own. Bad intraday ticks are a problem; they are especially prevalent in the New York markets. With *System One,* you never have to do any data management work. It even corrects its own intraday charts.

The *System One* is ready to show you monthly, weekly, daily, 60-minute, 30-minute, 15-minute, 10-, 9-, 8-, 7-, 6-, 5-, 4-, 3-, 2-, and 1-minute bar charts of virtually any contract of any commodity you desire, all current to the moment. It even saves its data automatically every day. Most people receive their real-time quotes with a discrete two-foot satellite dish. All the necessary hardware is included in the monthly price.

One very important feature of this package is that all three components—hardware, software, and data—come from the same source. This prevents one vendor from blaming another if something goes wrong. Such finger-pointing is common in the computer industry, and nothing is more frustrating to an unsophisticated user who just wants his system to work. If you ever have any problem, you know where to turn, and you know they will fix it immediately.

There are four basic components of the service. You can subscribe to the level of information your trading style requires. The components are: 1) quotes for futures, quotes for options, intraday charts and studies, time and sales, and CWN news; 2) daily charts; 3) weekly and monthly charts; and 4) Market Profile® and Volume Profile™ charts. You can also choose to receive prices from any of 16 available exchanges worldwide.

The *System One's* chart analyzing tools are more limited than on the *TQ 20/20* system, which has 17 different kinds of indicators. The

System One now has only five: RSI, slow Stochastics, two moving averages, oscillators, and tick volume. The first four are user-adjustable. We have said for many years, however, that such indicators are mostly redundant anyway. The *System One* has just added to its arsenal point and figure, spread, and ratio charts for both intraday and daily data. The one thing missing on both systems we would most like to see is total-volume and open interest charts. Another excellent addition would be a cycle finder feature that would display the mathematically derived dominant cycle for the chart on the screen.

Although news is available on the *TQ 20/20*, the only way to get it is to turn on your printer and have it all print out. This turns into a real annoyance and a waste of paper. With the *System One*, you can instead display news on the monitor, and then print only what you want. Each story is indexed, and there is a further subject matter index. It is thus easy to watch for stories that might interest you.

Like its predecessor, the *System One* has price alerts, which warn you when a price has been hit in a market you are following. It adds time-alert capability to remind you of Fed intervention time or an impending close. Neither system has study alerts. You can also get time and sales data to check those bad fills yourself.

For those who want to analyze the market using Steidlmayer's Market Profile charting concepts, the *System One* has the most comprehensive capabilities in this area. You can separate night and day sessions, adjust the scale, calculate TPO counts, and generate multiple running profiles. For non-Board of Trade markets, the system calculates and displays a running TPO value area. CQG has added their own unique Volume Profile charts for Board of Trade markets. That is the only exchange that currently provides volume breakdown information. The latest additions are profile charts of tick volume and spreads.

An important question for anyone contemplating the considerable investment required for intraday quotation/charting capability would be whether he could expect the investment to be returned in the form of more profitable trading. In other words, will the system pay for itself? If this is crucial to you, you should probably not make the investment. While you will have increased analytical capability, turning this into larger profits is not automatic. If you want to day-trade, remember that it is extremely stressful. I use the system constantly but never day trade (on purpose).

When you are ready to add intraday market-watching to your lifestyle, the reasonably-priced CQG *System One* is supreme in design and execution. Both the company and the product carry my highest recommendation.

You have now learned all the ingredients of a successful system, the computer software available to help you, how to create one, how to test it, and how to know whether it is any good. You are almost ready to begin choosing a system to trade. But should you trade with someone else's system or design your own? In the next chapter I'll show you how to decide.

14 Creating Your Own System

Most traders, especially inexperienced traders, overlook the importance of ego in trading. Yet it may be one of the most crucial factors in making trading decisions. Psychologists and psychiatrists have their own definition of ego as it relates to intellectual control of basic human instincts. I am using the term in its more popular sense, which refers to an individual's concept of his own importance and ability.

Looking from the outside at speculation, the perception is that its purpose is to make money. This is always the initial attraction. A person wants to increase his wealth without the usual efforts of a full-time job. The perception is that this is somehow going to be easy money.

Once a person moves from the theory to the actual practice of speculation, however, he learns several things. First, he learns that intelligent speculation is much more time-consuming than he thought. Second, he learns that he can derive much broader satisfaction from speculating than the easy profits that were his initial goal. Because successful speculation is so difficult, it offers a real challenge that stimulates most people all by itself.

There is great intellectual excitement from learning to be an expert trader. It makes for popular cocktail party conversation. A futures trader first explores trading and analysis in general. This is incredibly diverse and detailed subject matter. Plumbing its depths can take years. Then there is a choice among about 30 potential markets to trade. Each one offers additional unique research potential. The whole endeavor can keep an intellectually curious individual occupied seemingly forever.

Futures trading has a competitive aspect that is not present to such an extent in the stock market or real estate. Purchasers of common stock usually think of themselves as investing in the future of a company; real estate investors are also buying assets. To them, investing is a game where everyone can win except that some will win more than others. When you buy a stock or a building from someone else and its value subsequently goes up, the person who sold it to you does not lose money because of selling. He may take the proceeds, buy another stock or apartment house, and make even more money. Futures traders, on the other hand, are acutely aware that whenever they make money on a trade, someone somewhere else must lose. This can really get the competitive juices flowing in a society that exalts competition in both profit-seeking and pleasure-seeking activities.

Whereas the average person has natural limits that prevent him from being as skillful and competitive as he would want in other areas of life, there appear to be fewer natural handicaps in futures trading. In predicting whether the price of wheat will go up next week, there is no apparent disadvantage from limited capital. If you have enough for the margin for one contract, you have as much chance to make the right call as a millionaire who might trade a hundred contracts. Unlike the stock market, in which inside information governs every stock's value, there is very little inside information in commodities. The general consensus is that inside information is much less significant in the commodity world. I have heard stories from people who tried to trade on information they perceived to be ahead of the market. They failed. Weather is certainly an important piece of information that can influence commodity prices. To trained weather experts, a weather forecast is like inside information, yet I don't know of any weather forecaster who has made a fortune in the markets.

The would-be speculator quickly learns about those two non-monetary rewards of trading—intellectual stimulation and competition. The reality is that for most people these secondary satisfactions quickly become the primary reason for trading. That explains why so many people continue to trade after many years of financial disappointment. They enjoy the process of trading, and there is always the hope of success in the future.

Almost every trader, whether he knows it or not, trades more for the ego satisfaction than the money. I have given many seminars over the years, and I always try to ask the audience how many of them trade solely for the money. A number of years ago as many as 75 percent thought they were trading for the money. Lately, the proportion has reversed, and a great majority now realize that money may not be the most important factor. One time I asked whether people would continue trading if they knew they would not make money, but they also knew they would not lose very much. A surprising number admitted they would continue trading even with the certainty that they would not strike it rich.

The most essential aspect of ego in trading is the need to be right, i.e., to be smarter than the other guy. If you understand this paramount importance of ego, it can help you avoid some mistakes. A good example is failing to use a stop-loss for fear you will be stopped out of your position while being right about the market in the end.

The primary application to trading systems of the insight about the importance of ego is to understand a trader's reluctance to use someone else's system. The reason is that there is much less ego satisfaction in being successful with someone else's plan than your own. The inclination, therefore, is to make enough changes, even though minor, so that you can feel that it was your system that beat the market, rather than the other guy's. This concept also applies to advisory services. Very few traders will follow the advisor's recommendations to the letter. They either modify the orders or select among the trades. Even though they pay good money for the advice, they think they can do better. They want some of the glory. They end up following a profitable advisor and losing money. Instead of realizing the reason, they look for another advisor.

I am not passing judgment on anyone's decision to subordinate profits to ego. As long as they understand what they are doing, no one else should care. Since you are probably going to end up creating your own system anyway, you might as well recognize the realities and implications and go ahead and do it. However, if you believe you do not have the ability to create your own system, there is nothing wrong with trading someone else's. There can still be plenty of room for ego satisfaction. If the system you choose ultimately makes money, you will be ahead of almost everyone else who trades commodities. That is certainly something to be proud of. There are an infinite number of possible trading systems available. You had the good sense to pick a profitable system, even if the ideas weren't yours. They probably were not original with the system developer either. Even more important, you had the discipline to trade the system to a profitable result. I might also add that you can pat yourself on the back for realizing that it was more important to make money than to make a potentially futile effort at creating your own system.

As I hope this book has demonstrated, there is nothing particularly mysterious about creating a profitable trading system. So don't feel you need a Ph.D. in quantum mechanics to undertake the effort. There is a great amount of satisfaction to be derived from creating a system that makes money. Who knows? You might even sell the system or manage other people's money with it.

The real key to creating your own successful system is to understand the importance of proper testing. If you are going to make any changes at all in someone else's system, its track record is no longer applicable. You must test your system carefully before trading it. Remember also that testing serves an even more important purpose than just verifying that the system was profitable in the past. Your own testing will give you sufficient experience with the details of the system's past performance so that you will have confidence to keep trading it during the inevitable drawdowns. This is crucial to long-term success. So cut no corners in testing your ideas.

It may be possible to test some systems without a computer. If the system has rules that you can follow on charts you might be able to test it by obtaining back charts and going over them by hand. The best source for historical charts is a series of books called *The Encyclopedia of Historical Charts,* published by Commodity Perspective. It covers every popular trading market and contains weekly charts and daily charts for most delivery months. It starts in 1975, and every year they publish another volume, so you can keep up to date. The price is a remarkable bargain. For more information, contact Commodity Perspective, 30 South Wacker Drive, Suite 1820, Chicago, IL 60606; (312)-454–1801. It helps to have data to establish exact prices. I routinely save the commodity prices published every day in *The Wall*

Street Journal. It is a good habit to get into. When back-testing a system using charts, be very careful not to miss the losing signals. It is a psychological fact that when looking at a chart, we tend to see the profitable signals easily, while overlooking the losers. That is the big advantage of computer testing. The computer makes the test carefully and dispassionately. It will warn you away from a losing system that may have looked great when you tested by just eyeballing some charts.

Be wary of other people's testing. Be sure you know exactly how they conducted the test. Did it take account of opening gaps? If the system could have generated several signals during one day's trading, how did they know which one came first? Do the results include a reasonable deduction for slippage and commissions? What data did they use? Did they use the same system rules and parameters for each market? Review Chapter 5 for a complete discussion of all the considerations involved in accurate testing.

Be especially wary of systems or indicators that are illustrated by one or two charts. This is a favorite tactic of authors and system purveyors. It is easy to find several charts that will make just about any system look good. Do not get excited about such systems until you have tested them over much more data.

Luckily for traders, there are a number of computer programs available that permit you to test trading ideas and trading systems without any knowledge of computer programming. I have described some of the best in Chapter 13. These programs are terrific, but they do require that you be able to express the system in mathematical terms or in language the program understands. For complicated systems, this is not always easy. It is futile to use one of these programs if you cannot be sure you will describe the system correctly to the program. You may end up trading a system entirely different from the one the computer actually tested. Even professional programmers make mistakes in translating ideas to program code. I remember some giddy moments over the years when the results from computer-testing some trading ideas were too good to be true. After great excitement about big breakthroughs, it turned out that the testing program had errors that caused the exceptional results. It is a good idea to dissect the trade-by-trade results from the program to make sure it is testing the same system you intended to describe.

If you have a large enough budget, it might be worthwhile to hire your own programmer. Local colleges are a good source for skilled programmers who will work for a reasonable wage. People are willing to spend thousands of dollars for commercial software and willing to risk even more thousands trading, but they are unwilling to spend a little money for custom computer programming. If your programmer can convince you not to trade just a few losing ideas, the money you pay will be well spent. Once the programmer sets up the basic testing framework, it is relatively simple to incorporate different trading ideas or systems. This is an investment every serious trader should consider.

It might be useful to say a few words about the various kinds of systems you can create. If you have enough capital, you can trade several or even many systems at once. Which type or types you choose will depend on your personality and which trading style you feel comfortable with. In his excellent book *Beyond the Investor's Quotient* Jake Bernstein argues that this decision is one of the most important decisions a futures trader must make. Jake was a practicing psychologist before he was a commodity trader, and his insights in the area of trading psychology are more important to profitable trading than the usual books on market analysis. I strongly recommend both that book and his original book on the subject, *The Investor's Quotient.*

You can break all trading systems down into two identifiable types. A system can either wait for a trend to become established and then enter in the direction of the trend, or it can attempt to identify trend changes precisely and enter just before or just after assumed tops and bottoms. You can trade either of the two system types over roughly the following five time periods: one day, several days based on intraday data, up to one week based on daily data, one week to one month based on daily data, and over one month based on weekly data.

For various reasons a person can decide not to hold any trade overnight. Such a trade is called a day trade. You can day-trade, watching market activity during the day using intraday charts or without watching the market during the day. Intraday charts use data-point time periods ranging in length from one minute to one hour. To obtain them, you will need a computer connected to the exchanges by satellite dish, FM radio signal, or dedicated telephone line. Five-minute charts are very popular, as are 30-minute and one-hour charts. Those who trade using intraday charts must have the time, the discipline, and the emotional control to watch market action during the day. For most people this is incredibly stressful. At the end of the day, however, the trader can (theoretically) forget the markets until the next day. He does not have to worry about the effect of overnight news on his position. He can take time off when wants, more sure that he will not miss much. The required computer equipment and exchange fees to obtain intraday charts is less expensive than it used to be, but it still costs between $500 and $1,000 per month. Since per-trade profits will necessarily be smaller for short-term trading, the costs of trading are a bigger percentage of those profits. This leaves less margin for error than with longer-term trading. Even with all the relative disadvantages, some traders may prefer this kind of hyperactive involvement. It is the greatest challenge in futures trading.

You can also be a day-trader without watching the market during the day. You would trade with a system that analyzed past data and generated its signals before the market opened. The system would tell you what orders to place. Ideally, the orders would not be changed by what happens after the open, so that you could place the orders and go about your business. If the system requires monitoring the market during the day, a broker can do this for you. However, the cost of higher commissions for a full-service broker can be enough to cause such systems to fail. Because most markets do not have a large enough daily range to make this kind of trading feasible, you are restricted to the most volatile markets, like stock indexes and T-bonds. Since by definition you cannot let profits run longer than to the end of the day, you are violating one of the key tenets of good trading—letting your profits run. Profitable day-trading systems that work like this are the most difficult to create. The combination of the difficulty of predicting the likely market direction for the next day, the limited profit potential, and the costs of trading conspires to defeat these systems.

Trades made from intraday charts may be completed during the same day or may be held over several days or even longer, depending on the system and the current trends in the markets. Those who initiate trades using intraday chart patterns rather than daily chart patterns can cut losses shorter because they are using miniature charts with a smaller dollar scale. If they allow themselves to let profits run by holding successful positions as long as possible, they can have the best of both worlds—intraday chart stops and long-term profits.

The most popular time frame is represented by daily charts, where each data point is one day. Although, theoretically, there could be many time frames involving daily charts, most traders using daily charts fall into one of two categories. Either they are short-term traders, who normally do not hold a trade for more than a week, or intermediate-term traders, who look for trades lasting between one week and one month.

The longest-time-frame traders primarily use weekly charts, where each data point is one week. This is the least popular time frame, because such traders must have the greatest amount of discipline. It is arduous to wait patiently for a very long-term trade to develop. If you are watching and analyzing the markets, it is natural to want to do something. Because of the difficulty of picking advantageous entry points for long-term trades, the proficient long-term trader must learn not to be discouraged by being stopped out several times in an effort to establish his position. As difficult as it is to enter a long-term position, it is even more difficult to hold a profitable position for months or even years. Because such a trader takes positions infrequently and holds them for months, the average profit per trade should be large, and the costs of trading are inconsequential.

Over each of these different time frames, a trader may attempt to pick tops and bottoms and thus enter a new trend very early, or wait for the trend to become established before taking a position. Because the average trader is risk-averse, he most often tries to pick tops and bottoms. It appears to him that the risk is lower because he can place a solid stop fairly close to the entry point (above the top or below the bottom). In reality, this appearance is illusory. Although there may be less dollar risk, the probability of failure is far higher. There are many false tops and bottoms before the real one arrives. The likelihood is that a trader will be so discouraged by his losing attempts that by the time the real top or bottom arrives, he will be too scared to trade it. This is not a likely road to success. In fact, trying to pick tops and bottoms is at least in the first three of the biggest mistakes losers make. When trading an established trend, even if you have to place your stop further away, the strength of the trend will often rescue you from an injudicious entry. Thus, I believe trading an established trend, rather than trying to pick major tops and bottoms, is the best avenue to pursue. Others disagree. You will have to make your own decision based on experience and testing.

The most important consideration in creating your trading system is not to violate your own trading preferences so long as a profitable system can accommodate them. As in all aspects of life, it is essential to heed Polonius's dictum: "This above all: to thine own self be true, And it must follow, as the night the day, Thou canst not then be false to any man." On the other hand, it is futile to pursue a trading style that, while comfortable in the short run, will be unprofitable in the long run. Only rigorous testing can tell you. If your preferred style doesn't work, you'll have to change or stop trading. Don't try to pattern yourself after some famous trader or successful acquaintance unless you can do so comfortably. Other people's techniques, approaches, and methods can be and should be candidates for inclusion in your own system. You will have the best chance for success and reap the most rewards from trading when you trade *your* system that is consistent with your trading personality *and* historically profitable in careful testing.

You now know all the essentials for creating your own profitable trading system. It is time to relax and take a rest. Trading success is just around the corner. Or is it? Actually, the hardest part is yet to come. In the next chapter I will explain why creating a successful system is only the first step. The *really* hard part is trading it.

15 Follow Your System

If you think your problems are over when you find a profitable system, boy, are you in for a big surprise. The unfortunate truth is that your troubles are just beginning. As difficult as it may be to find or create a profitable system, it is even more difficult to follow the system once you do find it. There are three reasons for this. First, no one can ever know whether a system will continue to be profitable in the future. Second, profitable systems often act like unprofitable systems. Third, traders following mechanical systems are subject to exactly the same gut-wrenching emotions as those trading by the seat of their pants. This uncertainty and emotion is enough to cause the downfall of all but the most courageous and disciplined systems traders. This reality may be the overriding reason that system developers prefer to sell their systems to others rather than trade them themselves.

Greed and Fear

It is possible to explain virtually all speculative behavior in terms of two primary emotions, greed and fear. Although the word greed has a generally negative connotation in our society, I do not imply any negative value judgment by using it. We are all free to seek our own level of acquisitive satisfaction. I do not see why anyone needs to pass judgment on someone else's acquisitive goals by calling them greedy. No one ever refers to himself as greedy; it is always the other guy who is overreaching. However, in the context of trading, greed is the word commonly used to describe the desire to acquire more wealth. It seems as though traders are never satisfied, regardless of their success. If they have a losing trade, they criticize themselves for being so stupid to take it in the first place. If they have a winning trade, they criticize themselves for not having a bigger position. No matter how well they do, they can always rationalize why they should have done even better.

Although greed is the compelling factor that causes a trader to seek a profitable trading system, it is also one of the reasons that he will stray from following that system. It is difficult to trade the markets in a vacuum. The best speculators isolate themselves entirely from all distractions that might improperly influence their trading decisions. Pure technicians do not read newspapers or watch television news for fear they might, even subconsciously, be influenced. The rest of us are not so disciplined. Even though our system has not given an entry signal, we might be influenced by outside factors to want to take a position. We see an "expert" opinion predicting a strong move. The price chart itself may support the opinion. We do not want to miss a glorious profit opportunity, but our system is not giving the signal we want. Under the circumstances, we decide to cheat and second-guess the system.

Another way greed can cause cheating is to double up on certain signals that we believe will be especially profitable. This is dangerous because our instincts about which signals will be good or bad are usually wrong. A trader can also increase his level of trading in general because things have gone well lately. This is a common route to disaster. Greed can cause a person to override a system exit signal. Either he wants to hold onto a losing trade a while longer in hopes it will turn into a profit, or he wants to hold a profitable trade a while longer in hopes the profit will become a much bigger profit. The whole purpose of having a mechanical system is to block out all these kinds of emotional decisions that experience has taught us cause losses. Therefore, when following a system, do not succumb to the very poison you intend the system to supplant.

The second primary emotion governing the conduct of speculators is fear, the fear of failure and the fear of losing money. This emotion causes traders to pass up winning trades because they are afraid their entry signal is wrong. They know they are supposed to call their broker, but they freeze as they reach for the telephone. System traders can fall prey to the same emotion and temporarily abandon their system. Invariably, the the system signals you pass up will be profitable. Just as greed can interfere with the correct handling of a profitable trade, fear can induce a trader to exit before his system dictates. This is the fear that a profit will disappear or even become a loss. Your system should have been designed to let profits run, which is an even more difficult discipline to learn than cutting losses short. Don't let your emotions interfere with it. You need the occasional large profits to offset the usually greater number of small losses. The most pernicious fear in trading a system is the fear that the system will cause eventual losses rather than profits. This fear strikes during a drawdown period when the system has taken a number of losses in a row.

Coping with Drawdowns

The drawdown is the biggest bugaboo for systems traders. Drawdown refers to a period of time when the system suffers net trading losses. Every system, every method, every trader has drawdown periods. The only way to prevent drawdowns is to have a system that is profitable one hundred percent of the time. It is not possible to have a high percentage of profits without reducing the size of profits in relation to losses to the point where the system cannot hope to be profitable in the end. The drawdown of such a high-percentage system would be small in terms of the number of losing trades in a row, but large in terms of the size of losses in relation to the intervening strings of profits. The average successful trader or successful system is very lucky to achieve 50 percent winners. Many get by with 30 to 40 percent winners.

Under these circumstances, the laws of probability insure that even the best systems must at some point have *significant* drawdowns. If you keep flipping a coin, over time your heads and tails will be about the same, but in the short run there is a high likelihood of flipping 10 tails in a row. On average you will flip 10 heads or 10 tails in a row once every 1,024 times that you flip. If your system is less than 50 percent accurate, you will have large strings of losses even more often. As you might imagine, it takes far fewer than 10 losses in a row to scare the average system trader enough to abandon his system. If you are unable to trade a system through its inevitable strings of losses, you will spend your entire trading career going from one system to another. This is exactly what happens to almost everyone.

Underestimating the Impact of Drawdowns

Experienced systems traders understand the necessity to examine the maximum drawdown figure in an historical trading simulation summary report. Yet it is easy to overlook the psychological reality of experiencing that drawdown when you already know that the system is ultimately profitable. What makes trading through drawdowns so scary is that we do not know whether the system will continue to lose money and bankrupt us if we keep trading it.

One of my favorite exercises at seminars is to take a profitable system and demonstrate the difficulty of trading it. A day-trading system makes a good guinea pig because you usually trade it every day. (The best day-trading systems are more selective and do not trade every day.)

Several years ago I published a simple day-trading system for the S&P 500. I called it the *Bread and Butter System*. You could have called every morning just after the open and placed the orders, or your broker could have traded it for you. I followed it hypothetically for over a year, and it produced excellent results, considering that it was a day-trading system and so simple to trade.

In a year of trading beginning in July 1985 the *Bread and Butter System* traded 246 times. It was profitable 45 percent of the time, earning a gross profit of $30,150 per contract traded. The net profit after deducting $75 per trade for slippage and commissions was $11,700. When you consider that the margin at the time was $6,000, that's a pretty good return. The largest drawdown in net profits during the year was $5,100. That all sounds very acceptable when you consider it in hindsight. But suppose you had started trading the system on January 6, 1986. Let's see what your life might have been like following this system.

This is one of the most important parts of this book. I hope you will take about 10 minutes to follow this exercise exactly as I describe it. You will try to experience how you would have felt trading this profitable system for 10 of the weeks that I followed it. Cover Exhibit 15–1 with a piece of paper and move it down the page very slowly so you uncover one line at a time. Each line shows one day of trading with the day's profit or loss. At the end of each week, the table shows the week's total result and the cumulative profit or loss. Take at least five seconds to reflect on each day's result before you move the paper down again. Imagine your reaction had it been real money, *your* money. Think about whether you would have been comfortable trading the system the next day. After the end of each week, take a few more seconds to reflect on the week's results. Do your best to imagine how long you would have been trading the system and how well you would have done so far. Ask yourself whether you would continue trading the system the next week. Move the paper very slowly and be as honest about your probable reactions as you can. The whole exercise will take no more than 10 minutes. Do it now . . .

If you followed my instructions, you should have some idea of the difficulty of trading a system during a bad period. The trading rules and complete one-year track record for the *Bread and Butter System* are in Appendix 2.

When Has a System Failed?

It would be natural to ask at this point how you know when a system has failed and you should stop trading it. This is one of the most difficult questions that all systems traders must answer. How do you tell the difference between a normal drawdown and the beginning of a total disaster?

Since all systems (and traders) undergo serious drawdowns sooner or later in their careers, it is important to be ready for them. The usual trader assumes that after about three losses his system has failed. He then looks for a better system. He will be looking for a better system for the rest of his trading life. In addition, he will probably be abandoning his last one just before it begins a good string of profits.

There are two reasonable ways to decide that a system has failed and should be abandoned, at least temporarily. First, you should always set a dollar limit of losses at which you will stop trading the system. This kind of a stop-loss on a system is just as important as a stop-loss order on an individual trade. It is the only way to avoid trading a system to financial ruin. In addition, if you know and accept the approximate limit of your loss when you start, you can trade the system more confidently than if you have no idea what the dimensions of your loss might be. Just as you should know your stop-loss point when

EXHIBIT 15-1   Bread and Butter Day Trading System Hypothetical Results

DATE	DAILY PROFIT OR LOSS	SLIPPAGE AND COMMISSION	DAILY NET	WEEKLY NET	CUMULATIVE WEEKLY NET
860106	150	75	75		
860107	650	75	575		
860108	-250	75	-325		
860109	-250	75	-325		
860110	-250	75	-325	-325	-325
860113	150	75	75		
860114	525	75	450		
860115	150	75	75		
860116	-250	75	-325		
860117	150	75	75	350	25
860120	-250	75	-325		
860121	1,000	75	925		
860122	-250	75	-325		
860123	-250	75	-325		
860124	-250	75	-325	-375	-350
860127	-250	75	-325		
860128	-250	75	-325		
860129	150	75	75		
860130	-250	75	-325		
860131	1,325	75	1,250	350	0
860203	150	75	75		
860204	150	75	75		
860205	-250	75	-325		
860206	-250	75	-325		
860207	-250	75	-325	-825	-825
860210	-250	75	-325		
860211	-250	75	-325		
860212	-250	75	-325		
860213	150	75	75		
860214	-250	75	-325	-1,225	-2,050
860218	-250	75	-325		
860219	-250	75	-325		
860220	-250	75	-325		
860221	-250	75	-325	-1,300	-3,350
860224	-250	75	-325		
860225	-250	75	-325		
860226	150	75	75		
860227	-250	75	-325		
860228	150	75	75	-825	-4,175
860303	-250	75	-325		
860304	150	75	75		
860305	150	75	75		
860306	-250	75	-325		
860307	150	75	75	-425	-4,600

you initiate a trade, you should know your total limit of loss when you start trading a system. This prevents mind games when you are forced to make a decision at the failure point. At that time, you may have had a bad string of losses. It might be easy to convince yourself that the odds were in your favor at that point and you should trade on. With that attitude an acceptable loss can turn into a catastrophic one.

You should determine the fail-safe point from examining the system's historical record. The minimum amount of risk would be the maximum historical drawdown plus the margin required. Thus, if you were going to trade a T-bond system with a previous maximum drawdown of $5,900, since T-bonds has a margin that fluctuates between around $2,500 and $3,000, you might decide to allocate $10,000 in your account to trade the system and stop trading if the system lost $6,500 to $7,000. If you did not feel comfortable taking a loss of $6,500, you should set some lower amount as your fail-safe point. Of course, if your bail-out point is less than the maximum historical drawdown, your chances of trading the system successfully would be less.

You can consider a trading system like a small business. You will make an investment. You will manage the business. You will make a profit or a loss. Your fail-safe point is approximately the maximum amount you will lose if the business should fail. When you consider the required investment, the amount of time you will have to contribute to running the business and the potential return if the trading system is successful, investing in a trading system business compares very favorably to investing in the usual kind of small business. Since most small businesses fail, your chance of success may even be better than with a traditional business. Reflect for a moment on the headaches involved in running the usual business. Compare that to futures trading. Except perhaps for the emotional stress, trading is a very nice business to be in. You will need a relatively small investment. You won't need a fancy establishment or office. You won't need to advertise. You won't need to worry about employee problems. You won't have any inventory. The hours are good. You can reside anywhere in the world. You won't have to live or die by the competence of others. If your trading system is successful, you will have a high-return, easy-to-run business that can support you indefinitely.

There is also the question of whether to calculate the maximum drawdown you will accept before abandoning the system from the beginning investment or from the highest profit level the system reaches. While I can give you no precise formula, I would allow the system plenty of leeway at the beginning. Once the system has been running profitably for a time, it would be a good idea to withdraw the profits and spend them or invest them in something other than commodities. That way you will protect those profits from a future system failure. There is a tendency when trading a profitable system to want to increase the number of contracts traded after the system has been profitable for a while. I recommend against this. You will inevitably aggravate the drawdown that is sure to come. It is better to withdraw profits at least as great as your initial investment before increasing trading. Rather than increase the number of contracts traded on one system, it is better to diversify and start trading a different system, perhaps in an entirely different market.

The second way to judge whether a system has failed is to examine its recent performance. However, since all systems undergo draw-downs, losses alone will not tell you much of anything. You must look instead at the nature of the system and the nature of market price movement during the losing period. You cannot expect any system to work in all possible types of markets. A long-term, trend-following system will probably not be profitable during a period in which there are no sustained trends. The fact that it lost money during such a period tells you nothing about the system's continuing efficacy. On the other hand, if there has been a sustained trending period of the kind you designed the system to exploit and it still lost money, then you can legitimately question whether the system is a good one. Thus, the rule in judging performance is to compare the market activity to the system's design. If the system makes losses during an extended market period of the type in which it should have made profits, you should probably alter or abandon the system.

Traders Just Want to Have Fun

I should also mention another emotion that can lead you away from your system: the craving for action, excitement, and fun. There is certainly nothing wrong with having fun, but you should realize you will probably pay the price. Commodity trading *is* exciting, and many people get the same kind of rush from trading they get from riding a roller coaster.

The need for action causes people to overtrade. They do not have the patience to wait for the system to signal another trade. Greed has nothing to do with it. They are not afraid they are going to miss a profitable trade; they just miss the excitement of having a trade on.

Here are some recent quotes from a popular advisory service, Philip Gotthelf's *Commodity Futures Forecast,* which recognize this primal need of traders:

> There is no doubt the play was worth the exposure. Anyone who traded the meats with us had more fun in two weeks than we have seen in three months. I believe there is more to trading futures than making or losing money. The process should be exciting . . . and it was.
>
> I admit the trade is very risky. Exposure is moderate. But, every so often it is very exciting to pit skills against such a stubborn market. If every trade were easy, it would not be as much fun!

There are so many emotions and distractions pulling at a trader, it is no wonder even the best stray from their system or plan occasionally. Your monetary success, however, depends on how well you can overcome these temptations and stick to the system.

Understanding the Role of Luck

Paradoxically, one of the most important steps you can take to becoming a successful trader is to appreciate and accept the role of luck in trading. Whenever I mention this, I fear that I am misunderstood. I am not suggesting that profitable commodity traders are just lucky. Becoming a profitable trader is not a matter of luck. However, your short-term results will, to a great extent, depend on luck. The more you trade, the less luck will play a role in your success.

There is a great deal of randomness in short-term market activity. Because of the leverage, to avoid ruin commodity traders must succeed in the short term as well as the long term. Whether your next trade succeeds or not depends almost entirely on luck. Whether you will show a net profit after your next five trades also depends almost entirely on luck. Whether you will show a net profit on your trading for the next year depends mostly on skill, but there is still an element of luck involved. Only in the very long term will chance play no role in your success.

Understanding and accepting this reality is very important because it affects how you judge yourself as a trader and how you judge your system. If you blame yourself or your system for your next loss, you will probably assume you did something wrong or your system is flawed. You may tinker with your approach or your system when there is really nothing wrong. You can properly judge a trading method only after a relatively long period that will allow short-term random market action to cancel itself out.

If you accept the role of luck in the short term, you have to judge your profitable trades differently as well. You can no longer legitimately pat yourself on the back or brag to your spouse or best friend about your latest trade. Short-term success is more attributable to luck and the courage to trade in the first place. Well, I suppose they don't have to know that. Just be sure if you do brag that you don't start believing it yourself.

We have now covered the essentials of system design and testing. There are still several more important concepts you will need in order to round out your knowledge of commodity futures trading. The next chapter will outline the important considerations of money management. Most experts agree that money management is the most important part of an overall trading plan.

16 Money Management

One of the most important watersheds in the life of a commodity trader is the moment when he or she accepts the idea that proper money management is more important to profitability than trade selection. The natural tendency is to suppose that if you could only know the trend with greater precision or place stops more intelligently, it would make all the difference.

The reality is that entry and exit methods are more a method of imposing patience and discipline than remarkable insights into predicting future market behavior. Good trading systems (or trading plans) give you an edge because they force you to trade with the trend, cut your losses short, and let your profits run—the three cardinal rules of successful speculation. Bad trading systems don't measure up because of deficiencies in one or more of those three areas. Most losing traders have no system or plan. Thus, their emotions have free rein to prevent them from adhering to the cardinal rules.

Knowledgeable commodity traders have been suggesting for a number of years that with proper money management a person could pick his entry points by chance and still make money. For the average trader, spending hours and hours refining his analytical techniques to no avail, that is a depressing thought. How important is money management? Can it really make up for bad predictions? Very, and yes. For the mechanical system trader, the time to make sure the system adheres to proper money management principles is while you are creating and testing your system. Once you start trading, it is too late.

Money management. Nice buzz words—but what do they really mean? There are four important concepts in speculative money management: 1) Proper account size, 2) Diversification, 3) Risk management, and 4) Trading multiple contracts.

Proper Account Size

A common question from neophytes is, "How big an account do I need to trade commodities?" Because it is so important to understand the relationship of the amount of capital you commit to the effort and your chances of success, I have already discussed this in Chapter 2. In 1975, I started trading with a $3,000 account. I eventually graduated to multiple accounts many, many times bigger. My own experience reinforces my view that the more capital you can afford to commit, the greater your chances of ultimate success. Russell Wasendorf, whose work I greatly respect, wrote about this in his *Futures Factors* newsletter: "Informal studies have indicated that the larger the amount of investment capital placed in commodity trading, the greater the chance for success. The rough probabilities for success after one year are as follows: With $5,000, 10 percent; with $10,000, 20 percent; with $20,000, 30 percent; with $50,000, 50 percent; and with $100,000, 60 percent." Those are pretty sobering figures for small account traders.

The small trader can increase his odds considerably by having a realistic profit goal. As I indicated in Chapter 2, a reasonable goal is a consistent 50 percent return per year. In good years I would expect to make 100 percent and maybe more, but hopefully never much less than 50 percent. I am always content with that.

If a professional trader with many years' experience and a large account is happy with only 50 percent, a less experienced and less capitalized trader should be content with even less. But is the usual person with a $5,000 or $10,000 account satisfied with a 10 to 20 percent return his first year? Certainly not. That sounds like savings account interest rather than getting rich from commodity trading. He was enticed by the stories he read of cab drivers making a million in the sugar or coffee market. He figures that if some lucky stiff can make a million without knowing anything about technical analysis, he should be able to make $50,000 or $100,000 with the limited edition of Gann's secret techniques he just bought for $250. Good luck. Even though it looks easy, the chances that you will turn $10,000 into $50,000 in a year are very slim. The attempt is usually suicidal. That is why so many people lose money trading.

One reason that larger accounts tend to be more successful is diversification. I like to diversify among both trading systems and markets. There are advantages and disadvantages to diversification. At the same time that diversification limits your risk, it also limits your potential. (Remember there is an inexorable connection between risk and reward.) If you spread yourself around, you will dilute the effect of big gains in one or two markets. But you also dilute the adverse effect of losses in some markets. Preservation of capital is the most important consideration.

There is a less well-understood advantage to diversification. Since no one knows where the big moves will come, you increase your chances of catching a huge move by trading more markets. If we knew in advance where the fireworks were going to be, we would concentrate our trading there. We can make some educated guesses, but it seems that the big profits often come in the most unlikely places. Just as we never know which trades are going to be profitable, we never know which profits will turn into very big profits.

While it is important to diversify, you must be sensible about it and not trade low-probability markets just for the sake of diversification. A market can be classified as low probability for several reasons. It may be an inactive market that is going nowhere. Why waste your precious capital trading boring markets? There will be plenty of time to enter them if they suddenly come to life. Sticking to the more volatile markets is a good way to maximize return on capital.

There is an advisory service based on exactly this principle. *The Timing Device* had the highest profit per trade of any service *Commodity Traders Consumer Report* followed in 1986 and the second highest in 1987. Here is a provocative quotation about Editor Kelly Angle's trading philosophy: "Conventional wisdom assumes there is a direct relationship between volatility and risk. We have found there is little, if any, direct relationship. The only direct relationship high volatility has to your trading program is that it offers high profit potential. For example, strong trending markets can be relatively low-risk and yet offer excellent profit potential. The point is you can't make money in a flat market."

Another reason to classify a market as low-probability is because the odds are stacked against the off-the-floor speculator. Pork bellies is a prime example. Lumber is another floor traders' market. There are so many other markets to trade, why bother with those. It's like playing a crooked roulette wheel. You might win, but why give up any more of the odds than you have to?

Diversification in Markets and Systems

It is an axiom of prudent investing that one should diversify. Since no one can really know in advance which investments will win or lose, the conventional wisdom is that it is best to hedge your bets. The advantage of diversification is obvious. You need not be 100 percent right to come out ahead. You hope that the profits on the good investments will make up for all the losses on the bad ones, and there will be enough excess profits to make the entire portfolio yield a satisfactory return. The disadvantage of diversification is that you limit the potential profit of one or two very excellent investments by averaging them with some others that do not turn out so well. This assumes you know how to pick only high-returning investment vehicles. Almost no one can do that consistently.

Diversification is also prudent when trading commodities and when trading commodity systems. The real key to long-term staying power is to keep volatility as low as possible. That way you don't get scared and quit. A good way to damp volatility in your overall account is to trade many different markets and many different systems. When some markets are locked in trading ranges, others will be trending.

Diversification among trading systems or approaches is important because one approach cannot accommodate all types of markets. A good long-term, trend-following system will lose money when there are no sustained trends. A short-term system designed for trading-range markets will not do well during big moves. If you take systems of both types, that have tested well historically, and trade them in the same commodity at the same time, you should make a good return regardless of market conditions. When some systems are undergoing drawdown periods, others will be doing well. Each system's profits during periods it was designed to exploit will more than make up for its losses during incompatible periods. Both systems will be profitable over time, and the combination will have a much smoother equity curve than either system alone. Your overall return is guaranteed to be less than if you picked the best market and the best system, but who knows what that will be. Remember my initial warning to be willing to accept a reasonable return if you want to maximize your chances for profit.

There is no rule that says you cannot trade two or more systems in the same market at the same time. You do not have to worry whether one system is long and another is short at the same time. You put all the system orders into your account, and the result will reflect the overall performance of all the systems. If two systems go long and short *simultaneously,* you ignore those orders and wait for the next signal. You should have more capital in the account than if you just traded one system, but you will probably not need the capital you would need to trade all the systems separately. This is because when you trade a system separately you must allow for the maximum expected drawdown, but trading more than one dissimilar system, it is unlikely that the maximum drawdowns on all the systems will occur at once.

It is also possible to trade two systems in tandem with the same amount of capital as for one of them. This tandem method will guarantee that you achieve exactly half the net profits (or losses) as you would trading both systems separately. To trade two systems in tandem, go long only when both systems are long and go short only when both systems are short. When they disagree, do nothing or exit any current position. This is a good way to diversify without needing additional capital. If the systems are very different in approach, you should be able to damp the volatility of your equity curve substantially while still achieving good profits if the market cooperates.

Perhaps the ideal situation would be to trade two disparate systems in tandem in each of 10 or more diversified markets. Because the markets would be going through trending and non-trending periods at different times, you could do this with less than the total capital required to trade each market separately. You would give up any hope of a major killing, but increase substantially the chances of achieving a consistent, worthwhile return.

One the most compelling reasons that small traders fail is that insufficient trading capital makes adequate diversification impossible. One solution is to trade on the MidAmerica Exchange. This exchange is affiliated with the Chicago Board of Trade. Its purpose is to provide a place where traders can speculate using smaller contracts than those available on the regular exchanges; their contracts are typically one half to one fifth the size of regular contracts. There is a wide variety of markets. MidAmerica floor traders keep one eye on prices at the major exchanges so price movements are similar although the fills are usually not as good. You can operate your trading system, using major exchange prices, but have your broker place the orders at the Mid-America Exchange. Your results should be roughly proportional to what you would have achieved trading full-sized contracts. It is far better to trade MidAmerica contracts, accept slightly worse fills and proportionally smaller profits, but keep the risk proportional to your small account than to overtrade using full-sized contracts without proper diversification. Exhibit 16–1 lists the MidAmerica contract specifications. For more information and literature, write to Mid-America Commodity Exchange, Education and Marketing Services Department, LaSalle at Jackson, Chicago, IL 60604, or call (800)-843-2268 or (312)-435-3558.

EXHIBIT 16-1   MidAmerica Commodity Exchange, Contract Specifications as of January 1, 1988

	Ticker Symbol	Contract Size	Trading Hours* A.M. P.M.	Delivery Months
Corn	XC	1,000 bu.	9:30-1:30	Mch/May/Jul/Sep/Dec
Wheat	XW	1,000 bu.	9:30-1:30	Mch/May/Jul/Sep/Dec
Soybeans	XS	1,000 bu.	9:30-1:30	Jan/Mch/May/Jul/ Aug/Sep/Nov
Oats	XO	1,000 bu.	9:30-1:30	Mch/May/Jul/Sep/Dec
Cattle	XL	20,000 lbs.	9:05-1:15	Feb/Apr/Jun/ Aug/Oct/Dec
Hogs	XH	15,000 lbs.	9:10-1:15	Feb/Apr/Jun/Jul/ Aug/Oct/Dec
Soybean Meal	XE	20 tons (2,000 lbs./ton)	9:30-1:30	Jan/Mch/May/Jul/ Aug/Sep/Oct/Dec
NY Gold	XK	33.2 fine troy oz.	7:20-1:40	All months
NY Silver	XY	1,000 troy oz.	7:25-1:40	All months
Platinum	XU	25 fine troy oz.	7:20-1:40	Current three months and cycle months of Jan/Apr/Jul/Oct
British Pounds	XP	12,500 Pounds	7:20-1:34	Mch/Jun/Sep/Dec
Deutsche Marks	XM	62,500 Marks	7:20-1:30	Mch/Jun/Sep/Dec
Japanese Yen	XJ	6,250,000 Yen	7:20-1:32	Mch/Jun/Sep/Dec
Swiss Francs	XF	62,500 Francs	7:20-1:26	Mch/Jun/Sep/Dec
Canadian Dollars	XD	50,000 Canadian Dollars	7:20-1:36	Mch/Jun/Sep/Dec
Treasury Bonds	XB	$50,000 Face Value	7:20-3:15	Mch/Jun/Sep/Dec
Treasury Bills	XT	$500,000 Face Value	7:20-2:15	Mch/Jun/Sep/Dec

*Central Time

Risk Management

The third element of money management is risk management. Risk management has two separate components. First and most important is the idea of limiting your maximum loss on any one trade to an amount compatible with your trading method and account size. One of the most distinguishing features of the unsuccessful trader is the presence in his yearly trade summary of exceptionally large losses relative to his account size. Like all traders, I have gone through exactly the same thing.

Anyone who has made even the feeblest effort to learn how to trade knows you are supposed to cut your losses short. This rule appears in capital letters and bold type in most every commodity book ever written. And for a good reason, I should add. But knowing the axiom's importance has little effect on a trader's ability to follow it. No matter what you do, those big losses just manage to creep in there.

There are two reasons, and both are related to risk management. First, you may be psychologically unable to keep your losses small enough. Second, the market may overcome your well-meaning and properly-executed plan. The principal psychological impediment to loss control is ego. We don't want to take that loss because in our mind it implies failure. Sometimes we don't take a loss when we should, and the market bounces back and lets us off the hook. This only encourages us to do it again and again. Often, we allow an acceptable loss to become larger. Now it is bigger than our trading plan allows. We can't afford to take such a big loss. The market has to bail us out. This time it doesn't.

Almost all trading plans produce less than 50 percent winners. Professionals make big money because their average profit is significantly greater than their average loss. It doesn't take more than a few excessive losses to destroy this delicate balance. Large losses that cut into capital have an additional devastating impact. Assume you are starting with $20,000 and seek to make a 50 percent annual return. If you lose only 25 percent of your capital, you will have to double the productivity of your trading system (to 100 percent annual return) to achieve the same end result ($30,000). If you tried to do it, you would increase the risk by so much that your chance of success would be nil.

There is also a statistical reason that you must limit your losses to a small percentage of capital. It is known as the risk of ruin. This is a concept well known to statisticians but not so well known to commodity traders. The problem is that even a good trading system will eventually have a large number of losses in a row. There is no way to avoid this. If you risk too much on each trade, your account will be wiped out or you will not have sufficient margin to continue trading your system.

W. D. Gann and a number of other writers have suggested that traders not risk more than 10 percent of their account on any one trade. One well-known trading advisor wrote that if a trader "cannot get any wins in a string of 10 trades, he probably shouldn't be trading commodities in the first place." Yet *Commodity Traders Consumer Report* documented more than 10 losses in a row for that person's own advisory service! If any of these writers followed their own advice, they would have to be very lucky or long-since broke.

A statistician could demonstrate that if you flip a coin to decide a bet, on average you will lose 10 times in a row once for every 1,024 times you bet. Of course, it could happen sooner rather than later in the series of bets, so divide that figure by two to get the average time before the losing streak. If your trading system is 50 percent accurate, you can divide 512 by the number of trades you make in a year to see about how long you might be expected to last risking 10 percent of your capital on every trade. If your system is 55 percent accurate, you still have about a 12 percent chance of being wiped out before you double your capital. These figures all assume you win or lose the same amount on each trade, which is not realistic. But neither is it realistic to assume a 50 percent or 55 percent win ratio. An expert on commodity futures money managers recently estimated the average win ratio for professionals at only 35 percent. More complicated statistical formulas will accommodate more realistic representations of actual trading. However, the essential point remains. You must protect yourself against the inevitable string of losing trades.

The only way to do this is to limit losses to a very small percentage of your total risk capital. The smaller you can make it and still execute your trading plan, the better. Of course, you must take some risk to earn acceptable profits. If forced to name a figure, I would say in the neighborhood of 2 to 3 percent, depending on the success ratio of your system. This will at least insure you against the risk of statistical ruin.

If you are trading with a mechanical system, your maximum loss amount should be computed on the basis of beginning rather than existing risk capital. This means as you take losses and your account size decreases, you do not reduce the size of your maximum loss proportionally. If you did, you would be decreasing your trading after a drawdown. That is precisely the time your system has the greatest chance of returning to profitability. As you make profits and your account increases, you should not increase your maximum loss size (and thus the number of contracts you can trade at a time) because you would be doing so after a good winning streak. That is precisely the time your system has the greatest chance of starting a losing streak. After a good winning streak is the best time to take profits out of your account instead. It is a good thing to spend profits occasionally so you don't lose sight of the fact that you are dealing with real money and not just accounting entries.

The way to control excessive losses while using a trading system is to have enough reserves in your account so you can keep trading even after an historically large drawdown and to have a automatic cut-off point where you will stop trading the system. You should calculate the cut-off point in relation to the largest historical drawdown the system has suffered and the amount of capital you want to risk trading the system.

For instance, suppose the *Egghead System*'s largest drawdown in the last five years has been $6,500 and you need margin of $3,000 to trade the system; you should allow for at least a drawdown of $7,000. That would mean you would need $10,000 in your account to keep trading the system after a $7,000 drawdown. You would probably not want to risk more than half your total risk capital on any particular system. Remember, no matter how good they look historically, there's no guarantee for the future. Therefore, you should have at least $20,000 in your commodity account before beginning to trade with the *Egghead System*.

The second component of risk management is staying away from unnecessarily risky trades. I previously referred to the market's overcoming a well-meaning and properly executed plan. By this I meant that a trader takes an excessively large loss in spite of having a stop in the market at an acceptable point. Can a trader plead not guilty when he takes a pork belly position just before a Pig Crop Report and the market gaps through his stop with three or four limit days? Should a crude oil trader be surprised when he takes a big loss after guessing wrong about the outcome of an OPEC meeting? Is there any excuse for selling orange juice futures in January or coffee futures in August?

The mechanical system trader operating in these markets cannot just ignore the excessive seasonal risks. One prudent course would be to ignore system trades that subject you to the seasonal risk and take the trades that would benefit from a weather move. Like every other trading idea, you should have an objective rule to decide how to proceed and test it carefully before any actual trading. If an unexpected risk comes up in the middle of trading a mechanical system, the right thing to do is to step to the sidelines. Do not trade the system until the excessive risk no longer exists.

There is a popular superstition that commodity traders are always being victimized by limit moves. Yet I have traded actively since 1975, and the few limit moves against me have not resulted in serious losses. Perhaps I have been lucky. I prefer to attribute it to avoiding all trades where the gambling element is high. You should be a speculator, not a gambler.

The final element of limiting losses is having the discipline to follow your plan and actually exit losing trades when your system commands. As most traders can attest, this sounds easier than it is. The best teacher is experience. It helps to place your stop orders as open orders (good until canceled) when you initiate positions. I do this whenever possible. Never take a position without knowing the precise point where you will exit the trade or at least what circumstances (such as an indicator reading) will require ending a losing trade. A mechanical system automatically makes this decision for you. Your only problem is following the system rules. Rather than looking upon a loss as a personal failure, take pride in your ability to abandon losing positions ruthlessly. It will make all the difference in your bottom line.

Trading Multiple Contracts

The final element of money management is trading multiple contracts. My own experience has convinced me that exiting profitable positions at different levels is an important, though not essential, ingredient of success. It enables you to make money when markets are making medium- as well as long-trending moves. Although some experts disagree, my own and others' experience and testing suggests that using multiple fixed profit objectives is more profitable than exiting the whole position on a reverse signal.

You can implement this strategy only if you trade multiple contracts on each entry signal. To trade a mechanical system this way requires using several different systems in the same market at the same time. This is an excellent approach if you have sufficient capital.

Beginners should concentrate on trading one system and one contract at a time for each market you have chosen. When you are successful at that, you can graduate to multiple contract trading.

Use all the money management concepts in this chapter in planning an overall trading strategy. There are also some special tactics you can apply on a trade-by-trade basis to increase overall performance. I call these ideas *trade management,* and we will examine them in the next chapter.

17 Trade Management

The usual concepts of money management involve questions that can be decided before beginning to trade. I covered those in the last chapter. However, there also are some things you can do to improve your chances of success that depend upon the recent performance of your system. You cannot know this in advance. Even though you will not know beforehand exactly when you will implement these concepts, you should decide in advance what rules you will apply. It is important to decide in advance how you will proceed because otherwise your decisions will be influenced by the emotions caused by your trading performance.

Varying the Number of Contracts Traded

The purpose of this section is to examine whether you can improve results solely by adjusting the number of contracts traded in relation to how the system performed on the previous trade. Stated another way, I seek to answer the question: Given a profit or loss, should you change the number of contracts on the next trade? After a profit should you increase the number of contracts traded to take advantage of the additional capital you now have? After a loss should you increase the number of contracts traded on the theory that you are now more likely to get a profit on the next trade? Or, as most traders probably do, should you trade the same regardless of recent success or adversity?

One approach to a solution is through the study of betting systems developed for casino gaming. A multitude of money management strategies have been proposed for casino gambling. Mathematical studies have shown that ultimately, none will enable you to beat an unfavorable game. With the possible exception of advanced Blackjack, all casino games are unfavorable.

Such money management strategies have generally not been studied in connection with favorable games. A systematic and profitable approach to trading the futures markets constitutes a favorable game. Some of these ingenious casino techniques, therefore, might be able to improve commodity futures trading performance. With the help of Robert E. Lehman, I enlisted the aid of a computer to find out.

The Strategies

Whatever their details, all casino betting systems represent attempts to beat the inherent house advantage by some technique of money management. These techniques are a set of rules for increasing and decreasing bet size, depending on the outcome of the last or the most recent series of bets. The ones I studied are among the best-known of the classical approaches. If you want to read more about these and other similar approaches, I suggest the gambling section of your local library or bookstore. Here are the five strategies I examined:

1. Neutral Strategy (NT). You trade a constant number of contracts regardless of wins or losses. This neutral strategy is really no strategy, but it provides the benchmark against which to compare the other approaches.
2. Martingale (MG). The Martingale strategy is perhaps the best known of the casino gambling systems. You start with one betting unit, double your bet after each loss, and return to one unit after any win. The advantage, and seductiveness, of the Martingale strategy is that by doubling up after each loss, when you do win, you will always win back all your losses in that series plus one unit. (Try it on paper.) However, the bet size increases very rapidly during strings of losses, and you can be bankrupt before being rescued by a winning bet. To prevent heavily capitalized gamblers from using this strategy successfully, all casinos have a limit on the size of permissible bets.
3. Anti-Martingale (AM). The opposite approach is also possible. You start with one betting unit, double your bet after each win, but go back to one betting unit after each loss. The advantage of this strategy is that the risk is lower. The increased bet size is financed out of winnings, leaving your accumulated capital safe. The disadvantage is that you will always make your largest bets on the inevitable losers.
4. Progress-on-Loss (PL). Related to the Martingale strategies is a family of methods that systematically change bet size after each loss and after each win, progressing up and down a defined series. The simplest version, and the one I included here, is the unit progression. In the Progress-on-Loss you start with several betting units, increase your bet size by one unit after a loss, and decrease it by one unit after a win. Advantages and disadvantages are similar to the Martingale strategy, but the risk of ruin is reduced.
5. Progress-on-Win (PW). This is the inverse of the Progress-on-Loss strategy. You start with several betting units, decrease your bet size by one unit after a loss, and increase it by one unit after a win. Advantages and disadvantages are similar to the Anti-Martingale strategy, but the effects are more gradual.

The Research Method

What would happen if we applied these techniques to favorable games such as profitable futures trading systems? For the purposes of this study I investigated the effects of applying each trade management strategy to three different types of commodity trading systems, one of which should approximate your preferred style of trading:

1. Trend. The first system is the traditional longer-term, trend-following system. For this system I will assume the average profit is three times the average loss but only one third of the trades are profitable.
2. Intermediate. The second system falls between long-term trend following and short-term trading in its characteristics. For this approach I will assume the average profit is two times the average loss and one half the trades are profitable.
3. Trading. The third system has characteristics like a short-term system. I will assume the average profit is one and one half times the average loss and two thirds of the trades are profitable.

I had the computer study each of the five trade management strategies as applied to each of the three types of trading systems. The computer ran through all possible combinations of wins and losses in a series of 10 trades while factoring in the probability of wins and losses dictated by the system. Thus, I included in the study all outcomes that could have occurred in a series of 10 trades. (I originally started testing all possible combinations in a 15-trade series. Although the computer took much longer, the results were substantially the same.) The computer eventually looked at nearly 6 million trades.

I will use the term "series" to describe any possible combination of 10 sequential wins and losses. For each simulation I started trading with units of 10 contracts to allow for the possibility of 10 consecutive losses or wins using the Progress-on-Win or Progress-on-Loss strategies. I standardized the results by assuming a constant $500 risk of loss per contract. The average loss is thus $500, and the average profit varies from $750 to $1,000 to $1,500, according to the system being used.

The Results

The results appear in Exhibits 17–1 to 17–4 and in the graphs that follow. As you can see, the range of risk as well as the range of potential profitability was very large across the five money management strategies.

Explanation of Exhibit 17–1. Average Profits is the average of the total profits per series attained by each strategy after 10 trades across all the possible series.

Winning Series is the percentage of series that showed some profits after the 10 trades.

EXHIBIT 17–1   Trade Management Test, Overall Results

System = TREND Strategy:	Average Profits	Winning Series	Win/Loss Ratio	Extreme[/$1000] Win	Loss
Neutral	$16,666	70.09%	4.07	+150	−50
Martingale	$150,923	87.48%	2.02	+5125	−5115
Anti-Martingale	$28,425	58.38%	4.77	+15345	−50
Progress-on-Loss	$19,167	70.09%	3.95	+92	−73
Progress-on-Win	$14,166	65.10%	4.18	+217	−28

System = INTERMEDIATE Strategy:	Average Profits	Winning Series	Win/Loss Ratio	Extreme[/$1000] Win	Loss
Neutral	$25,000	82.81%	14.47	+100	−50
Martingale	$81,250	94.04%	5.85	+2565	−511
Anti-Martingale	$81,250	69.14%	22.01	+10230	−50
Progress-on-Loss	$25,000	83.89%	14.39	+58	−73
Progress-on-Win	$25,000	82.62%	14.47	+145	−28

System = TRADE Strategy:	Average Profits	Winning Series	Win/Loss Ratio	Extreme[/$1000] Win	Loss
Neutral	$33,335	92.34%	114.78	+75	−50
Martingale	$56,841	98.73%	41.90	+1285	−5115
Anti-Martingale	$301,842	84.15%	189.60	+7673	−50
Progress-on-Loss	$28,334	98.01%	93.62	+43	−73
Progress-on-Win	$38,322	92.34%	86.03	+109	−28

Win/Loss Ratio is the total amount won for all winning series divided by the total amount lost by all losing series.

Extreme Win/Extreme Loss is the highest profit achieved by any series using that strategy or the worst loss achieved by any series using that strategy (divided by $1,000). Multiply the numbers in the table by $1,000 to get the actual value.

Explanation of Exhibits 17–2 to 17–4.   These three tables show the average results after each trade (1–10) in a series. You can compare the average results for each trade management strategy applied to each system type at the end of the first, second, third, etc., trade in the series of 10. The columns show the Average Equity, the Extreme (largest) Win, the Extreme Loss, the Risk-Adjusted Average Equity, Highest Equity and Lowest Equity for all the possible combinations after each trade. Risk-adjusted figures are obtained by dividing by the largest drawdown in that series of trades.

Explanation of Charts.   The charts in Exhibit 17–5 are graphic representations of the fifth column in Exhibits 17–2 to 17–4. The worst drawdown is the measure of risk used to express Risk-Adjusted

EXHIBIT 17–2 Trade Management Test, Long-Term Strategy Results

	SYSTEM = TREND			PW=1/3	W/L=+1500/−500	
NEUTRAL STRATEGY		EXTREME		----- RISK	ADJUSTED	----
TRIAL NO.	AVG EQ	WIN	LOSS	AVG EQ	EQ HI	EQ LO
1	$ 1672	$ 15000	$ −5000	0.03	0.30	−0.10
2	3333	30000	−10000	0.07	0.60	−0.20
3	4992	45000	−15000	0.10	0.90	−0.30
4	6667	60000	−20000	0.13	1.20	−0.40
5	8337	75000	−25000	0.17	1.50	−0.50
6	10000	90000	−30000	0.20	1.80	−0.60
7	11669	105000	−35000	0.23	2.10	−0.70
8	13333	120000	−40000	0.27	2.40	−0.80
9	14996	135000	−45000	0.30	2.70	−0.90
10	16667	150000	−50000	0.33	3.00	−1.00
MARTINGALE STRATEGY						
1	1672	15000	−5000	0.00	0.00	0.00
2	4438	30000	−15000	0.00	0.01	0.00
3	8697	45000	−35000	0.00	0.01	−0.01
4	14936	85000	−75000	0.00	0.02	−0.01
5	23805	165000	−155000	0.00	0.03	−0.03
6	36183	325000	−315000	0.01	0.06	−0.06
7	53249	645000	−635000	0.01	0.13	−0.12
8	76556	1285000	−1275000	0.01	0.25	−0.25
9	108189	2565000	−2555000	0.02	0.50	−0.50
10	150923	5125000	−5115000	0.03	1.00	−1.00
ANTI-MARTINGALE STRATEGY						
1	1672	15000	−5000	0.03	0.30	−0.10
2	3889	45000	−10000	0.08	0.90	−0.20
3	6477	105000	−15000	0.13	2.10	−0.30
4	9325	225000	−20000	0.19	4.50	−0.40
5	12325	465000	−25000	0.25	9.30	−0.50
6	15441	945000	−30000	0.31	18.90	−0.60
7	18630	1905000	−35000	0.37	38.10	−0.70
8	21865	3825000	−40000	0.44	76.50	−0.80
9	25133	7665000	−45000	0.50	153.30	−0.90
10	28425	15345000	−50000	0.57	306.90	−1.00
PROGRESS-ON-LOSS STRATEGY						
1	1672	15000	−5000	0.02	0.21	−0.07
2	3387	28500	−1050	0.05	0.39	−0.01
3	5161	40500	−16500	0.07	0.56	−0.23
4	6999	51000	−23000	0.10	0.70	−0.32
5	8887	60000	−30000	0.12	0.83	−0.41
6	10833	67500	−37500	0.15	0.93	−0.52
7	12833	73500	−45500	0.18	1.01	−0.63
8	14889	79000	−54000	0.21	1.09	−0.74
9	17000	85000	−63000	0.23	1.17	−0.87
10	19167	91500	−72500	0.26	1.26	−1.00
PROGRESS-ON-WIN STRATEGY						
1	1672	15000	−5000	0.06	0.55	−0.18
2	3280	31500	−9500	0.12	1.15	−0.35
3	4831	49500	−13500	0.18	1.80	−0.49
4	6335	69000	−17000	0.23	2.51	−0.62
5	7777	90000	−20000	0.28	3.27	−0.73
6	9167	112500	−22500	0.33	4.09	−0.82
7	10498	136500	−24500	0.38	4.96	−0.89
8	11780	162000	−26000	0.43	5.89	−0.95
9	13000	189000	−27000	0.47	6.87	−0.98
10	14166	217500	−27500	0.52	7.91	−1.00

EXHIBIT 17–3 Trade Management Test, Intermediate-Term Strategy Results

	SYSTEM =	INTERMEDIATE		PW=1/2	W/L=+1000/-500	
NEUTRAL STRATEGY		EXTREME		----- RISK	ADJUSTED	----
TRIAL NO.	AVG EQ	WIN	LOSS	AVG EQ	EQ HI	EQ LO
1	$ 2500	$ 10000	$ -5000	0.05	0.20	-0.10
2	5000	20000	-10000	0.10	0.40	-0.20
3	7500	30000	-15000	0.15	0.60	-0.30
4	10000	40000	-20000	0.20	0.80	-0.40
5	12500	50000	-25000	0.25	1.00	-0.50
6	15000	60000	-30000	0.30	1.20	-0.60
7	17500	70000	-35000	0.35	1.40	-0.70
8	20000	80000	-40000	0.40	1.60	-0.80
9	22500	90000	-45000	0.45	1.80	-0.90
10	25000	100000	-50000	0.50	2.00	-1.00
MARTINGALE STRATEGY						
1	2500	10000	-5000	0.00	0.00	0.00
2	6250	20000	-15000	0.00	0.00	0.00
3	11250	30000	-35000	0.00	0.01	-0.01
4	17500	45000	-75000	0.00	0.01	-0.01
5	25000	85000	-155000	0.00	0.02	-0.03
6	33750	165000	-315000	0.01	0.03	-0.06
7	43750	325000	-635000	0.01	0.06	-0.12
8	55000	645000	-1275000	0.01	0.13	-0.25
9	67500	1285000	-2555000	0.01	0.25	-0.50
10	81250	2565000	-5115000	0.02	0.50	-1.00
ANTI-MARTINGALE SYSTEM						
1	2500	10000	-5000	0.05	0.20	-0.10
2	6250	30000	-10000	0.13	0.60	-0.20
3	11250	70000	-15000	0.23	1.40	-0.30
4	17500	150000	-20000	0.35	3.00	-0.40
5	25000	310000	-25000	0.50	6.20	-0.50
6	33750	630000	-30000	0.68	12.60	-0.60
7	43750	1270000	-35000	0.88	25.40	-0.70
8	55000	2550000	-40000	1.10	51.00	-0.80
9	67500	5110000	-45000	1.35	102.20	-0.90
10	81250	10230000	-50000	1.63	204.60	-1.00
PROGRESS-ON-LOSS STRATEGY						
1	2500	10000	-5000	0.03	0.14	-0.07
2	5000	19000	-10500	0.07	0.26	-0.14
3	7500	27000	-16500	0.10	0.37	-0.23
4	10000	34000	-23000	0.14	0.47	-0.32
5	12500	40000	-30000	0.17	0.55	-0.41
6	15000	45000	-37500	0.21	0.62	-0.52
7	17500	49000	-45500	0.24	0.68	-0.63
8	20000	52000	-54000	0.28	0.72	-0.74
9	22500	55000	-63000	0.31	0.76	-0.87
10	25000	58000	-72500	0.34	0.80	-1.00
PROGRESS-ON-WIN STRATEGY						
1	2500	10000	-5000	0.09	0.36	-0.18
2	5000	21000	-9500	0.18	0.76	-0.35
3	7500	33000	-13500	0.27	1.20	-0.49
4	10000	46000	-17000	0.36	1.67	-0.62
5	12500	60000	-20000	0.45	2.18	-0.73
6	15000	75000	-22500	0.55	2.73	-0.82
7	17500	91000	-24500	0.64	3.31	-0.89
8	20000	108000	-26000	0.73	3.93	-0.95
9	22500	125000	-27000	0.82	4.55	-0.98
10	25000	145000	-27500	0.91	5.27	-1.00

EXHIBIT 17–4 Trade Management Test, Short-Term Strategy Results

	SYSTEM = TRADING			PW=2/3	W/L=+750/-500	
NEUTRAL STRATEGY		EXTREME		-----	RISK ADJUSTED	----
TRIAL NO.	AVG EQ	WIN	LOSS	AVG EQ	EQ HI	EQ LO
1	$ 3337	$ 7500	$ -5000	0.07	0.15	-0.10
2	6669	15000	-10000	0.13	0.30	-0.20
3	9996	22500	-15000	0.20	0.45	-0.30
4	13329	30000	-20000	0.27	0.60	-0.40
5	16667	37500	-25000	0.33	0.75	-0.50
6	19997	45000	-30000	0.40	0.90	-0.60
7	23335	52500	-35000	0.47	1.05	-0.70
8	26662	60000	-40000	0.53	1.20	-0.80
9	29996	76500	-45000	0.60	1.53	-0.90
10	33336	75000	-50000	0.67	1.50	-1.00
MARTINGALE STRATEGY						
1	3337	7500	-5000	0.00	0.00	0.00
2	7776	15000	-15000	0.00	0.00	0.00
3	12953	22500	-35000	0.00	0.00	-0.01
4	18645	30000	-75000	0.00	0.01	-0.01
5	24653	45000	-155000	0.00	0.01	-0.03
6	30868	85000	-315000	0.01	0.02	-0.06
7	37244	165000	-635000	0.01	0.03	-0.12
8	43729	325000	-1275000	0.01	0.06	-0.25
9	50260	645000	-2555000	0.01	0.13	-0.50
10	56842	1285000	-5115000	0.01	0.25	-1.00
ANTI-MARTINGALE STRATEGY						
1	3337	7500	-5000	0.07	0.15	-0.10
2	88889	22500	-10000	1.78	0.45	-0.20
3	17401	52500	-15000	0.35	1.05	-0.30
4	29869	112500	-20000	0.60	2.25	-0.40
5	47619	232500	-25000	0.95	4.65	-0.50
6	72365	472500	-30000	1.45	9.45	-0.60
7	106496	952500	-35000	2.13	19.05	-0.70
8	153107	1912500	-40000	3.06	38.25	-0.80
9	216355	3832500	-45000	4.33	76.65	-0.90
10	301842	7672500	-50000	6.04	153.45	-1.00
PROGRESS-ON-LOSS STRATEGY						
1	3337	7500	-5000	0.05	0.10	-0.07
2	6560	14250	-10500	0.09	0.20	-0.14
3	9670	20250	-16500	0.13	0.28	-0.23
4	12670	25500	-23000	0.17	0.35	-0.32
5	15556	30000	-30000	0.21	0.41	-0.41
6	18331	33750	-37500	0.25	0.47	-0.52
7	21002	36750	-45500	0.29	0.51	-0.63
8	23558	39000	-54000	0.32	0.54	-0.74
9	25994	40500	-63000	0.36	0.56	-0.87
10	28334	42250	-72500	0.39	0.58	-1.00
PROGRESS-ON-WIN STRATEGY						
1	3337	7500	-5000	0.12	0.27	-0.18
2	6776	15750	-9500	0.25	0.57	-0.35
3	10330	24750	-13500	0.38	0.90	-0.49
4	13997	34500	-17000	0.51	1.25	-0.62
5	17782	45000	-20000	0.65	1.64	-0.73
6	21657	56250	-22500	0.79	2.05	-0.82
7	25672	68250	-24500	0.93	2.48	-0.89
8	29786	81000	-26000	1.08	2.95	-0.95
9	33999	94500	-27000	1.24	3.44	-0.98
10	38322	108750	-27500	1.39	3.95	-1.00

EXHIBIT 17–5   Trade Management, Overall Results (Graphs)

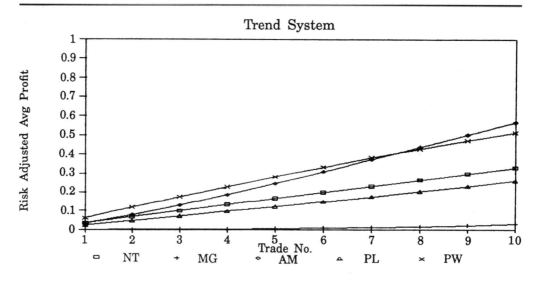

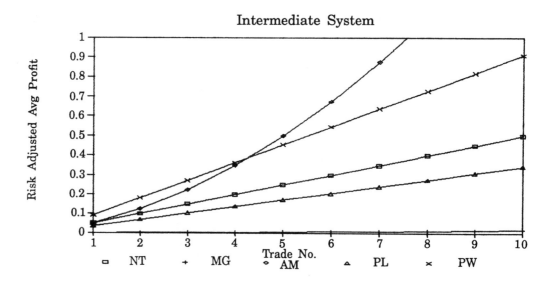

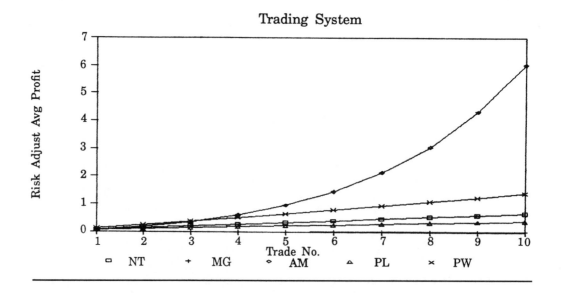

Average Profit. The horizontal axis shows the trade number in the series of 10. The vertical axis shows the average profit at that point for all series divided by the worst drawdown suffered. Below each chart is the legend, which identifies each line with the corresponding trade management strategy. The higher a line goes, the better is the strategy's reward/risk ratio. Thus, the longer you trade any strategy, the greater the reward/risk ratio. The Martingale strategy hardly gets above the zero line, while the Anti-Martingale strategy eventually outperforms all the others, regardless of system.

Analysis

The Martingale strategy stands out as providing the largest percentage of winning series and good potential profits, regardless of system. However, the risk is prohibitively large and makes the strategy useless for commodity trading.

The Anti-Martingale strategy, on the other hand, achieves the highest potential profits of these strategies and incurs less risk. The slightly lower percentage of winning series is the trade-off required to achieve these superior reward/risk levels.

The Progress-on-Loss and Progress-on-Win strategies generally fall in between the other two approaches with the Progress-on-Win strategy being the superior of the two. Progress-on-Win outperformed even Anti-Martingale for seven or fewer trades with the Trend system and for four or fewer trades with the Intermediate system.

To better visualize the reward/risk ratios of the different strategies, examine the performance graphs, which follow the Exhibits. These three graphs show the Risk-Adjusted Average Profit attained at each trade number taken across all series for each strategy and system.

In order to allow meaningful comparison between the strategies, I adjusted the raw performance figures to take account of the risk required in order to achieve the performance results. I adjusted for risk by dividing the performance measure under study by the worst loss that would have to be endured for that series, strategy and system. Thus, the risk-adjusted performance of the Martingale strategy, as shown on the graphs, is almost indistinguishable from the horizontal axis. This reflects the very large risk that that strategy entails.

Conclusions

The results of this study yield some valuable conclusions: First, two of the strategies, the Anti-Martingale and Progress-on-Win, outperformed the Neutral (or no strategy) approach to trade management. This is so because their risk (as measured by the extreme loss) was the same or less, while their return (as measured by the average amount of profits or the Win/Loss Ratio) was higher. However, the Progress-on-Win strategy does not appear practical for smaller traders because it requires trading with too many contracts. Your trading unit in contracts must be equal to the largest number of consecutive losses you could experience.

Second, the Anti-Martingale strategy increased performance quite dramatically, and did so without any increase in total risk. This is a practical approach for small traders because it allows initial trading in one-contract units with increases only after wins.

Third, there is a trade-off between a strategy's improved total reward/risk performance and the proportion of winning series it produces. In other words, in order to have a better chance of reaching the moon, you have to settle for a slightly increased chance of going nowhere at all.

Fourth, all these effects become more pronounced as we move from longer-term systems to shorter-term systems.

Fifth, only those strategies that increased the number of units traded after a win outperformed the Neutral strategy. Strategies that increased the number of trading units after a loss did worse than the Neutral strategy. This is further proof that you should resist the psychological temptation to double up or increase trading after a losing streak. The time to increase trading, if at all, is after a win, not a loss.

Finally, this study proves that, when applied to a profitable system, well-chosen trade management strategies can increase trading profits without a corresponding increase in risk. The potential benefits are real and worthwhile.

Application to Trading

I am not necessarily recommending that you always double the number of contracts after each winning trade. However, you should never increase trading size after a loss. You would probably be well-advised to consider increasing trading size after a win. Here are some additional factors you should keep in mind.

1. The advantage of the Anti-Martingale trade management strategy depends upon using a winning system. Remember, in the long run no trade management strategy can turn a losing system into a winner.
2. You can obtain the advantages of a trade management strategy without requiring that all trades have the same amount of risk.
3. The more your system trades and the higher its winning percentage, the more benefit you will receive from a trade management strategy.
4. The validity of this study is dependent upon a system in which the results of each trade are independent of one other. In other words, there must be no statistical correlation between the outcome of successive trades. In my opinion this is probably true for all commodity trading systems and methods.

As with everything else in commodity trading systems, the watchword is test. Back-test your current approach with these principles in mind. See whether your system performance would be improved by a more aggressive trade management approach. You might be pleasantly surprised.

Equity Curve Management

Anyone who has traded commodity futures for any length of time is aware of what is commonly referred to as the equity curve. This is the graphic representation of your account equity. The normal trader's equity never moves in a straight line. It goes up and down. For most people the overall trend is, unfortunately, down. However, even the good traders have periodic drawdowns in their equity.

The average trader comes to grips with the equity curve phenomenon most often when he decides to increase his trading. He makes this decision invariably after an exceptionally successful trading period. His equity curve has been rising dynamically. If this happens soon after he starts trading, he assumes he was born to trade and will always be relatively successful. If it happens after a longer learning period, he concludes that he has finally solved the problems of trading. In any case, he is lamenting the fact that he did not trade more contracts during his recent successful run.

Just as he corrects this problem by adding more contracts or more markets, his equity curve turns down and goes into a decline. Because of the increased trading, it takes a lot less time to lose all the profits than it took to make them. As his performance worsens, he begins to question his system. When the equity curve finally nears the bottom, performance has been so bad that the trader assumes the system no longer works or was no good in the first place. He stops trading it and looks for something better. As the system's equity curve begins to rise again, the trader is out of the market or trading some other system.

The very best way to trade would be to maximize exposure at the bottom of the equity curve, when everything looks the worst, and stop trading at the top of the equity curve, when everything looks the rosiest. Even if you could overcome the natural psychological barriers to such a strategy, would it be possible to identify in *advance* the appropriate points to start and stop trading?

With the assistance of a colleague, Joe Bristor, I conducted some research on the problem, using the equity curves of advisory services. However, equity curves are as applicable to mechanical systems as they are to any trading approach. Advisors, like systems, have definite periods of success and non-success. (I don't like to use the word failure because of its negative connotations. Failure implies some inadequacy on the part of the trader. He may have done everything exactly correctly but still not have been rewarded by the market. It is better to think of the situation as one that did not produce the intended results.) What if there was a way to trade several advisors or systems, or even one advisor or system, so as to maximize your exposure to profitable periods and minimize exposure to losing periods?

We set out to find such a mechanical method to apply to trading with advisory services. What we needed was a technique that would keep us from trading during months with abnormally large losses. The best way to miss the big losers is to wait on the sidelines for them to occur. Likewise, we needed a way to know when profits have become abnormal. We found two separate approaches that work well either separately or together.

We concentrated our research on the 16 advisory services followed by *CTCR* for the whole of the three-year period 1984 to 1986. (Two of them had slightly less than three years' data.) We chose for the measure of profitability what is listed in *CTCR* as Monthly Net Gain in Equity. This represents the profits or losses an account would have achieved during a month if it followed all the recommendations in the manner tracked by *CTCR*. It includes open equity at the end of the month because that represents accrued profits or losses that are marked to the market each day in an account. Open equity at the beginning of the month is deducted because it does not reflect actual profit or loss achieved during the month. The formula can be expressed as: This month's closed profits + This month's open equity − Last month's open equity.

Thus, if an advisor started a month with $10,000 in open equity, had $20,000 in closed trade profits during the month, and ended with $5,000 in open equity, his Net Gain for the month would be $15,000 ($20,000 + $5,000 − $10,000). If an advisor started a month with $5,000 in open losses, had $10,000 in closed trade losses, and ended with $15,000 in open equity, his Net Gain for the month would be $10,000 (−$10,000 + $15,000 + $5,000). You add the $5,000 because he started the month $5,000 in the hole, but he made it up during the month to end up with positive open equity.

Although we used Net Gain in Equity as our measure of monthly performance, there is no reason why you couldn't use some other reasonable measure, so long as you use it consistently. Closed trade profits might be another possibility.

In testing our system, we started out using all the advisors, whether they were profitable or not. We quickly discovered, however, that you cannot hope to make money following losing advisors, no matter what kind of money management scheme you follow. We therefore confined our testing to the 10 advisors who were profitable over the three-year period 1984 to 1986. This should not affect the application of the system because no one would trade an advisor who he did not believe would be profitable in the future. Although you can never know for sure in advance which advisors will be profitable, if you trade this approach with profitable advisors, you should reap the benefits. If you happen to choose unprofitable advisors, you will probably not be hurt by applying the system, although you shouldn't expect to end up with profits.

It should be noted that *CTCR*'s figures do not include any deductions for slippage and commissions. This is because we want to keep our figures as objective as possible and there is no objectively correct figure to deduct. Rather than make a subjective judgment that would distort the data, we present objective data and let our subscribers deduct an amount that they feel is appropriate.

In calculating your own figures for use in applying this approach, you should probably deduct an appropriate amount to reflect the slippage and commissions you actually incur or would be likely to incur in trading with the particular advisor. For purposes of establishing the rules for this approach, we don't think that slippage and commissions would make that big a difference. While the profit figures used in the supporting tables are overstated because of failure to deduct slippage and commissions, all figures are consistent in this regard. Note that services that trade more heavily will have proportionally greater reductions in profits on account of slippage and commissions. Again, we don't believe this affects the validity of the trading methods proposed.

Monthly Net Equity Changes of a Typical Profitable Advisor

Exhibits 17–6 and 17–7 are charts showing two different representations of the monthly net equity changes for *Commodity Closeup* for the 36 months between 1984 and 1986. (The horizontal and vertical lines labeled Standard Deviation and ACP will be explained later.)

The bar graph shows the size and timing of profitable and losing months. The bars for profitable months extend upward and those for losing months extend downward.

The line graph shows the distribution of profitable and losing months. Each small square represents the number of occurrences of months with different levels of profits (rounded to the nearest thousand dollars). For instance, looking at the top of the curve, the box labeled 7 represents seven different months in which the change in equity was between $0 and −$1,000. The curve resembles a normal distribution curve. As you would expect, the largest number of occurrences involved small changes, both plus and minus. The smallest number of occurrences involved large profits and large losses.

We used observations such as these graphs to establish rules for various trading approaches that would attempt to trade when the odds were the highest for achieving profits and to stop trading when the odds were the lowest. This would have the effect of trading near the bottom of the equity curve and staying on the sidelines near the top.

So how did these approaches stack up historically against just trading every newsletter recommendation? With these methods you would trade only about half the time. This would cut required margin considerably or enable you to trade more services with the same size account. Drawdown would also be cut about in half. This increases the comfort factor and makes it easier to follow all the trades. The methods retain a significant percentage of the profitability of trading every recommendation. This means that you can substantially increase your efficiency, measured in profits per actual month of trading.

EXHIBIT 17–6   Trade Management, Monthly Net Equity Changes

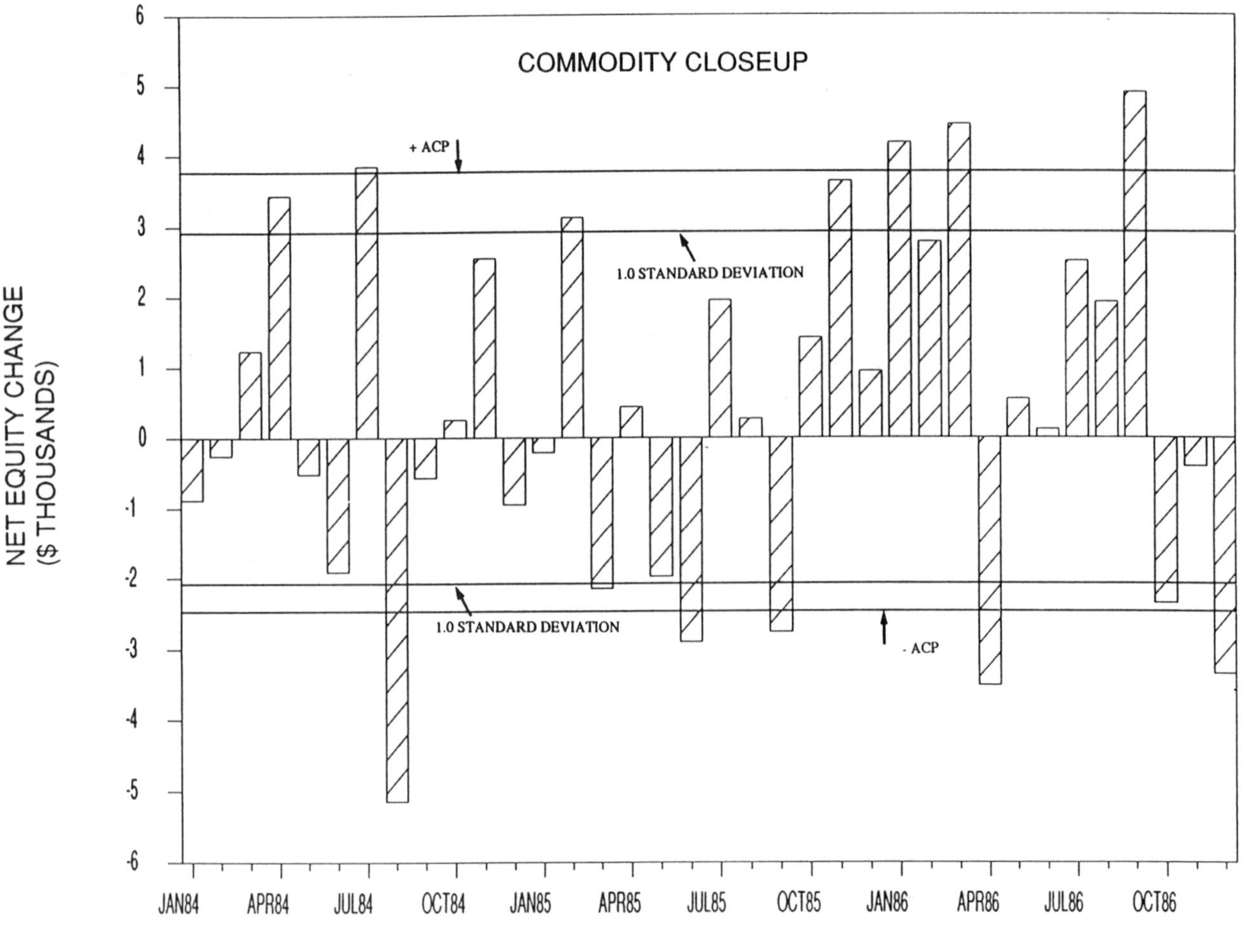

There are two parts to the system. Each may be employed alone or they may be employed together. The first approach uses monthly equity patterns to generate trading signals. The second approach uses the distribution of monthly equity changes to identify abnormally good months and abnormally bad months. These extreme levels generate signals to start and stop trading. The idea of the first approach is to avoid some of the inevitable losing months by waiting for them to occur before starting to trade. The second approach is based on the observation that extreme months, either winning or losing, usually represent a turning point in the equity curve. Thus, you want to start trading after an extremely bad month and stop trading after an extremely good one.

Trading Rules for the Equity Pattern Approach

1. Monitor the monthly equity changes of the service or system you are going to trade. For this approach you need at least 12 months of data, preferably more.

EXHIBIT 17–7   Trade Management, Distribution of Equity Changes

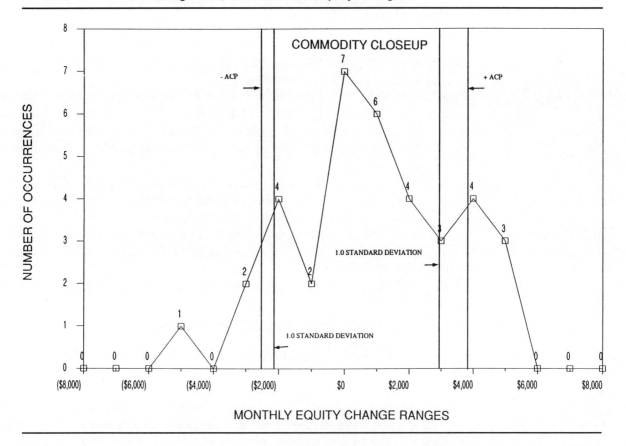

2. Wait until there are two *consecutive* losing months. Then start trading every recommendation. A break-even month is counted as a losing month.

3. Continue trading until there is at least one profitable month followed by one losing month. Stop trading. Thus, you keep trading through any number of profitable months until there is one losing month. Then stop trading and wait again for two losing months in a row. The losing month that causes you to stop trading may be the first of the two in a row that will signal you to resume trading.

The tables in Exhibit 17–8 show the expected performance in waiting for two (Column 1), three (Column 2), or four (Column 3) consecutive losing months before beginning to trade. While waiting for more than two consecutive losing months to start trading increases the percentage of profitable trading months, overall profits are less. Although it may be scary to keep trading after three and four losing months in a row, if the service is to be profitable, the odds favor a resumption of profitability. Thus, under our assumption of an overall profitable service, there is no reason to stop trading.

Trading Rules for the Equity Distribution Approach

1. Monitor the monthly equity changes of the service or system you are going to trade. For this approach you need at least 12 months of data, preferably more.
2. Calculate the standard deviation of the monthly equity changes.
3. Calculate the Abnormal Cutoff Point for Profitable (+ ACP) and Unprofitable (− ACP) months for the particular service or system.
4. Start trading after any month whose monthly equity change is less than − ACP.
5. Continue trading until either of two things happens. Either there is at least one profitable month followed by one losing month. (Thus, you keep trading through any number of profitable months until there is one losing month. Then stop trading.) Or there is a month whose equity change is greater than + ACP. Then stop trading.
6. Wait again for a month whose equity change is less than − ACP.

Calculating Standard Deviation

Standard deviation is a measure of the data's average deviation from the mean. Computer spread sheets and business or scientific calculators have built-in functions to calculate standard deviation. It is easiest just to use computers or calculators for the computation. For those who do not have access to such assistance or who are curious about how to calculate standard deviation by hand, Exhibit 17–9 shows the method. The data points are the monthly equity changes for *Commodity Closeup* during 1984 to 1986.

Trading Parameters for 10 Advisory Services

The following parameters were derived from 1984 to 1986 data for the profitable services followed by *CTCR* during that period.

Average Equity	Monthly Increase	Standard Deviation	Abnormal Cutoff Points	
			+ ACP	− ACP
Accu Comm	1,151	3,051	5,325	− 2,373
Bullish Consensus	2,037	4,086	7,627	− 2,682
Cambridge Marketletter	1,027	4,428	7,085	− 4,087
Commodex	4,504	12,121	21,085	− 9,496
Commodity Closeup	409	2,494	3,822	− 2,473
Davis-Zweig	789	11,170	16,070	− 12,112
DeMark Futures Forecast	8,155	16,769	31,095	− 11,213
Elliott Wave Theorist	1,894	6,340	10,567	− 5,429
The Factor Report	561	2,565	4,070	− 2,402
MBH Weekly Letter	423	2,689	4,102	− 2,683
Average	2,095	6,571	11,084	− 5,495

+ ACP = Average monthly increase + (1.368 × Standard deviation)
− ACP = Average monthly increase − (1.155 × Standard deviation)

EXHIBIT 17–8 **Equity Curve Management Strategy Results**

SYSTEM DRAWDOWN as a per cent of continuous trading of advisors (1984-86)

		CONTINUOUS	1	2	APPROACH 3	4	5	6
ACCU COMM	100%	-4972				30%	30%	30%
BULLISH CONSENSUS	100%	-9702				68%	90%	90%
CAMBRIDGE	100%	-14369				72%	16%	66%
COMMODITY CLOSEUP	100%	-8040				47%	34%	42%
COMMODEX	100%	-30485		[Not Tested]		77%	60%	78%
DAVIS-ZWEIG	100%	-25369				55%	40%	55%
DeMARK FUT FORECAST	100%	-31665				44%	41%	44%
ELLIOTT WV THEORIST	100%	-20068				81%	34%	81%
THE FACTOR REPORT	100%	-6635				20%	N/A	58%
MBH WEEKLY LETTER	100%	-15567				41%	80%	71%
AVERAGE OF ALL ADVISORS	100%					53%	47%	62%

TOTAL SYSTEM PROFITS as a per cent of continuous trading of advisors (1984-86)

		CONTINUOUS	1	2	APPROACH 3	4	5	6
ACCU COMM	100%	$35,699	39%	39%	50%	41%	9%	41%
BULLISH CONSENSUS	100%	$73,321	32%	32%	32%	71%	60%	60%
CAMBRIDGE	100%	$36,987	18%	2%	27%	54%	49%	50%
COMMODITY CLOSEUP	100%	$14,714	-24%	5%	5%	143%	142%	173%
COMMODEX	100%	$162,169	33%	36%	36%	41%	74%	63%
DAVIS-ZWEIG	100%	$28,396	118%	185%	185%	337%	304%	333%
DeMARK FUT FORECAST	100%	$220,196	-7%	91%	91%	47%	72%	76%
ELLIOTT WV THEORIST	100%	$68,197	-20%	26%	78%	27%	13%	47%
THE FACTOR REPORT	100%	$20,201	-6%	-16%	46%	23%	0%	107%
MBH WEEKLY LETTER	100%	$15,248	121%	105%	105%	-22%	-74%	63%
TOTAL OF ALL ADVISORS		$675,128	$115,666	$380,865	$441,885	$391,099	$449,738	$529,513
AVERAGE OF ALL ADVISORS	100%		31%	51%	65%	76%	65%	101%

AVERAGE MONTHLY NET EQUITY as a per cent of continuous trading of advisors (1984-86)

		CONTINUOUS	1	2	APPROACH 3	4	5	6
ACCU COMM	100%	$1,151	135%	152%	120%	97%	69%	97%
BULLISH CONSENSUS	100%	$2,037	96%	96%	96%	128%	103%	103%
CAMBRIDGE	100%	$1,027	64%	5%	60%	121%	160%	113%
COMMODITY CLOSEUP	100%	$409	-65%	11%	11%	215%	320%	249%
COMMODEX	100%	$4,505	117%	107%	107%	86%	157%	125%
DAVIS-ZWEIG	100%	$789	388%	371%	371%	606%	1093%	546%
DeMARK FUT FORECAST	100%	$8,155	-94%	145%	145%	90%	178%	137%
ELLIOTT WV THEORIST	100%	$1,894	-177%	63%	134%	51%	53%	74%
THE FACTOR REPORT	100%	$561	-68%	-93%	126%	91%	0%	240%
MBH WEEKLY LETTER	100%	$424	336%	270%	252%	-53%	-267%	109%
AVERAGE MONTHLY EQUITY		$2,095	$229	$2,518	$2,788	$2,307	$3,590	$2,969
AVERAGE OF ALL ADVISORS	100%		73%	113%	142%	143%	187%	179%
PERCENTAGE OF MONTHS TRADING	96%		24%	36%	43%	46%	30%	49%

EXHIBIT 17–9 Calculating Standard Deviation

	MONTHLY EQUITY	EQUITY SQUARED
JAN84	(880)	774,400
FEB84	(258)	66,564
MAR84	1,242	1,542,564
APR84	3,448	11,888,704
MAY84	(522)	272,484
JUN84	(1,910)	3,648,100
JUL84	3,854	14,853,316
AUG84	(5,137)	26,388,769
SEP84	(564)	318,096
OCT84	257	66,049
NOV84	2,546	6,482,116
DEC84	(948)	898,704
JAN85	(210)	44,100
FEB85	3,128	9,784,384
MAR85	(2,146)	4,605,316
APR85	438	191,844
MAY85	(1,973)	3,892,729
JUN85	(2,890)	8,352,100
JUL85	1,948	3,794,704
AUG85	268	71,824
SEP85	(2,757)	7,601,049
OCT85	1,425	2,030,625
NOV85	3,643	13,271,449
DEC85	942	887,364
JAN86	4,188	17,539,344
FEB86	2,780	7,728,400
MAR86	4,435	19,669,225
APR86	(3,512)	12,334,144
MAY86	545	297,025
JUN86	113	12,769
JUL86	2,506	6,280,036
AUG86	1,925	3,705,625
SEP86	4,892	23,931,664
OCT86	(2,349)	5,517,801
NOV86	(406)	164,836
DEC86	(3,347)	11,202,409
TOTALS	14,714	230,110,632

A = 230,110,632
B = (14,714 * 14,714) = 216,501,800
N = NUMBER OF DATA POINTS [36]

FORMULA FOR STANDARD DEVIATION

$$SD = \sqrt{\frac{A - (B/N)}{N}} \qquad \sqrt{} \text{ means square root of}$$

$$SD = \sqrt{\frac{230,110,632 - (216,501,800 / 36)}{36}}$$

$$SD = 2,494$$

ACP points represent abnormal monthly profit and loss levels. Our research showed that when a service has an abnormally good month, it is a good idea to stop trading immediately. Conversely, when a profitable service has an abnormally bad month, it is a good idea to start trading immediately.

We found two methods of calculating $+ACP$ and $-ACP$ that worked well. The first used just the standard deviation. The second involved using a multiple of the standard deviation. For $+ACP$, we recommend using 1.368 times the standard deviation. For $-ACP$, we recommend using 1.155 times the standard deviation.

Exhibit 17–8 shows the performance of each of these methods, compared with following all trades of a profitable service. Exhibit 17–8 shows three measures of performance: drawdown, total profits, and average monthly net equity gain or loss. The first two columns show how a trader would have done by taking all recommendations of the service. The next six columns show how the trader would have done by trading six different equity curve management approaches. This comparative performance is expressed as a percentage of the performance achieved following all recommendations. Thus, if the comparison shows 100 percent, the results would have been exactly equal to those achieved by following all recommendations. If the comparison shows 50 percent, the results would have been half as good as those achieved by following all recommendations. If the comparison shows 200 percent, the results would have been twice as good as those achieved by following all recommendations.

The six different equity curve management approaches are as follows.

Approach 1: Two-Consecutive Test. Begin trading after two consecutive losing months. Continue only if the third month is profitable. Stop trading upon the first losing month after a winning month or string of winning months. (Named after the fact that you allow only two consecutive losers.)

Approach 2: Three-Consecutive Test. Begin trading after two consecutive losing months. Continue only if the third or fourth month is profitable. Stop trading upon the first losing month after a winning month or string of winning months. (Named after the fact that you allow three consecutive losers.)

Approach 3: Four-Consecutive Test. Begin trading after two consecutive losing months. Continue if the third, fourth, or fifth month is profitable. Stop trading upon the first losing month after a winning month or string of winning months. (Named after the fact that you allow four consecutive losers.)

[We do not show results of trading after five consecutive losing months because there were only a few such occurrences. However, we suggest continuing even after five losing months. Remember, if you are working with a profitable advisor, his slump will end.]

Approach 4: 1.0 Standard Deviation Test. Begin trading as explained in Approach 3 above. Or begin trading if any monthly equity value penetrates the lower standard deviation line. Stop trading upon the first losing month after a winning month or string of winning months or upon penetration of the upper standard deviation line.

Approach 5: ACP Test. This test uses the upper and lower Abnormal Cutoff Points to toggle trading activity. Begin trading upon penetration of the lower −ACP line. Stop trading upon penetration of the upper +ACP line. You do, however, still stop trading upon the first losing month after a winning month or string of winning months.

Approach 6: The Equity Curve System. A combination of the best of Approaches 4 and 5. Begin trading as explained in Approach 3 or begin upon penetration of the lower −ACP line. Stop trading upon penetration of the upper +ACP line or upon the first losing month following a winning month or string of winning months.

If you look at the average for all advisors and compare Approach 6 to following all recommendations, you find that you would have traded only half the time but made slightly higher profits with a considerably smaller drawdown. This was exactly the effect we sought to achieve in designing the system!

Although the other approaches made lower total profits, remember that you were trading less than half the time. Therefore, your average monthly return was considerably higher and your drawdown was much lower. You can increase the total profits by using the equity curve management approach and trading more advisors or more contracts.

Two Approaches for Real-Time Trading

But wait a minute, you are probably saying. Trading the equity curve is all very well and good in hindsight, but how can I trade that way in real time? That would mean assuming all of an advisor's (or system's) open positions at the beginning of a month. I would be coming in right in the middle of a trade. The stops at that time would probably be much farther away than they would at the time of entry.

While it is true that assuming a position in the middle of a trade would be a novel and perhaps scary way to proceed, if our research has any value, it shows that this is actually better than just entering all trades at the beginning. While it is true that some positions would be assumed late in the move with large open profits and perhaps distant stops, others would be assumed with open losses and closer stops. If an advisor is going to be turning profitable, you might as well assume his open positions, because they are just as likely to generate immediate profits as a new position. However, for those who would be uncomfortable jumping into the middle of an open trade, I have an alternate suggestion.

When the system tells you to begin trading the next month, you do not need to assume all existing open positions. Instead, start taking new recommendations. Continue to take all new recommendations until the system tells you to stop trading. At that point, stop taking new recommendations. Do not close out current open positions immediately, however. Hold all current positions until the advisor (or system) recommends exit. I will call this the *New Trade Method* as opposed to the *Equity Curve Method*.

I can hear the howls of protest. It is true that the tables of statistical data already presented were based on assuming all existing positions at the beginning of a month when you started trading and exiting all existing positions at the end of a month when you stopped trading. However, to insist that historical research of an idea be based exactly on the same kind of trading that you will employ in the future is to perpetuate the same kind of mistake about commodity futures price data that has caused so many traders to come to grief in the past.

Traders always assume that as long as some approach worked well in the past, regardless of how it was created, it will probably work well in the future. This is just not so. Prices in the future will not behave exactly as they did in the past. It is really true that past performance is no guarantee of future profitability.

If the idea behind this system—stopping and starting trading with an advisor or system based on recent profitability—has merit, it should work in numerous different ways. Therefore, I am not concerned whether you trade the actual equity curve precisely or use some other roughly equivalent method to approximate the idea.

In order to test this concept, we looked at the results for our 10 advisors during 1986 based on trading to conclusion all recommendations entered in the months designated for trading while ignoring recommendations made to enter during months designated for no trading. As I predicted, they were almost as good as using the rigid *Equity Curve Method*. This lends added credibility to the general approach of starting and stopping trading on the basis of recent performance.

Taking all trades in 1986, the 10 advisors collectively would have earned $282,575 in total profits. Following Approach 6, using the *Equity Curve Method* would have yielded 72 percent of the total all trades profits but almost doubled (180 percent) the profit per month actually traded. Following Approach 6, but using the *New Trade Method* described above, you would have earned 64 percent of the possible all trades total profits but 160 percent of the profit per month actually traded. Thus, your trading would have been 60 percent more efficient than if you had taken all trades. Following Approach 6 and using the *New Trade Method,* the percentage of winning trades increased to 48 percent from 43 percent for taking all trades.

As an example for a particular advisor, the *Davis-Zweig Futures Hotline* lost over $10,000 during 1986 trading all 12 months. If you followed the *Equity Curve Method,* using Approach 6, you would have made $46,586 and traded only during eight months. Using the *New Trade Method,* you would have made $32,716. *Commodity Closeup* made $11,770 trading all 12 months in 1986. Using Approach 6 with the *Equity Curve Method,* you would have traded only seven months but still made $10,822. Using the *New Trade Method,* you would have made $6,391, achieving about the same efficiency as taking all recommendations but with greater accuracy and lower drawdown.

While all the above figures represent only hypothetical trading, they are internally consistent. I have shown that you can increase trading efficiency and reduce drawdowns by being more selective in trading an advisor or system. It is beneficial to wait until after some losing months before starting to trade. It is beneficial to start trading after an especially bad losing month. It is beneficial to stop trading after an especially good period and wait again for a losing period before resuming trading. There are many more unexplored ways to implement such an approach. I hope you will be moved to do some additional research on your own.

I have now covered all the essential elements of successful commodity futures trading and mechanical system design. You are now ready to design and trade your own system, using ideas in this book or from other sources. The possibilities are truly endless. To help you recall all that you have learned, the next chapter will recapitulate and summarize the important points in this book. It also contains some new surprises.

18 Summary and Conclusion

If you have made it this far with me, you realize that while there are many details involved in successful commodity trading, the essence is not complicated. It takes effort but not inordinate intelligence. Reasonable profits are within the grasp of anyone who has accumulated sufficient capital to open an account and has the patience and discipline to preserve it.

Commodity speculation is nothing more than intelligent gambling on the future direction of price movement. Speculators don't own or deal in the products they trade. Leverage makes possible incredible profits, and just-as-incredible losses. However, while enormous losses are common, the commodity markets need not be as risky as popular superstition suggests. How much risk you take is within your control. Your chances of long-term success depend on whether you want to get rich quick or are willing to settle for a reasonable return on your capital. The more profit you expect and the more impatient you are to earn it, the lower is your likelihood of eventual success. If you have reasonable goals and can master yourself, you can master the markets.

Although it appears that profitable speculation depends on accurate price forecasting, the reality is that consistently accurate price predictions (with the precision necessary in leveraged commodity trading) are impossible. Luckily, they are not necessary. The key to profits is not to anticipate trends, but to follow them. A trader will do the best when he positions himself in the direction of a strong trend and stays with the trade as long as the trend persists. A trend is relevant only in the time period in which it exists. There can be conflicting short, intermediate, and long-term trends in the same market at the same time. Each trader must operate in the time frame that matches his trading personality. Slippage and commissions are an overhead cost that must be added to every trade. Therefore, long-term systems, which trade infrequently, tend to be the most profitable.

There are three cardinal rules of successful commodity trading: follow the trend, cut losses short, and let profits run. They are as old as trading itself, emphasized in every book on the subject and well-known to every trader. Even though every losing trader knows these principles, he is nevertheless unable to follow them.

There are six essential reasons that commodity traders have such a low success rate. Lack of understanding is probably the least important factor. Although knowledge is usually power, knowledge is not enough in commodity trading. The hardest part is the doing. The two biggest trader misconceptions are the subliminal effect of ego in ruining a good trading plan and misplaced reliance on technical analysis as a means of predicting the markets. Technical analysis is useful but imperfect.

The only reason for failure beyond a trader's control is lack of capital. Lack of capital is relative. The more money you have deposited in your trading account, the more flexible and diversified you can be in your trading. The more you have and the more you are truly willing to lose, the better will be your chance for success, provided you manage your trading properly.

One of the biggest obstacles on the road to profits is unrealistic expectations. A reasonable goal for commodity traders is a consistent return of 50 percent a year on the total amount in your trading account. That is the goal for an experienced trader. The novice should have a lower target. If a new trader broke even in his first year, he would be way ahead of most others. If he was able to do that, he could go for perhaps a 20 percent return his second year. Then he would be ready to shoot for 50 percent his third year and thereafter. Although 50 percent is the goal, in good years you might do considerably better.

A related problem is lack of patience. It most often manifests itself in two ways: overtrading and overrisking. These are both caused by trying to make too much money too quickly.

Another well-known reason traders fail is lack of discipline. Discipline is the most popular word used to describe the quintessence of good commodity trading. We know what we are supposed to do. We may even have a specific plan, replete with details about how to react in every possible situation. Yet even professionals find ways to deviate from their plan. Amateurs don't even have a plan. Great traders not only have the best plans, they stray from their plan the least often.

The last stumbling block is the least mentioned and least understood. It is high risk aversion. Most human beings are naturally averse to risk. The best commodity traders are like financial race-car drivers, sky divers, and ski jumpers. They are not afraid of taking big financial risks; they actually enjoy it. Recent scientific evidence suggests there is a biochemical difference between the brains of risk takers and non-risk takers. If that is so, it means there is only so much that risk-averse traders can do to feel more comfortable with high-risk trading. One of the most important steps you can take to profitable trading is to come to terms with your level of financial risk aversion and accommodate it.

In Chapter 3, we looked at the typical way a beginning trader approaches the markets. He tends to move haphazardly from one approach to the next, always looking for something better. He has no trading guidelines and no overall plan. On the other hand, a professional trader is highly organized and has his own unique way to identify potential trades. He enters the market when his plan dictates. He tends to follow the direction of the market in his time frame rather than anticipate a change in trend. The professional has learned to handle the inevitability of losses. He knows he can never avoid them.

For all traders there is a continuum between 0 percent mechanical trading and 100 percent mechanical trading. Someone who trades 100 percent mechanically never has to make any trading decision. He has a plan that tells him precisely what to do in any situation. Successful traders all have a relatively mechanical approach. The average person has the best chance to be a profitable trader if he or she adopts a 100 percent mechanical approach. If profit is your goal rather than massaging your ego or having fun, I recommend that you find one or more good mathematical systems and trade them in a diversified group of markets. You will also need sufficient capital and courage to withstand the inevitable equity drawdowns that occur regardless of trading approach.

A mechanical approach is the only way to avoid the destructive emotionalism that permeates trading. Human nature is such that left to your own devices, you will succumb to the twin villains of fear and greed and invariably make the wrong decisions.

Here is what I mean by a strictly mechanical approach. You will have a predetermined group of markets that you will follow. You will have mathematical formulas to apply to previous prices that will tell you when to buy and when to sell. There will be entry rules, exit rules for losing trades, and exit rules for profitable trades. There will be rules for when to start trading and stop trading each system. Your only tasks will be to choose initially the systems and markets to trade and to apply the system rules to market price action. If your system is computerized, you will have to provide data to the computer, run the system software, and place the orders the system dictates. This should not take very much of your time. You can hire someone to do it for you.

The key to creating a mechanical system that will work in the markets is to avoid creating a curve-fitted system. A curve-fitted system is one that has been expressly designed so that it would have been profitable trading the past. It is easy to identify such systems created without a computer because of the many complicated rules with endless exceptions and exceptions to exceptions. Using a computer to optimize trading rule parameters disguises the process so well that most people don't realize that by finding the best-performing parameters, they may be inadvertently creating a curve-fitted system.

When doing historical testing, it is essential to remember what the goal is. It is not to create a system that will generate the most hypothetical profits trading in the past. It is to create a system that will generate the most profits trading in the future. The future is the only arena where you can make real money.

Chapters 5 and 6 discussed the many issues involved in historical testing of trading systems. They include such problems as what data interval to use, what type of data, the appropriate test period length, and which markets to test. The key is to make the test as realistic as possible within the limits of the data. One important ingredient of fair testing is an appropriate deduction from every trade for the inherent costs of trading—slippage and commissions. Using a realistic cost deduction often makes the difference between whether a system appears to be profitable or not.

There are numerous criteria that you can use to assess the effectiveness of a system's historical performance. The decision is not crucial, because the best systems tend to perform better in every category. The quickest way to evaluate a system's potential is to look at the average profit per trade.

In Chapter 7, we took a stroll through the wonderland of system merchandising. You saw the way clever vendors can turn the subject of profitable trading into a mystical search for trading's Holy Grail. This book should convince you that there are no magic secrets only the professionals know, and there is no way to buy guaranteed success. The analytical tools you have learned should help you make a realistic assessment of the likely value of any system promotion. Above all, remember that price and value are not necessarily related when you are dealing with commodity trading products.

This book presented, for the first time ever, a systematic exploration of the effectiveness of accepted trading techniques. In Chapter 8, I showed you the historical performance of several popular trading approaches and a new long-term system I designed just for this book. Using the same standard testing, I evaluated all aspects of trading systems. In Chapter 9, you learned the theory behind various kinds of entry techniques. In Chapter 10, I explained how to cut losses short with strategically placed stop-loss orders. In Chapter 11, you saw the effect of various profit-taking schemes.

The Babcock Long-term System demonstrated its superiority in comparison with all the techniques described and tested in this book. Since the uniform test period ran between July 1982 and June 1987, you may be wondering how it did in the succeeding year. Exhibit 18–1 shows its performance over that year. Although the table shows losses, the system would probably have been profitable for anyone who actually traded it. The biggest loss was a $28,225 hit in the S&P 500, which occurred on October 22, 1987. The system was flat going into the October 19 crash, but then flashed a buy signal on October 21. In that incredibly volatile environment, it would not have been prudent to take that signal. The excessive loss over the $2,500

EXHIBIT 18–1   Performance Report, Babcock Long-term System (July 1, 1987 to June 30, 1988)

	S&P 500	T-Bonds	Euro dollars	Swiss Francs	Japanese Yen	Comex Gold	Heating Oil	Soy beans	Sugar	Live Cattle	Average
Number of Closed Trades	3	4	3	2	4	1	4	3	4	5	3
Number of Profitable Trades	0	1	1	2	1	1	1	2	3	1	1
Percent Profitable	0%	25%	33%	100%	25%	100%	25%	67%	75%	20%	39%
Total Profit or Loss	-33,425	-6,025	-5,375	20,437	-6,600	4,300	-5,508	12,125	1,042	-5,780	-2,481
Average Profitable Trade	0	3,744	2,225	10,219	1,213	4,300	219	7,363	1,214	110	3,893
Average Losing Trade	-11,142	-3,256	-3,800	0	-2,604	0	-1,909	-2,600	-2,600	-1,473	-3,771
Maximum Drawdown	-33,425	-7,169	-7,600	0	-7,813	0	-5,727	-2,600	-2,600	-5,780	-7,271
Average Profit Per Trade	-11,142	-1,506	-1,792	10,219	-1,650	4,300	-1,377	4,042	261	-1,156	-752

stop resulted from an immense gap down on the next day's opening. That kind of unpredictable price action is precisely the reason to stay out of the market during such periods. Without that one huge S&P loss and without including the cattle market, which no one should trade with the system, the overall profit was $9,196, a respectable $340 per trade.

You may also be wondering how well it might have done trading some other markets not included in the uniform testing plan. Exhibit 18–2 shows its hypothetical performance in 11 additional markets between January 1, 1983, and June 30, 1988. I chose the later starting date for these tests because for many of these additional markets, I do not have data before December 1, 1982. There are still five full years of trading there since the system needs a minimum of six months of data to begin generating signals. The crude oil market did not start trading until 1983. This test begins on March 30, 1983.

I know of no publicly available trading system that has been profitable over so many markets and such a long time period using the same parameters for each market. There are many systems being sold for thousands of dollars that cannot use the same parameters in more than *one* market and still show profits. That smacks of curve-fitting, which lessens the likelihood of profitable performance in the future. I created the Babcock Long-term System without curve-fitting, so its performance is much more likely to continue in the future. This is especially true if you trade it over a diversified group of markets. So that you can further examine its performance, I have included in the Appendix a trade-by-trade summary of the Babcock Long-term System in each of the 21 markets covered in Exhibits 8–10, 18–1, and 18–2. Remember that the prices came from a continuous contract file, so the entry and exit price levels will not match the actual contracts that would have been traded.

The best-performing system that came through the testing in Chapters 9 and 10 also continued to perform well in the succeeding year after the five-year test period ended. Exhibit 18–3 shows that its profitability actually increased. Although this ended up as the best-performing system, I made no effort to find the best parameters for the various entry and stop-loss rules. Under the circumstances, that this system was profitable over such a long period and over so many

EXHIBIT 18–2 Performance Report, Babcock Long-term System, 11 Additional Markets
(January 1, 1983 to June 30, 1988)

	Treasury Bills	British Pounds	Deutshe-marks	Copper	Crude Oil	Corn	Soybean Meal	Soybean Oil	Live Hogs	Orange Juice	Cotton
Number of Closed Trades	12	14	15	12	11	13	14	13	14	14	16
Number of Profitable Trades	6	5	6	7	5	7	6	8	8	7	8
Percent Profitable	50%	36%	40%	58%	45%	54%	43%	62%	57%	50%	50%
Total Profit or Loss	4,425	2,378	3,588	6,800	2,330	1,188	3,280	10,174	600	9,335	14,845
Average Profitable Trade	2,675	3,753	4,258	2,070	3,106	970	3,137	2,307	1,422	3,508	3,895
Average Losing Trade	-1,937	-1,821	-2,440	-1,538	-2,200	-933	-1,943	-1,656	-1,795	-2,174	-2,039
Maximum Drawdown	-6,450	-5,200	-14,713	-3,725	-5,360	-3,525	-5,450	-4,480	-5,102	-7,273	-8,290
Average Profit Per Trade	369	170	239	567	212	91	234	783	43	667	928

EXHIBIT 18–3 Performance Report, Exhibit 10-11 System (July 1, 1987 to June 30, 1988)

	S&P 500	T-Bonds	Euro dollars	Swiss Francs	Japanese Yen	Comex Gold	Heating Oil	Soy beans	Sugar	Live Cattle	Average
Number of Closed Trades	14	10	4	9	10	13	9	4	8	9	9
Number of Profitable Trades	1	3	2	3	4	2	3	3	4	4	3
Percent Profitable	7%	30%	50%	33%	40%	15%	33%	75%	50%	44%	32%
Total Profit or Loss	4,900	-6,000	-625	14,600	5,512	-7,650	1,150	20,200	4,386	1,830	3,830
Average Profitable Trade	18,625	931	938	6,229	3,137	1,920	1,467	7,129	1,672	1,295	3,311
Average Losing Trade	-1,056	-1,256	-1,250	-681	-1,173	-1,045	-542	-1,188	-576	-670	-946
Maximum Drawdown	-7,125	-6,631	-2,500	-2,300	-4,637	-8,380	-3,250	-1,188	-1,800	-2,280	-4,009
Average Profit Per Trade	350	-600	-156	1,622	551	-588	128	5,050	548	203	426

markets without curve-fitting demonstrates the power of system trading in the commodity markets. With more intensive research, you should be able to produce an even better system for your own trading.

In Chapter 12, I discussed the personalities of the various markets and how they might affect system performance. One of the most important influences on profitability is the character of the market over the time period tested. In other words, it is most often the market that makes the system profitable rather than the other way around. I introduced an approach that, rather than trade each market individually, trades all the markets at once. Since any particular market makes a good tradeable move only infrequently, a great deal of effort can be wasted (and losses incurred) waiting for those profitable spurts. This relative-strength approach concentrates all your efforts on the markets that are likely to make a tradeable move right now.

Mechanical trading systems work best in the commodity markets, where there is greater volatility, greater leverage, and a far lower cost of trading than for common stocks. Since trading commodities need not be more risky in terms of the potential return than trading common stocks, there should be no reason that you should want to trade systems in stocks rather than commodities. However, the right mechanical approach can also work in volatile stocks.

Do not fall prey to the deceptive attraction of trading options rather than futures. Buying puts and calls is a sucker play. The brokerage industry sells them to the public as a way to participate in the profit potential of commodities without assuming so much risk. Because of the excessive premiums and decaying time-value, in my opinion, it is impossible to make money in the long term buying puts and calls. The odds favor the professionals who are selling, not buying, naked options.

The principal change in futures trading over the last 10 years has been the availability of powerful computers. Any trader who has sufficient capital to trade can afford one. Trading software has made such strides during this time that it is mind-boggling to imagine what the next 10 years may bring. In Chapter 13, you learned about the various kinds of software products available to assist in research and trading.

Although a computer will increase your analytical ability and no doubt add enjoyment to your trading, it is not an automatic guarantee of better trading results. Don't assume that if you buy a computer, it will pay for itself in increased profits. The computer cannot help you with the most crucial parts of trading—patience, discipline, courage, and proper money management.

Looking from the outside at speculation, the perception is that its purpose is to make money. This is always the initial attraction. A person wants to increase his wealth without the usual efforts of a full-time job. However, once he gets into it he finds out that trading is much more time-consuming than he thought. He also learns that he can derive much broader satisfaction from the challenge than the easy profits that were his initial goal. The intellectual stimulation and competition become even more important than profit.

The ego involved in trading makes most people reluctant to use someone else's system. They will always want to make little changes and "improvements." Since you are probably going to create your own system in the end, you might as well recognize the implications and get on with it. There is nothing mysterious involved. The real key is understanding the significance of proper testing. Testing serves an even more important purpose than just verifying that the system was profitable in the past. Your own testing will give you sufficient experience with the details of the system's past performance so that you will have confidence to keep trading it during the inevitable drawdowns. Be wary of other people's testing. Be sure you know exactly how they conducted their tests.

You can break all trading systems down into two identifiable types. A system can either wait for a trend to become established and then enter in the direction of the trend or it can attempt to identify trend changes precisely and enter just before or just after assumed tops and bottoms. You can trade either of the two system types over roughly the following five time periods: one day, several days on the basis of intra-day data, up to one week on the basis of daily data, one week to one month on the basis of daily data, and over one month on the basis of weekly data. The most important consideration in creating your trading system is not to violate your own trading preferences so long as a profitable system can accommodate them. Creating a successful system is only the first step. The *really* hard part is trading it.

As difficult as it may be to find or create a profitable system, it is even more difficult to follow the system once you do find it. There are three reasons for this. All relate to the frightening phenomenon of equity drawdown. First, no one can ever know whether a system will continue to be profitable in the future. Second, profitable systems often act like unprofitable systems. Third, traders following mechanical systems are subject to exactly the same gut-wrenching emotions as those trading by the seat of their pants. The inevitable uncertainty and emotion are enough to cause the downfall of all but the most courageous and disciplined system traders. This reality may be the overriding reason that system developers prefer to sell their systems to others rather than trade them themselves. Watch out for a natural craving for action and fun. The need for action causes people to overtrade and stray from their systems.

Knowing when a system has failed is one of the most difficult questions that all system traders must answer. You should always set a dollar limit of losses at which you will stop trading a system. This kind of stop-loss on a system is just as important as a stop-loss order on an individual trade. In addition, you can reasonably conclude that a system has failed if it makes losses during the kind of market period it was designed to exploit. No system can make money in all kinds of markets, so be tolerant if your system loses during bad market periods.

Trying to figure out where the market is going next is a fascinating, if futile, endeavor. Proper money management is not mysterious, however, and it is far more important to profitability than trade selection. Sound money management involves trading in correct proportion to your capital and managing risk so as to preserve capital. If you can manage your losses properly, the profits will come. When, in addition to managing losses, you can milk your profitable trades to the maximum, you will be a trading superstar.

Finally, in Chapter 17, you saw a statistical exploration of trade management techniques. These are advanced strategies that depend on a system's recent performance. One approach varies the number of contracts traded; the other turns trading on and off completely to exploit the equity cycle, which alternates between winning and losing periods.

Do not underestimate the importance of luck—both good and bad—in short-term trading performance. The randomness in market behavior means you can do all the wrong things and make money . . . for a while. You can do all the right things and still lose. Over time, however, if you follow the essential principles, you should make a reasonable return for your efforts. Don't be too hard on yourself if things go wrong. At the same time, don't get cocky when things are going well. The markets have a way of humbling everyone sooner or later.

If you understand the ideas and concepts presented in this book, you are eligible for an advanced degree in trading system theory. But the real payoff is not in the learning but in the trading. That takes capital, courage, and determination. The best advice I can give you in closing is something Casey Kasem used to say at the end of his weekly top-40 radio show: "Keep your feet on the ground and reach for the stars." Good luck, good trading, and may the trend be with you.

* * * *

Anyone who wants to pursue system trading ideas further can contact my company for information about our library of trading systems. If you have an IBM or compatible computer and want to experiment further with the ideas in this book, we also have software that can help you. Write me at CTCR Products, P.O. Box 254480, Sacramento, CA 95825, or call (916)–677–7562.

1 Long-Term Weekly Charts (1978–1988)

EXHIBIT A1-1 S&P 500 Stock Index

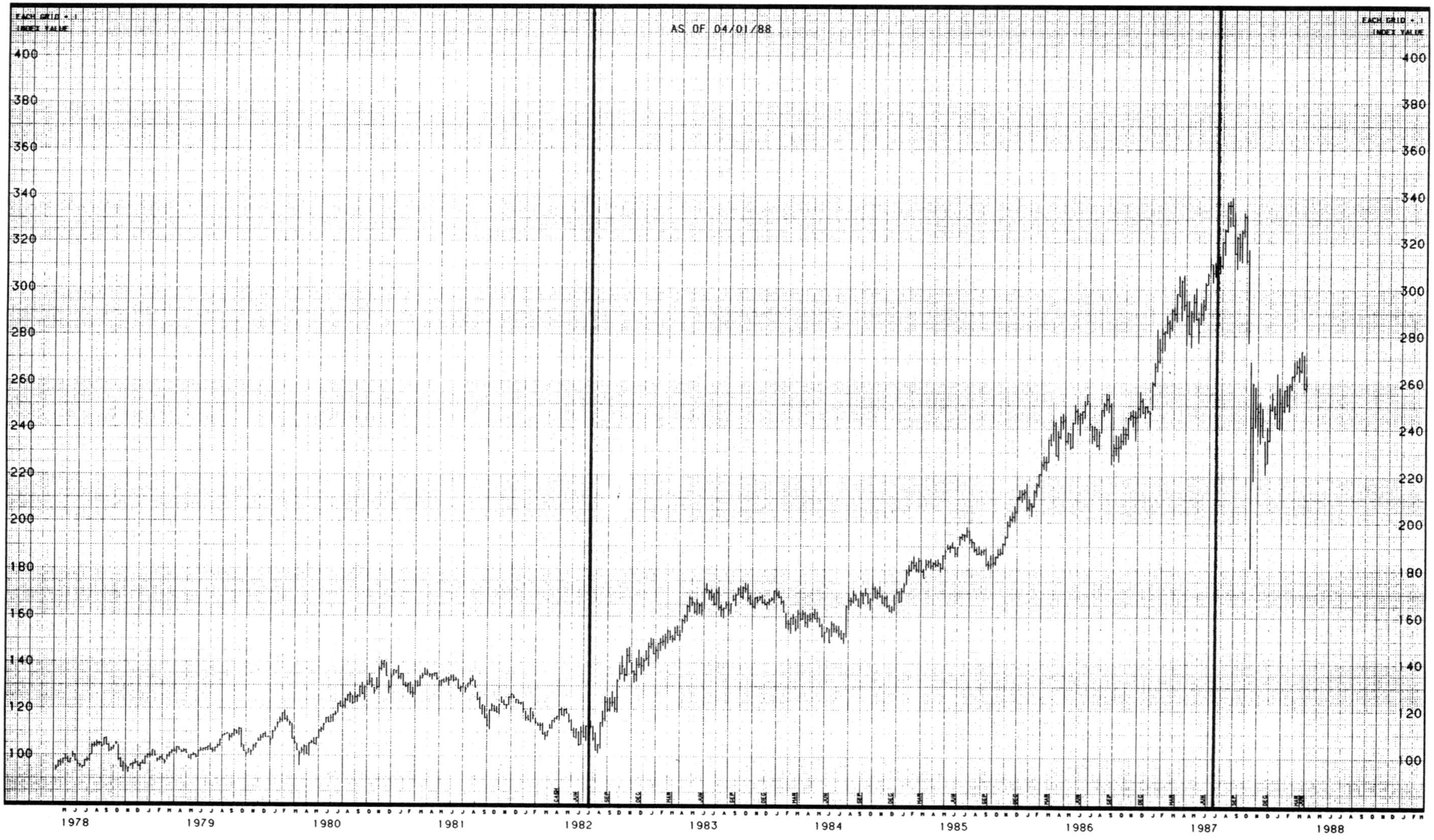

AS OF 04/01/88

Reprinted with permission. © 1988 by *Commodity Perspective*, 20 South Wacker Drive, Suite 1820, Chicago, IL 60606

EXHIBIT A1-2   T-Bonds

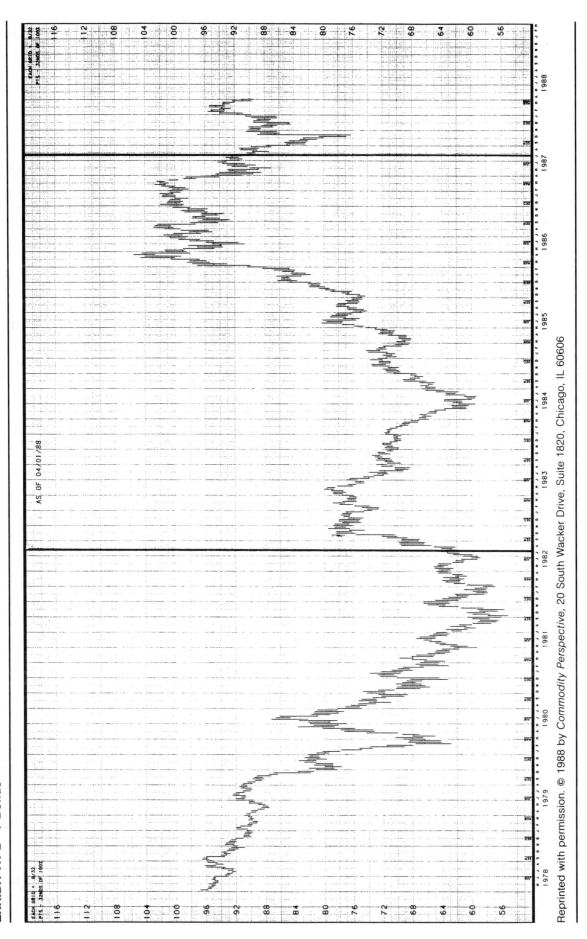

EXHIBIT A1-3 Eurodollars

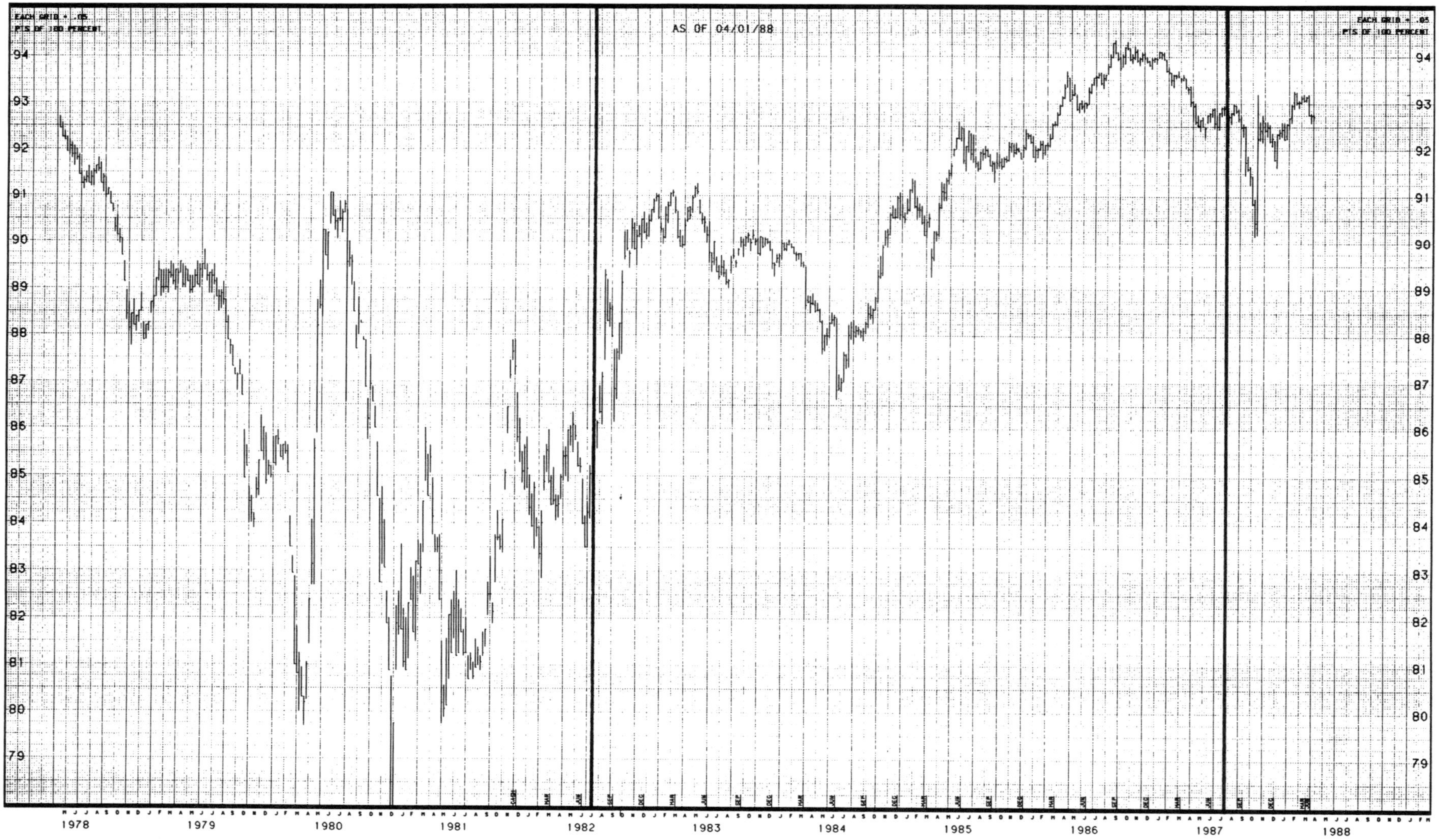

AS OF 04/01/88

EACH GRID = .05
PTS OF 100 PERCENT

EXHIBIT A1-4 Swiss Franc

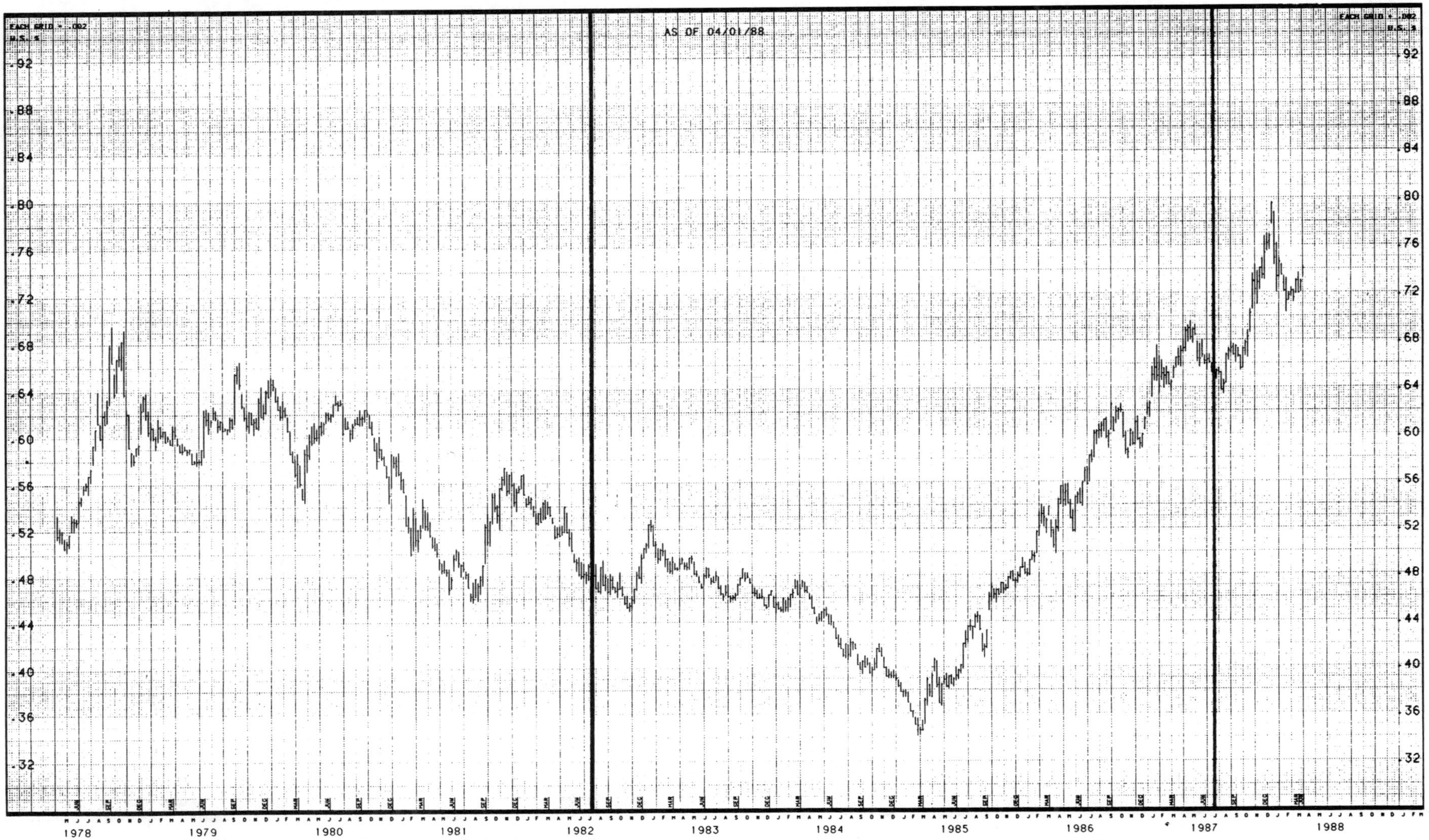

AS OF 04/01/88.

Reprinted with permission. © 1988 by Commodity Perspective, 20 South Wacker Drive, Suite 1820, Chicago, IL 60606

EXHIBIT A1-5 Japanese Yen

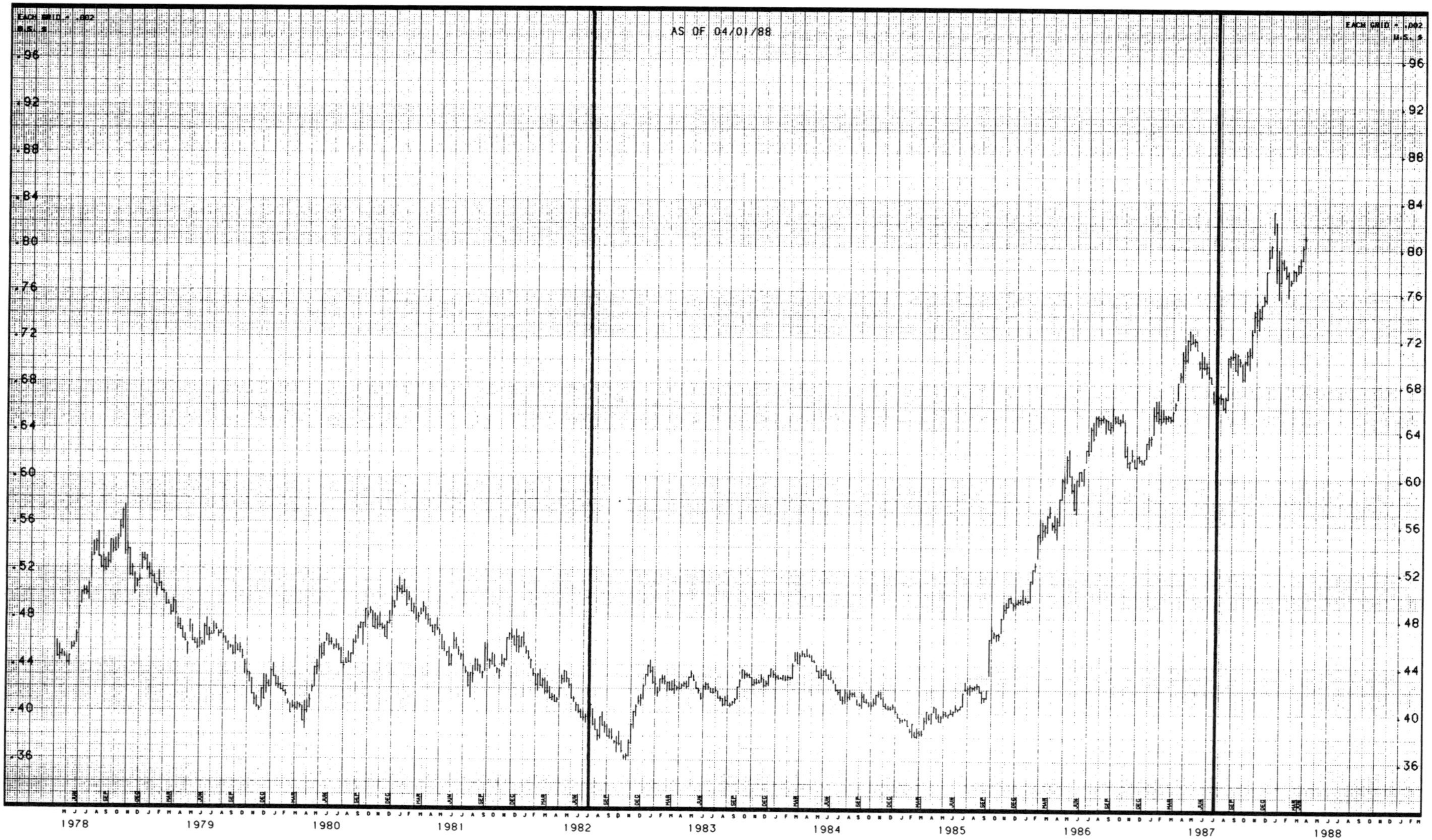

Reprinted with permission. © 1988 by *Commodity Perspective*, 20 South Wacker Drive, Suite 1820, Chicago, IL 60606

EXHIBIT A1-6 Gold

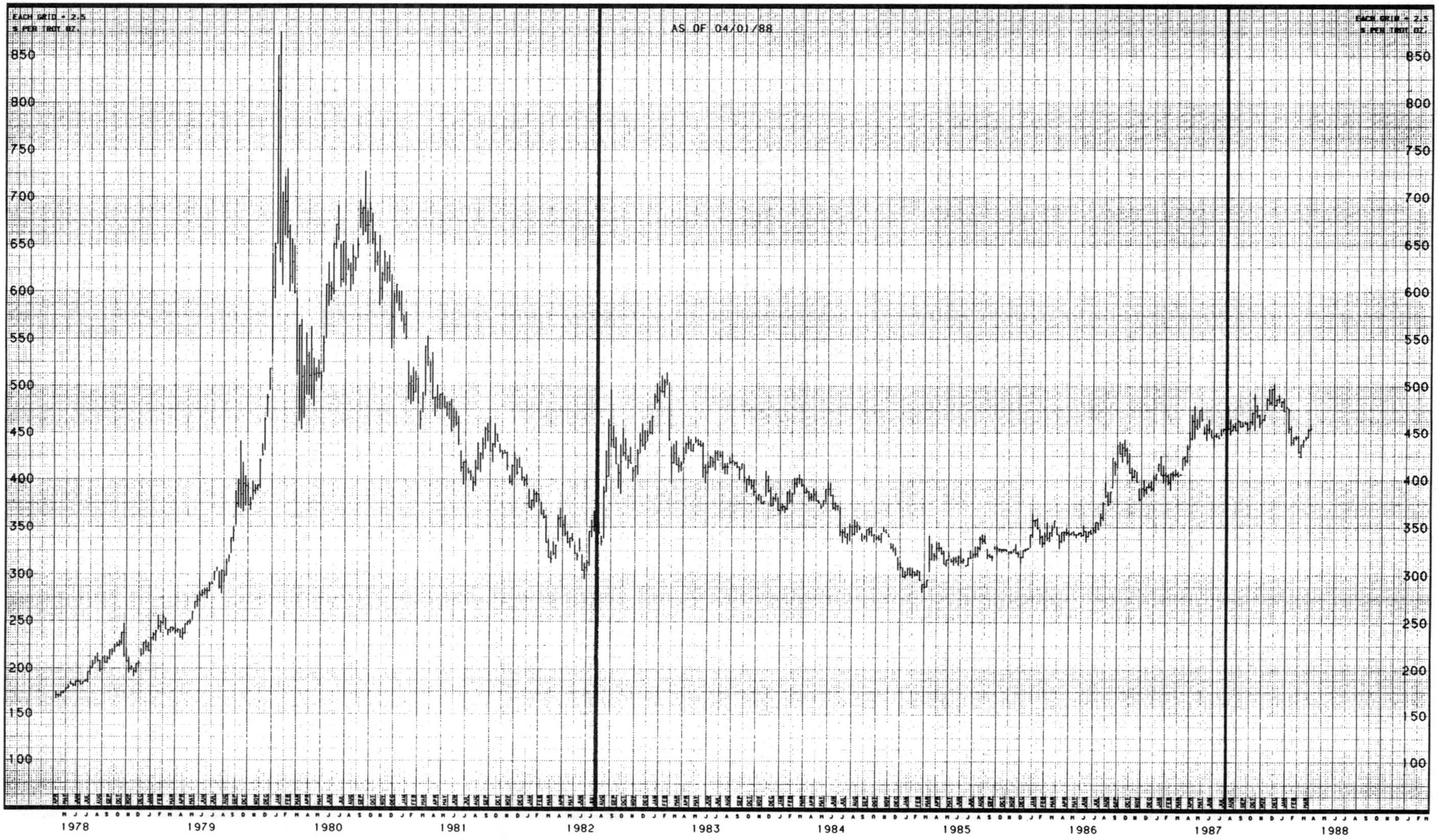

AS OF 04/01/88

Reprinted with permission. © 1988 by *Commodity Perspective*, 20 South Wacker Drive, Suite 1820, Chicago, IL 60606

277

EXHIBIT A1-7   Heating Oil

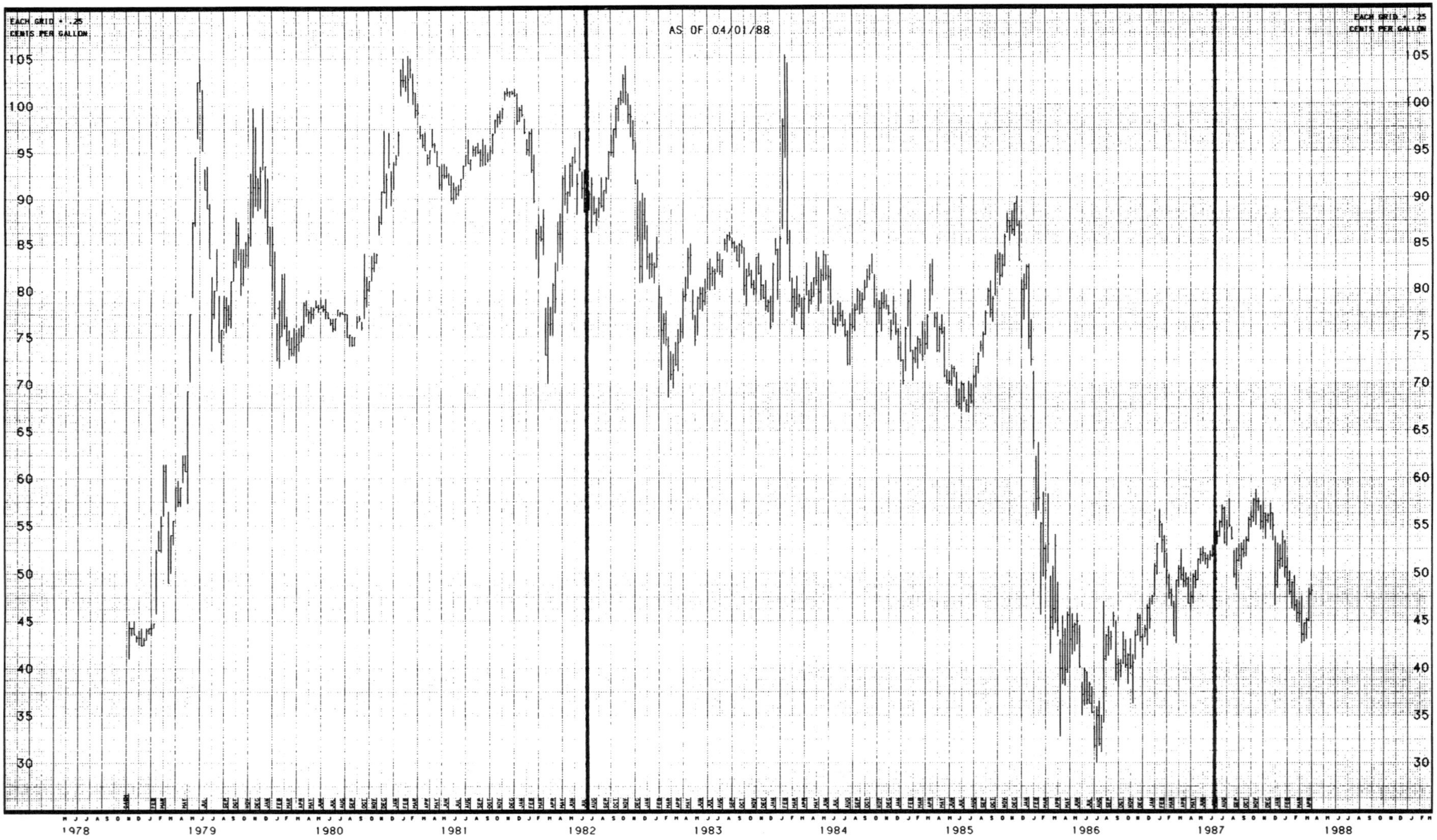

Reprinted with permission. © 1988 by *Commodity Perspective*, 20 South Wacker Drive, Suite 1820, Chicago, IL 60606

EXHIBIT A1-8 Soybeans

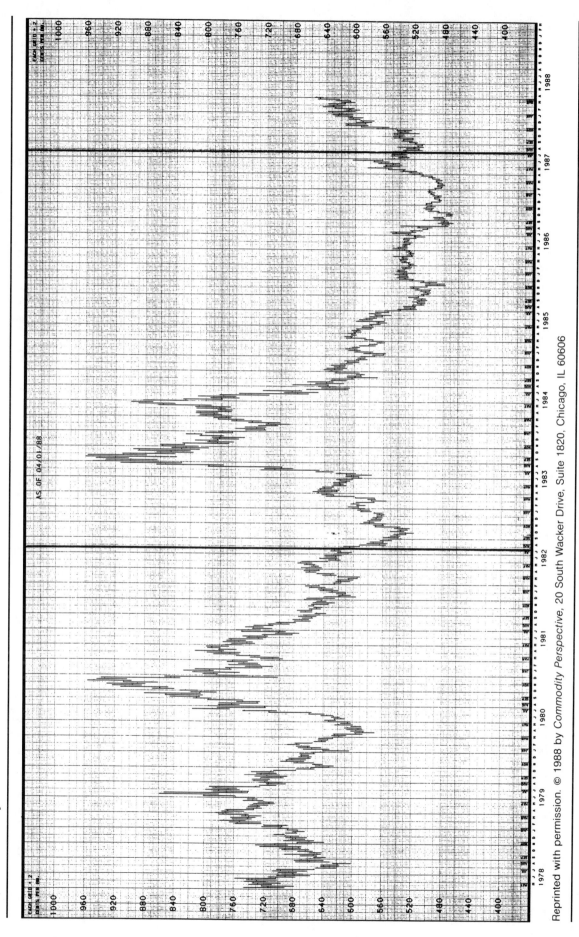

Reprinted with permission. © 1988 by *Commodity Perspective*, 20 South Wacker Drive, Suite 1820, Chicago, IL 60606

EXHIBIT A1-9 Sugar

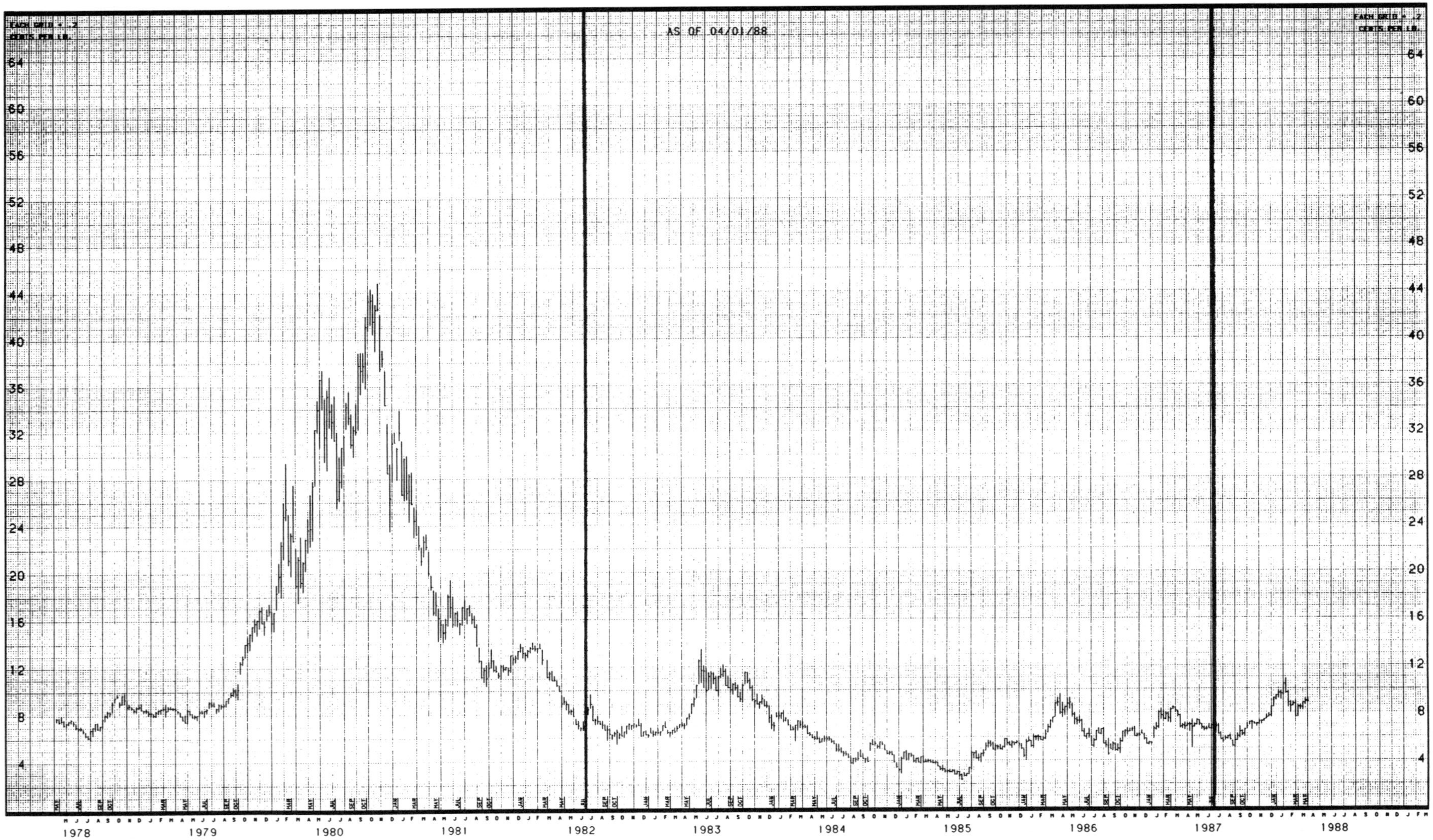

AS OF 04/01/88

Reprinted with permission. © 1988 by *Commodity Perspective*, 20 South Wacker Drive, Suite 1820, Chicago, IL 60606

EXHIBIT A1-10 Live Cattle

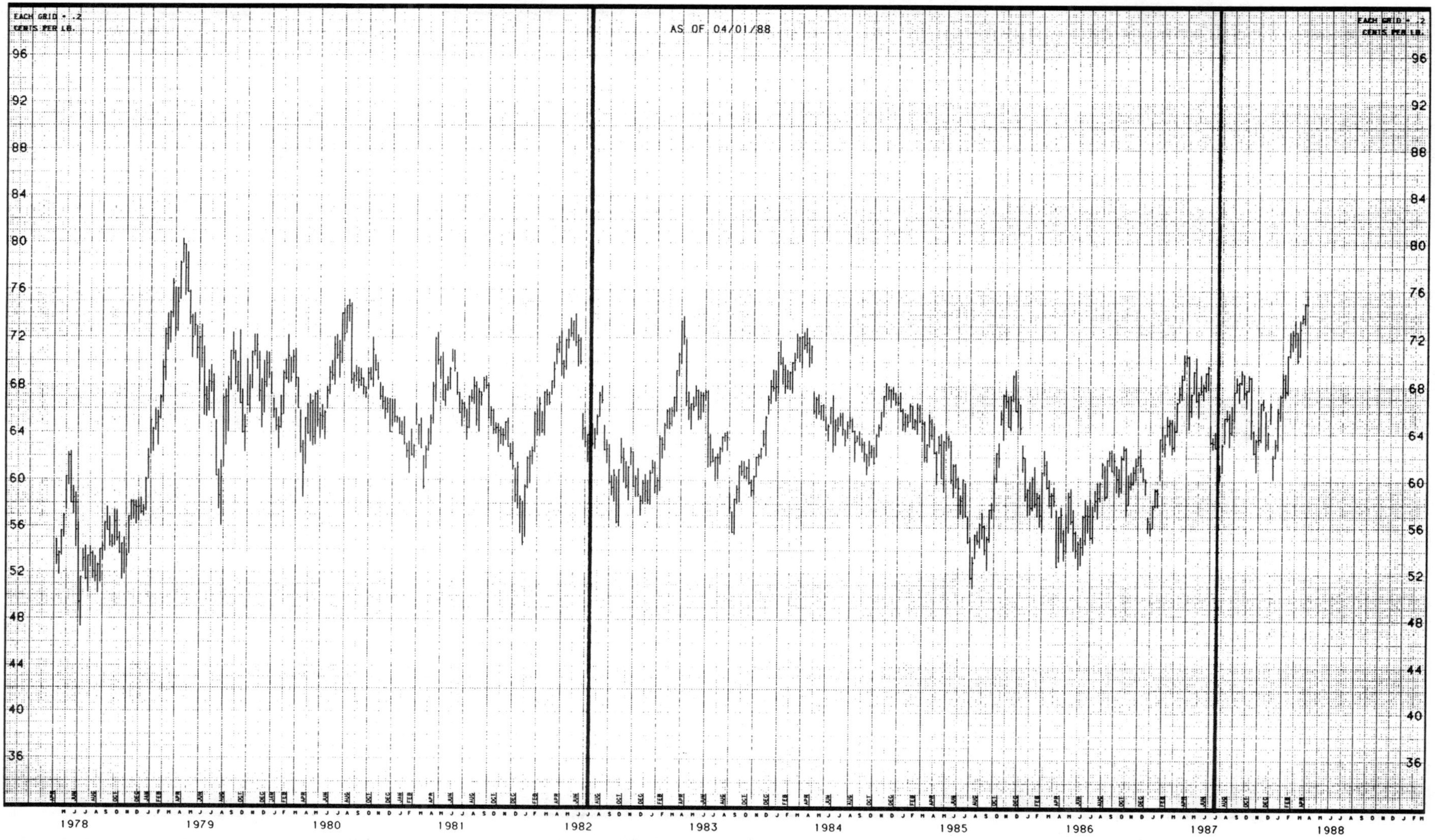

EXHIBIT A1-11   T-Bills

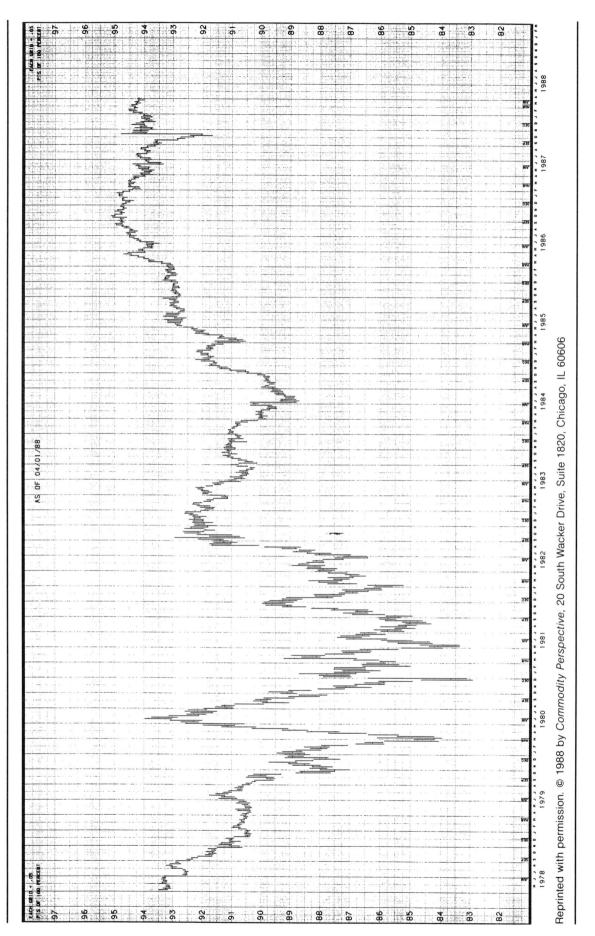

EXHIBIT A1-12   British Pound

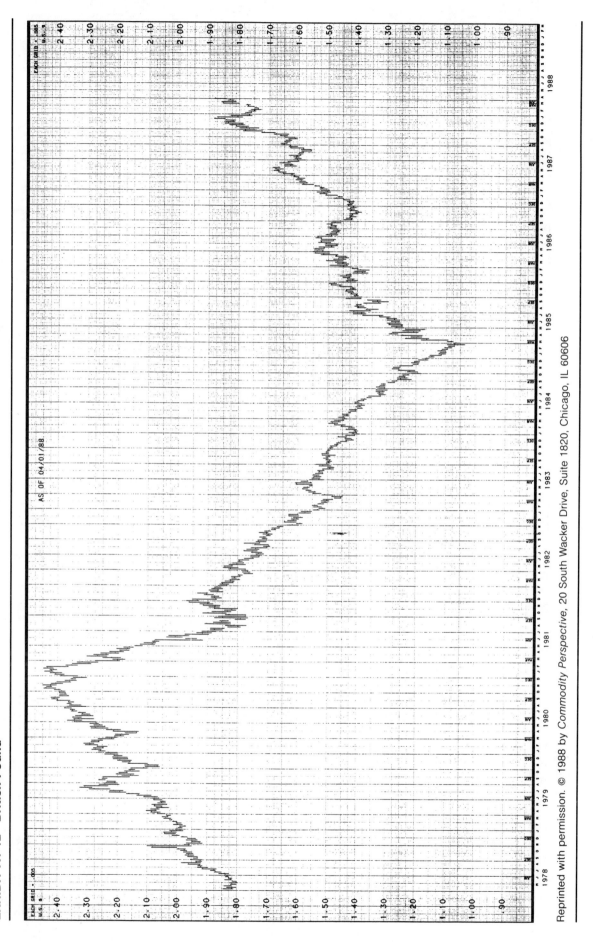

EXHIBIT A1-13 Deutschemark

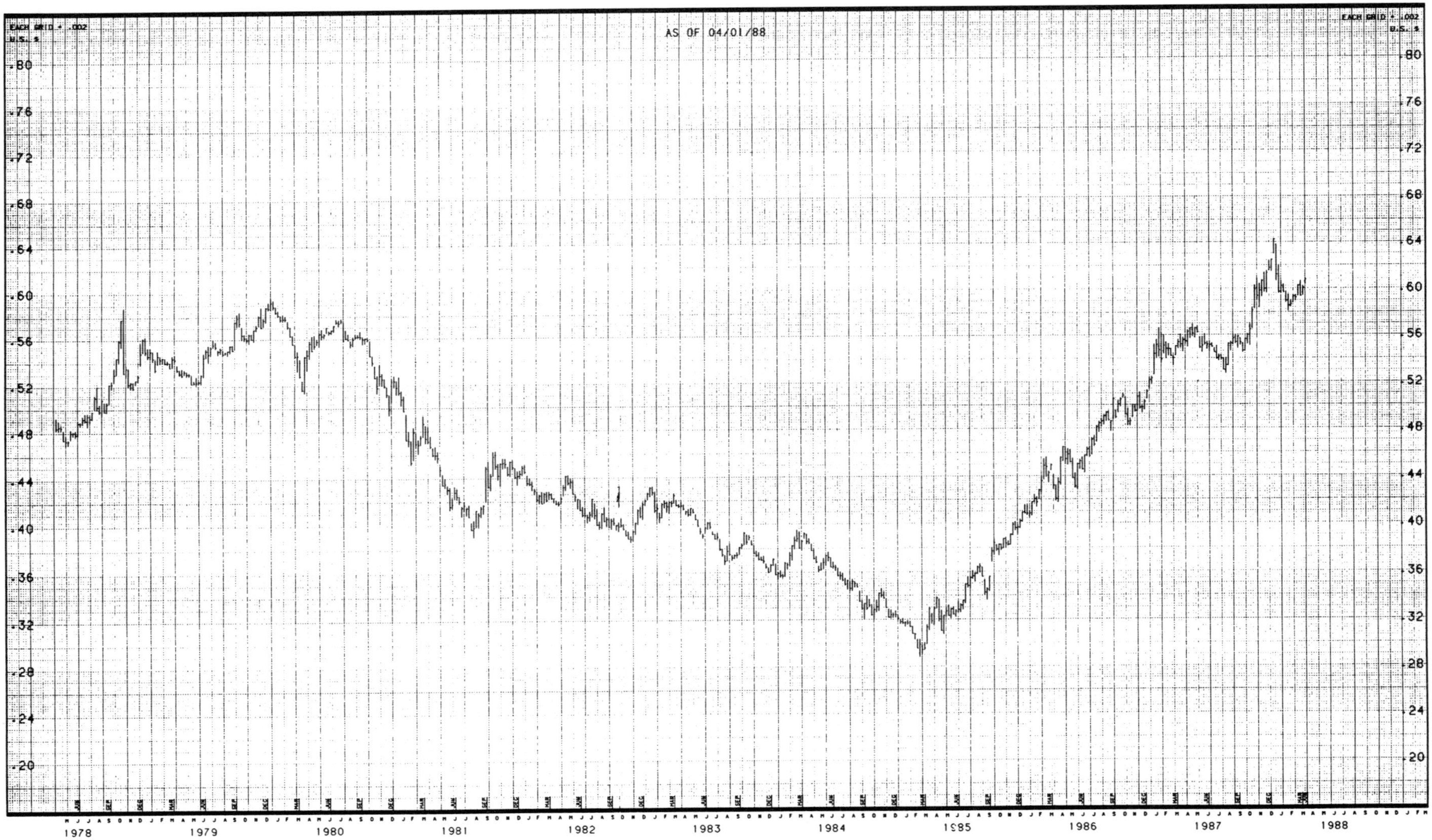

Reprinted with permission. © 1988 by *Commodity Perspective*, 20 South Wacker Drive, Suite 1820, Chicago, IL 60606

284

EXHIBIT A1-14   Copper

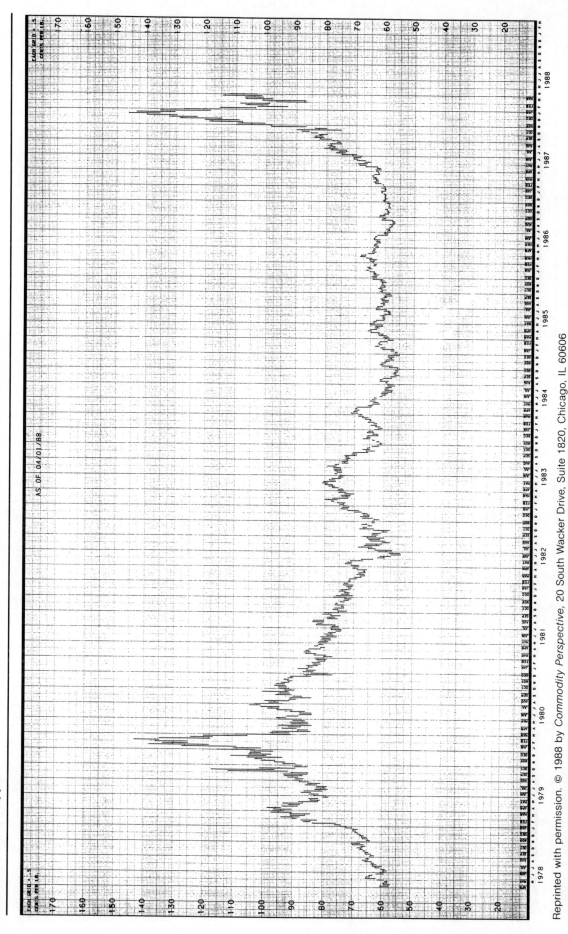

EXHIBIT A1-15 Crude Oil

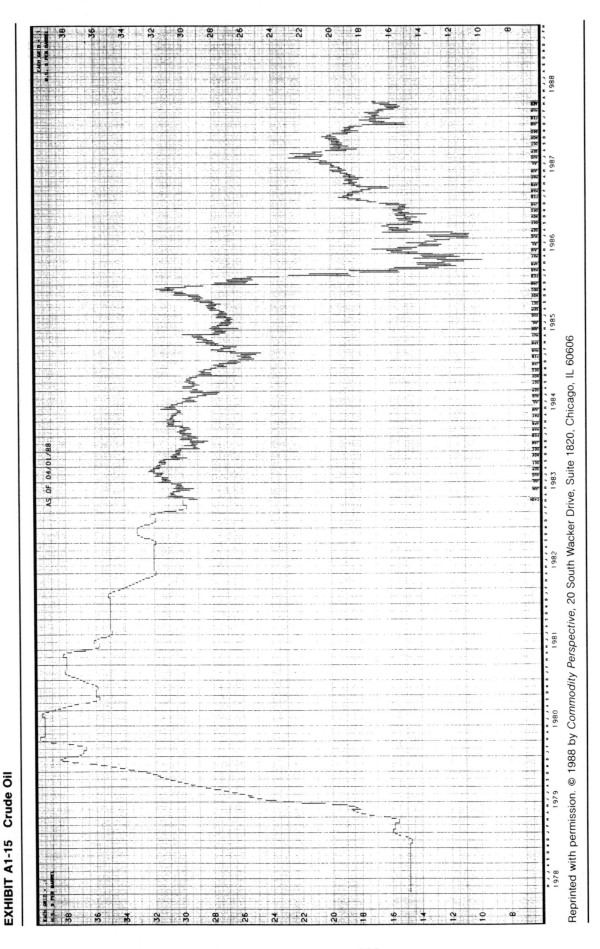

AS OF 04/01/88

EXHIBIT A1-16 Corn

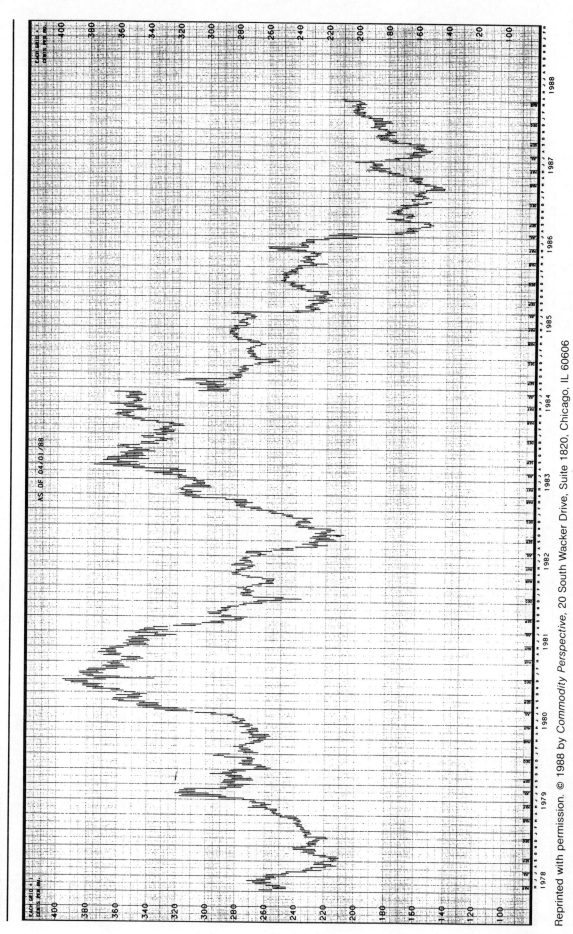

EXHIBIT A1-17 Soybean Meal

AS OF 04/01/88

Reprinted with permission. © 1988 by *Commodity Perspective*, 20 South Wacker Drive, Suite 1820, Chicago, IL 60606

288

EXHIBIT A1-18 Soybean Oil

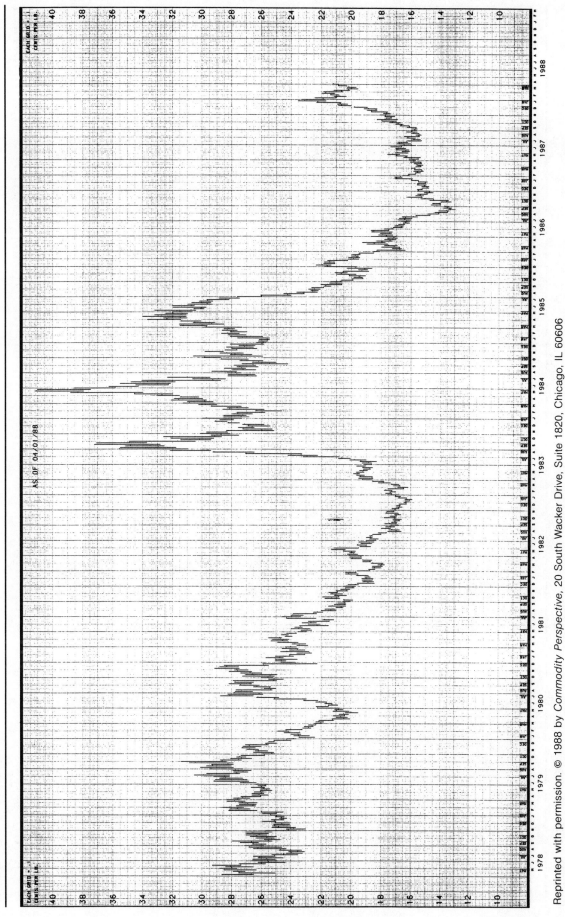

EXHIBIT A1-19 Live Hogs

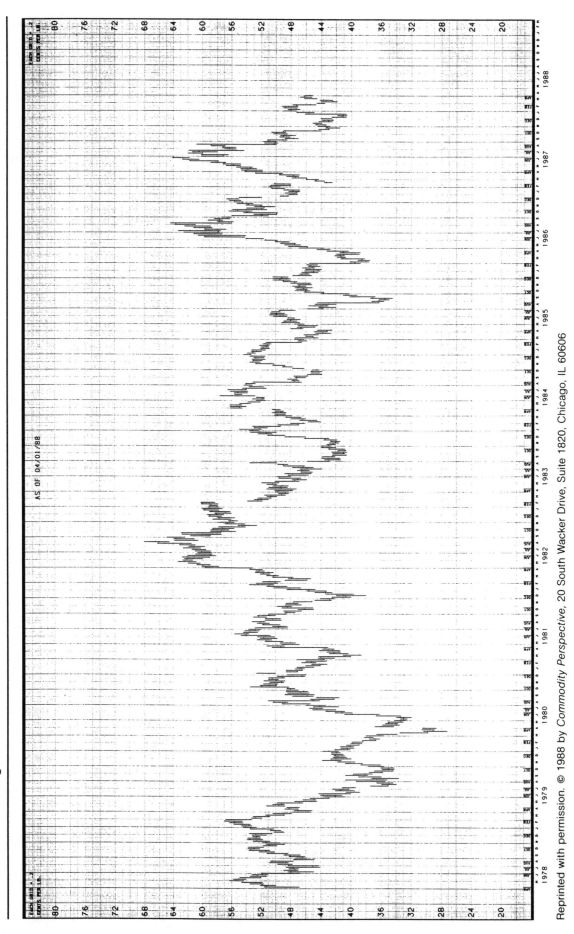

AS OF 04/01/88

Reprinted with permission. © 1988 by *Commodity Perspective*, 20 South Wacker Drive, Suite 1820, Chicago, IL 60606

290

EXHIBIT A1-20 Cotton

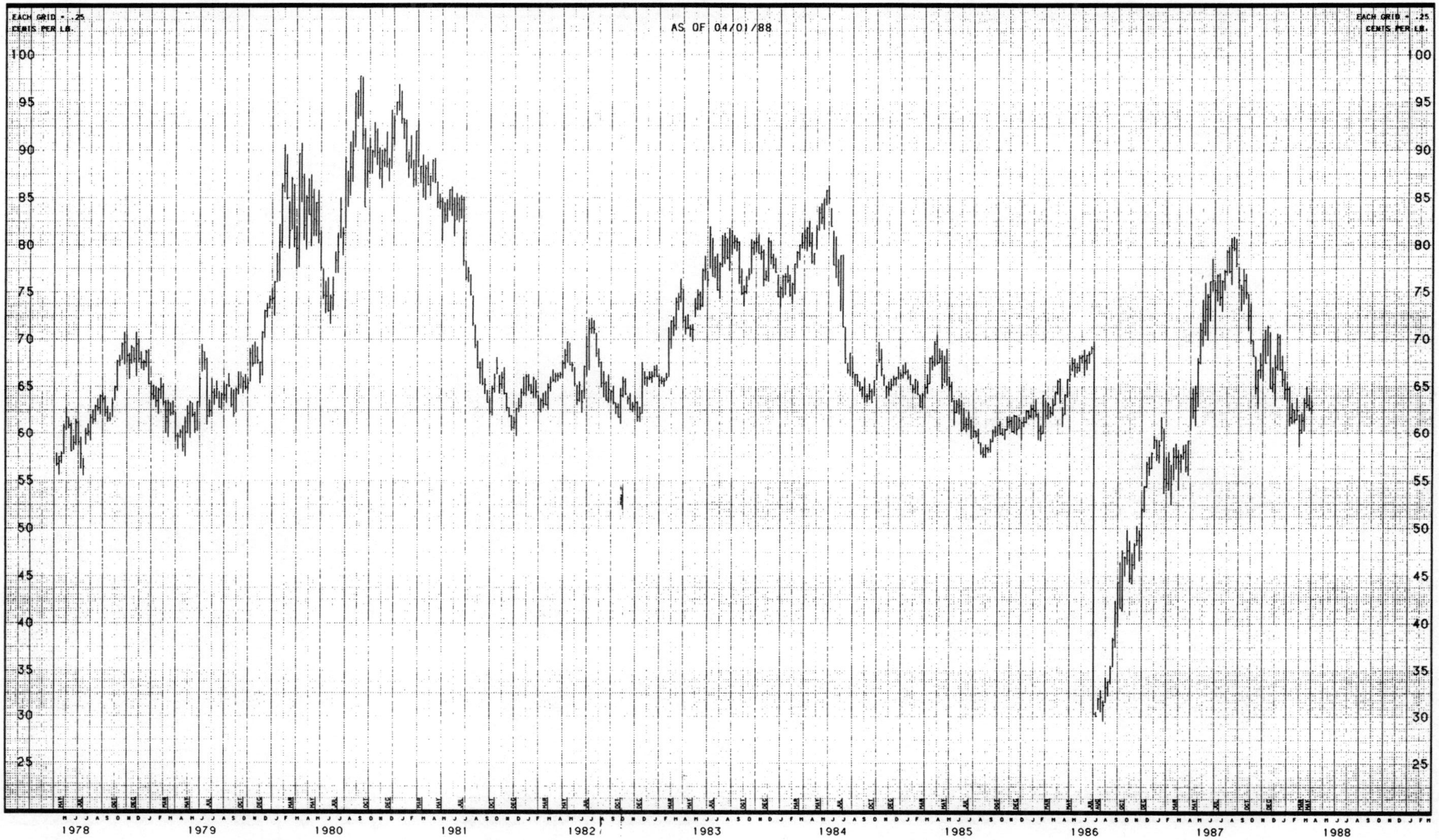

EXHIBIT A1-21   Canadian Dollar

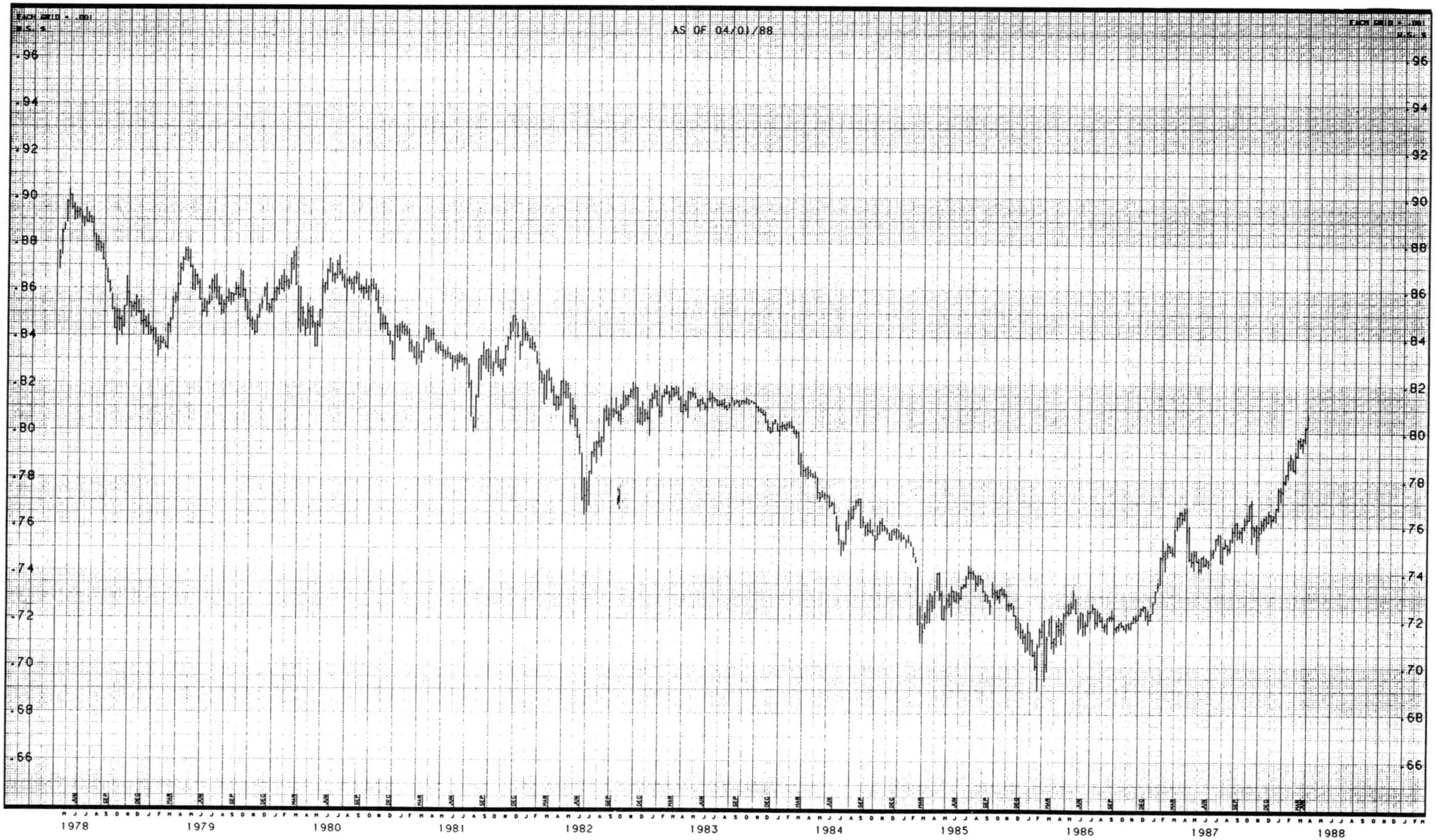

AS OF 04/01/88

Reprinted with permission. © 1988 by *Commodity Perspective*, 20 South Wacker Drive, Suite 1820, Chicago, IL 60606

EXHIBIT A1-22 Silver

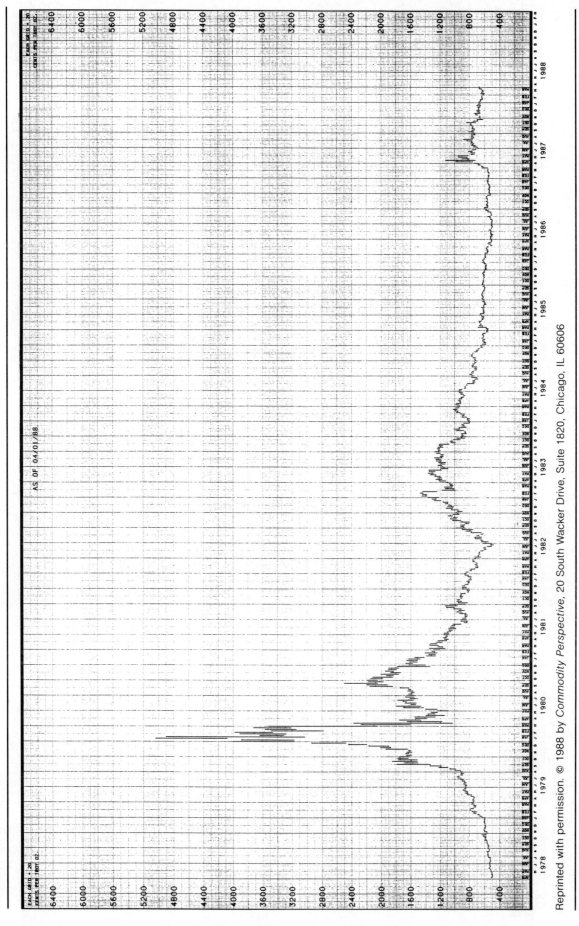

EXHIBIT A1-23 Wheat

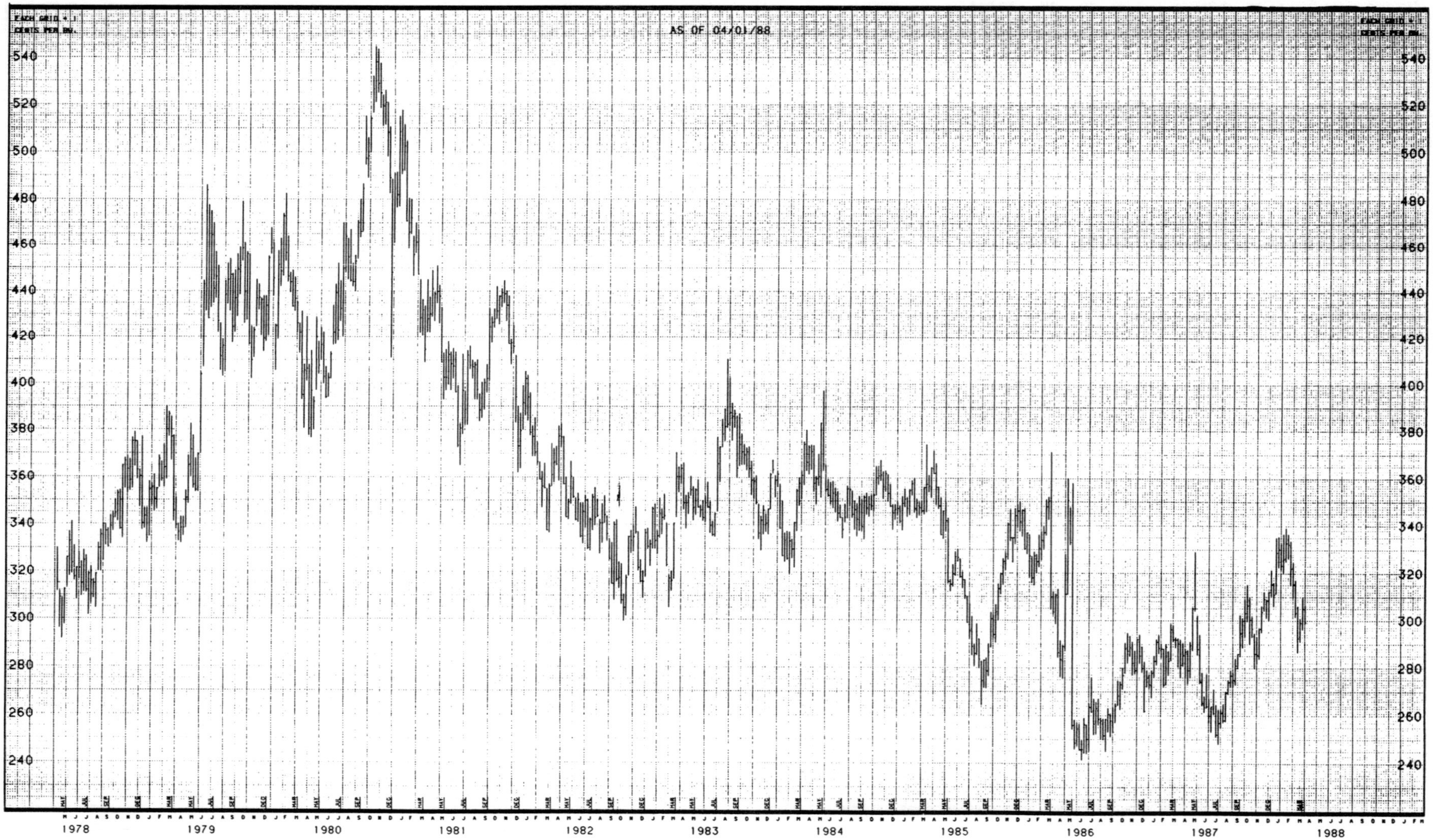

AS OF 04/01/88

Reprinted with permission. © 1988 by *Commodity Perspective*, 20 South Wacker Drive, Suite 1820, Chicago, IL 60606

EXHIBIT A1-24   Pork Bellies

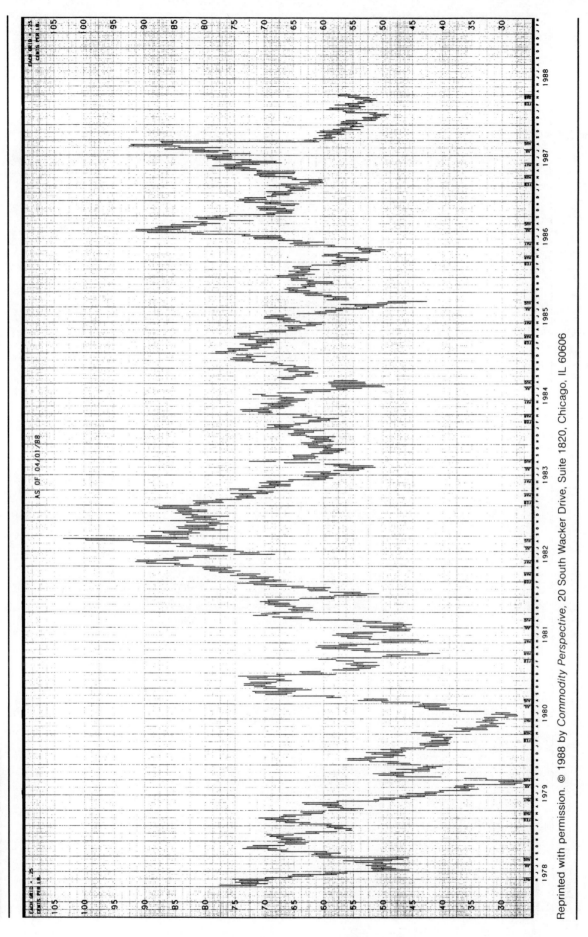

AS OF 04/01/88

Reprinted with permission. © 1988 by *Commodity Perspective*, 20 South Wacker Drive, Suite 1820, Chicago, IL 60606

EXHIBIT A1-25   Cocoa

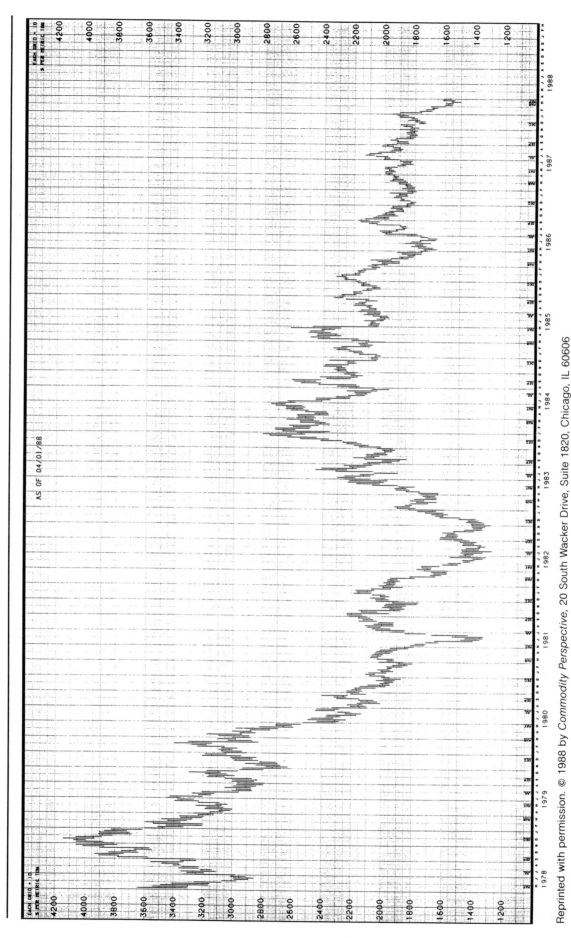

2 Bread and Butter S&P Day Trading System*

Trading Rules

1. Determine the opening price. I use the price of the first trade that occurs. This is the figure carried by the exchange as the opening. It may be anywhere in the opening range. [I see nothing wrong with tinkering with the system by using the mid-point of the opening range. You might also use the high of the opening range to calculate the buy price and the low of the opening range to calculate the sell price.]

2. Place an OCO order (one side being filled cancels the other) to buy on stop 50 points above the opening or to sell on stop 50 points below the opening. You will go long or short depending on which side is filled first. That will be your only trade for the day, so be sure the other side is canceled. [You might consider using stop-limit orders to prevent any slippage. This could result in missing a good trade, however.]

3. Place a stop 50 points from your fill. This will limit your loss to $250 plus any slippage on the stop order. [You may want to amend the system to place your stop at the opening or one tick beyond the opening. The opening is a natural support or resistance point. I have seen the market return to the opening price (stopping out the system), from where it turned around and made a big gain. Putting the stop one tick beyond the opening would have turned that day from a loser into a big winner. However, you will add $25 to all losses this way.]

4. If you ever have a 100-point profit during the day ($500), move your stop 80 points towards the price. This will protect $150 of your profit. [You may want to experiment with this rule, but it is definitely a good idea to protect a significant profit. The S&P has a way of quickly turning a nice profit into a loss.]

5. If not stopped out before the close, exit on the close. Your stop order should be a day-only order, so it automatically expires. If the price is near the stop just before the close, use an OCO order to get out on your stop or on the close (one cancels the other).

Here is the hypothetical record between July 15, 1985, and July 11, 1986. The net profit column includes a $75 per trade deduction for slippage and commissions; the other columns include no deduction.

Date	Profit or Loss	Weekly Profit or Loss	Cumulative Weekly Profit	Cumulative Trades	Cumulative Average Trade	Cumulative Number of Profits	Cumulative Percent of Winners	Cumulative Net Profits
850715	−250							
850716	−250							
850717	−250							
850718	−250							
850719	−250	−1250	−1250	5	−250	0	0%	−1,625
850722	175							
850723	−250							
850724	125							
850725	−250							
850726	−250	−450	−1700	10	−170	2	20	−2,450
850729	1125							
850730	0							
850731	75							
850801	400							
850802	225	1825	125	15	8	6	40	−1,000
850805	150							
850806	1675							
850807	−250							
850808	−250							
850809	100	1425	1550	20	78	9	45	50
850812	−250							
850813	−250							
850814	−250							
850815	125							
850816	−250	−875	675	25	27	10	40	−1,200
850819	50							
850820	500							
850821	−100							
850822	800							
850823	−50	1200	1875	30	63	13	43	−375
850826	−250							
850827	−250							
850828	N/T							
850829	N/T							
850830	25	−475	1400	33	42	14	42	−1,075
850903	25							
850904	25							
850905	−250							
850906	25	−175	1225	37	33	17	46	−1,550
850909	−250							
850910	725							
850911	550							
850912	−250							
850913	275	1050	2275	42	54	20	48	−875
850916	−250							
850917	1075							
850918	−250							
850919	750							
850920	−250	1075	3350	47	71	22	47	−175
850923	100							
850924	400							
850925	1075							
850927	N/T	1325	4675	51	92	25	49	850

Date	Profit or Loss	Weekly Profit or Loss	Cumulative Weekly Profit	Cumulative Trades	Cumulative Average Trade	Cumulative Number of Profits	Cumulative Percent of Winners	Cumulative Net Profits
850930	−250							
851001	1625							
851002	−250							
851003	−250							
851004	125	1000	5675	56	101	27	48	1,475
851007	−250							
851008	−250							
851009	150							
851010	−250							
851011	−250	−850	4825	61	79	28	46	250
851014	600							
851015	150							
851016	−250							
851017	−250							
851018	225	475	5300	66	80	31	47	350
851021								
851022	325							
851023	500							
851024	−250							
851025	−100	475	5775	70	83	33	47	525
851028	−250							
851029	325							
851030	−125							
851031	0							
851101	150	100	5875	75	78	35	47	250
851104	−250							
851105	25							
851106	−250							
851107	N/T							
851108	500	25	5900	79	75	37	47	−25
851111	2025							
851112	150							
851113	−250							
851114	750							
851115	150	2825	8725	84	104	41	49	2,425
851118	−250							
851119	150							
851120	−250							
851121	675							
851122	−250	75	8800	89	99	43	48	2,125
851125	−175							
851126	−250							
851127	1375							
851129	725	1675	10475	93	113	45	48	3,500
851202	550							
851203	225							
851204	1300							
851205	−250							
851206	−250	1575	12050	98	123	48	49	4,700
851209	−250							
851210	−250							
851211	−250							
851212	−250							
851213	1275	275	12325	103	120	49	48	4,600
851216	−250							
851217	150							
851218	150							
851220	150	−50	12275	108	114	52	48	4,175

Date	Profit or Loss	Weekly Profit or Loss	Cumulative Weekly Profit	Cumulative Trades	Cumulative Average Trade	Cumulative Number of Profits	Cumulative Percent of Winners	Cumulative Net Profits
851223	1,275							
851224	525							
851226	N/T							
851227	475	2,275	14,550	111	131	55	50	6,225
851230	150							
851231	−250							
860102	−250							
860103	150	−200	14,350	115	125	57	50	5,725
860106	150							
860107	650							
860108	−250							
860109	−250							
860110	−250	50	14,400	120	120	59	49	5,400
860113	150							
860114	525							
860115	150							
860116	−250							
860117	150	725	15,125	125	121	63	50	5,750
860120	−250							
860121	1,000							
860122	−250							
860123	−250							
860124	−250	0	15,125	130	116	64	49	5,375
860127	−250							
860128	−250							
860129	150							
860130	−250							
860131	1,325	725	15,850	135	117	66	49	5,725
860203	150							
860204	150							
860205	−250							
860206	−250							
860207	−250	−450	15,400	140	110	68	49	4,900
860210	−250							
860211	−250							
860212	−250							
860213	150							
860214	−250	−850	14,550	145	100	69	48	3,675
860218	−250							
860219	−250							
860220	−250							
860221	−250	−1,000	13,550	149	91	69	46	2,375
860224	−250							
860225	−250							
860226	150							
860227	−250							
860228	150	−450	13,100	154	85	71	46	1,550
860303	−250							
860304	150							
860305	150							
860306	−250							
860307	150	−50	13,050	159	82	74	47	1,125
860310	150							
860311	2,250							
860312	−250							
860313	900							
860314	150	3,200	16,250	164	99	78	48	3,950

Date	Profit or Loss	Weekly Profit or Loss	Cumulative Weekly Profit	Cumulative Trades	Cumulative Average Trade	Cumulative Number of Profits	Cumulative Percent of Winners	Cumulative Net Profits
860317	150							
860318	1,450							
860319	−250							
860320	−250							
860321	−250	850	17,100	169	101	80	47	4,425
860324	150							
860325	−250							
860326	1,250							
860327	−250	900	18,000	173	104	82	47	5,025
860331	−250							
860401	−250							
860402	−250							
860403	−250							
860404	−250	−1,250	16,750	178	94	82	46	3,400
860407	−250							
860408	2,350							
860409	−250							
860410	−250							
860411	−250	1,350	18,100	183	99	83	45	4,375
860414	−250							
860415	150							
860416	−250							
860417	−250							
860418	−250	−850	17,250	188	92	84	45	3,150
860421	150							
860422	−250							
860423	−250							
860424	−250							
860425	−250	−850	16,400	193	85	85	44	1,925
860428	−250							
860429	2,125							
860430	2,600							
860501	−250							
860502	150	4,375	20,775	198	105	88	44	5,925
860505	150							
860506	150							
860507	150							
860508	−250							
860509	150	350	21,125	203	104	92	45	5,900
860512	−250							
860513	−250							
860514	150							
860515	−250							
860516	150	−450	20,675	208	99	94	45	5,075
860519	−250							
860520	1,625							
860521	−250							
860522	2,200							
860523	150	3,475	24,150	213	113	97	46	8,175
860527	−250							
860528	150							
860529	150							
860530	−250	−200	23,950	217	110	99	46	7,675
860602	150							
860603	−250							
860604	−250							
860605	−250							
860606	−250	−850	23,100	222	104	100	45	6,450

Date	Profit or Loss	Weekly Profit or Loss	Cumulative Weekly Profit	Cumulative Trades	Cumulative Average Trade	Cumulative Number of Profits	Cumulative Percent of Winners	Cumulative Net Profits
860609	2,550							
860610	−250							
860611	−250							
860612	−250							
860613	1,700	3,500	26,600	227	117	102	45	9,575
860616	−250							
860617	1,125							
860618	150							
860619	−250							
860620	−250	525	27,125	232	117	104	45	9,725
860623	−250							
860624	−250							
860625	150							
860626	−250							
860627	−250	−850	26,275	237	111	105	44	8,500
860630	150							
860701	−250							
860702	150							
860703	950	1,000	27,275	241	113	108	45	9,200
860707	3,475							
860708	−250							
860709	−250							
860710	150							
860711	−250	2,875	30,150	246	123	110	45	11,700

Babcock Long-Term System Hypothetical Trades*

Date	Position	Action Price	Profit or Loss	Cumulative Profit
S&P 500				
830420	LONG	205.70		
830804	SHORT	205.85	-25	-25
830906	FLAT	211.05	-2700	-2725
840524	SHORT	190.50		
840802	LONG	194.45	-2075	-4800
841009	SHORT	197.85	1600	-3200
841015	FLAT	202.85	-2600	-5800
850213	LONG	214.60		
850222	FLAT	209.60	-2600	-8400
850806	SHORT	210.40		
851105	LONG	211.95	-875	-9275
860708	SHORT	254.20	21025	11750
860813	FLAT	259.20	-2600	9150
860912	SHORT	240.85		
860922	FLAT	245.85	-2600	6550
870112	LONG	270.95		
870413	SHORT	293.15	11000	17550
870416	FLAT	298.15	-2600	14950
870803	LONG	325.75		
870908	FLAT	320.75	-2600	12350
870908	SHORT	320.95		
870911	FLAT	325.95	-2600	9750
871021	LONG	262.45		
871022	FLAT	206.20	-28225	-18475
T-BONDS				
830519	SHORT	58.84375		
840725	LONG	49.40625	9338	9338
850222	SHORT	56.03125	6525	15863
850416	FLAT	58.53125	-2600	13263

*Using artificial, continuous contract prices and assuming open trades were closed out on the last day

Date	Position	Action Price	Profit or Loss	Cumulative Profit
850528	LONG	63.56250		
860516	SHORT	86.06250	22400	35663
860527	FLAT	88.56250	-2600	33063
870409	SHORT	90.93750		
870615	LONG	88.84375	1994	35056
870722	FLAT	86.34375	-2600	32456
871012	SHORT	76.43750		
871021	FLAT	80.90625	-4569	27888
871021	LONG	80.87500		
880518	SHORT	84.71875	3744	31631
880606	FLAT	87.21875	-2600	29031

EURODOLLARS

Date	Position	Action Price	Profit or Loss	Cumulative Profit
830202	SHORT	81.97		
830429	FLAT	82.97	-2,600	-2,600
830531	SHORT	82.31		
830822	LONG	82.24	75	-2,525
831215	SHORT	82.74	1,150	-1,375
840615	LONG	82.94	-600	-1,975
850208	SHORT	87.29	10,775	8,800
850412	FLAT	88.29	-2,600	6,200
850503	LONG	88.79		
860113	SHORT	89.80	2,425	8,625
860327	FLAT	90.80	-2,600	6,025
860401	LONG	90.91		
860516	SHORT	90.76	-475	5,550
860813	FLAT	91.76	-2,600	2,950
860821	LONG	92.03		
870130	SHORT	91.60	-1,175	1,775
870610	LONG	90.78	1,950	3,725
871014	FLAT	89.78	-2,600	1,125
871014	SHORT	89.85		
871020	FLAT	91.81	-5,000	-3,875
871020	LONG	91.11		
880630	FLAT	92.04	2,225	-1,650

SWISS FRANCS

Date	Position	Action Price	Profit or Loss	Cumulative Profit
830321	SHORT	60.15		
831003	LONG	58.25	2,275	2,275
831118	FLAT	56.25	-2,600	-325
831212	SHORT	55.47		
840224	LONG	56.12	-912	-1,237
840427	FLAT	54.12	-2,600	-3,837
840615	SHORT	52.75		
841102	LONG	48.90	4,712	875
841126	FLAT	46.90	-2,600	-1,725
850111	SHORT	44.57		

Date	Position	Action Price	Profit or Loss	Cumulative Profit
850327	LONG	44.23	325	-1,400
850905	SHORT	48.44	5,162	3,763
850923	FLAT	51.41	-3,813	-50
851004	LONG	52.72		
860908	SHORT	63.57	13,463	13,413
860917	FLAT	65.57	-2,600	10,813
861030	SHORT	63.20		
861128	FLAT	65.20	-2,600	8,213
870113	LONG	67.73		
870601	SHORT	69.55	2,175	10,388
870610	FLAT	71.60	-2,662	7,725
870821	LONG	69.81		
880106	SHORT	76.70	8,513	16,238
880630	FLAT	67.08	11,925	28,163

JAPANESE YEN

Date	Position	Action Price	Profit or Loss	Cumulative Profit
830805	SHORT	49.11		
830923	LONG	49.67	-800	-800
840509	SHORT	50.55	1,000	200
841107	LONG	47.49	3,725	3,925
841227	FLAT	45.49	-2,600	1,325
850103	SHORT	45.15		
850319	LONG	44.79	350	1,675
860103	SHORT	53.87	11,250	12,925
860124	LONG	55.78	-2,488	10,438
860407	SHORT	59.19	4,163	14,600
860416	FLAT	61.19	-2,600	12,000
860423	LONG	63.77		
860530	FLAT	61.77	-2,600	9,400
861023	SHORT	66.61		
870114	FLAT	68.68	-2,688	6,713
870119	LONG	69.74		
870630	FLAT	71.18	1,700	8,413

GOLD

Date	Position	Action Price	Profit or Loss	Cumulative Profit
830223	SHORT	634.60		
831130	LONG	537.50	9,610	9,610
831215	FLAT	512.50	-2,600	7,010
840222	LONG	524.90		
840403	FLAT	499.90	-2,600	4,410
840601	LONG	504.80		
840705	FLAT	475.50	-3,030	1,380
840705	SHORT	471.90		
850318	LONG	388.50	8,240	9,620
861117	SHORT	436.20	4,670	14,290
870114	FLAT	461.20	-2,600	11,690

Date	Position	Action Price	Profit or Loss	Cumulative Profit
880127	SHORT	481.70		
880630	FLAT	437.70	4,300	15,990

HEATING OIL

Date	Position	Action Price	Profit or Loss	Cumulative Profit
830405	LONG	56.66		
830906	SHORT	61.42	1,898	1,898
831221	LONG	55.13	2,541	4,439
840611	SHORT	59.68	1,810	6,250
840822	LONG	59.97	-223	6,027
841016	FLAT	54.02	-2,600	3,427
850128	SHORT	47.37		
850226	FLAT	53.32	-2,600	827
850226	LONG	53.36		
850605	SHORT	55.28	706	1,533
850821	FLAT	61.23	-2,600	-1,067
850925	LONG	68.02		
851202	SHORT	73.93	2,381	1,315
860507	LONG	38.24	14,889	16,204
860702	FLAT	32.29	-2,600	13,604
860818	LONG	39.09		
861013	FLAT	33.14	-2,600	11,004
870629	LONG	47.84		
870817	SHORT	44.90	-1,336	9,668
880418	LONG	48.93	-1,793	7,875
880627	FLAT	42.98	-2,600	5,275
880629	SHORT	41.84		
880630	FLAT	41.08	218	5,494

SOYBEANS

Date	Position	Action Price	Profit or Loss	Cumulative Profit
830615	SHORT	735.00		
830706	LONG	763.50	-1,525	-1,525
831117	SHORT	912.50	7,350	5,825
840229	LONG	841.50	3,450	9,275
840705	FLAT	789.50	-2,700	6,575
840725	SHORT	733.00		
851106	LONG	576.00	7,750	14,325
851118	SHORT	540.00	-1,900	12,425
851212	LONG	572.25	-1,713	10,713
860813	FLAT	520.00	-2,713	8,000
870409	LONG	549.50		
870708	SHORT	570.00	925	8,925
871120	FLAT	620.00	-2,600	6,325
880404	LONG	693.50		
880630	FLAT	971.50	13,800	20,125

Date	Position	Action Price	Profit or Loss	Cumulative Profit
SUGAR				
830211	LONG	15.68		
830926	SHORT	16.86	1,222	1,222
840828	LONG	9.91	7,684	8,906
841217	SHORT	8.28	-1,926	6,980
850719	LONG	6.31	2,106	9,086
851226	SHORT	8.13	1,938	11,025
860318	LONG	9.82	-1,993	9,032
860529	SHORT	10.01	113	9,145
861010	LONG	8.42	1,681	10,826
870324	SHORT	8.50	-10	10,815
870916	LONG	7.21	1,345	12,160
880201	SHORT	9.16	2,084	14,244
880627	FLAT	11.39	-2,600	11,644
880628	LONG	12.35		
880630	FLAT	12.63	214	11,858
LIVE CATTLE				
830322	SHORT	45.07		
830808	LONG	44.27	220	220
830830	SHORT	39.87	-1,860	-1,640
831128	FLAT	46.12	-2,600	-4,240
831128	LONG	46.22		-4,240
840210	SHORT	47.10	248	-3,992
840306	LONG	50.10	-1,300	-5,292
840425	SHORT	47.27	-1,228	-6,520
841123	FLAT	53.55	-2,608	-9,128
850204	LONG	53.65		-9,128
850225	SHORT	50.32	-1,432	-10,560
850514	LONG	48.55	612	-9,948
850624	FLAT	42.22	-2,632	-12,580
850715	SHORT	39.37		-12,580
850930	LONG	38.05	432	-12,152
860403	FLAT	31.80	-2,600	-14,752
860424	SHORT	29.90		-14,752
860513	LONG	34.20	-1,820	-16,572
861002	SHORT	37.50	1,220	-15,352
870127	FLAT	43.75	-2,600	-17,952
870128	LONG	44.37		-17,952
870520	SHORT	50.82	2,480	-15,472
870825	FLAT	57.07	-2,600	-18,072
870825	LONG	56.75		-18,072
871022	SHORT	55.62	-552	-18,624
880115	FLAT	61.87	-2,600	-21,224
880203	LONG	63.97		-21,224
880615	SHORT	64.50	112	-21,116
880630	FLAT	64.60	-140	-21,256

Date	Position	Action Price	Profit or Loss	Cumulative Profit
T-BILLS				
830818	LONG	84.55		
840322	SHORT	85.22	1,575	1,575
840525	LONG	85.52	-850	725
850208	SHORT	89.41	9,625	10,350
850417	FLAT	90.41	-2,600	7,750
850418	LONG	90.50		
860113	SHORT	91.67	2,825	10,575
860327	LONG	92.52	-2,225	8,350
860516	SHORT	92.26	-750	7,600
860825	FLAT	93.26	-2,600	5,000
861212	SHORT	92.92		
870601	LONG	92.31	1,425	6,425
870902	SHORT	92.47	300	6,725
871020	FLAT	93.47	-2,600	4,125
871020	LONG	93.14		
880630	FLAT	93.30	300	4,425
BRITISH POUNDS				
831207	SHORT	131.45		
840217	LONG	132.45	-350	-350
840625	FLAT	122.20	-2,663	-3,013
840703	SHORT	120.20		
841102	LONG	111.45	2,088	-925
841231	FLAT	101.40	-2,613	-3,537
850114	SHORT	96.30		
850318	LONG	97.35	-362	-3,900
851211	SHORT	131.20	8,363	4,463
860321	FLAT	141.20	-2,600	1,863
860428	LONG	146.40		
860922	SHORT	137.70	-2,275	-412
861222	LONG	138.60	-325	-737
870527	SHORT	158.10	4,775	4,038
871027	FLAT	168.10	-2,600	1,438
871029	LONG	169.75		
880115	SHORT	175.30	1,288	2,725
880328	FLAT	185.30	-2,600	125
880602	SHORT	179.85		
880630	FLAT	170.44	2,253	2,378
DEUTSCHEMARKS				
830801	SHORT	45.72		
840203	LONG	44.09	1,938	1,938
840705	FLAT	42.08	-2,612	-675
840723	SHORT	41.39		
841102	LONG	39.98	1,663	988

Date	Position	Action Price	Profit or Loss	Cumulative Profit
841130	FLAT	37.98	-2,600	-1,612
850205	SHORT	36.59		
850327	LONG	37.35	-1,050	-2,662
850906	SHORT	39.27	2,300	-362
850923	FLAT	41.99	-3,500	-3,862
851004	LONG	43.08		
860403	SHORT	45.79	3,287	-575
860416	FLAT	48.04	-2,913	-3,487
860821	LONG	52.40		
860911	SHORT	51.21	-1,588	-5,075
860918	FLAT	53.21	-2,600	-7,675
860918	LONG	53.66		
861030	SHORT	51.96	-2,225	-9,900
861201	FLAT	54.18	-2,875	-12,775
870112	LONG	55.88		
880106	SHORT	62.33	7,963	-4,812
880630	FLAT	55.53	8,400	3,588

COPPER

Date	Position	Action Price	Profit or Loss	Cumulative Profit
830928	SHORT	57.90		
840305	LONG	52.85	1,163	1,163
840620	FLAT	42.85	-2,600	-1,437
840705	SHORT	41.60		
841025	LONG	39.35	463	-975
850626	SHORT	36.25	-875	-1,850
851003	LONG	37.35	-375	-2,225
860211	SHORT	38.35	150	-2,075
860902	LONG	33.95	1,000	-1,075
870331	SHORT	34.55	50	-1,025
870515	LONG	39.10	-1,237	-2,262
871020	SHORT	48.70	2,300	38
871102	FLAT	58.70	-2,600	-2,562
871102	LONG	60.15		
880630	FLAT	98.00	9,363	6,800

CRUDE OIL

Date	Position	Action Price	Profit or Loss	Cumulative Profit
831227	LONG	20.84		
840622	SHORT	21.20	109	109
840822	LONG	21.65	-231	-122
841018	FLAT	18.33	-1,436	-1,558
850102	SHORT	17.79		
850304	LONG	19.08	-584	-2,142
851210	SHORT	22.50	1,394	-748
860516	LONG	13.64	3,679	2,932
860604	FLAT	11.10	-1,109	1,823
860916	SHORT	13.03		
861215	FLAT	15.53	-1,092	731

Date	Position	Action Price	Profit or Loss	Cumulative Profit
861231	LONG	16.68		
870819	SHORT	19.39	1,096	1,827
880412	LONG	18.71	244	2,071
880624	FLAT	16.21	-1,092	979

CORN

Date	Position	Action Price	Profit or Loss	Cumulative Profit
830720	LONG	316.25		
840725	SHORT	309.25	-450	-450
850321	LONG	291.25	800	350
850722	SHORT	269.50	-1,188	-838
851010	LONG	258.75	438	-400
860902	SHORT	239.00	-1,088	-1,488
860924	LONG	248.75	-588	-2,075
861219	SHORT	229.25	-1,075	-3,150
870325	LONG	225.50	88	-3,063
870629	SHORT	233.50	300	-2,763
870918	LONG	223.75	388	-2,375
880414	SHORT	234.00	413	-1,963
880603	LONG	256.25	-1,213	-3,175
880630	FLAT	345.50	4,363	1,188

SOYBEAN MEAL

Date	Position	Action Price	Profit or Loss	Cumulative Profit
830811	LONG	254.10		
831121	FLAT	229.10	-2,600	-2,600
840109	SHORT	211.50		
840302	LONG	207.00	350	-2,250
840607	FLAT	182.00	-2,600	-4,850
840611	SHORT	180.50		
841022	LONG	140.30	3,920	-930
841227	SHORT	120.40	-2,090	-3,020
850708	LONG	88.20	3,120	100
851115	SHORT	88.60	-60	40
860107	LONG	108.90	-2,130	-2,090
860515	SHORT	101.30	-860	-2,950
860715	LONG	98.40	190	-2,760
870622	SHORT	125.50	2,610	-150
871109	FLAT	150.50	-2,600	-2,750
871127	LONG	185.40		
880127	FLAT	160.40	-2,600	-5,350
880511	LONG	197.40		
880630	FLAT	284.70	8,630	3,280

SOYBEAN OIL

Date	Position	Action Price	Profit or Loss	Cumulative Profit
830721	LONG	18.83		
831005	SHORT	26.17	4,304	4,304
840224	LONG	23.19	1,688	5,992

Date	Position	Action Price	Profit or Loss	Cumulative Profit
840703	SHORT	25.76	1,442	7,434
841106	LONG	27.56	-1,180	6,254
850719	SHORT	31.40	2,204	8,458
851211	LONG	26.36	2,924	11,382
860225	SHORT	22.85	-2,206	9,176
870123	LONG	20.30	1,430	10,606
870717	SHORT	17.91	-1,534	9,072
870925	LONG	19.01	-760	8,312
880309	SHORT	21.16	1,190	9,502
880516	FLAT	25.33	-2,600	6,902
880607	LONG	26.53		
880630	FLAT	32.15	3,272	10,174

LIVE HOGS

Date	Position	Action Price	Profit or Loss	Cumulative Profit
830728	LONG	21.55		
840213	SHORT	22.95	320	320
841105	LONG	18.57	1,213	1,533
850415	SHORT	13.62	-1,585	-52
850918	LONG	5.95	2,203	2,150
860213	SHORT	9.10	845	2,995
860508	LONG	13.75	-1,495	1,500
860925	SHORT	27.95	4,160	5,660
870424	FLAT	36.27	-2,600	3,060
870506	LONG	37.22		
870911	SHORT	45.95	2,518	5,578
880108	LONG	45.37	73	5,650
880303	SHORT	44.62	-325	5,325
880531	LONG	52.80	-2,552	2,773
880615	SHORT	45.75	-2,215	558
880630	FLAT	45.27	42	600

ORANGE JUICE

Date	Position	Action Price	Profit or Loss	Cumulative Profit
830912	LONG	87.80		
840612	SHORT	150.00	9,230	9,230
840919	FLAT	166.65	-2,600	6,630
841015	SHORT	152.45		
850118	LONG	145.85	890	7,520
850408	SHORT	132.95	-2,035	5,485
850913	LONG	119.95	1,850	7,335
851014	FLAT	102.20	-2,763	4,572
851014	SHORT	102.10		
851210	LONG	103.35	-288	4,285
860102	SHORT	88.50	-2,328	1,957
860325	LONG	74.75	1,962	3,920
870109	SHORT	98.00	3,387	7,307
870908	FLAT	114.65	-2,600	4,707
870910	LONG	115.75		

Date	Position	Action Price	Profit or Loss	Cumulative Profit
880223	SHORT	147.40	4,647	9,355
880516	FLAT	164.10	-2,605	6,750
880603	LONG	165.70		
880630	FLAT	183.60	2,585	9,335

COTTON

Date	Position	Action Price	Profit or Loss	Cumulative Profit
830915	SHORT	28.65		
840302	LONG	27.47	490	490
840611	SHORT	28.41	370	860
841015	LONG	17.77	5,220	6,080
850219	SHORT	13.86	-2,055	4,025
850313	LONG	16.03	-1,185	2,840
850711	FLAT	11.03	-2,600	240
850719	SHORT	9.89		
851002	LONG	9.84	-75	165
860127	SHORT	10.49	225	390
860430	FLAT	15.49	-2,600	-2,210
860430	LONG	15.79		
870128	SHORT	39.57	11,790	9,580
870313	FLAT	44.57	-2,600	6,980
870414	LONG	49.27		
870624	SHORT	58.29	4,410	11,390
870630	FLAT	63.29	-2,600	8,790
870827	LONG	71.54		
870903	FLAT	66.54	-2,600	6,190
870909	SHORT	64.37		
880314	LONG	53.88	5,145	11,335
880630	FLAT	61.10	3,510	14,845

Index